W9-BTP-763

NON-CIRCULATING

THE MERTON ANNUAL

10

THE MERTON ANNUAL

Studies in Culture, Spirituality, and Social Concerns

THE MERTON ANNUAL publishes articles about Thomas Merton and about related matters of major concern to his life and work. Its purpose is to enhance Merton's reputation as a writer and monk, to continue to develop his message for our times, and to provide a regular outlet for substantial Merton-related scholarship. *THE MERTON ANNUAL* includes as regular features reviews, review-essays, a bibliographic survey, interviews, and first appearances of unpublished, or obscurely published, Merton materials, photographs, and art. Essays about related literary and spiritual matters will also be considered. Manuscripts and books for review may be sent to any of the editors.

EDITORS

Michael Downey
Saint John's Seminary
Camarillo, CA 93012-2598

George A. Kilcourse
Theology Department
Bellarmine College
2001 Newburg Road
Louisville, KY 40205-0671

Victor A. Kramer
English Department
Georgia State University
University Plaza
Atlanta, GA 30303-3083

Volume editorship rotates on a yearly basis.

ADVISORY BOARD

THE MERTON ANNUAL

Studies in Culture, Spirituality, and Social Concerns

Volume 10   1997

Edited by

Victor A. Kramer

A Liturgical Press Book

THE LITURGICAL PRESS
Collegeville, Minnesota

Cover design by Ann Blattner. *Artwork:* "Jerusalem" by Thomas Merton.

"The School of the Spirit" by Thomas Merton, O.C.S.O., is printed with the permission of The Trustees of the Merton Legacy Trust.

ISBN 0-8146-2254-2

1   2   3   4   5   6   7   8   9

The Merton Annual

Volume 10	1997

REVIEWS

Introduction

Fragmentation and the Quest for the Spiritual in the Late Twentieth Century

Victor A. Kramer

In Czeslaw Milosz's journal *A Year of the Hunter,* his chronicle of 1987 and 1988, he ponders his desire to identify a novel which would provide insight into the contemporary cultural scene just as Thomas Mann's *The Magic Mountain* had earlier served as metaphor for the illness of the earliest years of the century. Such a book would, perhaps, provide insight into the spiritual condition of today's civilization. Mann's bleak sanitarium novel, we remember, helped Walker Percy form his own initial fictional inquiry about spiritual disorder and contemporary times, but Thomas Merton, already in his *The Secular Journal,* professed to finding Mann's novel too formulaic. Maybe that is why Milosz imagines he himself might compose a novel which would reflect the complexity of the strivings and contradictions of the present age, but within a completely different setting.

Surprisingly, his imagined locus for such fiction which could delineate essential features of the spiritual landscape might be, he speculates, either in Rome or at the Abbey of Gethsemani where Merton lived. Milosz's entry then also discusses many of the persons Merton himself was reading in the 1960s (Maritain, Arendt, Heidegger), and further it speculates that the Kentucky abbey where so many persons had come to visit Merton would work especially well as setting.

This seems at first an extreme suggestion, but in fact it triggers still other stimulating and imaginative possibilities. In many ways Merton was someone who would fit well into such a novel. His gregariousness and the vast body of his energetic writings and letters continues to provide a meeting place for thousands of readers today. In a fictional setting Merton's sometimes paradoxical insights into contemporary culture's longing could provide an excellent oblique commentary. It is also quite possible to imagine his particular monastery as a meeting place and setting because writers—poets, intellectuals, artists, philosophers—as different as Jacques Maritain, Walker Percy, Denise Levertov, Douglass T. Steer, and Joan Baez—did indeed visit there along with many others. Percy, in a 1980 interview about his admiration for Merton, lamented that he had not chosen to ask Merton more specific questions when they had met at Gethsemani in 1967, yet the point is that as seekers of spiritual truth they were on the same quest.

Milosz's insight about a projected novel which would reflect the present age is an excellent one because a figure like Merton could serve as a catalyst. Merton, we remember, had read *The Moviegoer* in 1965 and sent Percy a fan letter. He found the novel a key to our contemporary moment's distress. Just like the hero, Binx Bolling, of that novel, Merton realized that all persons in this culture are displaced, yet in continuing to question, they find glimmers of the sacred. Questioning was at the heart of all Thomas Merton's continuing work as he examined the wider culture, and this is part of his legacy. Thus, this marginal monk's work remains important in relation to the core of our own culture's fundamental questions about how to live and love in an age which seems so radically different from earlier ages.

If we are to make sense of how to reintegrate the spiritual into our fragmented lives, contemplative need (perceived by commentators like Milosz, Percy, and Merton) and aspects of a solitary mode of life may indeed be parts of the answer. Yes, such reappraisal, and certainly within a novel, could include a character resembling Thomas Merton, but it would because such a character would be thinking and writing about aspects of the world beyond the monastic. Appropriately, many of the papers in this volume of *The Merton Annual* were planned to deal with aspects of lay and everyday spirituality. Therefore, each of the three articles which constitute the opening part of this book, articles by Patrick O'Connell, Wendy M. Wright, and Beatrice Bruteau, examine crucial issues which relate to day by day living. These papers stand at the core of today's inquiry concerning what might be described as the dilemma of contemporary spirituality, and Merton is their impetus.

As O'Connell systematically explains, the issue of the relationship of monastic spirituality to life outside the monastery became increasingly important for Merton as his understanding of monasticism developed, and this same type of relationship, Merton knew, was of fundamental importance for each person as life unfolds in the ordinary contexts of experience. Each of these three opening essays was planned to demonstrate, as a unit, that at the heart of our developing understanding of spirituality is the fact of the individual's active involvement moment by moment. It may take decades of pondering, but it is eventually clear that spirituality will not be divorced from, but is always integrated with, all aspects of life.

O'Connell demonstrates that for Merton's mature spirituality it became much less a matter of just following institutional patterns. Similar points are quietly made by Professor Wright in her essay which demonstrates that much of what Merton articulated also can be lived out in ordinary lay life "becoming aware of the natural contemplative moments and rhythms." The third essay, by Beatrice Bruteau, uses Merton as a springboard to assure us that in all creation, there is unity, and thus, ultimately "eucharistic cosmos."

Read together these essays provide overlapping examinations which build upon the legacy of Thomas Merton. Clearly, Father Louis came to see that many unnecessary distinctions between lay and monastic existence, or between Christian and non-Christian belief, clouded our ability to live contemplatively. O'Connell, Wright, and Bruteau each, therefore, help us to see that the presence of God is a matter of "energy sharing." Finally, full sharing means sharing on all levels: the monk, the mother, and mediator, cannot be separate. Many of the remaining essays included in this book were designed to examine related issues.

The three essays which follow all deal with Merton as poet. In completely different ways they seem almost to build upon the general points made about spirituality in the opening three articles. This is because of the honesty in Merton's poetry. His poetic development was one of continual change and an ever greater openness to mystery. Alan Altany's article shows how this poet, the Merton of the 1960s, transcended some of his earlier assumptions. Several of the remaining essays in this volume deal more specifically with the intersection of the transcendent with the ordinary, of the everyday with the theological, of the infusion of the ordinary life with a radiance beyond the ordinary. Poetry was, for Merton, the very best manifestation of this developing interplay.

The three essays by Altany, Archer, and Cooper examine how Merton realized this unfolding of mystery and insight, and how this was illuminated by the gift of poetic skill which allows the ordinary to shine. Altany's essay documents Merton's own poetic transformation. Archer's article demonstrates parallels between Merton and his contemporary Denise Levertov as they lived through the same era. Her analysis of parallels between Merton's poetry and Denise Levertov's is appropriately followed by the examination by David Cooper about the decades-long relationship between Merton and his poetry publisher, James Laughlin (who has also served as Levertov's publisher for decades as well).

The Cooper article illustrates how Merton was stimulated by, and engaged with, his editor, Laughlin, throughout a quarter of a century. Their correspondence was voluminous. One regrets that it was necessary for Cooper to select from this rather large correspondence of Merton with his publisher-friend for the *Selected Letters* which Cooper edited and describes here. What one can clearly see is that this was a two-way relationship and that Merton, would not, could not, be sealed off from contemporary life and interests, and that his writing profited from stimulation beyond the monastery.

In the three additional examinations which follow of Merton as a man of letters fruitfully engaged with the world, other scholars here also study the many ways Father Louis apparently profited from being involved with questions about writing about the world. Using the Working Notebooks as her springboard, Claire Badaracco makes the very substantial point that throughout his reading notebooks Merton was engaged in a kind of creative tension and that a similar kind of engagement serves as a model for contemporary feminine spiritual writers who question traditional paradigms. Bradford Stull's article provides still more specific evidence about how particularities of Merton's metaphorical language in his "theo-political essays" function to draw the reader in. Ultimately Merton could not not be involved. As a non-systematic, yet often metaphorical writer, he also draws his reader into a questioning stance like his own. In the related essay by David Belcastro we see how Merton came to be more and more engaged with the writings of Albert Camus. Not unlike Milosz (who Belcastro reminds us urged Merton to read Camus) Camus was fascinated with the complexity of modern culture with and without Christian belief. Whether one is a believer or not, both Camus and Merton would agree one cannot avoid raising spiritual questions.

My final grouping of three essays demonstrates still other aspects of Merton's importance for today's reader and his continuing quest to make sense of what it means to live well. If the opening essays by O'Connell, Wright, and Bruteau demonstrate Merton's importance in relation to a developing spirituality beyond the cloister, and the second group by Altany, Archer, and Cooper demonstrate his growing abilities as poet, and the third grouping by Badaracco, Stull, and Belcastro shows how he was ever more involved with the world through his reading and writing, these final three studies emphasize that his life and writings continue to provide fuel for important discussions within today's world.

In Mark O'Keefe's essay about Merton's "true self" and the "fundamental option" we see that Merton's examinations of the true self provide a key for contemporary theology to discuss the holistic structure of Christian life. We are also reminded in the essays by Johan Seynnaeve and John Wu, Jr. that the true spiritual seeker must keep looking, searching, questioning. The parallels between Merton and Dom Thomas Verner Moore, as they both drew nearer the isolation of a Carthusian life, are examined by Seynnaeve who reminds us that Merton's desire to become a Carthusian was not encouraged by Moore, and that apparently Dom Moore was not so much thwarting Merton as expressing that he sensed Merton was not ready for such a life. Clearly in 1947 Merton was still dealing with fundamental questions about his vocation which could not then be easily resolved and certainly not by leaving the Abbey of Gethsemani.

The essay by John Wu, Jr. brings us back to many of the same fundamental connections examined by O'Connell, Wright, and Bruteau, and reminds us how fortunate it was for Merton, and subsequent generations of readers that he kept struggling with fundamental questions about his necessary relationships to society.

In addition to the articles discussed in this introduction, this volume of *The Merton Annual* includes several other valuable items. As has been the custom for these ten years of the existence of the *Annual*, we are again able to provide an edited version of a previously unavailable Merton manuscript. It has been ably edited by Patrick Hart, and in "The School of the Spirit" we have valuable evidence of the young, energetic Merton literally preparing his way (and ours) for the later mature contemplative who related much more openly to the world. In the interview, different than the preceding interviews in earlier volumes which concentrated on persons who knew Merton personally, we have evidence of Merton's influence and insight into the present moment. Conducted and edited by Jonathan Montaldo, with the Merton scholar Anthony Padavano, this interview provides still more connections between Merton's legacy and the present age.

Certainly, in a very real sense all the reading and study of, and writing about, Merton, thirty years after his death exists as a kind of enactment of what Ceslaw Milosz imagined as an ideal meeting place for the interaction of persons who are seeking ways to integrate the spiritual into their post-modern lives.

The bibliographical survey-analysis of the significant books and articles by and about Merton which appeared during 1996, another reflection of Merton's speaking to a wide variety of persons, has been prepared by fellow editor George Kilcourse. The book reviews, which include reviews of three more complete Merton Journals (volumes 2, 3, and 4) have been coordinated by Michael Downey, who, with this volume of *The Merton Annual*, is completing five years of association with the Annual. His contribution, and that of all the editors in the first series (Volumes 1 through 5) and the second series (Volumes 6–10) have assisted to make this decade of Merton scholarship fruitful. We hope that the work of the Annual during the past ten years has provided assistance toward the world's understanding of Merton's quest for the spiritual in the late twentieth century.

Thanks is expressed to the Board of the Aquinas Center of Theology (Center for Catholic Studies at Emory University, Atlanta, Georgia) for the support which has been provided through editorial and secretarial services while this volume was in production. A special word of thanks is expressed to Carrie J. Griffin who helped with typing and correspondence from January through December, 1997, while the volume's editor served as Senior Fulbright Lecturer at The University of Heidelberg in Germany.

EDITORIAL NOTE:

In *The Merton Annual*, Vol. 9 (1996) within the article by Patrick Hart, O.C.S.O., "Editing the Journals of Thomas Merton," the impression was mistakenly made that the "Macaronic Lyric" (p. 234) is part of the entry which begins on page 330 of *Run to the Mountain*. In fact, the poem is a separate work. For more information, see *The Merton Seasonal*, Vol. 21, No. 1 (Spring 1996), pp. 7–8.

Foreword

The School of the Spirit
by Thomas Merton

Patrick Hart, O.C.S.O.

Following on the heels of the phenomenal success of *The Seven Storey Mountain*, Thomas Merton made several attempts to begin a new book in early 1949. On February 15 he confides to his journal that he has written some forty pages, "mostly in blood," since the end of the retreat, and he was not happy with the results. . . . Five days later, on February 20, he seems to have had a breakthrough, as he writes: ". . . *[The Cloud and the Fire]*, now changed and called *The School of the Spirit* goes quite smoothly. I have to simply sit down at the typewriter with what I want to say planned out. That is the *sine qua non*—even if I write something completely different, as I did today."[1] Merton was attempting to write a book on the beauties of the contemplative life for all, a life based on the perfection of love.

Apparently his enthusiasm did not last long, because after having written three chapters, a total of about seventy pages, he abandoned the manuscript once again. This time it was not to be revived. What we have here are the first two chapters of *The School of the Spirit*, which were discovered shortly after Merton's death in the collection of Sr. Thérèse Lentfoehr, S.D.S., in Racine, Wisconsin. She had written to me about another unpublished manuscript called *The Inner Experience*, which she was anxious to read. We had the original here, and I agreed

---

1. Jonathan Montaldo, ed. *Entering the Silence: Becoming a Monk and Writer: The Journals of Thomas Merton*, Volume Two 1941–1952 (San Francisco: Harper San Francisco 1996) 282–3.

to send her a copy in exchange for a copy of *The School of the Spirit*. Thus we bartered! And fortunately for Bellarmine College, since I was able later to provide a copy for their Merton collection as well.

On November 14, 1967, the year before Merton embarked on his pilgrimage to the Far East, he finally signed a legal document establishing the Merton Legacy Trust with Naomi Burton Stone, Thomasine O'Callaghan, and James Laughlin as trustees. One of the many duties was outlined in this document under "A. Trustees Powers: d) Publish my drafts of books in manuscript form which have not been published with specific exceptions of *The Inner Experience* and *The School of the Spirit* which are not to be published as books. Even though these specific manuscripts are not to be published [as books], the Trustees may permit qualified scholars to quote from said works."[2]

Fortunately, the Trustees interpreted the last line of the above document as allowing the publication of these two restricted manuscripts in a scholarly journal, but not in book form. Thus, *The Inner Experience,* which was revised any number of times by Merton during the last decade of his life, as indicated by the various colors of ink used in the revisions, first appeared in eight numbers of *Cistercian Studies* (1983–1984).[3] It has become very popular and still in demand by readers.

The School of the Spirit on the other hand had no revisions, and the sources in Latin were not indicated. Merton had simply abandoned the typescript and sent a copy to Sister Thérèse for her collection, which she later gave to Columbia University. I had originally planned to run it in *Cistercian Studies,* and had obtained permission from the Merton Trust, but I then abandoned the idea since I had resigned as editor of *Cistercian Studies* after ten years in that service. Thus, it remained on the shelf until Dr. Victor Kramer, current editor of *The Merton Annual,* asked me if I knew of some unpublished Merton material that could be used in *The Merton Annual 10.* I immediately thought of *The School of the Spirit,* and after securing permission from the Merton Legacy Trust, sent a copy of the manuscript to him. He and I thought it best to publish only the first two chapters, since there was a missing page in the third and last chapter which was left unfinished.

2. Unpublished manuscript: *Merton Legacy Trust,* 14 November 1967, Louisville, Kentucky, eight pages.

3. *Cistercian Studies Quarterly:* the eight numbers that comprise *The Inner Experience,* are available in offprint form from CSQ Administration: Sr. Sheryl Chen, O.C.S.O., Santa Rita Abbey, HC 1 Box 929, Sonoita, AZ 85637-9705.

He asked me to arrange for translations of the Latin in the text, and to provide a foreword, giving the historical background of this incomplete and until now unpublished Merton work.

I am happy to see the opening two chapters of *The School of the Spirit* finally see the light of day. I want to thank Dr. Robert Urekew of Saint Catherine's College, Springfield, Kentucky, for his assistance in tracking down the sources and providing the translations. Finally, a word of gratitude is in order to the Trustees of the Merton Legacy Trust for making this manuscript available to readers of *The Merton Annual*.

The School of the Spirit

Thomas Merton

Chapter One: The Contemplative Life

Love, says Hugh of St. Victor, is the life of a rational soul. Without love, a soul cannot exist. *Vita animae dilectio est et sine dilectione esse non potest.* [The life of the soul is love, and without love the soul cannot exist.] But a soul that gives its love to the wrong object, throws its life away. Love dictates a man's freedom to the object of his love. And if a man consecrates his freedom to something that cannot fulfil the deepest capacities of his rational being, he throws his freedom away. He is a captive. He remains in darkness and in sorrow and his whole life is a defeat.

The secret of life and of happiness is to love a reality in which there is no defect to betray and cheat our love. There is only one such: God.

There are many different ways of loving God: but ultimately they all tend to a perfect and all-exclusive absorption in Him alone. If they do not, then they are not really love of God. Men can dedicate their lives to God by taking care of sick people or teaching in schools: for they see His image reflected in the souls of other men and they wish to serve Him by imitating and carrying on the works of mercy that Christ performed on earth. A married life, lived in a deep spirit of Christian faith, can become a more or less conscious and continuous participation in the mystery of creation, in which the most important and mysterious factor is the cooperation, by human beings, in the shaping of young souls as God's likeness develops in them. Other men can serve God and prove their love for Him by trying to direct the destinies of states or communities according to divinely ordained principles on which peace and justice depend, in the affairs of men. Still others love God by seeking His reflection in the forms of created things and paying Him intellectual homage by works of their own creation: sculpture, painting, poetry, architecture. And there are others who love God in the intellectual structures of philosophies and theologies which express the deepest and most fundamental realities of the spirit in terms which human reason deals with as its own.

These ways of loving God bring men peace on earth, and satisfy, to some extent, their free souls: but they are not final. And the satisfaction they bring with them, at certain moments of high intensity and connatural fulfilment, is the satisfaction rather of hope than of possession. The joy that comes with the exercise of talent, the peace that belongs to human love, fulfilled in line with the vital economy of the Church's sacramental system, and the deeply rewarding happiness that accompanies the performance of God's will and in doing good on earth: all these things are only pledges of a greater and more perfect fulfilment. They satisfy us not because they are ends, but because they bring with them the assurance that they can be adequate means to the only true end—something which lies beyond and above them and belongs to a much higher order.

Transient activity, however good, only satisfies our souls in so far as it is the promise of a supreme activity that transcends the passage of time, an activity without labor and frustration, in which there is no longer any shadow of obstacle: an activity which is pure, spiritual and full, and entirely realized in one instant which will remain forever and never cease. Transient moments of human love are only pledges of a spiritual love that can unite our souls with the infinite Truth forever: for the marriage of human lovers has this dignity, that it is able to remind us that we were made to love with our whole being in a love which endows and enriches us in proportion to our gift and abandonment of ourselves. The clean creative fire that furnishes incandescent intellectual forms to the mind of the artist should symbolize, for him, the fire of the Word which blazes forth from the depths of the infinite God, and is the glory and the truth of God, and is God. And we were made to play for ever in the flame of that eternal and uncircumscribed intuition, where all causes are gathered in the Art of God. All the art that is on earth can only satisfy us in so far as it draws us inward and delivers us from the cravings of sense and leaves us for a moment in the depths of that intellectual peace which can foreshadow, even in the order of nature, the eternal contemplation of heaven.

And now we have come to the concept of contemplation.

There is possible, on earth, an experience of the highest reality, an obscure but immediate contact with the very substance of Him Who is Truth. At the moment of such contact the intellect and will of man, drawn down into their own depths, meeting one another in the soul's essence, in which they are naturally united, are, as it were, liquified, dissolve and flow into the spiritual immensity Who is darkness to us because He is Pure Light. In a tremendous and fruitful silence, an abyss of pure freedom, the soul discovers, in an incommunicable experience, what is going to happen to it, one day, when it passes over into God forever to be transformed into Him and become one spirit with Him forever.

The return of such a soul from the unity and peace of its contemplation into the multiplicity and movement and unfulfilment which mark the activities of earthly life brings with it the keenest anguish of exile. But there remains some savor of the experience of an unforgettable pledge of the contemplation for which we were all created to which we are destined in heaven if we make use of the means God has given us to get there.

All these are ways of loving God on earth: ways that involve action of the body or of the spirit: ways that traffic in pledges of eternity. The most perfect of these ways, by far, is that which concerns itself most exclusively with contemplation.

All the other lives dedicated to God's love are good, but they are imperfect because they only reach Him indirectly. The active lives (unless they flow from the very fullness of contemplation) only direct our minds and wills to God obliquely. They occupy us chiefly with created things and with transient movements and intermediary ends. Ultimately they end in God, but it often requires some effort to recover the memory of that end by a reflex movement of the mind. The contemplative life, simple, perfect, in its unified tendency to the one supreme end, seeks God in Himself alone. Creatures have to be used as means as long as men are outside paradise: but the mind does not so easily stop in them or allow them to cloud it over. The whole existence of a contemplative is regulated by successive active or passive movements of interior purification in which the mind overleaps the multiplicity of created images and seeks God in an obscure and unified gaze of love. And, when God wills, it finds Him and clings to Him resting immediately in Him somewhat as it is destined to do in heaven. For contemplation attains to God as He is in Himself, in the obscurity of faith, and it is the beginnings of eternal life: *quaedam inchoatio vitae aeternae.* [a kind of beginning of eternal life.]

* * *

The contemplative life, then, is a life of the most perfect love—the love of the highest reality, for the contemplative seeks nothing but to lose himself in the fruition of the supreme actuality: God's Truth. St. Thomas situates the essence of the contemplation at its intellectual peak, but the marriage of the intellect with infinite light can only begin and end in love, and therefore it is a vision which is cradled in the heart of a furnace of infused love.

How could it be otherwise? *Deus caritas est!* [God is love! 1 Jn 4:16.] Since God is love there is no other way of knowing him by experience than by loving. "Everyone that loveth is born of God, and knoweth God. He that loveth not, knoweth not God, for God is charity."

To say that the contemplative life is one that is constantly aimed, in the most direct way, to immediate union with God as He is in Himself, is to say that it sums up and includes every other human striving and aspires to the one adequate fulfilment towards which all other aspirations of our soul either blindly or consciously tend.

Indeed, wherever there is love, there is bound to be some kind of contemplation. Even loves whose objects are unreality or sin, tend to occupy and obsess the mind with the images of their objects. The man who loves physical pleasure is obsessed with the idea of the things he enjoys, and his obsession ends up by being a caricature of the contemplative life. This is not surprising: he was given a soul that was made for nothing else than to be obsessed with the supreme object of all love. Divorced from Truth, the soul still has to love something and devote itself to something, even if its object is bound to deceive and frustrate it.

And that gives us the explanation of the term contemplative life. How is the word "life" used in such a context? Life, in general, is the capacity for self-motion, self-determination. Living things are distinguished from inanimate beings by the fact that they are the principles of their own vital acts. Plants nourish themselves and grow because of something inherent in themselves. Animals do not get up and move around only when they are pushed. The characteristic of rational life is a higher self-movement still: for our acts are free. We can determine ourselves to one action or another on the basis of rational choices. The highest expressions of rational life are intellection and love. Which brings us back to where we started, when we said that love is the life of the soul and that without love the soul cannot exist.

To say that a man lives the contemplative life is to say what he lives for, what he loves. The act of contemplation, in which the whole being of man is united to God's Truth in a union of vision and fruition, in the one thing to which his whole life tends. It is this object, that unifies and directs all other strivings of that one life. This work, or "operation", is what is characteristic of the contemplative. It identifies him. It dominates him by its attraction. And thus it gives him his name.

In the same way the active life is principally concerned with temporal activities. A man who lives for his work, whether it be teaching or writing or healing the sick or governing a community—or even sanctifying his own soul by the labor of virtue, is concentrated in the active rather than the contemplative life. But it must be remembered that in each of these lives, what is principally intended does not exclude a secondary intention.

The contemplative life does not exclude all external activity, but it regulates that activity in view of contemplation. In fact, the contemplative life, in its highest degrees, tends to overflow into apostolic action in which the fruits and truths of contemplation are shared with others. But even this activity itself can be so closely related to contemplation that it is almost another form of love and union with God and of vision of God. A contemplation that would freeze and congeal in total incaptivity would cease to be a life at all: and the union with God Who is Love means participation in one of the characteristics of that Love, which is to share itself and pour itself out and communicate itself to others. But this activity is so much in the service of contemplation that it tends to perfect it, by bringing us back to the depths and the silence of God's light, richer in love, richer in merit, rich in the fruits of our apostolate (that is to say in souls) and with our own being dilated and renewed in a profounder capacity for vision and for love.

On the other hand, an active life that does not include in itself some element of contemplation, cannot be called Christian, because it in not directed to God. Obviously, if our activity is directed ultimately to God as our last end, we must keep Him in view and do whatever we do at least virtually for the love of Him. This involves contemplation in the broad sense of cultivating a deep interior life, meditation, recollection, prayer, reading, as a reservoir for strength and resources in fruitful activity.

One does not have to be in a cloister or a hermitage to lead the contemplative life. It is possible to professional men in the world, to be married people: although for these it will always be more difficult, because of the division in their lives which St. Paul foresaw. "He that is with a wife is solicitous for the things of the world . . . and he is divided."

Just as theologians speak of the "state of perfection" in the technical, juridical sense of the religious state, in which everyone is bound to the pursuit of perfection (although many may, in fact, be far from perfect) so they also speak of the contemplative state, in which men bind themselves, for instance, to some religious Order which has, as its end, the contemplative life only in theory. And do not mistake me: they may sanctify their souls by doing so, if what they are doing is imposed upon them by the will of God, and if they do what they can to maintain the essential balance between the interior and exterior lives.

It is necessary to get these abstract terms clear, and not to assume that no one in an active state of life can be a contemplative, or that everyone in a contemplative Order is a contemplative in actual fact. The contemplative state is merely one in which obligations and rules conspire to make the contemplative life easy and safe. In fact, they should make it so easy that it ought to become a matter of course. Outside the special ambiance created by enclosure, silence, poverty, obedience, and constant prayer, the act of contemplation is not impossible and there are, in fact, many contemplatives in the world. For the Spirit blows where he wills, *ubi vult spirat,* and forms contemplatives wherever He pleases, without consulting human wisdom or the opinions and judgements of men.

* * *

The contemplative life, wherever it may be had, whether in a cloister or out of it, is the most perfect life that a man can lead on earth because it brings him into the closest and most immediate contact with God Who is our last end.

This was clearly stated by St. Thomas. *Vita contemplativa simplicite est melior quam activa.* [The contemplative is simply better than the active life.] He gave the same reasons for thinking so that Aristotle had given before him. The contemplative life calls into action the highest faculties of man, and applies them to their highest object. It delivers him, at least to some extent, from vicissitude and change and movement, fills his soul with a deeper peace and a purer delight than can be found in physical action, frees him, at least partially, from dependence on material things, brings him closer to his end and elevates him to a higher degree of participation in the life of God.

And since the contemplative life is principally concerned with the love of God, it is the most meritorious life that we can lead because love is the root of merit. *Radix meriti est charitas . . . Deum diligere secundum se est magis meritorium quam diligere proximum . . . Vita contemplativa directe et immediate pertinet ad dilectionem Dei . . . ideo ex suo genere contemplativa vita est majoris meriti quam activa.* [The root of merit is love . . . Loving God in and of itself is worth more than loving one's neighbor . . . The contemplative life directly and immediately leads to the love of God . . . thus, but its very nature, the contemplative life brings greater merit than the active life.]

To sacrifice the pleasure of contemplation for the sake of an action demanded by duty or charity can be accidentally more meritorious than contemplation itself, but only in so far as it represents a greater and purer love for God. And since the root of merit is not work or hardship or difficulty but love, St. Thomas answers those who think the active life more meritorious because of the labor it involves: "to undergo external labors for Christ may be a sign of the love which is the basis of merit: but a much more evident sign of that love is for a man to turn aside from everything pertaining to this mortal life and to take his delight in nothing else but the contemplation of God."

In short, the contemplative life is the most perfect that a man can lead because it is the evidence of a more perfect love, gives scope for more perfect love, sets a man free from things that are apt to be relatively trivial and concentrates all that is best and most vital in his soul upon the purest of God.

That this life is not selfish we have already seen to some degree and we shall see later on in greater detail. It is enough to repeat, here, that this love, in its highest intensity, tends to pour itself out and gather other souls into the circle of its one tremendously fruitful activity that is purely of the spirit and shares in the society of the blessed and the infinite beatitude of God.

It is because the preaching life should be, by rights, the overflow of the fulness of contemplation that St. Thomas said that the Orders devoted to preaching and teaching were, in the abstract, the most perfect in the Church of God.

* * *

It is clear that the contemplation of which we speak is more than the highest intuitions of the artist or philosopher. It goes beyond intellectual speculation to possess truth, not merely with the mind but with one's whole being and to grasp reality not in its abstract and speculative reduction to an idea, but by an affective identification of the whole soul with Truth as such.

But it is something more: it is supernatural. And therefore it must not be confused with the highest forms of natural "contemplation" which sometimes resemble mystical experience and are often called "mystical" by the uninformed. Since the romantic revival in literature sought to liberate the deepest springs of artistic perception from what were felt to be the trammels of formalism, anyone who was capable of manifesting some immediate artistic grasp of the concreteness of things by a short-cut that ignores the processes of discourse, was apt to be called a mystic. What is even worse, it is not unusual to find people calling anyone whose thought or writing is a bit obscure, a mystic. The term mystic has, in fact, so far degenerated that it is given to all those who exalt the emotions and human passion over the intellect. The name, thus corrupted, has been applied to people like Hitler, D. H. Lawrence, Nietzsche, Robert Browning(!), Mary Baker Eddy, and a hundred others. By such standards every fortune teller becomes a mystic.

Contemplation as it is understood in the Catholic Church, is not a denial of the intellect in favor of the deification of "dark forces" and inexpressible urges that well up from the depths of a man's being. It transcends and sublimates the speculation of the mind by lifting its operation to a higher place where, drawn into unity with the will and directly moved by the infused light and power of God, it receives a supreme perfection of wisdom and understanding which "the eye hath not seen, nor the ear heard, nor hath it entered into the heart of man to conceive."

While stressing the absolute primacy of the supernatural Order, Catholic philosophers and theologians take nothing away from nature that is really due to it or really perfects it. Consequently, they are also the ones who preserve intact all the highest natural rights of the intellect and will. In fact, the Church is practically the only teacher who still defends an epistemology that allows the intellect any valid knowledge of exterior things in their objective reality. Therefore it is the Catholic philosopher who generally holds the highest estimate of what the unaided natural powers of man can do in the way of contemplation.

Besides teaching that human reason can arrive at a perfectly valid knowledge not only of the existence of God but also of many of His attributes, through the analogies offered by His creation, Catholic philosophers have not forgotten the heights of natural contemplation that were reached by Plato, Aristotle, Proclus, Porphyry, Plotinus, and others who are called mystics—in a loose but with far more justice than those we listed a moment ago.

Jacques Maritain has analyzed, with singular accuracy and acuteness, that "metaphysical intuition of the act of existing" which is the root of all real philosophy and the one thing capable of making the philosopher's vision an analogue of the contemplative experience. This vivid and concrete and personal intuition of existence, immediately apprehended in existing things or in one's own soul, is one of the most exciting and beautiful experiences of which our nature, left to its own resources, is capable. So vital is this experience that it cannot help communicating something of the peace and satisfaction that comes with true and supernatural contemplation. Psychologically it resembles the act of simple contemplation in some of its elementary forms: but the big difference is that it does not produce the same living and lasting effects in the soul.

This apprehension of existence as such sounds esoteric, perhaps, in the language of the philosopher: but it is accessible to any intelligent child. It is an experience which, like so many others of the same order, happens to many who are incapable of understanding it. It fills them with wonder and leaves them inarticulate. It is something the untrained mind cannot cope with, and it tends to remain intact, inviolate in the memory. One does not tell anyone about it because one cannot find any words in which to begin to talk about such a thing.

Typical of this experimental grasp of existence in its concreteness is the sudden awareness of one's own identity that may come over a child as it enters the years of reason. In the middle of play, a little boy of seven or eight becomes suddenly and unaccountably aware that he is a person. His little soul, fresh and clean and made for deep and beautiful illuminations, suddenly becomes radiant with the appreciation of its own being and capacity and dignity. Do not mistake me: this is not a movement of coarse self-assertion. It is intellectual and pure. It is a simple reflection of the truth, and because it is so purely and clearly true it arouses a movement of wonder and gratitude and love, which is in its beautiful candor and immediacy, a profound homage to the God of truth.

A child whose soul has been struck by this warm flash of reality can never forget it. When it strikes him, it leaves him under a spell.

For several minutes he stops his play; he can hardly move, held prisoner by the beautiful inarticulate wonder of the thought that he *exists*. His whole being feels as if it were momentarily caught into a golden cloud. It is an intellectual act of the greatest natural simplicity, a pure intuition, involving no steps of reasoning, and in which the whole soul is suddenly assembled in one active light and there rests.

I wonder how many there are in the world who have had something like this happen to them and have never been able to tell anybody about it. Perhaps they have never even been able to tell themselves about it. They have not realized what a potency for supernatural contemplation and prayer was implied by this capacity for a direct and simple view of existence as such. It has never been developed. Grace could have made something wonderful out of that power. The Holy Spirit put this image of the godhead in us precisely in order to develop it and endow it with tremendous riches. He means to endow us even while we are on earth. It is His plan to enlarge this natural capacity, by contemplation, in this life, in order to fit us for the supreme weight of glory which is the contemplation of God in the beatific vision of heaven.

* * *

Not even the highest and purest natural contemplation can be called mystical in the strict sense. Mystical contemplation implies the direct intervention of God Himself, moving the intellect and will immediately. The metaphysical intuition that was just described is the product of a natural act: it is a reaction, if you will, of the intellect in the presence of a datum of sense experience. The mind, acting on a light of the senses, and realizing its own activity by something more than a mere reflection, apprehends its own peculiar identity in the concreteness of its own action. All this implies the natural concourse of God, of Whose light the human intellect is a participation.

In mystical contemplation the soul reacts to an altogether different light and impulsion, and these are communicated directly to the mind and will, without the direct influence of any sensible species. God Himself produces the effect in the soul without the intervention of any natural agent, except perhaps as an accident or condition or occasion. In a truly mystical experience, the soul cooperates indeed with God, but only passively. That is to say, it acts, but is not the principle of its own action.

The details of all this must be left to a later chapter. What is important here is to understand that human nature, by virtue of its intellectual and spiritual character, is radically in potency for the highest of mystical contemplation and the economy of divine grace is clearly established in such a way as to endow every baptized Christian with the seeds from which can grow the fullness of supernatural and contemplative life.

The baptized infant begins already to share in the inner life of God. The Christian who lives up to his faith, who loves God better than he loves business and money and reputation and pleasure, is certainly developing this participation of God's life in his soul. Neither he nor the infant realizes what is going on. At best, it is a matter of dark belief, of an assent without any sensible appreciation of what he possesses in his soul.

There comes a stage in the spiritual life in which faith gives place to a deeper and spiritual understanding. At this stage the Christian may be gifted with a new and quasi-experimental sense of the presence of God in his soul. Psychologically the same natural forces are apt to be called in to play as in the metaphysical intuition of existence. The faculties of the soul are unified into a mirror which receives the intimation of Being in a simple and undivided light, baffling analysis. But here is the difference. The being apprehended is not the fact of one's own existence, or of existence concretized and seized in one's own mind; nor is it Being as such, nor even infinite Being, Pure Act. Considered as philosopher's abstractions. In this simple light, which is not evident because it is an intensification of the inevident "light" of faith, is "seen" God. In this simple light is grasped something of the meaning that can lie hidden in a mystery of faith. The light is not the product of any natural act. It is produced in the passive soul—a fact which sometimes gives it a breathtaking simplicity and clarity which makes the laborious knowledge acquired by human effort seem gross and slightly absurd. In fact this, which is one of the highest supernatural perfections of the natural faculties, so far transcends the operations of nature as to apparently supersede and "annihilate" them altogether. All the paradoxes of mystical language have to be brought into play to explain this mode of "seeing without seeing," "knowing in darkness," "possessing without possessing" which fills the soul by emptying it. In the end, what is grasped is "touched" rather than seen: what has taken place is an obscure and vital contact with Truth Itself, not the Truth of the Philosopher but the Living God, One in Three Persons, in Whose presence all other truths and judgements vanish into insignificance.

Most important of all, this mystical contact with God is effected in the immediacy of personal love. I stress the word personal; the Truth is Three Persons. All Three giving themselves at once in mystical love to the soul which, perhaps, does not at first realize them as Triune but only as One. But what is realized is the fact that the *purest Truth comes to us only in the form of love.*

It is only because you love that you "touch" or "realize" or "grasp" the most absolute of all Truth in the blind obscurity of transfigured faith which, under the influence of God's vitalizing presence, is endowed the most profound and penetrating conviction and power. And all this is communicated to the depths of the soul without reflection, without effort, without strain, without hesitation, without doubt or the slightest shadow of uncertainty.

Finally, this mystical perception of God is a pure gift of God. We can do nothing to obtain it or to deserve it. Our acts of virtue, of faith and supernatural love, our trust in God, our humility and our acceptance of trial, can dispose us for its reception but cannot strictly merit it, still less provoke it. True, the purest intuitions of the philosopher and the few clean flashes of genuine inspiration that come to a poet are also beyond the immediate command of the will. Yet they can be remotely "willed" in the sense that anyone with the proper gifts can prepare the way and warm himself up to the pitch at which his own faculties, stimulated by favorable circumstances, can produce the final flash of genius out of their own resources.

* * *

The contemplation of God is the reason for our creation. And this contemplation demands the conscious fruition of God made present to the soul in mystical experience. In its perfection it coincides with the integral perfection of charity in which we are "transformed" into God and become "one spirit" with Him according to the language of St. Paul. *Qui adhaeret Domino, unus spiritus est.* [Whoever is joined to the Lord becomes one spirit (with the Lord) 1 Cor 6:17.]

Adam, in Eden, was the type of the perfect contemplative. The Fathers of the Church all considered him as such, and looked on the whole Christian life on earth as a laborious effort to recapture, through the merits of the Passion of the Second Adam, the liberty and integrity and contemplation, the *apatheia* and *gnosis* that were enjoyed by the first. [*apatheia* = absence of concupiscence, passionlessness] [*gnosis* = knowledge of God].

The essence of beatitude, our last end, is described by the teaching authority of the Church as a "vision of God and fruition of His beauty . . . it consists in two things: that we shall see God as He is in His nature and substance and that we shall become as gods. For all those who have fruition of His substance, even though they retain their own substance, they take on a marvelous and almost divine form so that they seem to be gods rather than men." The same authority continues and explains that this is effected by an immediate union of the soul with God, and concludes that the essence of beatitude is to be sought in the actual possession of God.

It would be easy, but perhaps tiresome, to multiply the statements of Fathers and Doctors of the Church that man is created for contemplation.

No one could be clearer than St. Thomas on this point. Speaking of the contemplative life in the question of the *Summa* which treats it *ex professo* [officially], he says that the contemplative life is concerned above all with the contemplation of God's truth because this contemplation is the end of all human life, *finis totius humanae vitae.* [the end of all human life.] He quotes St. Augustine to the effect that the contemplation of God "is promised to us as the end of all our actions and the everlasting perfection of joy," and concludes by telling us that the contemplative life on earth is the beginning of the eternal beatitude of heaven *quae hic incipitu ut in futuro continuetur.* [which, beginning here, will be continued in the future.] This leaves us no doubt that he is talking of contemplation in the strict sense.

St. Bonaventure and Richard of St. Victor, along with St. Thomas himself, find in human nature itself the testimony of the end for which it was created. If we have minds and wills, it is because we were meant to know and love the most perfect Truth and Goodness of God. Indeed, as St. Augustine said, and every Christian mystic repeated after him, "Thou hast made us, O Lord, for thyself, and our hearts are restless until they rest in Thee." And the Bishop of Hippo adds, very succinctly that just as the soul is the life of the body, so the blessed life of the soul is God Himself. *Ut vita carnis anima est, ita beata vita hominis Deus est.* [Just as the spirit give life to the flesh, so the blessed life of man is God.]

This statement is strictly accurate. In fact it is more correct to say that the end for which we are created is not contemplation but *God Himself*. Contemplation is, after all, a created activity. It is the characteristic activity by which free and intellectual beings are united to the

God Who is, Himself, the last end of all things. The end of all our striv-ings is outside the created order. The last step in the line of created things by which we arrive at Him is contemplation: but it is really God who is the end of the journey. Contemplation is simply the station where we alight and pass out into the city of heaven, which is God's own substance and essence.

But besides being the end of our journey, God is also the way. He Himself told us: I am the way. It is the Truth of God made Man Who is, strictly speaking, the way. And yet we cannot even travel by that way, to the Father, through Christ, unless another Divine Person comes to help us and endow us with light and strength. The Holy Ghost comes down to us by the way which we must take to go up to the Father: through the Son, through Jesus Christ. The Holy Ghost is sent to "teach us all things." He purifies our hearts, teaches us love, teaches us prayer, by being Himself our purity, our love and our prayer. He above all is the teacher of the Divine Contemplation for which we were created. It is through Him, and is the bond of His Love, that we will be destined to be married to the Word, Who is the Father's glory and contemplation. In Him, we shall not only contemplate Truth and possess it, but we shall *become* Truth. We shall not only love Truth, but truly *become* Love, in the Spirit of Love Who united Light with His Father and Glory with the Father of Glory.

Chapter Two

O Israel, How great is the house of God and how vast is the place of His possession! It is great, and hath no end. It is high and im-mense. There were the giants, those renowned men, that were from the beginning, of great stature, expert in war. The Lord chose them not, neither did they find the way of knowledge: therefore did they perish. And because they had not wisdom, they perished through their folly.

There are words the prophet sang knowing that the wisdom and the power and the craft of men is madness and weakness and in-eptitude compared with the wisdom that is taught by God alone. And yet it is only in that highest of all wisdoms that we can find peace and fulfillment.

> For if thou hadst walked in the way of God, hadst surely dwelt in peace forever. Learn where is wisdom, where is strength, where is understanding, that thou mayest know also where is length of days and life, where is the light of the eyes and peace.

But man can not find that wisdom by himself alone. The great men of the world have never known it—or else they would never have crucified the Lord of glory. To the pagans it is foolishness, and to the self-complacent doctor of the law, who trusts in his own learning, God's wisdom is scandalous and dark.

> Who hath found out wisdom's place and who hath gone into her treasures? Where are the princes of the nations and they that rule over the beasts that are upon the earth, that take their diversion with the birds of the air, that hoard up silver and gold, wherein men trust? . . . They are cut off and gone down to hell and others are risen up in their place. Young men have seen the light and dwelt upon the earth: but the way of knowledge they have not known . . . The children of Agar also that search after the wisdom that is of the earth, the merchants of Merrha and of Theman, and the tellers of fables and the searchers of prudence and under-standing: but the way of wisdom they have not known, nor have they remembered her paths.

How can anyone scale heaven and capture that wisdom which is inaccessible to the minds and thoughts of men? Can any merchant bring back contemplation in ships from the ends of the earth?

> Who hath gone up into heaven and taken wisdom, and brought her down from the clouds? Who hath passed over the sea and found her and bought her, preferably to chosen gold? *There is none that is able to know her ways, nor that can search out her paths.*

But if no man can find out the wisdom in which all our happi-ness is hidden, we are condemned to die in a strange land, defiled with the dead, feeding our souls with the husks of swine. There is One Who knows wisdom because He is Wisdom. It is He Who can, if He so wills, pour out into our hearts something of His own tremendous light. More than that, He can come down from heaven and teach us Himself the ways of wisdom. And all the Old Testament prophets cried out to Him imploring Him to "tear open the sky and come down." For they too realized that "No one knows the Son but the Father, and no one knows the Father but the Son and he to whom it shall please the Son to reveal Him." The anguish and urgency of their impatience was born of their realization that God had, indeed, decreed to come down to men, for His delights were to be with the children of men. He would take flesh and dwell among us, and whoever would then see Him would see the

Father in heaven. So Baruch sang of Him, of the only One Who really knew wisdom:

> He that knoweth all things knoweth her and hath found her out with His understanding. He that prepared the earth for evermore and filled it with cattle and fourfooted beasts. He that sendeth forth light and it goeth: and called it, and it obeyeth Him with trembling. And the stars have given light in their watches and rejoiced: and they were called and they said, Here we are: and with cheerfulness they have shined forth to Him that made them.

> *This is our God, and there shall no other be accounted of in comparison to Him. He hath found out all the way of knowledge and gave it to Jacob His servant and to Israel His beloved.*

> *Afterwards He was seen upon earth, and conversed with men.*

* * *

The anguish and the desire of the prophets of the Old Testament is lost in the triumph and exultation of the Apostles and Evangelists of the New who went forth to the four corners of the earth proclaiming that God had indeed come down, the Word had in all truth been made flesh and had dwelt among them, and that they had seen His glory, the glory of the only-begotten Son of the Father, full of grace and truth.

The Gospel must be looked at in its wholeness, to be understood. It is something far more than an ethical code, more than a mere body of theological doctrines. It is more than the record of mystical teaching, and a set of practices for arriving at perfection. It is not sufficient to believe that Jesus was the Son of God and to accept the Gospels, therefore, as a unique witness to His life on earth. The Gospels are more than a witness, more than a mine of apologetic and dogmatic proofs for the truth of Christian faith.

The Gospels are the word of God, *Verbum Dei.* And "word" here, *Verbum* [Word], *Logos* [Reason], is something more than a sign of an idea. The word of God is dynamic; it is a force. By means of this force, God produces an effect in the soul. He reveals Himself to the mind that accepts His word and preserves it to "bring forth fruit in patience." For the Words spoken by Christ "are spirit and life." *Verba quae ego loquor vobis spiritus et vita sunt.* [The words that I spoke to you are spirit and life. Jn 6:63.] They do not die with the sound that conveys them: "heaven and earth shall pass away, but My word shall not pass away." The word of God in the Gospel is an instrument by which God effects salvation in the soul that accepts it fully, in the simplicity of faith. And since salvation is the possession of God, God really and actually communicates Himself to the soul in His word, His revelation of His will for men.

When men speak to men, they communicate ideas from one mind to another but when God speaks to men He communicates Himself, His own Truth, in its wholeness, to the wholeness of their being: if they "hear" His words, He enters into their lives and transforms their spirit so that now their whole existence is centered on Him. He becomes the life of their life, and their lives from then on are "built" upon Him.

The Gospels are therefore a sacramental. *Per evangelica dicta deleantur nostra delicta.*

[Through the spoken words of the Gospel (proclamation) may our sins be erased. (Roman Missal)]

But the word of God does not merely justify men. Justification, sanctifying grace, is only the beginning of God's economy of salvation. Salvation is not merely a negative thing: the liberation from sin and from enslavement to the devil and to the passions of our flesh. It is also positive. The positive element is far more important than the negative. God does not separate us from the world, the flesh and the devil merely in order to leave us to ourselves: He endows us with a new life in Him. He is Himself that new life. He gives Himself that new life. He gives Himself to us in order to be the blessedness of our souls, illuminated by His glory.

The word of God, in the Gospels, is eternal life. *Verba mea spiritus et vita sunt.* [My words are spirit and life. Jn 6:63] Eternal life is to know the One true God and Jesus Christ Whom He has sent. The word of God in the Gospel is therefore the seed of the highest and most perfect contemplation. Just as it effects faith in the properly disposed soul, so it will go on and produce much higher effects still, in those who receive it in a "good and perfect heart, in which it will bring forth fruit a hundredfold."

Or, to change the metaphor, the word of God is "living water" and in everyone who receives it, it becomes a "fountain of water springing up into life everlasting." More than that, the word of the Gospel becomes a "river of living water" which is not of this earth but of heaven, and is nothing less than the Holy Spirit, or God Himself.

Therefore the new life promised by Christ to His disciples was not merely a new morality. It was not merely the cessation of sin, followed by normal natural activities performed with a certain piety and decorum. True, our natural life is sanctified by charity, but the economy of the Gospels does not end there. The fulness of Christian life is something more than the sanctification of naturally virtuous acts in view of a reward in the other world. The word of God should begin here on earth to flower into the life of heaven. *Quae sursum sunt sapite, non quae super terran.* [Savor what is above, not what is earthly.] The Douay version translates this as "*seek* the things that are above." But there is more in *sapite* than seeking. It means savoring, and suggests fruition. It is the classical term for the loving knowledge that is at the heart of contemplation. No doubt it does not have all the fulness of contemplation in this context, and in that respect the notion of "seeking" is justified. What it really means is: "realize that your last end is to know and enjoy the things of heaven, and aspire to that knowledge and enjoyment, rather than the fruition of earthly satisfactions."

Christ did not leave His Apostles any doubts about the fulness and dignity of life that had been communicated to them. "To you it is given to know the mysteries of the Kingdom of Heaven." And "all things, whatsoever I have heard of My Father, I have made known to you." He told them they were no longer His servants but His friends, sharing in His own heritage, His own knowledge and love of His Father. More than that, they are the Sons of God and it has not yet appeared what they shall be . . . for they shall be like Him, because they shall see Him as He is. But this sonship, this promise of transformation, is more than an extrinsic qualification: it is the expression of an interior sanctity that flows from union with God Himself, and this union is guaranteed within us by the Holy Spirit of God, the Third Person of the Holy Trinity, Who is given to us and Who constitutes us sons of God, crying out in our souls "Abba, Father!" Indeed, it is through Christ, the Word that we are actually united, by the Holy Spirit, to the Father *per ipsum habemus accessum in uno Spiritu ad Patrem.* [through him we have access to the Father in one Spirit. Eph 2:18.]

* * *

The Apostles and Evangelists and the Disciples of Christ came forth from the cenacle at the third hour, the first Pentecost after Christ ascended into heaven, and the crowd that listened to their preaching and recognized all the tongues of the known world soon realized that these Galileans were filled with something that was more than an ideal.

St. John, the greatest of the Evangelists, the Eagle, and the Son of Thunder, began both his Gospel and his first Epistle with summaries of the whole content of revelation. Theologian and contemplative that he was he wrote out a theology of contemplation in words of fire that are still the foundation of all Christian doctrine. *In principio erat Verbum, et Verbum erat apud Deum. . .* [In the beginning was the Word, and the Word was with God. . . Jn 1:1.] The tremendous chords that open the fourth Gospel and close all Masses, echo what John heard of eternity when he rested his head upon the Heart of Christ. Purer, clearer, more speculative than the first sentences of his Epistle, the Prologue of St. John's Gospel nevertheless lacks one thing which we find in the first Chapter of the *Epistola Prima*. [First letter.] There is a matchlessly urgent power of conviction in the simplicity with which he announces his subject: *"That which was from the beginning, which we have heard, which we have seen with our eyes, which we have looked upon and our hands have handled, of the word of life."* The Word of Life is not merely the Gospel, but the Second Person, the Fire whose sparks the Evangelists were to scatter all over the earth in their writing and the Apostles in their preaching, and mark, they have *touched* the uncreated Word, "seen with their eyes," "handled with their hands". It is from the immediacy of this experience that their preaching draws its dynamism, for they had touched Him from Whom power went out to heal all. *Virtus ex illon exibat et sanabat omnes.* [Power went out from him and healed all. Lk. 6:19.]

From then on, the Apostles could only go through the world crying out as John the Baptist cried out on the banks of Jordan: *"Ecce!"* "Look!" and as John the Evangelist repeats time after time in the few pages of his epistle: *Vidata!* "Look! See!" *Apparuit!* He has appeared! They are conscious of their mission to wake up the whole world not to the secrets of some esoteric cult but to a glory and magnificence which are all about us, in the midst of us, and which we know not.

What is this glory that we are to lift up our heads and see? What is this that we are called to look upon and understand? The Apostles bombard us with huge, fundamental terms which to us are distinct from one another but to them seem to meet in one central focus of synonymous meaning: Life, Light, Truth, and *Caritas,* Love. These, it appears, are all one. They are God, and they are made flesh in Jesus Christ. Light, Life, Truth and Love are so much one that to Love is to be enlightened, to live, and to possess the Truth. "Every one that loveth is born of God, and knoweth God." To be more exact, to Love Christ, the whole Mystical Christ, Jesus and all those who share His divine life, is to see and possess God. Why is this? Because Christ is the Word of God, eternal, "Who was in the Beginning."

Now the Word of God is the glory of the Father, the splendor of the divine substance, proceeding from the Father by intellectual generation from all eternity. The Word and the Father are one substance, one nature: they are one infinite Truth, but they are distinct in their personal relations for the same Truth begets itself as Father and proceeds intellectual from itself as its own Word or idea or contemplation of itself. Thus this infinite Truth is One and at the same time distinct not in two persons only but in three, for there is another relation of origin springing forth from the relation already existing between Father and the Son. For now the Truth having generated itself intellectually, proceeds from itself freely, in the mode proper to volition, or in our language, by an "act of will." This third Person is the love of the Truth for its own Splendor. And so there is One God in Three Persons: the Truth, Father or Origin; the Splendor and Glory and Figure of the Truth, originating in the Truth; and the Joy, the Exultation, the uncompassed and magnificent of the Freedom of the Truth which proceeds, as an act of Love, from the twin origin of Truth reflected in Truth.

This is the contemplative Life which is God. Infinite Actuality realizing Himself in a blaze of absolutely unlimited intelligence and manifesting His perfection in a Freedom, a Love, an uncompassed substantial generosity which is so magnificently pure as to be absolutely inconceivable to anyone but Himself!

The spiritual genius of the Apostles, illuminated by the Holy Ghost, saw through the wide open doors of revelation into the furnace of contemplation which is the mutual relations of the Father, Son and Holy Ghost. They ran out into the streets shouting like men who were drunk. Spreading the news of what they had seen, they overthrew a whole empire of seemingly invincible darkness and error and sin. They broke the whole tremendous power of hell with the words of their Gospel, with a little clean water and the sign of the Cross, with bread and wine and some words spoken by the Savior, with oil and chrism and with a few simple sentences and gestures of prayer. For, "last of all in these days God has spoken to us by His Son, whom He hath appointed heir of all things, by whom also He made the world. Who, being the brightness of His glory and the figure of His substance, upholding all things by the word of His power, making purgation of sins, sitteth at the right hand of the majesty on high.

* * *

The Apostles were not content to share with others the Truths they themselves had learned in contemplation. Their mission was also to teach others how to learn the same truths from experience, as they themselves had learned them. It was not enough to make known the doctrines of revelation merely as abstract and speculative truths: for as long as these things were only theories, to be reduced to practice through the medium of an ethical code, Christianity would not achieve its full maturity in the souls of men. For Christianity, let us repeat, was not another philosophy like the stoicism of the ancients or a mystery cult like those of Orpheus and Mithras. It was not to be a "system" of thought completed by a code of action. It was something infinitely more: a Life, a more abundant Life which was a sharing in the infinite Life of God, and contained in itself the meaning of all existence and all activity. For the Christian, to live this highest of all lives in its fulness also automatically brought with it the contemplation of the highest truth and the enjoyment of the most perfect joy.

Ultimately, Christianity does not even teach a way to God that is distinct from God Himself: for Christ—the Word of God—revealed unmistakably that He is both the end of all our strivings, the Truth in which our minds rest, containing in Himself all doctrine, and the way to the Truth our end. *Ego sum via, veritas et vita.* [I am the way, the truth and the life. Jn. 14:6] St. Bernard paraphrases and explains: "I am the way leading to Truth: I am the Truth, Who promises Life: and I am the Life which I give."

The Christian Life is not so much a doctrine, even a doctrine practiced and lived. It is Christ Himself, living in us. *Vivo, iam non ego, vivit vero in me Christus.* [I live, now no longer I, but Christ lives in me. Gal 2:20]

This life begins at baptism, and it can be lived in the depths of our souls without our having any consciousness of being different from what we were before. Nevertheless, the fulness of the Christian life is achieved when grace possesses the highest faculties of the soul, illuminating the intellect, purifying and transforming the will and raising both above the normal operations of nature, unifying them in a supernatural activity in which they become at least obscurely conscious of the new existence which is theirs.

Not only do we accept the fact of divine revelation and the new life of faith blindly, on the authority of others, but we begin to realize what all these things mean, we enter into ineffable communion with the Truth dwelling in our souls, and we find ourselves gifted, through absolutely no merit or effort of our own, with an insight into divine things which is rightly called "understanding" although its mode of penetrating the divine mysteries makes their content accessible to us without making it any less obscure.

This understanding is sometimes called a "sense," *sensum,* in the Vulgate. "We know that the Son of God is come and He hath given us His understanding, *dedit nobis sensum* [he gave us meaning], that we may know the True God and may be in His true Son." This "sense" is what Jesus gave to the Disciples with whom He walked to Emmaus on the day of His Resurrection. They did not know Him at first. He spoke to them of the words and prophecies of Scripture, and while they were talking together, their "hearts burned within them"—in the first un-recognized movements of the contemplative gift. The significant thing is that although they had already begun to have an interior and exper-imental recognition of the Divine Word, it did not yet make them con-templative because they had no means of appreciating what it was. It took another and more definite infusion of the Gift of Understanding and Wisdom—in the reception of the Holy Eucharist—to open their eyes altogether. St. Luke also tells us in the same chapter how Jesus, before His Ascension, opened the understanding of the Apostles and Disciples: *aperuit illis sensum* [he opened this meaning to them. Lk 24:27], to give them a sure and affective knowledge of the meaning of Scripture. Contemplation, in the New Testament and among the Fathers too, is inseparable from Scripture. It is through the word of Scripture that we reach the Word Who is God. The Gift of contempla-tion, to the early Church, meant the acquisition of an inward eye to which the obscure, outward envelope of Scripture became transparent and the word of revelation gave place to the Word Who is generated eternally in the Bosom of the Father. and Who comes to us hidden in the words of Scripture as though in a Sacrament.

St. Paul repeatedly urged his converts—many of whom had been numbered among the wildest inhabitants of the seaports of the Levant—to aspire to this contemplative insight that would unite them with the Word in deep vision and love. He prayed the Father of Glory to give them "the spirit of wisdom and revelation in the knowledge of Him, the eyes of your heart enlightened *(illuminatos oculos cordis)* [enlightened eyes of the heart. Eph 1:8] that you may know what the hope is of His calling. That Christ may dwell by faith in your hearts; that being rooted and founded in charity you may be able to comprehend with all the saints what is the breadth and length and height and depth, to know also the charity of Christ which surpasseth all knowledge that you may be filled unto the fulness of God." Over and over again the Apostle urges them on by telling them of his prayers that they may abound in this mysterious inward gift of enlightenment which is inseparable from the perfect love of God, which increases with love and penetrates the mysteries of revelation with the vision of love to possess God *in omni sapientia et intellectu spirituali* [in all wisdom and spiritual understanding. Eph 1:8], to become, at last, one spirit with Him.

The mystical contemplation of God is clearly associated in the doctrine of St. Paul, with the fulness of the Christian life and the integrity of Christian perfection.

St. Thomas epitomizes Christian tradition on this point by interpreting the word *sensus,* "mind", as the *wisdom* of Christ. When St. Paul says that those who are mature in the Christian life have the "mind" of Christ, he means that they share the contemplation of the Word. It is no merely abstract, intellectual knowledge of God, but a concrete apprehension of Him, by that loving and fruitive knowledge properly called wisdom. The Angelic Doctor explains that the term *sense (sensus)* in the Vulgate is philosophically correct even though there is question here only of spiritual and intellective perception, and nothing within reach of the interior or exterior senses. And he gives a deep reason. It is appropriate, he says, that this loving knowledge should be called a *sense,* for although it is intellectual and therefore above all sense or feeling, it apprehends God, its object, in His singular, particular being.

This wisdom, this "sense of God" says St. Thomas, is one of the elements of Christian perfection. He flatly declares: "He who has this sense is perfect." *Qui sentit quae Dei sunt, perfectus est.* [Who understands what is of God, is perfect]. On the other hand, the "sense" the appreciative knowledge of worldly things, which seeks fruition in them as ends in themselves is a wisdom damnable in the eyes of God, because it makes union with Him impossible. *Qui non sentiunt nisi carnalia Deo placare non possunt.* [Those who only understand what is of the flesh cannot please God.]

The perfection conferred on the soul by this wisdom is twofold. It fulfils all the capacities of our highest faculties: intellect and will. It separates both of these from earthly things and unites them with God. It delivers the intellect from a knowledge depending on sense species and human discourse, and it frees the will from attachment to created things and dedicates it entirely to God. *Est perfectio caritatis ubi nulla est cupiditas.* [It is perfect love when there is no attachment.] Finally, this perfection is evident from the fact that in this "sense" of God, the soul apprehends the things of God and judges all other things under the direct guidance of the Holy Spirit.

Just as carnal wisdom proceeds to its conclusions under the guidance of the "spirit of the world," so Christian wisdom, impelled and illuminated by the Spirit of God arrives at God Himself. What is more, this wisdom is not only from God, but it *is* God. *Haec sapientia Deus est et a Deo.* [this wisdom is God and is from God. 1 Cor 1:30.]

Hence it is quite understandable that St. Thomas should describe this "sense" of God as the contemplation of those who "being subject to the spirit of God, *enjoy a most sure and certain knowledge of spiritual things.*

It is certainly not surprising that this should be so, when Jesus Himself so clearly determined this bequest to His Church when opening to His Apostles His spiritual testament at the Last Supper.

"From henceforth you shall know Him, (the Father) . . . Yet a little while and the world seeth me no more, But you see me, because I live and you shall live . . . you shall know Him (the Spirit of Truth) because He shall abide with you and be in you . . . You shall know that I am in my father and you in me and I in you."

He does not say that we are merely to *believe* these things, but that we shall have a deeper and greater certitude even than the assent of faith can give us. The term *knowledge* is not considered too strong to apply to this penetration of the deepest of all mysteries, the inner life of the One God in Three Persons. There can be no doubt that this implies a real manifestation of the Divine Life, because Jesus uses that very word: "He that loveth me shall be loved of my Father and *I will manifest myself to Him* . . . and my Father will love him and we will come to him and will make our abode with him."

Finally, lifting up His eyes to His Father in heaven, Jesus declared that He had communicated to men the very glory which is His own infinite Truth, the reflection of His Father, and that by this communication they would be drawn in to the circle of subsistent relations which are the contemplation and love of God Himself, in the Most Blessed Trinity:

"The glory which thou has given to me, I have given them; that they may be one as we also are one: I in them and thou in me, that they may be made perfect in one."

* * *

There is a problem about Christ's promise of the Holy Ghost to His Apostles. After all, they certainly had faith in Him, they loved Him with a supernatural love. They possessed sanctifying grace, they were living supernatural lives. All these things would have been impossible unless the Holy Ghost were already present in their souls. Why did Christ tell them that He would send them the Holy Ghost?

The answer is that although their faith had made them Christians the supernatural life was simply in an embryonic, or at least an immature state in their souls. They had faith, charity, their lives were virtuous enough, but their outlook was still too human. They judged all things according to the values of the world, according to the life of the senses or, at best, of reason, and as a result they had no real appreciation of their supernatural calling. They could not yet conceive what it meant to be heirs of the Kingdom of heaven. They had no sense of their great spiritual destiny. On the contrary, they wrangled among themselves about precedence in the messianic kingdom. They wanted to know who would have first place, who would sit at the right and left of the King. The supernatural life meant, to them, casting out devils and working miracles and they thought themselves entitled to make use of their power to punish their enemies: it was St. John himself, he who was later to become the eagle among contemplatives, who, in his spiritual immaturity wanted to call down fire upon some Samaritans who had hurt his feelings.

Before Pentecost, and above all before the Resurrection of Christ, the Apostles were in pretty much the same condition as those Corinthians and Hebrews whom St. Paul rebuked for their imperfection and their superficial Christianity.

And therefore St. Augustine explains why the Holy Ghost had to be "sent" to them when they already had Him in their souls. The reason is this. Since the Apostles did not possess the Spirit of God in the measure in which they needed to possess Him, they might as well not have possessed Him at all. In other words, the Holy Spirit was dwelling in their souls, but since He did not exercise a sufficiently strong influence in their lives it was as if He were not there. He was obscured and hidden. He could not manifest His presence to them because they were still guided by a totally different wisdom, a wisdom which is contrary to the wisdom of God. They had the Spirit of God in their hearts by grace, but in all the practical conduct of their lives they were largely guided and dominated by quite another spirit, which the Scriptures call the "spirit of the world," the "wisdom of the flesh." And the "Wisdom of the flesh is the enemy of God, for it is not subject to the law of God, nor can it be."

St. Augustine contemplates this sorry situation, and his line of reasoning follows that taken by St. Thomas in the consideration we have just quoted on the "sense" of Christ. St. Augustine comes to much the same conclusion. The perfection of our supernatural life depends on our love of God and our union with the will of God. This love and obedience depend, in turn, on the action of the Holy Ghost in our souls. And the action of the Holy Ghost increases in proportion to our appreciation of His presence, His love and His power to assist and perfect us in the ways of divine love. Hence, where there is no thought of the Holy Ghost, no awareness of God's presence, no interest in His love, no concern for His help, and no desire to see His face, our supernatural life is bound to be feeble and obscure. But where infused love has awakened our souls to a deep and constant desire of God and where the light of faith, knowledge and understanding keep our minds awake and we tend to grow rapidly in the secret life which we have from Him, in Christ, and our supernatural stature increases beyond measure and beyond all human accounting, without our being half aware of what is going on. And so, St. Augustine argues that Christ promised to give His Apostles the Holy Ghost in such a way that they would *know* His presence and live in intimate union with Him and be taught and directed by Him. This awareness, this intimacy, this wakeful and attentive appreciation would transform their lives. It would introduce them into the fulness of Christian perfection.

In the economy of salvation, it is the Holy Ghost Who is charged with the sanctification and the perfection of men. This work is appropriated above all to the Third Person, Who is the love of the other Two Persons of the Blessed Trinity and thus, in a sense, the "perfection" of the Trinity, for "charity is the bond of perfection."

In the first place, the Spirit of God is given to us by Christ to deliver us from the blindness and hopeless futility of passion which makes us the slaves of our natural desires and fears. Dominated by emotion and the confusion of conflicting appetite man cannot have peace until he is set free from this servitude of corruption. The Holy

Spirit sets us free from sin, and, indeed, without His direct intervention there is no escape from the "law of sin and of death". But this is
only the beginning of the work of grace in our souls. The Holy Spirit
does not liberate us from sin merely in order to leave us on the human
plane of existence, leading humdrum lives of bourgeois virtue, practicing thrift, not eating or drinking more than we can decently contain,
and being cheerful in our relations with people who really annoy us
intensely. No doubt it is an asset to be able to be pleasant as well as
civil under trying circumstances: but the Holy Ghost has much more
to do in our souls than produce such tame effects as these.

His work of liberation does not stop with the checking of
grosser disorders. It is God's will that we should be completely purified of all the motives which turn us away from the peace and clarity
of His own wisdom. We must be completely and immovably established in His will, so that nothing may cloud the clarity of our vision
of Him, nothing may shake the peace of our wills united with Him and
resting in His infinite peace. Therefore the Holy Spirit makes war without respite upon all the forces that oppose His complete domination of
our souls. He is the Spirit of Life, and as long as there remain in our
soul the faintest traces of those elements of death which manifest
themselves as the "wisdom of the flesh," He will be at work counter-
acting their influence and purifying the mind and will of their infec-
tion. Nevertheless we remain free under His action, and if we choose
to prefer sickness and death, to health and life, He will not compel us
to live. He will not force His happiness upon us. But if we receive His
grace—a thing which we cannot do without grace itself, working effi-
caciously in us—He will move us to deny the "prudence of the flesh"
and to serve as His instruments in the work of our own salvation by
"mortifying the deeds of the flesh."

The Spirit of God, then, is the chief Master and Guide of all
Christian asceticism. He is the only safe guide. Without Him, asceticism is a distortion, a form of spiritual gymnastics, and as such it is
nothing but another form of the "wisdom of the world" which is our
own worst enemy and His. But the work of the Spirit does not end in
the negative labor of self-denial and correction. His chief function is
positive. Besides removing whatever is harmful or even merely useless
in our interior life, He strengthens and fosters everything that is good:
He develops in us the nascent capacities for spiritual and contemplative life. He helps our weakness, *adjuvat infirmitatem nostram* [Rom
8:14] and while we are too blind and too stupid to know what is good

[line missing ms. p. 37]. In fact, it may happen that he asks God to send us quite the opposite to what we ourselves would naturally ask for. As long as we are only superficially Christian, our prayers tend to be formulated according to the standards of human prudence, and they express our ambition, our sluggishness in spiritual things, our fear of labor, our love of comfort and pleasure. The Holy Spirit sometimes obtains for us things that our nature does not at all desire.

The Holy Spirit, Who lives in our souls by grace, demands insistently to be allowed to work in us without impediment. If we listen to Him, it is bound to cost us many sacrifices. He will lead us into difficulties, and make us do hard and unpleasant things. He will begin to cut away our pride and self-complacency. He will starve out our love of pleasure, and shame our cowardice by carrying us through trials we never dreamed we could stand. He will do all this in order to burn and purify our souls and cast out the wisdom that is opposed to His wisdom. He will exercise, with the sign of the Cross, all the prudence of the flesh and of the world. And in proportion as we allow Him to cleanse and empty our souls of this false wisdom, He will fill them with His own wisdom, and we will begin to learn something of the peace which the world cannot give, the peace of the children of God.

In proportion as we give ourselves over to the power of the Spirit of God, Whose love urges us on through the darkness of hardship and sacrifice, where the price of every advance is with great faiths, we begin to acquire an unexpected sense of freedom and ease, a mysterious sureness and capacity to perform difficult and unfamiliar actions. And this liberty, carrying with it a deeper assurance of supernatural life, begins to make us obscurely aware of that connaturality with God which merits for sanctifying grace the qualification of "divine sonship." For the Spirit of Liberty gives testimony to our spirit that we are the Sons of God, provided we suffer with Christ, that we may be glorified with Him.

The more we are subject to the movement and guidance of grace, the more we are liberated from the influence and direction of selfish and sensual motives. The whole object of the economy of grace is to perfect our liberation from the flesh by completing our subjection to the Holy Spirit, so that all our motives may become supernatural and all the activity of our minds and wills may be directed by an immediate influx of intellectual light and spiritual energy from the depths of the divine Truth and Love. This progressive divinization of our interior activity elevates us above our own natural plane and gives us participation in God's life which is no mere metaphor, no mere moral union but a real and physical actuality. *Qui Spiritu Dei agantur, sunt filii Dei.* [Those who are moved by the Spirit of God are sons of God. Rom 8:14]

St. Paul, whose exposition we are still analyzing, clearly shows that the Holy Spirit develops in us a keener and more lively sense of our supernatural participation in God's life, as He gains a surer grasp upon our souls. The two normally go together: union with the Holy Spirit, by love and obedience to His secret guidance might logically be expected to bring with them an experimental appreciation of the new life that is flooding our spiritual faculties with its energy. *Qui secundum spiritum sunt, quae sunt spiritus sontiunt.* [Those who are according to the Spirit are those who understand what is of the Spirit. Rom 8:5] The classical chapter in which the Apostle works out this doctrine is in the First Epistle to the Corinthians, where the contrast between the Spirit of God and the Spirit of the world is accompanied by a clear statement that the perfection of the Christian life brings with it a conscious participation in God's own contemplation of the splendors of His divine essence. And this vision of divine things is given to us in the gift of the Holy Spirit "who searcheth all things, even the deep things of God."

The term of this activity of the Holy Spirit in the Christian soul is described as a mystical transformation into God. This transformation terminates not in a complete physical identity of the soul and God in one substance, because that would be metaphysically impossible. The abyss that exists between an infinite Being Who is Pure Act, and a contingent creature held in being by His power forbids a substantial union between the two. A human nature cannot become the divine nature. Yet in the miracle of the Incarnation the two natures, divine and human, were united in one divine Person. Next to this hypostatic union, which is the unique privilege of Christ alone, the closest possible union between God and a created substance is the mystical transformation in which a soul capable of contemplation becomes perfectly identified with God in *all its spiritual activities.*

To love God as God loves Himself because you see Him as He sees Himself: this is the inconceivable exaltation which is promised to the Christian as the term of all the work of the Holy Spirit in his soul. Such a consummation means, for all practical purposes, that man becomes a god in everything except by right. He is a god in fact because he is living the perfect life of God, in God and with God. The only thing that God retains for Himself is the fact that this life is His by nature, while it is granted to the beatified soul only by participation. This perfect union, consummated in heaven, and already realized to a great extent on earth in the lives of the greatest saints, is summed up by St. Paul in the words: "But we, beholding the glory of the Lord with open face, are transformed into the same image, from glory to glory, as by the Spirit of the Lord."

The word image reminds us here that one most important thing remains to be said about the role attributed to the Holy Ghost, by Scripture, in raising men to the perfection of the contemplative life. It is this: Just as the Holy Ghost proceeds from the Father and the Son, all his operations in the souls of men are explicitly referred to the Father through the Son. The Holy Spirit proceeds from the Father and the Son and the work attributed to Him outside God takes its character from the internal origin of the Holy Spirit within God. By His Love He reaches out from the depths of the Godhead to draw us into the divine life and fix us, as it were, in the two Persons Who are the One principle of His own procession. It is therefore his function, above all, to draw us to Christ, because all our destiny begins and ends in Christ. It was from the Word that the Holy Spirit drew forth the exemplar causes for our creation, and it is in the Word that we are to come to rest at last, beholding the Father in the mirror of His glory. "Through Him, Christ, the Word) We have access in One Spirit to the Father."

The whole work of the Holy Spirit on earth is centered and focused on the Person Who is the Word, Jesus Christ. His function begins with his "testimony" to Christ in Scripture continues with reminding us of everything Christ taught and teaching us all things by His unction, that is by His infused light and love. The final term of the work is to fulfil the purpose of our creation by glorifying us, in the Word, in heaven. The place of the Holy Spirit in the economy of salvation is then to make us saints, to make us contemplatives, in Christ. That is, to unite us to the Word of God in a union of perfect likeness by contemplation. His purpose in our regard is that we, in the words of the Vulgate, may be identified with the image of the Son: *conformes fieri imaginis Filii.* [conformed to the image of the Son. Rom 8:28]

"What I Wear Is Pants":
Monasticism as "Lay" Spirituality
in Merton's Later Life and Work

Patrick O'Connell

In his correspondence with Rosemary Ruether, we find Thomas Merton making some rather disconcerting comments about his life as a hermit. The solitude he had sought for years as the fulfillment of his monastic vocation now seems to be presented virtually as a repudiation of that vocation. On February 14, 1967, he writes, "I am in a position where I am practically laicized and de-institutionalized, and living like all the other old bats who live alone in the hills in this part of the country and I feel like a human being again. My hermit life is expressly a *lay* life. I never wear the habit except when at the monastery and I try to be as much on my own as I can and like the people around the country."[1] Three weeks later, he refers again to his "'secularized' existence as a hermit" and explains, "I am not only leading a more 'worldly' life (me and the rabbits), but am subtly infecting the monastery with worldly ideas,"[2] through, he may mean, his weekly talks to the community on political and literary topics. Such remarks may be interpreted as an expression of Merton's disillusion with institutionalized monastic life in general and with the Gethsemani community in particular, or as a rather disingenuous, even somewhat duplicitous, attempt to justify his present vocation to a particularly fierce critic of

1. Thomas Merton, *The Hidden Ground of Love: Letters on Religious Experience and Social Concerns,* ed. William H. Shannon (New York: Farrar, Straus, Giroux, 1985) 501; the same letter is also found in Mary Tardiff, OP, ed., *At Home in the World: The Letters of Thomas Merton and Rosemary Radford Ruether* (Maryknoll, N.Y.: Orbis, 1995) 23.

2. *Hidden Ground of Love,* 505; *At Home in the World,* 38.

monasticism.[3] Both of these motives are no doubt present to some extent. But I would like to propose that underlying the disillusion and/or the defensiveness there is a more complex, and ultimately more satisfying, explanation for Merton's use of this sort of language: his studies and his own experience had convinced him that a "lay" spirituality was not only compatible with monasticism but from a certain perspective was an integral part of monastic history and identity.

Such a proposal may initially strike one as illogical if not absurd: lay and monastic states would seem to be polar opposites, mutually exclusive, and in one sense they certainly are. By definition the vowed religious life is distinguished from the lay, secular state, and monks are religious par excellence. But "lay" can also be used to contrast with "clerical," a state which is by no means identical with "religious," though in popular perception they are easily confused. Merton himself makes note of the difference, and indicates its significance for a proper understanding of monastic life, in reflecting on Dietrich Bonhoeffer's *Prison Letters,* which he calls "very monastic in their own way." By this surprising statement he apparently means that Bonhoeffer's vision of "religionless Christianity," which does not publicly call attention to itself, has a dimension of hiddenness comparable to the "desert" quality of monasticism. "His 'worldliness,'" Merton continues, "can only be understood in the light of this 'monastic' seri-

3. Though Ruether's criticism of monastic "withdrawal" is intense, particularly in the early letters to Merton (see the letter of early March, 1967 [*At Home in the World,* 27–30]), in a generally overlooked article entitled "Monks and Marxists: A Look at the Catholic Left" (*Christianity and Crisis,* 33:7 [April 30, 1973] 75–9) she explicitly credits the "monastic spirituality of Thomas Merton" (along with Dorothy Day and the Catholic Worker movement) with being at the root of U.S. Catholic involvement in work for peace and justice; see particularly 76: "Here it was the probing mind of Thomas Merton that provided the hermeneutic for the spirituality taking place in Dan Berrigan, Jim Forest, Jim Douglas [sic] and others. In retreats at Gethsemane [sic], through his writings and voluminous correspondence, Merton helped to form a spirituality that transformed prayer into protest, contemplation into resistance to the powers and principalities of a murderous world. . . . Thus, in the monastic spirituality of Thomas Merton, traditional Christian rejection of 'this world' took on new and concrete meaning, not as a struggle against flesh and blood, but as a struggle against the powers and principalities of the great empires, with America as their most recent representative. Here monastic spirituality was reconnected with its apocalyptic root." Ruether goes on to compare this personalistic, "prophetic" stance with the more praxis-oriented, Marxist-influenced approach found in Latin America and elsewhere (what would come to be known as liberation theology), using each to critique what she perceives as the shortcomings of the other.

ousness, which is, however, not . . . a withdrawal, a denial. It is a mode of presence." He concludes his reflection by aligning monasticism with this stance rather than a more public, ecclesiastical witness: "Paradoxically, then, Bonhoeffer's mode of unnoticed presence in the world is basically monastic as opposed to the 'clerical' or 'priestly' presence, which is official, draws attention to itself and issues its formal message of institutional triumph."[4] Thus if the term "lay" is contrasted not with "religious" but with "clerical," it would seem that Merton is locating monasticism on the "lay" side of the division, where it is well situated, not incidentally, to enter into dialogue not only with the "secular" Christianity of a Bonhoeffer but with persons of other faiths, or even of no religious faith at all.

I

The foundation for this position is not merely eccentric or idiosyncratic personal preference or practice on Merton's part. It is a conclusion grounded in his study of monastic origins. He notes, "The monk was originally a *layman* (priests were exceptional) who lived alone in the desert outside the framework of any institution, even of the Christian and Ecclesial institution."[5] This statement should not be taken to imply

4. Thomas Merton, *A Vow of Conversation: Journals 1964–1965* (New York: Farrar, Straus, Giroux, 1988) 65–6; a slightly different version of this passage is found in Thomas Merton, *Dancing in the Water of Life: Seeking Peace in the Hermitage—Journals, Volume Five: 1963–1965*, ed. Robert E. Daggy, (San Francisco: HarperCollins, 1997) 129. In *Contemplation in a World of Action* (Garden City, N.Y.: Doubleday, 1971), Merton relates this "monastic" dimension of Bonhoeffer's thought to his imprisonment: "Bonhoeffer, regarded as an opponent of all that monasticism stands for, himself realized the need for certain 'monastic' conditions in order to maintain a true perspective in and on the world. He developed these ideas when he was awaiting his execution in a Nazi prison" (7–8). Reflecting on Bonhoeffer's *Ethics* in his *Working Notebook #16*, from the second half of 1965, Merton writes, "The monk originally *broke out* of the clerical 'space' of the Church. To roam in the desert, the ultimate of the world, the place relegated to the devil—to restore the desert to condition of paradise—by showing it is *not* a space belonging to the devil. This is the real spirit of Vatican II—as opposed to Vat I, etc., when this was not at all clear yet" (48).
5. *Contemplation in a World of Action*, 239; see also *The Inner Experience* (VIII): "the first monks of all, the Egyptian desert Fathers, the pioneers of the monastic and contemplative lives, were *lay people*" (*Cistercian Studies Quarterly*, 19:4 [1984] 338). In *A History of Christian Spirituality I: The Spirituality of the New Testament and the Fathers* (1960; trans. Mary P. Ryan [London: Burns & Oates, 1963]), Louis Bouyer writes: "The monk was simply a Christian, and, more precisely, a devout layman, who limited

a separation from the wider Church, but simply that the monk's participation in the Church does not consist in fulfilling a specific organizational role.[6] "Christian solitude," Merton emphasizes, is "essentially an
expression of the mystery of the Church, even when in some sense it implies a certain freedom from institutional structures."[7] But this "freedom
is never a freedom *from* the Church but always a freedom *in* the Church
and a contribution to the Church's own charismatic heritage."[8]

This charismatic dimension, the willingness to be led, like Jesus,
by the Spirit into the desert, to allow all familiar roles and usual com-
forts and securities to be stripped away so that God alone might be
one's sole protection and child of God one's only identity, was the hall-

himself to taking the most radical means to make his Christianity integral" (317). In
his authoritative history of early monasticism, *The Desert a City: An Introduction to the
Study of Egyptian and Palestinian Monasticism under the Christian Empire* (Oxford:
Blackwell, 1966), Derwas J. Chitty likewise refers to the lay character of early monasticism: about the first major figure of monasticism, he writes, "Antony was an illiter-
ate layman, and the majority of the Egyptian monks were much the same" (86), and
summarizes, "At the beginning of that period, the monastic movement was a new
enterprise, a lay movement with no literature but Holy Scripture—a determination,
in renunciation of the world, to live the full evangelical life, whether in solitude or
community" (179). (Merton was familiar with both these works: Bouyer is cited in the
1961 novitiate lectures, *Notes on Ascetical and Mystical Theology*, 23 and passim; Chitty
is quoted on 135 of *Working Notebook #24*, from late May, 1967.)

6. See the opening words of the Preface to Louis Bouyer's *The Meaning of
the Monastic Life*, trans. Kathleen Pond (New York: P. J. Kenedy, 1955), a work that
Merton himself called "fundamental" and "standard" (Thomas Merton, *The School
of Charity: Letters on Religious Renewal and Spiritual Direction*, ed. Patrick Hart,
O.C.S.O. [New York: Farrar, Straus, Giroux, 1990] 119, 145): "The purpose of this
book is primarily to point out to monks that their vocation in the Church is not, and
never has been, a special vocation. The vocation of the monk is, but is no more than,
the vocation of the baptized man. But it is the vocation of the baptized man carried,
I would say, to the farthest limits of its irresistible demands" (ix); see likewise the
statements on page 13: "monastic life is nothing else, no more and no less, than a
Christian life whose Christianity has penetrated every part of it. It is a Christian life
which is completely open, without refusal or delay, to the Word, which opens itself
and abandons itself to it"; and page 22: "To be a monk, then, is simply to be an integral Christian." Merton himself writes, "The monk is not defined by his task, his
usefulness. In a certain sense he is supposed to be 'useless' because his mission is
not to *do* this or that but to *be* a man of God. He does not live in order to exercise a
specific function: his business is life itself" (*Contemplation in a World of Action*, 7).

7. *Contemplation in a World of Action*, 251; for Merton, "to be called to a totally different mode of existence, outside of secular categories and *outside of the religious establishment* . . . is the very heart of monasticism" (23).

8. *Contemplation in a World of Action*, 251.

mark of primitive monasticism. "In the earliest days of desert monasticism," Merton writes, "there were no vows, no written rules, and institutional structure was kept at a minimum. The monastic commitment was taken with extreme and passionate seriousness, but this commitment was not protected by judicial sanctions or by institutional control."[9] Monastic formation depended on personal authority, "the charismatic authority of wisdom, experience and love,"[10] rather than formal office, on relationships rather than regulations: "There was strict obedience on the part of the novice who sought to reproduce in his own life all the actions and thoughts of his spiritual master or 'spiritual father.' But the spiritual father had been chosen freely because of his own experience and his evident charism of renunciation and vision."[11]

Of course such a situation could not continue indefinitely, and the institutionalization of monasticism was both inevitable and necessary, as Merton himself recognized, noting that "it must be admitted that communal structures have a value that must not be underestimated."[12] But he also consistently maintained that the structure was for the sake of the charism, not vice versa. To equate monasticism simply

9. Ibid., 191–2; see also Merton's Introduction to *The Wisdom of the Desert* (New York: New Directions, 1960): "An Abbot was not then, as now, a canonically elected superior of a community, but any monk or hermit who had been tried by years in the desert and proved himself a servant of God" (15). In *A History of Christian Spirituality I*, Bouyer writes: "Later on, the canonists would tend to see [monasticism] only as a state of life, defined once for all by the vows. But at this stage, the vows were still unknown and the monastic life seemed, on the contrary, to be a commitment to detachments and correlative ascents which were to have no end here below" (308).

10. *The Wisdom of the Desert*, 5; in *Contemplation in a World of Action*, Merton cites the teaching of Antony: "There was nothing to which they had to 'conform' except the secret, hidden, inscrutable will of God. . . . It is very significant that . . . the authority of St. Anthony is adduced for what is the basic principle of desert life: that God is the authority and that apart from His manifest will there are few or no principles" (6–7).

11. *Contemplation in a World of Action*, 192 (see also 271); in *A History of Christian Spirituality I*, Bouyer writes: "In the beginning, . . . the superior, or more precisely, the 'abbot,' that is, the spiritual father, was not a personage endowed with an official function: he was simply the perfected spiritual man. The anchorite whose anchoritism had been fruitful, so to say, made no difficulties about allowing other men to join him and consented willingly to communicate to them everything he had received in solitude. The 'abbots', whose sayings and the examples that illustrate them are collected in the *Apophthegms*, were precisely this" (321).

12. Thomas Merton, *Contemplative Prayer* (1969; Garden City, N.Y.: Doubleday Image, 1971) 28; see also *Contemplation in a World of Action*, 17, 25.

with adherence to a rule is to confuse means with ends, for the purpose of monastic life is to serve as a solitary witness to the essentially paschal character of Christian discipleship, conformity not to a system or to an official function but to the person of Christ: "His loneliness had a prophetic and mysterious quality, something almost in the nature of a sacramental sign, because it was a particular charismatic way of participating in the death and resurrection of Christ. . . . To confront the emptiness, the void, the apparent hopelessness of this desert and to encounter there the miracle of new life in Christ, the joy of eschatological hope already fulfilled in mystery—this was the monastic vocation."[13]

As he considered the history of religious life, Merton discovered repeated instances of a return to this more charismatic, lay-oriented approach, typically associated with a more eremitic style of life. The tenth-century hermit movement is an impressive example of this renewal of the primitive monastic vision, which arose, as it would have to, outside the confines of institutional monasticism: "Lay people or secular clerics began to withdraw directly into solitude without passing through a period of monastic formation. Living in the woods and developing as best they could their own mode of life, they remained in rather close contact with the poor (that is, generally speaking, with their own class), with outlaws and outcasts and with the itinerants who were always numerous in the Middle Ages."[14] By their very withdrawal from the accepted roles of society, whether civil or ecclesial, these solitaries were paradoxically united in solidarity with those marginalized by the prevailing social structure: "Closely identified as the hermits were with the underprivileged, the oppressed and those for whom the official institutions of society showed little real concern, the nonmonastic hermitage quickly became a place of refuge for the desperately perplexed who sought guidance and hope—if not also a hiding place and physical safety. Thus the nonmonastic hermit by the very fact of his isolation

---

13. *Contemplation in a World of Action,* 239 (see also 10).

14. Ibid., 261; Merton specifically mentions "the very significant lay-hermit movement in the eleventh-century-lay solitaries who were also itinerant preachers to the poor and to the outcasts who had no one to preach to them" in his March 9, 1967 letter to Ruether (*Hidden Ground of Love,* 504; *At Home in the World,* 37). Paradoxically, Merton notes in a February 26, 1966 entry in his *Reading Notebook #17,* the hermit movement eventually became a catalyst for monastic ordination: "Historical point— ordination of monks to priesthood became very common in 11th–12th centuries precisely in view of hermit life. Priest-hermit considered his mass primarily as the perfect means of uniting his sacrifice-passion with the Passion of Christ" (88).

from the world became open to the world in a new and special way."[15] Though the movement was "tamed," as it were, by the thirteenth century,[16] and "absorbed back into monasticism," its spirit continued to remain alive in such forms as the early Cistercian lay brotherhood, which "had something of an eremitical as well as a distinctly 'lay' character,"[17] especially for those brothers who spent long periods of time in solitude on monastic lands outside the enclosure. But the most significant heirs of this charism were the early Franciscans, "nonmonastic and completely open to the world of the poor and outcast,"[18] who were nevertheless, in Merton's judgement, the genuine exemplars in the Middle Ages of "the authentic freedom of early monasticism."[19] Merton suggests "that actually the ideal of St. Francis was more purely *monastic* in the true original primitive sense than the life lived by the big Benedictine and Cistercian commmunities of the thirteenth century where everything was so highly organized behind walls."[20] It is worth noting in this connection that Francis and many of his first followers were never ordained priests, that they claimed no name but Christian and no status but *fratres minores*, lesser brothers.

Thus when Merton refers to himself offhandedly in a letter to Ruether as "a tramp and not much else"[21] he is actually laying claim to a rich heritage of witness to the priority of Gospel to Law. When he tells the fellows at the Center for the Study of Democratic Institutions, just before departing for Asia, that "the monk should not be a priest," and even says, "I should not be a priest," adding, "I didn't want to be a priest, but it was part of the system, so I became one,"[22] this should

15. *Contemplation in a World of Action*, 261.

16. But see Merton's comments on the non-monastic hermits of fourteenth-century England, of whom Richard Rolle is the most famous example (*Contemplation in a World of Action*, 302).

17. Ibid., 262.

18. Ibid., 263.

19. Ibid., 358.

20. Ibid.

21. *Hidden Ground of Love*, 501; *At Home in the World*, 24.

22. Thomas Merton, *Preview of the Asian Journey*, ed. Walter H. Capps (New York: Crossroad, 1989) 49; see also the reference in *Contemplation in a World of Action* to the "Primitive Benedictine" foundations that returned to "a community of simple monks in one class, only a few of whom were priests" (11). In *Working Notebook #14* (undated, but evidently from the mid-1960s since it includes drafts of poems that would be incorporated into *Cables to the Ace*), Merton quotes from an unpublished conference given by Edward Schillebeekx: "Monasticism is not situ-

be interpreted, I think, not as a rejection or denigration of his own priesthood, which continued to be an integral and valued part of his spirituality throughout the hermitage years and right up to the time of his death, but as the recognition of a confusion of roles, an institutionalizing of the charismatic, a clericalizing of what was originally and essentially a lay movement.[23] As he explained during this dialogue, "The monk is a layperson in the desert, who is not incorporated into the hierarchy. The monk has nothing to do with the establishment."[24] In call-

---

ated on a functional level, either lay or priestly. It is solely a taking after God. And in the measure that monks lose sight of this & accept an apostolic ministry, in the measure that they seek to found a monastic life on the priesthood & to orient their spirituality in this way, then monks deviate from their state, deviate from monasticism. And so the Church is at the same time more & more deprived of a state of which she has great need—pure monasticism" (75).

23. In *The Meaning of the Monastic Life*, Bouyer writes: "If, in fact, at the present day, monks have become an important part of the clergy, such a circumstance, whatever proportions it may assume, remains accidental. All great monastic legislators, from St Benedict downwards, pass it over" (5); he later refers to the "gibe" found in the apophthegms of the desert fathers: "the two kinds of persons whom the monk must flee more than all others, it is said humorously, are bishops and women" (133; Merton himself refers to "Desert Fathers" who "fled from bishops" in his correspondence with Ronald Roloff, O.S.B. in *The School of Charity* [155]); on a more serious note Bouyer cites the teaching of the great Eastern Fathers: "we have only to read St John Chrysostom's *De Sacerdote*, or, if you prefer, the correspondence and poems of St Gregory Nazianzen to discover how acute the conflict created by a priestly vocation superimposed upon a monastic vocation, appeared to them" (165). Chitty notes that "Both Antony and Pachomius avoided ordination" and cites Pachomius' custom of "call[ing] in a priest of one of the neighbouring churches, not wishing any of the brethren to seek ordination—for . . . 'the beginning of the thought of love of command is ordination'" (*The Desert a City*, 31, 23); see also the anecdotes of Macarius, who "moved to another village to escape enrol[l]ment in the clergy," and of Peter of Iberia, who, "getting wind" of plans to ordain him, "jumped down from a roof . . . and escaped" (temporarily, as it turned out) (13, 87); Merton translates a slightly different version of the former story as the last of the sayings in *The Wisdom of the Desert* (79–81); see also the story of Abbot Isaac's efforts to avoid ordination (thwarted by an ass!) (65).

24. *Preview of the Asian Journey*, 49. Merton's most extensive consideration of early monasticism and ordination comes in *Reading Notebook #57*, in his notes on the sixth chapter of Adalbert de Vogüé's *La Communauté et l'Abbé dans la Règle de saint Benoît* (Paris-Brussels: Desclée-de-Brouwer, 1961); Merton summarizes de Vogüé's findings that both the Benedictine Rule and the earlier *Regula Magistri* are "suspicious of priests" within the monastery, and goes on to abstract eleven points drawn from the chapter, with extensive citation of primary sources, including: "Monks fly from priesthood as an *honor* . . . and as a *distraction*" (#5); "Refusals to cooperate in ordination or in exercise of priestly functions" (#6); "However—need of monastic

ing attention to the "lay" character of his life as a hermit, then, Merton was not expressing a simple rejection of monasticism but claiming the recovery of an important strand of authentic monastic and religious life.

II

To affirm the "lay" dimension of monasticism is therefore to resist the temptation to equate one's identity with one's role, one's worth with one's status, the meaning of one's life with one's office. It means the rejection of all idealized projections and socially acceptable images of oneself, including even the image of monk. "The monk does not come into the desert to reinforce his own ego-image, but to be deliv-

---

priests for sacramental life of community" (#8); "Hence monks wanted a holy Abba to be also ordained priest—since he already exercised spiritual authority" (#9); "Still—in west the priest-abbot not common; certainly still doubtful that St Benedict consented to ordination" (#10). De Vogüé's overall position, very similar to that of Bouyer in *The Meaning of the Monastic Life*, is that monasticism is essentially a lay rather than a clerical vocation: "Priesthood and monasticism are two different things. The former is ordained for the government of the people of God, the latter consists of a break with the present world. . . . Monasticism is therefore in line with baptism. It is nothing else but a supreme effort to die with Christ and live in him, in other words to realize daily the sacramental action of baptism. It can therefore be said that monasticism is in line with the function of the laity. Not only is it not confined to clerics, but the tendency to solitude, which defines its nature, runs counter in principle to the pastoral vocation of the priest" (Adalbert de Vogüé, *Community and Abbot in the Rule of St Benedict*, trans. Charles Philippi & Ethel Rae Perkins, 2 vols., Cistercian Studies Series 5 [Kalamazoo, MI: Cistercian Publications, 1988] 2:294-5). De Vogüé concludes his chapter by noting the relevance of this distinction between cleric and monk for contemporary monastic renewal: "the Rule provides a place for priesthood only in cases of real necessity. The priest-monk, far from constituting the ideal type of monk, is conceived rather as an anomaly, fraught with danger, but inevitable, of which efforts are made to mitigate the inconveniences by means of severe warnings. In our day, in a completely changed situation, these inconveniences no longer make themselves felt, but if the practice of general ordination to the priesthood has brought about their cessation, it has also created new difficulties, which the Benedictine Rule was not able to foresee. So it is true that monasticism, on the whole, cannot renounce its lay character without casting a slur on one of the essential features of its vocation" (*Community and Abbot*, 2:303). Given Merton's extensive notes on this work, read in the early 1960s (*Reading Notebook #57* is undated, but the article cited immediately following the notes on de Vogüé was published in 1963), it is highly probable that it served as the principal source for Merton's comments on monasticism and priesthood, and indeed on the specifically lay character of monasticism in general.

ered from it."[25] Merton finds the truth of this insight exemplifed in one of the stories of the Desert Fathers, in which a restless apprentice monk asks permission to go visit the sick, but is told by his spiritual father, his *abba*, to stay put in his cell. A clue to the meaning of the story, Merton notes, is the Greek word used for visiting the sick, *episkopein*, with its connotations of superiority and condescension: "'looking them over as if one were a bishop' we would be inclined to say."[26] It is a story about trying to find oneself, to affirm one's own worth, by adopting a conventionally approved role; the young man's motive for performing a work of charity, however admirable in itself, is to feel good about himself, but the wise elder refuses to allow his disciple to take refuge in this self-deception. Merton comments,

> Afflicted with boredom and hardly knowing what to do with him-self, the disciple represents to himself a more fruitful and familiar way of life, in which he appears to himself to "be someone" and to have a fully recognizable and acceptable identity, a "place in the Church," but the Elder tells him that his place in the Church will never be found by following these ideas and images of a plausible identity. Rather it is found by traveling a way that is new and dis-concerting because it has never been imagined by us before, or at least we have never conceived it as useful or even credible for a true Christian—a way in which we seem to lose our identity and become nothing.[27]

The truth, of course, is that the self constructed according to social norms is not the self created in the image of God, and that false self must die in order for the authentic self, the mysterious, hidden iden-tity known only to its Creator, to emerge. To call a monk a "lay" Christian is to recognize that at least one essential aspect of the mo-nastic vocation is to be a standing warning that the very notion of an "official" Christian, a "professional" Christian, is in grave danger of confusing outward function with inner identity; it risks substituting appearance for reality. Both the cleric and the non-monastic lay person need the monk as a salutary reminder that to be a Christian, a disciple, is not a matter of playing a role or of filling an office but of committing one's entire life to the person of Jesus.

This "lay" character also has a liberating aspect to it: the monk is not confined to a fixed role, a limited set of duties or obligations. The very

25. *Contemplation in a World of Action*, 285.
26. Ibid., 254.
27. Ibid.

nature of the monastic life, insofar as it is not "clerical," not provided with a definite niche in the ecclesial structure, testifies to the freedom of the Christian. Contrary to Luther's critique, however accurate it may have been in the historical circumstances of his time,[28] monasticism is intended to be a sign of sheer grace, of salvation by faith not works, by a person not a system. According to Merton, "The monastic vocation is traditionally regarded as a charism of liberty in which the monk does not simply turn his back on the world, but on the contrary becomes free with the perfect freedom of the sons of God by virtue of the fact that, having followed Christ into the wilderness and shared in His temptations and sufferings, he can also follow Him wherever else He may go."[29] Such freedom is risky, because it places the monk in the desert, "where the secure routines of man's city offer no support,"[30] but it is precisely from these "secure routines," which stifle vitality and creativity and try to domesticate the Spirit that blows where it wills, that one needs to be liberated: "The world needs men who are free from its demands, men who are not alienated by its servitudes in any way."[31] The monk is, or should be, such a person. In his final talk in Bangkok, Merton goes so far as to define a monk as "essentially someone who takes up a critical attitude toward the world and its structures, . . . somebody who says, in one way or another, that the claims of the world are fraudulent."[32]

Here, of course, the prophetic, counter-cultural dimension of the monastic life is evident. The monk "retains the eschatological privilege and duty of smashing idols—worldly, ecclesiastical, secular and even monastic"[33] because his detachment from all that is provisional and secondary allows him "to gaze steadily at the whole truth of Christ"[34] and so to reject the absolute claims that any institution or structure or authority makes about itself. The monk is one "who at once loves the world yet stands apart from it with a critical objectivity which refuses to become involved in its transient fashions and its more manifest absurdities."[35] Hence Merton's description in Calcutta of the

---

28. See Ibid., 181–6, and 360–1, for a discussion of Luther and monasticism.

29. Ibid., 227 (see also 360–1).

30. *Contemplative Prayer*, 27.

31. *Contemplation in a World of Action*, 227.

32. Thomas Merton, *The Asian Journal*, ed. Naomi Burton, Patrick Hart and James Laughlin (New York: New Directions, 1973) 329.

33. *Contemplation in a World of Action*, 189.

34. Ibid., 188.

35. Ibid., 227 (see also 8–9, 92–3).

monk as "a marginal person, . . . essentially outside of all establish-ments,"[36] at the periphery of contemporary "mass society" with its ten-dency to depersonalize and dehumanize, yet thereby in a unique position not simply to withdraw from society but to offer it a chal-lenging and life-affirming critique—the vision of a new humanism rooted in the dignity of the person as image of God.

If from one perspective, that of status, efficiency, productivity, the monk is marginal, from another he is at the very heart of the human enterprise. "The monk," Merton said in Bangkok, "dwells in the center of society as one who has attained realization—he . . . has come to experience the ground of his own being in such a way that he knows the secret of liberation and can somehow communicate it to others."[37] In discovering his own true center he is in communion with all other human beings through compassionate identification. The monk affirms authentic human values by incarnating them himself and by recognizing and defending them in others, especially when they are threatened or violated. "The monastic life today stands over against the world with a mission to affirm not only the message of sal-vation but also those most basic human values which the world most desperately needs to regain: personal integrity, inner peace, authentic-ity, inner depth, spiritual joy, the capacity to love, the capacity to enjoy God's creation and give thanks."[38] For Merton there is no conflict be-tween these common human aspirations and a specifically Christian and monastic identity and vocation because the central Christian doc-trines of creation, incarnation and redemption are a repeated, ever deepening revelation and affirmation of human dignity. "Monastic spirituality today," Merton believes, "must be a personalistic and Christian humanism that seeks and saves man's intimate truth, his personal identity, in order to consecrate it entirely to God."[39] It is more essential, in other words, to focus on how monks can contribute to the full humanization, which is also the divinization, of all people, than to stress what differentiates the monk from "the laity." While the monk participates in the project of human transformation in a unique way, the way of solitude and inner exploration, he is nevertheless partici-pating in a project common to the entire *laos*, all the people of God.

---

36. *Asian Journal*, 305.
37. Ibid., 333.
38. *Contemplation in a World of Action*, 81.
39. Ibid., 82.

"What is essential in the monastic life," Merton declared on the last day of his life, "is not embedded in buildings, is not embedded in clothing, is not necessarily embedded even in a rule. It is . . . something deeper than a rule. It is concerned with this business of total inner transformation. All other things serve that end."[40]

III

It is in this context that Merton's concern for monastic renewal must be situated. The perennial temptation of monasticism is to substitute an alternate set of "secure routines" for those of the world, to make institutional structures rather than charismatic freedom the defining characteristic of monastic life. Comparing the contemporary monk with the Desert Fathers, Merton notes: "With us it is often rather a case of men leaving the society of the 'world' in order to fit themselves into another kind of society, that of the religious family which they enter. . . . The social 'norms' of a monastic family are also apt to be conventional, and to live by them does not involve a leap into the void—only a radical change of customs and standards."[41] When monastic life becomes a form of security rather than a challenge to risk, to grow, to die and rise with Christ, it betrays its essential meaning.

An even more serious danger is that "The institution is identified with God, and becomes an end in itself."[42] This is, of course, a form of idolatry, in which the basic humanity of the individual is sacrificed to the requirements of the institution: "the monk is given to understand that there is *no alternative* for him but to regard this institutional life in all its detail, however arbitrary, however archaic, however meaningless to him, as the *only way* for him to be perfect in love and sincere in his quest for God."[43] The corollary of this approach is that the way of the nonmonastic world is often regarded as a corrupting system that must be rejected totally, as exemplified, for example, by "the rigid, authoritarian, self-righteous, ascetic" monk Ferrapont in Dostoevsky's *The Brothers Karamazov*, "who delivers himself from the world by sheer effort, and then feels qualified to call down curses

40. *Asian Journal*, 340.
41. *The Wisdom of the Desert*, 9–10.
42. *Contemplation in a World of Action*, 19.
43. Ibid.

upon it."[44] By denying and rejecting the human element outside the monastery, one ends by suppressing and rejecting the humanity in oneself and in the monastic community.

While this temptation to reduce monasticism to its formal components is a perennial one, its consequences are particularly harmful in the contemporary period when the structure and routine are in large part relics of a past era with very little connection to the monks' former, "lay" lives. The problem is merely compounded when "updating" consists in adopting structures and practices of secular society that are basically depersonalizing: "if the monastery comes to resemble a big business and a plant surrounded by noise and clatter, the monks . . . will tend to be more and more alienated, taking refuge from routines in which they cannot take a serious human interest because they are the same impersonal and organized routines they left in the world."[45] Renewal cannot consist merely in the substitution of one set of structures for another: it must "concentrate on the *charism of the monastic vocation* rather than on the *structure of monastic institutions or the patterns of monastic observance.*"[46] The recollection and recovery of the "lay" dimension of monastic history and identity function as a check on the tendency of structure to replace charism; it counteracts the temptation to substitute for a life of authentic human freedom a closed, self-sufficient "societas perfecta" which replaces and judges life in "the world."

IV

Merton's hermitage is a response to the dilemma of contemporary monasticism, which is of course his own dilemma as well. "Doubtless," he writes, "this can be seen as a perfecting of my monastic life and also as a final disillusionment with monastic life."[47] Ironically, it is a perfecting precisely by its recovery of some degree of the primitive "lay" freedom from

44. *Contemplative Prayer,* 28 (Merton calls Dostoevsky's monk "Therapont" here); it is Ferrapont's opposite, the Staretz Zossima, "the kind, compassionate man of prayer who identifies himself with the sinful world in order to call down God's blessing upon it," and whose "monastic spirit is charismatic rather than institutional," whom Merton sees as the model "in the present era of monastic renewal" (28).

45. *Contemplation in a World of Action,* 81.

46. Ibid., 14.

47. *Vow of Conversation,* 190; for a slightly different version of this passage, see *Dancing in the Water of Life,* 256.

the artificiality of structure and the tyranny of routine, which are of course the primary source of the disillusion.[48] His new life is an affirmation of his ordinariness: "'Solitude' becomes for me less and less of a specialty, more and more just 'life' itself. I do not seek to 'be a solitary' or anything else, for 'being' anything is a distraction. It is enough to 'be' in an ordinary human mode with one's hunger and sleep, one's cold and warmth, rising and going to bed, putting on blankets and taking them off."[49] The simplicity here may be somewhat misleading. Merton's words echo, perhaps deliberately, D. T. Suzuki's concluding words in his dialogue with Merton about the Desert Fathers: "*Q.* What is Tao? (We may take Tao as meaning the ultimate truth or reality.) *A.* It is one's everyday mind. *Q.* What is one's everyday mind? *A.* When tired, you sleep; when hungry, you eat."[50] Merton's response puts the Zen master's paradox in a Christian context:

> Christianity moves in an essentially historical dimension toward the "restoration of all things in Christ." Yet with Christ's conquest of death and the sending of the Holy Spirit that restoration has already been accomplished. What remains is for it to be made manifest. . . . To one who has seen it, the most obvious thing is to do what Dr. Suzuki suggests: to live one's ordinary life. In the words of the first Christians, to praise God and to take one's food "in simplicity of heart." The simplicity referred to here is the complete absence of all legalistic preoccupation about right and wrong ways of living. "When tired you sleep, when hungry you eat."[51]

In this attentiveness to the ordinary, this mindfulness, revelation appears in the most unexpected places, as in the lovely final entry of *A Vow of Conversation*, the journal of Merton's entry into solitude, when Merton sees deer grazing near the hermitage:

48. In *Contemplation in a World of Action* Merton notes that Dom Jacques Winandy proposes a canonical separation of the eremitical life from the religious state, bringing it "closer to the lay state than to the status of religious or of monk" (295); while he himself is concerned, both theoretically and practically, "with the possibility of a renewal of eremitism within the religious state itself" (Ibid.), his recognition of the ambiguities of the hermit's position relative to the monastic community allows him both to define the hermit as "the monk par excellence" (296) and to call the "hermit life . . . expressly a lay life" (*Hidden Ground of Love*, 501; *At Home in the World*, 23).

49. *Vow of Conversation*, 192; for a slightly different version of this passage see *Dancing in the Water of Life*, 257.

50. Thomas Merton, *Zen and the Birds of Appetite* (New York: New Directions, 1968) 134.

51. Ibid., 138.

The thing that struck me most—when you look at them directly and in movement, you see what the primitive cave painters saw. Something you never see in a photograph. It is most awe-inspiring. The *muntu* or the "spirit" is shown in the running of the deer. The "deerness" that sums up everything and is sacred and marvelous. A contemplative intuition, yet this is perfectly ordinary, everyday seeing—what everybody ought to see all the time. The deer reveals to me something essential, not only in itself, but also in myself. Something beyond the trivialities of my everyday being, my individual existence. Something profound. The face of that which is both in the deer and in myself.[52]

In this experience is the proof that the Tao is indeed one's everyday mind, that the mystery of reality is hidden in the depths of the ordinary, that the contemplative vision is available to all, though few will notice. The gift of the hermitage for Merton himself, and his gift to others, is this overcoming of the dichotomy between the everyday and the transcendent.

The voice of God is not clearly heard at every moment; and part of the "work of the cell" is *attention,* so that one may not miss any sound of that voice. What this means, therefore, is not only attention to inner grace but to external reality and to one's self as a completely integrated part of that reality. Hence, this implies also a forgetfulness of oneself as totally apart from outer objects, standing back from outer objects; it demands an integration of one's own life in the stream of natural and human and cultural life of the moment.[53]

It demands a reappropriation of the fundamentally human capacity to encounter the sacred in the midst of the ordinary, which is authentically but not exclusively monastic. Far from isolating him from the rest of humanity, Merton's move to the hermitage had the effect of attuning him more sensitively and perceptively to the common needs and aspirations of every person, which he experienced in himself. The paradox of Merton's last years, which found him at once seeking and finding greater solitude and more in touch with the political, social and cultural crises of the time, is resolved in his existential awareness of this integration of self and world as complementary, interpenetrating signs and instruments of the divine presence, concealed in plain sight.

52. *Vow of Conversation,* 208; for a slightly different version of this passage, see *Dancing in the Water of Life,* 291.

53. *Vow of Conversation,* 189; an earlier, less developed version of this passage is found in *Dancing in the Water of Life,* 255.

V

Probably the most appealing, and most revealing, description of the "lay" character of Merton's solitary life is found in his essay "Day of a Stranger," originally written, he tells us, "in answer to a request from a South American editor to describe a 'typical day' in my life."[54] The day chosen was in May 1965 when Merton was on the threshold of his permanent removal to the hermitage, and the essay reveals the essential elements of the life of solitude as Merton had already begun to experience it. In describing his day Merton clearly intends that the distinctions between lay and religious, monastic and nonmonastic be relativized and transcended. His life is presented as a unique way of experiencing a common humanity.

At least five dimensions of this life that integrate him with the world shared with the rest of humanity are interwoven throughout the essay. Most immediately apparent is the question of his own identity, evident even in the title, where the word "stranger" might initially suggest someone whose way of life is strange or exotic, but which eventually takes on the connotations of one who doesn't "fit in," whose identity cannot be defined by a public role, a recognized place in society at large or monastic society in particular—cannot in fact be defined at all. Merton takes pains to dispel the impression of strangeness in the first sense by emphasizing that in fundamental ways his life is no different from anybody else's. He pointedly and humorously demythologizes any mystique of the monk as superior to or set apart from ordinary people: "This is not a hermitage—it is a house. ('Who was that hermitage I seen you with last night?. . .') What I wear is pants. What I do is live. How I pray is breathe."[55] But this very ordinariness protects

---

54. Quoted by Robert E. Daggy in his Introduction to Thomas Merton, *Day of a Stranger* (Salt Lake City: Gibbs M. Smith, 1981) 7; all references will be to this edition, but the essay can also be found in *A Thomas Merton Reader*, revised edition, ed. Thomas P. McDonnell (Garden City, N.Y.: Doubleday Image, 1974) 431–8, and in *Thomas Merton: Spiritual Master: The Essential Writings*, ed. Lawrence S. Cunningham (New York: Paulist, 1992) 214–22. It should be noted that the final version of this essay, as found in these sources, is considerably revised and expanded from the initial draft, now available in *Dancing in the Water of Life*, 239–42 (for a helpful discussion of the successive drafts, see the Introduction to *Day of a Stranger*, 17–21). Much of the material quoted in the following discussion was added by Merton in the process of revision; exceptions will be cited in the notes.

55. *Day of a Stranger*, 41; see the similar language in Merton's March 9, 1967

and nurtures the mystery of identity.[56] As he had not yet been relieved of the office of novice master, he still had a "public" self, but this does not constitute his deepest, truest identity: "I have duties, obligations, since here I am a monk. When I have accomplished them, I return to the woods where I am nobody."[57] Like "all the silent Tzu's and Fu's" that surround him in spirit, he is a "[man] without office and without obligation,"[58] whose identity cannot be defined by what he does, or how society classifies him: "I live in the woods as a reminder that I am free not to be a number."[59] His deepest identity is hidden even from himself, and does not become available through introspective self-examination: "In an age when there is much talk about 'being yourself' I reserve to myself the right to forget about being myself, since in any case there is little chance of my being anybody else. Rather it seems to me that when one is too intent on 'being himself' he runs the risk of impersonating a shadow."[60] His identity remains a mystery, but the mystery is constituted not by his being a hermit, but because he is a human being. His life is a reminder to others that they too are free not to be numbers, that they too risk impersonating shadows, but are not inevitably doomed to do so. His life is a sign that no one's life is, in essence, or should be, in practice, reduced to the function they perform or the role they play.

This rejection of a superior, esoteric existence is reinforced by the attention paid to the ordinary rhythms and routines of everyday life, from which the hermit is not exempt. Merton deliberately, and slyly, uses the term "rituals," with its associations with religious rites, to describe the most "secular" of activities, not excluding even a visit to the outdoor privy:

letter to Ruether: "All you do is breathe and look around and wash dishes, type, etc. Or just listen to the birds" (*Hidden Ground of Love*, 502–3; *At Home in the World*, 34).

56. See Merton's Introduction to *The Wisdom of the Desert*: "These monks insisted on remaining human and 'ordinary.' This may seem to be a paradox, but it is very important. If we reflect a moment, we will see that to fly into the desert in order to be extraordinary is only to carry the world with you as an implicit standard of comparison. . . . The simple men who lived their lives out to a good old age among the rocks and sands only did so because they had come into the desert to be themselves, their *ordinary* selves, and to forget a world that divided them from themselves. There can be no other valid reason for seeking solitude" (22–3).

57. *Day of a Stranger*, 57; for an earlier version of this passage, see *Dancing in the Water of Life*, 241.

58. *Day of a Stranger*, 63.

59. Ibid., 31.

60. Ibid.

Rituals. Washing out the coffee pot in the rain bucket. Approaching the outhouse with circumspection on account of the king snake who likes to curl up on one of the beams inside. Addressing the possible king snake in the outhouse and informing him that he should not be in there. Asking the formal ritual question that is asked at this time every morning: "Are you in there, you bastard?" More rituals. Spray bedroom (cockroaches and mosquitoes). Close all the windows on south side (heat). Leave windows open on north and east sides (cool). Leave windows open on west side until maybe June when it gets very hot on all sides. Pull down shades. Get water bottle. Rosary. Watch. Library book to be returned.[61]

A passage such as this is a reminder that grace builds on nature but does not replace it. Human life is inescapably incarnate, fleshly, and part of the value of even the most ordinary activities is to keep one rooted in concrete actuality, to guard against the fatal self-deception that the "religious" person lives on a different plane of reality from everyone else.[62] In performing his "rituals," Merton is attuned to the rhythms of the day—closing the south windows as the sun rises while leaving north and east windows open for cross-ventilation—and the rhythms of the season—leaving west windows open until the heats of June. There is a sense of correspondence with the natural patterns of time—the watch is picked up only when he is ready to make his daily trip down to the monastery. At the same time, the presence of cockroaches and mosquitoes (not to mention the king snake) makes clear that the hermitage is no idyllic, edenic, self-enclosed world; it is part of the normal, ambiguous environment in which all people find themselves, and so signifies an inevitable yet freely accepted solidarity with the human condition. Yet there is something different as well, at least from the standard middle-class experience and expectation. If the hermit participates in routines common to all, he is also a sign of contradiction to the busyness, the noise, the technological gadgetry taken for granted in contemporary society but in fact not necessary at all. "Washing out the coffee pot in the rain bucket" reminds those who rely on the dishwasher, or even on hot and cold running water, that full humanity does not depend on access to the latest conveniences. Both familiar and unfamiliar, the hermit's rituals are not a glorification of the primitive—Merton was quite grateful when modern plumbing and electricity arrived at the hermitage—but a subtle admonition not to

61. Ibid., 53.
62. In *Contemplation in a World of Action*, Merton writes, "Transformation is not a repudiation of ordinary life but its definitive recovery in Christ" (100).

absolutize the relative, not to confuse the natural with the artificial, the necessary with the optional.

This passage already suggests a third aspect of this "lay" existence, immersion in the natural world in all its concrete particularity. Merton locates himself in a setting that is not reducible to a set of mapmaker's coordinates: it is "in Kentucky" but that is not its essential defining characteristic: "Do I have a 'day'? Do I spend my 'day' in a 'place'? I know there are trees here. I know there are birds here. I know the birds in fact very well, for there are precise pairs of birds (two each of fifteen or twenty species) living in the immediate area of my cabin. I share this particular place with them: we form an ecological balance. This harmony gives the idea of 'place' a new configuration."[63] There is a sense of respect here, a recognition that the trees and birds were in this place before he was and will continue to be there when he is no more; therefore it is his responsibility not to impose his pattern on them but to become aware of and participate in their pattern, their harmony. This relationship is humorously expressed later in the essay in the delightful variation on St. Francis' sermon to the birds: "'Esteemed friends, birds of noble lineage, I have no message to you except this: be what you are: be *birds*. Thus you will be your own sermon to yourselves!' Reply: 'even this is one sermon too many!'"[64] It is not the birds but the preacher who needs to hear and heed the instruction "be what you are," which could in fact be considered the sermon *of* the birds.

This appreciation of harmony does not exclude an awareness of dissonance in nature, a sense that it too participates in some way in the fallenness of creation. "As to the crows," Merton notes, "they form part of a different pattern. They are vociferous and self-justifying, like humans. They are not two, they are many. They fight each other and the other birds, in a constant state of war."[65] But if nature at times parallels the conflicts and confusion of the human world (and so serves as an object lesson undermining the pretensions and posturing of human arrogance), it also stands as a sign of contradiction to the getting and spending in which the great world looks to find its meaning. Birds and business are on different schedules: "The birds begin to wake. It will

63. *Day of a Stranger,* 33; for an earlier version of this passage, see *Dancing in the Water of Life,* 239.

64. *Day of a Stranger,* 51.

65. Ibid., 33; for an earlier version of this passage, see *Dancing in the Water of Life,* 239.

soon be dawn. In an hour or two the towns will wake, and men will enjoy everywhere the great luminous smiles of production and business."[66] Like the birds, the hermit is attuned to other rhythms than those presented by the commercial world. He is sensitive not only to *chronos*, clock-time, but to *kairos*, the decisive moment of revelation and transfiguration: "It is necessary for me to see the first point of light which begins to be dawn. It is necessary to be present alone at the resurrection of Day, in the black silence when the sun appears. In this completely neutral instant I receive from the Eastern woods, the tall oaks, the one word 'DAY,' which is never the same. It is never spoken in any human language."[67] This responsiveness to nature is not intended to substitute for or to exclude human contact. Rather, in Merton's view, the ecological balance of his physical environment provides a pattern for "a mental ecology too, a living balance of spirits in this corner of the woods. There is room here for many other songs than those of birds," voices of poets singing in many languages, voices of eastern sages and western Church Fathers, voices of Hebrew prophets and "feminine voices from Angela of Foligno to Flannery O'Connor, Teresa of Avila, Julian of Norwich, and, more personally and warmly still, Raissa Maritain."[68] The natural world provides a context in which the wisdom of the human world can be properly heard and appreciated: "It is good to choose the voices that will be heard in these woods, but they also choose themselves, and send themselves here to be present in this silence."[69]

But the human world penetrates the hermit's existence not only through the insights of artists and visionaries. A fourth element of Merton's life in the hermitage that is shared with all humanity is the necessity to confront the dilemmas of social and political life. Merton frames his essay with references to airplanes. After a sardonic opening paragraph on the pseudo-mystical elevation of modern jets, in which

---

66. *Day of a Stranger*, 45.

67. Ibid., 51; for an earlier version of this passage, see *Dancing in the Water of Life*, 241. Merton writes to Ruether, "One of the things I love about my life, and, therefore, one of the reasons why I would not change it for anything, is the fact that I live in the woods and according to a tempo of sun and moon and season in which it is naturally easy and possible to walk in God's light, so to speak, in and through his creation" (*Hidden Ground of Love*, 502; *At Home in the World*, 34).

68. *Day of a Stranger*, 35; for an earlier version of this passage, see *Dancing in the Water of Life*, 239–40.

69. *Day of a Stranger*, 35, 37.

passengers are suspended in a moving stillness "with timeless cock-tails . . . contemplation that *gets you somewhere!*"[70] he turns to "Other jets, with other contemplations,"[71] the grotesquely perverted mimicry of "the SAC plane, the metal bird with a scientific egg in its breast!"[72] The essay, and the day, end with the same image: "Meanwhile the metal cherub of the apocalypse passes over me in the clouds, treasur-ing its egg and its message."[73] Merton permits himself and his reader no illusion that withdrawal into solitude means escape from the perils human society has created for itself: "like everyone else, I live in the shadow of the apocalyptic cherub."[74] If there were ever a time when the monk had the luxury of ignoring the problems of the wider world, that time is forever gone. Monks, and even hermits, live in the same world as everyone else, and therefore have the same obligations and responsibilities to defend life and resist the forces of death. The hermit is able to address the struggle between light and darkness in society because he has experienced that same struggle in his own heart, and he is able to articulate a word of hope because he knows that the dark-ness has not finally overcome the light:

> In the formlessness of night and silence a word then pronounces itself: Mercy. It is surrounded by other words of lesser conse-quence: "destroy iniquity," "wash me," "purify," "I know my iniq-uity." *Peccavi.* Concepts without interest in the world of business, war, politics, culture, etc. Concepts also often without interest to ecclesiastics. Other words: Blood. Guile. Anger. The way that is not good. The way of blood, guile, anger, war. Out there the hills in the dark lie southward. The way over the hills is blood, guile, dark, anger, death. Selma, Birmingham, Mississippi. Nearer than these, the atomic city, from which each day a freight car of fission-able material is brought to be hid carefully beside the gold in the underground vault which is at the heart of this nation. "Their mouth is the opening of the grave; their tongues are set in motion by lies; their heart is void." Blood, lies, fire, hate, the opening of the grave, void. Mercy, great mercy.[75]

70. Ibid., 29.

71. Ibid.

72. Ibid., 31; the original version of this passage does not use the bird/egg image: see *Dancing in the Water of Life*, 239.

73. *Day of a Stranger*, 63.

74. Ibid., 31.

75. Ibid., 43, 45.

The final word is mercy, but its power is revealed not by refusing to hear the other words but by confronting them, knowing the full extent of their ugliness, and refusing to be overwhelmed by them because one has learned, through no merit of one's own, that there is a deeper, more lasting reality than hate and death.

Though the term is not used, this passage is of course a description of the divine office, as "psalms grow up silently by themselves without effort in this light which is favorable to them."[76] Throughout "Day of a Stranger" the explicitly spiritual, religious, Christian dimension discloses itself unobtrusively, woven into the pattern of personal identity, of ordinary routines, of natural harmonies, or as here, of social and political confusions and threats. It is the final integrating factor that unites the hermit with his brothers and sisters, but only because it has itself been integrated with the rest of life. It is the "one central tonic note that is unheard and unuttered" but which makes possible the harmony of all creation, "the *consonantia* of heat, fragrant pine, quiet wind, bird song."[77] Viewed in isolation, Merton "the stranger" comments, "Spiritual life is guilt," but when the artificial separation between worldly and spiritual aspects of life is overcome, when religion is not restricted to formal rituals at specified times, all life is recognized as holy: "Up here in the woods is seen the New Testament: that is to say, the wind comes through the trees and you breathe it."[78] The divine presence, the *pneuma* that blows where it wills, is as "natural," and as essential, as breathing.

At the heart of the call to solitude is the invitation to recognize and embrace the Love hidden in the depth of all that is real. "One might say I had decided to marry the silence of the forest. The sweet dark warmth of the whole world will have to be my wife. Out of the heart of that dark warmth comes the secret that is heard only in silence, but it is the root of all the secrets that are whispered by all the lovers in their beds all over the world."[79] The secret is that all particular loves, in so far as they are authentic, are participations in the one Love; that all particular surrenders are concrete ways of participating in the primal and primary surrender of self to Absolute Reality, the

76. Ibid., 43.

77. Ibid., 61; for an earlier version of this passage, see *Dancing in the Water of Life*, 242.

78. *Day of a Stranger*, 41.

79. Ibid., 49; for an earlier version of this passage, see *Dancing in the Water of Life*, 240.

Fullness of Truth. It is the assurance of the unity that grounds all diversity, the One manifested in the many, the "hidden wholeness" of creation as the epiphany of the divine, what Merton calls Sophia, Holy Wisdom.[80] Merton's vocation to solitude is not exclusive but inclusive, not something to distinguish him from others but a sign of the easily overlooked significance of each life and all life. "So perhaps I have an obligation to preserve the stillness, the silence, the poverty, the virginal point of pure nothingness which is at the center of all other loves." This is not an obligation imposed by any institution or required by any rule. It is an expression of charismatic freedom, love responding to Love, heart speaking to Heart. "I attempt to cultivate this plant without comment in the middle of the night and water it with psalms and prophecies in silence. It becomes the most rare of all the trees in the garden, at once the primordial paradise tree, the *axis mundi,* the cosmic axle, and the Cross. *Nulla silva talem profert.* There is only one such tree. It cannot be multiplied."[81] There are not, finally, many trees but one Tree, many loves but one Love, many lives but one Life. At this still point, the distinctions between secular and sacred, lay and monastic, are transcended in a contemplative intuition that is also ordinary, everyday awareness of a common humanity,[82] sharing the same earth, revolving around the same center, redeemed by the same Cross in order to live the same freedom of the children of God.

---

80. See Merton's prose poem "Hagia Sophia" in Thomas Merton, *The Collected Poems* (New York: New Directions, 1977) 363–71; also in *A Thomas Merton Reader,* 506–11, and *Thomas Merton: Spiritual Master,* 257–64. The phrase "hidden wholeness" is from the opening sentence of this work.

81. *Day of a Stranger,* 49; for an earlier version of this passage, see *Dancing in the Water of Life,* 240.

82. Merton writes to Ruether, "my own small concerns with monasticism may seem completely irrelevant. And I am not defending them. Because they are not just monastic concerns, they are human and universal. What makes it difficult to express this is the fact that, for instance, 'being a hermit' seems to mean trying to be a very peculiar and special kind of artificial man, whereas for me what it means is being nothing but man, or nothing but a mere man reduced to his simple condition as man, that is to say as a non-monk even, a non-layman, a non-categorized man, a plain simple man. . . . What would seem to others to be the final step into total alienation seems to me to be the beginning of the resolution of all alienation and the preparation for a real return without masks and without defenses into the world, as mere man" (*Hidden Ground of Love,* 508; *At Home in the World,* 46).

Living Contemplatively*

Wendy M. Wright

This past summer I paid a visit to a friend of mine in France, an American Trappestine, who was midway in her year sabbatical with a sister monastic community located in the countryside outside of Grenoble. Three traveling companions and I had left the mountainous region of Savoy early that morning, taken the autoroute south and passed onto narrowing roads as we neared the monastery of Chambarand. The September mid-morning sunlight showed the rolling French pasturage and quaint antique villages we passed through quickly to advantage. In keeping with the classic Cistercian spirit, the monastery was far removed from any population center. For miles all we saw were fields, a few farm houses, an occasional village church, centuries old and still witness to the never changing cycles of rural life: planting and harvest; sunrise and set; spring turning to summer turning to fall; birth, marriage, and death. Overarching the entire landscape was a deep stillness in which the buzzing of a bee, the trickle of a nearby stream or a chill breeze were the only sounds to compose a chant in the waiting air. As we wheeled up the graveled drive the rotation of our auto tires burst upon the hush of contemplative silence that encompassed the monastery grounds.

The Chambarand Trappistines support themselves by making cheese, we gleaned from the displays of rounds, cubes and rectangles prominent in the gift shop window. Passing by the shop, which was closed for midday prayer and meal, we made our way to the main

*Editor's note: *This essay is an expanded version of an address given at a conference about "Everyday Spirituality" at the Aquinas Center for Catholic Studies, Emory University, March 9, 1996.*

entrance and inquired after my American friend. She was expecting us. As the three of us waited, the stillness of the place laid its mantle on us and we stood without speaking. A community member met us pleasantly at the door and ushered us apologetically (she spoke no English) into a chill parlor where my friend was to meet us. Thick stone walls built against winter's onslaught also kept the autumn sun from penetrating the room. But the shuttered windows that opened out onto the inner cloister were flung open, and harvest vegetables growing green and yellow in the sunlight were visible there.

My friend arrived in full habit, taking off the work apron she had been wearing while turning cheeses in the factory. As it was almost noon, she led us through the massive stone corridors of the monastery complex to the church for the midday office. There in the great, spare stone sanctuary the ancient rhythms played themself out for perhaps the hundred-thousandth time. Summoned by the peels of the bell that rang out solemnly over the countryside, the community of fifty-two women gathered, gliding noiselessly into their respective choir stalls. All stood, bowed, and knelt in concert. Knees, shoulders, heads in common gesture, kinesthetic memory bending the body, and thus the spirit, to prayer. All listened attentively as the spoken word of Scripture called out bead after bead of ancient, depthless wisdom, fingered by the mind, the lips, the heart. All opened throats and with a single sound breathed a melody that has reverberated through cloisters for nearly a millennium.

The entire structure of monastic life, its rhythms, architecture, customs and disciplines, is designed to foster contemplation. It is designed to encourage the silent inward turning that ushers one finally into the silence of God. This silence undergirds all reality. Monastic life witnesses to that silence as the fundamental reality undergirding all our lives. But what of that silence outside the cloister? What of its disclosure in the fabric of daily life "in the world"? In this article I will explore the sort of contemplative experience that is not explicitly monastic, yet which breathes in a similar, suspended air that radiated that summer day from the Cistercian monastery at Chambarand. My intent is first, to consider the nature of contemplation and the contemplative dimension of life and to suggest what living contemplatively apart from the monastic structure might be like, and second, to turn to the arena of contemporary family life and explore its contemplative dimension. In the process, I will draw upon stories and illustrations of my own and suggest ways in which Thomas Merton's world, the world open to what he called "the hidden ground of love,"[1] can be part of all of our worlds.

I. Drawn to the Life of the Life of the Soul

The summer visit to Chambarand was not my first monastic experience. I have for over a quarter of a century been a frequent visitor to any number of monastic foundations. If my visitations point to an ongoing quest to deepen my relation with God through the contemplative path, and I think they do, it is not true that monasticism has been the primary environment in which I have nurtured that relationship. I did not first learn to pray in the monastic context, nor do I now live in a manner that can in any way be construed as formally contemplative. My husband and I have three children ranging at present from twelve to nineteen years of age. I teach full time in the theology department at a Jesuit university in the field of history of spirituality and overfill too many days with the details of the academy—committees, advising, editing, writing, attending conferences. On top of this, I have been drawn to take on, in great part because of the labile nature of the field of spirituality, a variety of pastoral roles—retreat leader, spiritual director, author of inspirational literature.[2]

1. Merton makes reference to the "hidden ground of love" as that reality for which there can be no explanation and in which we discover the happiness of being one with everything in a 1967 address to students at Smith College in Northampton, Massachusetts. The phrase occurs, as well, throughout his letters and provided editor William H. Shannon with a title for his volume of Merton's selected letters. See *The Hidden Ground of Love: The Letters of Thomas Merton on Religious Experience and Social Concerns*, selected and edited by William H. Shannon (New York: Farrar, Strauss, Giroux, 1985).

2. My books include *Bond of Perfection: Jeanne de Chantal and François de Sales* (Mahwah, N.J.: Paulist Press, 1985); *Francis de Sales and Jane de Chantal: Letters of Spiritual Direction*, Classics of Western Spirituality Series, with Joseph F. Power, O.S.F.S., and Peronne-Marie Thibert, V.H.M. (Mahwah, N.J.: Paulist Press, 1988); *Sacred Dwelling: A Spirituality of Family Life* (New York: Crossroad, 1989), second edition (Leavenworth, Kansas: Forest of Peace, 1993); *Francis de Sales: Introduction to the Devout Life and Treatise on the Love of God*, Spiritual Legacy Series (New York: Crossroad, 1993); *The Vigil: Keeping Watch in the Season of Christ's Coming* (Nashville: Upper Room, 1992); *The Rising: Living the Mysteries of Lent, Easter and Pentecost* (Nashville: Upper Room, 1994); *A Retreat With Francis de Sales, Jane de Chantal and Aelred of Rievaulx: Befriending Each Other in God* (Cincinnatti: St. Anthony Messenger, 1996).

Yet it was the monks and others in our history such as medieval holy women and desert hermits, kin to the monks in their quest for the contemplative life, who taught me, through the testimonies of their lives, that the deep down ache that would not go away and which compelled me at one and the same time to restless peregrinations and simply sitting still, was as important as I sensed it must be. This despite the fact that little else in my environment encouraged its cultivation.

It was as a late-blooming graduate student and after being keenly wounded enough in life's battles to have come to impasse on all fronts, that I first discovered the voices of those who we deem part of our Christian contemplative tradition—Augustine, the anonymous author of *The Cloud of Unknowing*, Br. Lawrence of the Resurrection—the familiar figures. These ancient witnesses spoke a language, uttered words from a fund of wisdom that resonated so insistently with my as-yet inchoate longings, that the pursuit of them became a passion. These ancient ones lived splendidly, even sensuously, into the deep place I sensed was central to my own life. Augustine gave it a name: "He is the Life of the Life of my soul."[3]

Further graduate work, which allowed an immersion into the lives of Jane de Chantal and Francis de Sales, turn-of-the- seventeenth-century saints whose spiritual friendship I chronicled, allowed me to become more familiar with the languages and practices of the Christian contemplative life. Chronicling became more than an academic pursuit, it also became the occasion for self-investigation. I felt drawn—inexorably, palpably—to the still, full atmosphere of monasteries. Trappistine. Visitandine. Benedictine. Carmelite. Franciscan. I visited them all. Along the way I met Thomas Merton. First through a rather cursory reading of *The Seven Story Mountain* (whose excessive convert zeal verbiage I had a difficult time wading through). Then through a more attentive reading of *Contemplation in a World of Action* and *The Asian Journal*.[4] I have one vivid memory of spending an afternoon trapped between floors in a university elevator, taking comfort in

---

3. Augustine of Hippo, *Confessions*, book 10, chapter 6.

4. It was especially the famous passage in the *Asian Journal* penned when Merton visited the Buddhist statues at Polonnaruwa that spoke to me. "Looking at these figures I was suddenly, forcibly, jerked clean out of the habitual, half-tied vision of things, and an inner clearness, clarity, as if exploding from the rocks themselves, became evident and obvious. . . The rock, all matter, all life, is charged with dharmakaya. . . everything is emptiness and everything is compassion." *The Asian Journal of Thomas Merton* (New York: New Directions, 1973) 233–5.

the fact that I had Merton's words as companion for my inforced er-
meticism.[5] But mostly, it was Merton's life that fascinated me, as it has
generations of American spiritual seekers. He was someone who had
followed the deepest demands of his heart. I longed to do the same.

It was during a prolonged stay at a Trappistine community in
the redwood forests of Northern California during the winter of 1976
that clearer sense of what it might mean to live contemplatively began
to emerge for me. This was the community Merton had visited just before embarking on his Asian journey, and he was still present in the
anecdotal memory of the sisters. It gave the place a certain aura, as
though this place was a fitting launching pad for a journey from which
one might never return.

That winter was a graced time in many respects. I lived a quasi-
hermit's life, participating in the liturgical rhythm of the hours and in
some form of manual labor during scheduled work hours. Beyond
that, I was left free to rest in the impulse that had brought me there in
the first place: the call to deeper solitude, the call to listen. I had been
well advised by a psychologist friend before coming: "Don't think you
even know the question you are asking by going. Just listen." Allow
the various levels of conversation that constantly spin around in your
head to gradually fall away. To the point where silence itself is its own
question. Never mind the answer.

So I went. And listened. In that wonderful way that refuses to
yield to analysis, commentary or interpretation. Where wind is wind.
And the beating of a heart is the beating of a heart. But where you realize you have never genuinely heard wind or a heartbeat before.

Winter is off-season for the community so there were few
guests. One week was even dedicated to a community retreat. A monk
from a Trappist monastery on the East Coast arrived to conduct the
days of reflection. In my listening mode, two things he said struck my
ear with clarion clarity and became the basis for my later understanding of what the contemplative life is not, and what it is. He began by
evoking an image of a young woman seated in a meadow alone,
breathing in the beauty around her. In fairness to the monk, I'm not

---

5. I believe at the time I was reading his *Monastic Journey*. The section on
the solitary life was especially pertinent. "The *eremos*, the desert wilderness 'where
evil and curse prevail', where nothing grows, where the very existence of man is
constantly threatened, is also the place specially chosen by God to manifest
Himself in His 'mighty acts' of mercy and salvation." See *The Monastic Journey*,
edited by Br. Patrick Hart (Garden City, N.Y.: Doubleday Image Books, 1987) 190.

sure what his intent was in bringing this particular, albeit classic, image to the attention of the community. But it provided me with an image for understanding what the contemplative life is not. A contemplative life may in part be about the withdrawl to solitude and the aesthetic gaze upon the created universe. But it is not a life of idyllic fantasy, not something "other," not a safe haven from the harshness of the world. Nor is it equatable with a stress-free existence or a state of unalterable calm. "Being centered" we would call it today.[6]

The other idea the monk presented has served me well in reflecting upon a contemplative life. He said that such a life is about facts. It is about what is. But what we deem "factual" is shaped by our perception. And the contemplative eye sees "facts" with a certain stunning clarity. It "sees" into the various levels of reality down to the core where the deep silence pertains.

This contemplative approach I speak of is not necessarily synonymous with the term "contemplation" used in traditional discussions of spiritual theology (based especially on the writings of the Carmelite mystics Teresa of Avila and John of the Cross). In these a distinction is made between "acquired" and "infused" contemplation, and the contemplative life proper is equated with a lifestyle of withdrawal and an advanced state of interiority in which all human activity has ceased and the operation of God alone is evident. I am using the term rather in the way earlier authors like Augustine, Gregory the Great, or Bernard of Clairvaux used it.[7] As a way of perceiving the world—a simplified, whole seeing—that gives birth to faith, hope and love. A way that tends to wordlessness and the unification of thought, feeling, and desire so that the energies of the whole person are gathered into focus. Contemplation, in this early Christian use of the term, might be defined as a listening awareness that allows the Word to take root in the heart and transform it.

---

6. The way the casual phrase "being centered" is often used today is quite different from the practice of Centering Prayer that Merton's fellow Cistercians have made popular in the years since Merton's death. That practice, associated especially with the names Thomas Keating and Basil Pennington, is a modern adaptation of the contemplative practice advocated by the anonymous author of the fourteenth-century *Cloud of Unknowing*.

7. On this point see the classic work by Edward Cuthbert Butler, *Western Mysticism: The Teachings of SS Augustine, Gregory and Bernard on Contemplation and the Contemplative Life* (London: Constable, 1927).

It is easy to recognize the monastic roots of this idea the way I have defined it. The ancient Benedictine practice of lectio divina, to which Merton as a Cistercian was heir, involves the cultivation of a distinct sort of listening awareness. In the profound and sustained silence of monastic enclosure, where words are few and those words uttered are primal—they are God's Word—one cultivates a sense of the sources of a given word's origin. One hones a sensitivity to the primal utterance. In the measured discipline of monastic routine, with life's maintenance pared to a minimum, one can give oneself to the formative process of growing into the Word, letting the Word become the vessel into which one's life is poured. Or, to change the metaphor, and stay even closer to the ancient tradition's self-understanding, the contemplative life is, first and foremost, a life of becoming a receptive vessel into which the divine Word is poured. Bernard of Clairvaux and his twelfth century compatriots, along with a host of other pray-ers in the tradition, Merton among them, likened themselves to Mary at the moment of the Annunciation. Receptive, assenting, open to welcome the Spirit-seed which would inhabit, grow, and be born in her. The Virgin Mary is the model of the contemplative soul opening itself to God.[8]

The contemplative life is a life of prayer, but a distinctive sort of prayer. While related to other forms of prayer such as praise, petition, lament, intercession or meditation, contemplative prayer has a quality distinctively its own. To put it plainly: in contemplation one allows oneself to be acted upon rather than acting as an agent. This allowing is not passivity, neither is it a cowering nor a resignation to let what ever will be, be. Rather, it is a ready receptivity. Much like the readiness of the non-leading partner in a couple's dance. One must be infinitely alert, instantaneously responsive, quick to dip and flow with the surge of the music and the practiced yet unpredictable step of one's partner. Such is the responsive readiness of contemplative prayer.

Such prayer risks much. To remain open to the influx of Spirit is to be formed. To be formed is to enter into transformation. And contemplative prayer is about transformation, about being reshaped in the image and likeness of God which in humanity was originally created. To pray this way is to see, to hear, to perceive anew. The process of such a transformation is guided by the symbolic language of the cumulative tradition but it is always unique, always irrepeatably particular. It is

8. As an example see Merton's early poem, "The Blessed Virgin Mary Compared to a Window" in *Collected Poems* (New York: New Directions, 1977) 46–8.

played out anew in each individual life. What can be said in all cases, is that such a transformation allows one to enter into a particular relationship with what is. Reality is thus not approached primarily as a problem to be solved, a cipher to be decoded, or data meant to be analyzed and controlled. Rather, reality is approached as a mystery to be plumbed, an astonishment etching its meaning into the marrows of our hearts. This does not imply that contemplative prayer does not ever issue in action, or prompt us to wrestle vigorously with the problems of our world. On the contrary, the action that flows from contemplation can be focused and impassioned, intent on transforming the world. But the seeing of what is, the listening, the running of the heart's tentative fingers over the terrain of the real, is done with reverence and as an encounter with mystery.

Perhaps one of the most distinctive aspects of contemplative prayer is that, while we ourselves are being refashioned, God, as we previously know God, also undergoes transformation. Or, to put it more accurately, we are led in contemplation beyond our earlier images and experiences of the divine. We are invited to continually let go of our familiar ways of knowing and encountering God. As we die to what we have been, God too seems to die. Thus the contemplative experience of dying, of penetrating deeper into reality and leaving behind all we have previously known, even at the seemingly most stable and foundational of levels, is simultaneously an entry into new, unfamiliar, less immediately apprehensible, encounters with God.

To approach it from another vantage point: contemplative prayer has to do with allowing oneself to be formed by and into an image that challenges the present images with which one lives. Contemplation invites vision that is constantly expanding, it offers a lens through which to gaze upon life that inverts and subverts present perception and gives at least partial access to a "God's eye" view. Contemplation is that risky and radical opening of self to be changed by and into God's own self. Thus it is a life of continual dying, of being stripped over and over again of the comfortable and familiar, of letting a reality beyond our own shape us. From another perspective, it is a life of emerging spaciousness, of being made wide and broad and empty enough to hold the vast and magnificent and excruciating paradoxes of created life in the crucible of love.[9]

---

9. Merton's most explicit work on the dynamics of contemplation is *Contemplative Prayer* (New York: Herder and Herder, 1969).

On one monastic excursion to a Trappist foundation in upstate Oregon, during my graduate school years, I was given a fresh image of the contemplative life that I find myself coming back to again and again. I had gone partly as an academic exercise, to become familiar with monastic praxis. But I also came with my heart trained on the inward dynamics I was experiencing. A long inner greyness, a keen sense of absence had long plagued me. Analysis of the situation from many vantage points yielded nothing. I found it difficult to characterize what had been my sense of God for perhaps five years. "Gone" was perhaps the best description. I felt confused and alone, perhaps deluded. No one seemed to know what I meant. Then, during this classroom field trip, the young monk appointed to dialogue with our class illuminated my experience for me. We had been going around the circle, introducing ourselves, speaking in general ways about our religious backgrounds. I don't remember what I said, but he shot back, "Yes, I know what you mean. I've been there for a long time too." And I knew that he knew exactly what I meant—knew that our truest experiences mirrored one another. I was immediately confirmed and given hope. I recall little of the rest of his conference except one phrase, which I later learned was a paraphrase of the poet Rilke.[10] But that phrase spoke volumes about where he and I found ourselves and about the nature of the contemplative life. "To be a Christian," he said, "is not to know all the answers. To be a Christian is to live in the part of the self where the question is being born." To live into the questions. To push the horizon of self back so insistently that one's reference point is the ever present act of birthing itself. To live in the presence of what can never be finished, found or known. To live in God's time. Open utterly to what is.

Contemplation is not an escape from the burdens of human existence. Rather, it brings us deeply into the heart of the world. Facts are the stuff of contemplation. But we must approach those facts with reverence, not primarily as problem-solvers, armed with our arsenals of established preconceptions, but as people willing to allow God, through our practices and the events of our lives, to pry us open so that our seeing and our loving begins to mirror the clarity and compassion of God's.

10. The Oregon Trappist was not the only devotee of Rilke. Merton spoke highly of him. See for example the audio cassette recording *Poetry and Imagination: Thomas Merton,* produced by Credence Cassettes, 60 min. (Kansas City Mo.: National Catholic Reporter, 1988).

II. A Contemplative Approach to Family Life

Very little in the structure and pace of modern American family life obviously lends itself to a classic life of contemplation such as I have begun to outline here. If silence, solitude, and an unchanging daily rhythm has been understood in our tradition as the essential matrix within which to form contemplative awareness, ordinary family life would seem an unlikely context in which to speak of such formation. And, we are all acutely aware, historic Christianity emphatically affirmed that the monastery and the family were two dramatically opposed institutions. One was for prayer. The other was for populating a Christian society. I will never forget, as a youthful, recently-married graduate student, picking up St. Jerome and reading his hurled invectives against the lot of the housewife: she flying from one end of the house to the other, fretful over her spouse, her children and her domestic duties. Where, fumed Jerome, is there time in all of this for thought of God?[11]

This is not the place to chronicle the Christian religion's gradual positive affirmation of marriage and family life as first, a sacrament, and second, a place of prayer and the cultivation of a genuine spiritual life. This has occurred.[12] The thundering rhetoric about family values that issues from the pulpits of all denominations is evidence enough of this. Yet there still remains much hesitancy about the compatibility between a contemplative life and familied experience. To the extent that we equate contemplative with monastic, the hesitancy is an appropriate one. Familied life, even if some members carve out solitary time and space or adopt rules about silence or follow daily rhythms of shared prayer, is intrinsically different from its monastic counterpart. The spirituality born of monastic experience is primarily vertical and one-on-one (God and the individual); it implies a going apart, a renunciation of a life of intimacy with spouse and children, a relinquishment of property and the burdens of caretaking; it implies a certain

---

11. The passage is found in St. Jerome, "Against Helvidius: The Perpetual of Blessed Virgin Mary," in *Nicene and Post-Nicene Fathers of the Christian Church*, vol. 6 *St. Jerome: Letters and Select Works* (Grand Rapids, Mich.: Wm.B.Eerdmans, 1954).

12. An overview of the development of the sacramental theology of marriage within the tradition is found in Joseph Martos, *Doors to the Sacred: An Historical Introduction to Sacraments in the Catholic Church* (Garden City, N.Y.: Doubleday, 1981).

marginality, a view from the critical distance that silence and solitude and spacious time allows.

A spirituality forged from the experience of familied life, in contrast, is intensely horizontal; it is about the in-betweenness of persons, of relationships, about bodies and lives intertwined, the intimate proximity of others; it is about the busyness of tending and providing, about the stewarding of property, it allows for very little of the distanced perspective that silence and solitude offer.

Yet while monasticism and familied life proceed from distinct and different human contexts and thus tend to give articulation to distinct spiritualities, there is nonetheless a sense, a significant sense, in which both may be said to be mediums through which a contemplative approach can be cultivated.

While I would suggest that specifically monastic practices, such as extended solitude and silence, might be intentionally integrated into family life, it is not necessarily being quasi-monastic that lends itself to contemplation, but rather becoming aware of the natural contemplative moments and rhythms that present themselves in the daily course of life. Before I speak to these, however, I would observe that many contemporary practices work against this openness: the prevalence of constant noise—the omnipresent television, radio, and music as well as the constant din of city traffic so many of us live with; the lack of opportunity for self-reflection in most of our work days; the frenetic pace of modern life, filled as it is with meetings, schedules, car-pools, interruptions from e-mail, voice-mail, cellulars, internet, and answering machines. Contemporary family life is crosshatched by all of these obstacles to the simple steady awareness of what is.

Blessedly, family life is not only about mortgages, grocery shopping, college education accounts, dance lessons, PTAs, childcare, discipline, soccer leagues, toilet training, or carpools. It is first and foremost about the intense and tender and often fierce interrelatedness of human beings. It is about the astonishment of being with each other. It is especially through parenting that I have come to appreciate the contemplative dimension of my life. And although I have perhaps had more opportunity to be articulate, both to myself and others, about the nature of such a contemplative path, I am not alone in my intuitions. I have rarely met a reflective parent who does not immediately resonate with my descriptions of the contemplative nature of parenthood even if their specific experiences or language is not quite mine.

As human beings, we locate the sacred. We discover the holy in space—in rivers, mountains, cathedral, grottos, and shrines. We sense sacred presence in time—as we enter the Sabbath, as we celebrate sacred seasons such as Advent or Lent or as we mark the anniversary of a loved one's death. We sense the sacred in certain people. Certain spaces. Certain times. Certain people. They are charged with a numinous aura that we respond to with awe. They are treasured. They are sacred. They are holy.

So too we locate the sacred in the times, place and people of family life. I have a favorite exercise I do with people on retreat. After defining family as any configuration of people with whom one finds oneself intimately connected through the course of one's life, I ask them to name the place in their own family's experience where they discover the "more," the experience of being greater that the sum of the individual parts. Ninety percent of respondents name the dining room or kitchen table. When I ask what is characteristic of that place, people say that they share more than food there, that there they tell of the day's events, that extended generations gather together. The table thus becomes a place of encounter with the deeper springs of mystery from which we drink. Tables are places of communion, of mutual need and nourishment acted out on several levels simultaneously. Our physical, emotional, and spiritual hungers are fed in a mealtime ritual as ancient as humankind. The table itself becomes the sacred spot where the ritual is accomplished. That this is keenly felt by people has become obvious to me in the way people speak of tables. One gentleman recounted that he owned the dining room table that had belonged to his grandfather. Every time he passed that table, he felt the presence of all the family members who had gathered there over the years. They were discovered in the presence of the table.

Tables are not the only sacred spaces of family life. Gardens, cars, bathrooms, vacation homes, tractors: the list is endless and varied. What they have in common is the fact that they are places of deep communion, of encountering others in a manner that exposes our primal vulnerability and hungers, and makes of us both feeders and fed. We enact the mystery of our deep interconnectedness. This ushers us ultimately into our shared hunger for God.

Sacred times in family life have a quality similar to sacred places. Entering them, we discover the depth of our connectedness to spirit. Holiday celebrations and anniversaries are chief among family sacred times. They function for family members much the way the rhythm of the liturgical year functions in monastic life. They sanctify time. They pierce the opaqueness of ordinary time with a latticework of windows through which we peer into the depth dimension of our lives. Year after year we pierce more deeply, the celebration gaining in richness with each successive encounter. For each time we are greeted with all our previous experience. Layer on layer. A wedding anniversary gains texture and weight through the seasons of a marriage. Encoded in that celebrative time are all the varied experiences of the years—the first flush of romance, the busy nurturance of birthing and childrearing, the excitement of the first house, the new job, the disappointments and failures, the reconciliations, the shared labors. The cumulative story is contained in time: not only of a couple's life together but of their most profound dreams, the music of the spirit, their dance with God.

If the contemplative life is about the steady gaze upon the facts of existence, a gaze that searches for the still "I am" that undergirds all, then the family is certainly an arena which offers an uncushioned encounter with facts. To hold one's newborn child for the first time. To wait at the bedside of a dying parent. To suffer the agony of a life threatening childhood illness. To delight completely in and with a beloved spouse. To hold ancient, treasured memories in common with a brother or sister. These are the simple facts of family. They are also sure gateways into the astonishing, painful, joy-filled facts of human existence, an existence whose very fabric is woven through with the threads of divinity.

Perhaps it is because love binds us so closely in family that this deep piercing is possible. Love, that gravitational pull that draws us out of the illusion that we are isolated selves. Love, that primal knowledge of our common identity. Love, that binder and healer of our shared alienation. Our false selves, resistant though they are, can be stripped away in the crucible of geniune love.[13]

Family life does not have to be churchy or quasi-monastic to reveal its contemplative dimension. Some cultivation of self-reflection and the claiming of naturally solitary, silent moments would seem to be essential. But these moments do not have to be superimposed. Rather, they need to be recognized, protected and entered into.

---

13. The notion of the false self was, of course, made famous by Merton. See especially chapter 2 of his *New Seeds of Contemplation* (New York: New Directions, 1961).

Routines of folding laundry, rituals of putting a child to bed with a song or story, fishing together on vacation, walking the dog on a summer's evening, an automobile drive in the country, watching the sun set from a porch swing, sleeping out under the stars. All these and a myriad of others thread through our lives together. They are breathing spaces, opportunities for the simple factuality of what is to present itself in all its unspeakable fullness.

Certainly, more formal disciplines of prayer can encourage the listening attention of contemplation. These will differ from family to family. Some may be overtly contemplative. A husband and wife may be students of centering prayer and spell each other in babysitting duties so that they might each find time for their practice. Another family might have a shared ritual of morning prayer, dipping down into the vast well of the church's ancient liturgies to bring up the Word as a spring of living water. But not all members of a family may find cultivation of a specifically contemplative mode of prayer life-giving. Some may have their faith energized through the exercise of social justice—through contact with the poor at a soup kitchen or through community service. Others may find the path of intellectual engagement fruitful—through a study of the spiritual and theological classics of our tradition. In any of these cases, the contemplative undercurrent of our existence must be attended to in some way. That deep knowing is a portion of all experience. Awareness of it must thread through our study, our actions, and our interactions.

Nor does a family have to fit the description of the perfect, functional family to give access to the sustaining hidden ground of love that Merton described.[14] The persistent, onward thrusting of life itself seems determined to find its truest expression. Most families have their contemplative glimpses, their acknowledgement of that foundational love. Most families can name sacred times and places unique to them. I think of a single mother who had escaped from a severely abusive marriage and who, along with her teenaged children, had grappled with substance abuse. This family's sacred space was at the kitchen counter, where two by two they would stand side by side, one washing and one drying the dishes. There, she claimed, they could begin to speak and cultivate the communion they had lost for so long. Not facing one another (it was too soon for that) they experienced

---

14. Cf. note 1.

themselves "in a bubble," a time out of time, where they could begin together to heal.

If I were asked to give a formal name to this contemplative living in family, and to link it to the greater heritage of Christian prayer, I would first turn to the pages of the little Carmelite classic from late seventeenth-century France, *The Practice of the Presence of God* by Brother Lawrence of the Resurrection. Lawrence was a lay brother of the Paris Carmel. His work in the community varied over the years. Among the jobs he held were sandalmaker and cook. Despite his obscure origins and the even more obscure role he played in his monastic community and the religious affairs of his era, Brother Lawrence had a wide reputation and was consulted for his spiritual counsel by many. He promoted a simple path which he termed "the practice of the presence of God."[15]

It is that simple practice of finding God alive in the hustle and bustle, the burdens and delights, the wrenching sorrow and unspeakable joy that is common to us all, monastic and lay alike. The contexts differ and thus the dynamics and insights as well. But the loving attention, the refusal to engage with life primarily as a problem to be solved, a cyper to be decoded or a formula to be analyzed, the embrace of the facts of our existence as a question into which we live, a mystery we allow to enter and shape us, this we share. This is the contemplative life.

I will close with two images, drawn from my own experience. I trust they will encourage a contemplative claiming of our lives as familied people. The first image is one that I came to parenthood with. The second is one given to me in the course of being a parent. The first emerged during my first pregnancy. This was a luminous time for me, despite much fatigue and persistent sickness. I felt like I was at the center of the universe, aligned with the most powerful generative forces of life itself—which of course I was. Fantasizing ahead to an unknown future, I imaged an idyllic future with my child-to-be. In retrospect, it was rather like the image of contemplation presented by the Trappist father—of the young woman in a meadow rapt in reverie. I saw myself as the mother of a cherubic, tow-headed toddler, sitting on a park

---

15. The latest English edition of Br. Lawrence's classic is Brother Lawrence of the Resurrection, *The Practice of the Presence of God*, critical edition by Conrad De Meester, O.C.D., trans. by Salvatore Sciurba, O.C.D. (Washington D.C.: ICS Publications, Institute of Carmelite Studies, 1994).

bench as her child plays on the grassy knoll in the near distance. The whole scene was bathed in peace. Sunlight. Joy. I, free to reflect, was collected within myself, settled in delicious stillness as the beauteous young life cavorted in a pristine grassy, flower-filled park. Real motherhood soon taught me that it is never like that. One is never free as a mother of a toddler, or a grade school child or adolescent for that matter, to simply sit back and observe. An outing to a park has to be negotiated around naps and meals. And one is always on one's feet, trailing or restraining an unsteady walker, alert for dog droppings, for obstacles that may cause tripping, for enticing glittering objects that may end up in the mouth. And one is burdened with extra jackets, diapers, snacks, drinks, a treasured toy that cannot be left at home, aware that fatigue, hunger, frustration, tears, or the need to use the restroom might strike at any minute.

Yet to see the world through the eyes of a child is to begin a lesson in wonder. To radically entrust your heart to another growing, changing human being is to risk living into the question. To know yourself as inextricably joined to another is to cross the threshold of the vast, inexpressible network of mystery that conjoins us all.

It is that mystery that brings me to my last image. This past fall, my husband and I sent our first child to college. An ordinary action, performed by hundreds of thousands of parents each year. Yet for each parent-child configuration, the event is unique. Our daughter chose a Catholic university on the coast, halfway across the nation from our home. So the preparations and the dislocation were major. I went with her to see her settled in her dorm room, to hook up the computer, to help shop for what seemed like a thousand articles she needed to equip her to live independently from us. The university provided an excellent orientation program for new students and parents with just the right mixture of launching activities for students and letting go pep talks for parents.

It was a good weekend but one in which I found myself struggling with the welter of paradoxical emotions that threaten to swamp one at a time of such profound transition. As the weekend progressed, my daughter was less and less at my side. A residence hall meeting, a first year ice breaker, a dance, these claimed her, as they should. Late afternoon of the weekend's end, I took a solitary walk out to the campus edge. Her university is situated on a wide bluff that overlooks the central city in one direction and the ocean in the other. Dusk was gathering, and I found myself full throated with an explosive mixture of pride, sorrow, joy, grief, anxiety and relief. I watched for a long time as the sun grew crimson over the sea, then started back to the central campus. As I rounded a tree on a grassy knoll, I noted a statue I had neglected previously. At first glance, it seemed a statue of the Virgin Mary, which in fact it was. But a Virgin as I had never seen her before. Standing, her body thrust slightly forward, arms lifted high, she offered up to the expansive sky an infant child. The gesture was at once tender and anguished, charged with the inexpressible protective love of motherhood that must relinquish to an unknown future that which is more precious to her than life itself. The statue was dedicated to the mothers of the university's students.

The statue imaged for me a familied variant of the contemplative life. Here was Mary, the classic Christian embodiment of contemplation, not before the conception, at the moment of annunciation, but after the gestation, birth and nurture. Offering all—her love, her life itself—back into the arms of the unknown. A radical entrusting to what is. Risking the mystery. Living into the question.

Eucharistic Cosmos

Beatrice Bruteau

Thomas Merton was always trying to situate his religion in a larger context: psychological development, social justice, other religions. To extend the basic notions of Christianity in a cosmic context would be a congenial continuation of Merton's expansion. I here propose to describe the cosmos as an energy-sharing, self-organizing, symbiotic, Trinity-imaging reality—which is what I take the real (as distinguished from the ceremonial and symbolic) Eucharist to be. Eucharist is life-sharing. Life is organized energy-sharing. Trinity is agape-sharing, by which Persons, though distinct, are One.

The essence of Christianity is to see—and therefore to live in terms of—a total Reality that is expressive of the God who is Trinity and who is Incarnation. If this is the heart of the Christian religion, then it behooves the contemplative, especially, to be conscious of the great universe, an expression of God's trinitarian and incarnational presence every way we look, on all levels of organization from quarks to humans, and in everything that happens, from exploding stars through the struggles of life (including point-of-view "good" and "evil") to sublime moments of art and mystical union.

This article will sketch briefly my ideas on Trinity as community, Incarnation as God's ecstasy, and the universe as self-organizing and symbiotic. This will prepare the way for a discussion of the human being (brain and consciousness), a proposal to see the cosmos on the model of the Incarnation, and a conclusion regarding the practice of a trinitarian eucharistic spirituality.

The Trinitarian Community

Many metaphysicians have taken as their starting point the fact that Being is somehow both one and many. This is the context in which

I appropriate the concept of God as Trinity, develop it as a Person-Community, and extend it as a paradigm for the universe.

I think that the greatest advantage of the concept of God as Trinity over other approaches is that it recognizes that plurality cannot be reduced to unity nor derived from unity. It is almost truer to say that unity derives from plurality, or rather from the interactivity that plurality makes possible. For the coincidence of unity and plurality in the Godhead comes from the nature of God as agape. Agape has the unique feature of establishing both differentiation and unity by the same principle. Agape, as seeking the good of the beloved, requires that there be an other to love. But, as love, it also seeks union and is not satisfied until complete union is achieved. It is the nature of that union, which must not destroy the differentiation, that is of interest as a paradigm for the Trinity's creative expression in the universe.

Here I share some background with Thomas Merton. We were both exposed to the ideas of Daniel Walsh. I find Walsh's way of talking about Person very helpful for the way I want to talk about the Trinity. Also, it was Walsh who said that choice of starting point is all-important, and the place to start is "God is Love." He even said, "Love is so intense that it expresses itself as the Trinity. The Trinity is not God; the Trinity is the first expression of Love, who is God."[1] A remarkable utterance.

For me, this is saying something that is the key for a theology of the cosmos. The central reality is *interaction*. Not just (static) relationship. Not attitude or orientation. Love is essentially dynamic. It is the donation or the sharing of whatever "energy" is the relevant "selfhood" of the participating parties. It itself is the union of plurality and unity.

Although the agape that is God is not self-seeking but self-giving and Being-giving, it is nevertheless reciprocal. No one gives only and does not receive. Thus agape defines a community, and this community has the characteristics of a *system:* all parties contribute and all parties receive. There is no starting point and no concluding point.[2] The interactivity of all the parties constitutes the reality of the union-being of the whole as a whole.

---

1. Daniel Walsh, "Person and Community," Gethsemani Archives Document 5 (Trappist, Ky.: Abbey of Gethsemani, Nov. 6, 1971) 4.

2. This neglects, for purposes of establishing a paradigm for creation, the non-reciprocal order of the processions.

The "parties" to the Love interaction are Persons, says Walsh. Persons are distinguished from natures. Nature answers 'what?'; Person answers 'who?'. Natures are created by the free will of God. Persons arise from the being of God. Persons are uncreated. That applies to all Persons, including those who afterwards express through created natures, such as angels and human beings.[3]

Walsh himself suggested two "effusions" of Persons from the being of God (Love): the traditional Trinity of the divine Persons, and a second effusion of Persons who would be endowed with finite natures.[4] However that may be, it seems clear to me that ultimately there must be a single community in the divine life. The affirmation of such a community of Oneness among the Persons and the achievement of such a community among the created natures is what we are all about. The divine intent is "that they may be one as we are one" (John 17:22). And how are the divine Persons one? Through their mutual indwelling. The total reality of each divine Person is Love, agape, self-giving, being-giving. Thus each Person is active with an ecstatic movement to give itself, to give full being, to each other Person. This is eucharist inside God, each "feeding" each other with each one's own being.[5] My contention is that this interaction—which is Love—is the Oneness of God, and is the paradigm for creation. All that is made is made in the image of God, and this image is of the divine interactive eucharistic Community.

Incarnation as God's Ecstasy

The eucharistic movement is ecstatic. The incarnational movement is ecstatic. I want to see the cosmic interaction as eucharistic and incarnational, see it as God's ecstasy. We have two applicable texts.

> Philippians 2:4-7: Let each of you look not (only) to your own interests but (also) to the interests of each other. Have the attitude

3. D. Walsh, Gethsemani Document 3, "Anselm and Duns Scotus on Faith and the Person," (The Catholic University of America, 1966) 23. For fuller discussion, see B. Bruteau, Feature Book Review of Robert Imperato, *Merton and Walsh on the Person*, in *International Philosophical Quarterly* XXXI:3 (Sept. 1991) 353–63.

4. D. Walsh, Gethsemani Document 14, "Chapter Talk," June 1967, 3–4.

5. Expanded discussion of this can be found in B. Bruteau, "Trinitarian Personhood," *Cistercian Studies* XXII:3 (1987) and in "The One and the Many: Communitarian Non-Dualism," in B. Bruteau, ed., *The Other Half of My Soul: Bede Griffiths and the Hindu-Christian Dialogue* (Wheaton, Ill.: Quest, 1996) 268–307.

among yourselves that is also in Christ Jesus, who subsisting in the form of God, did not deem it robbery to be equal with God, but emptied himself, taking the form of a slave, being generated in the likeness of human beings.

There are two words here that can be interpreted in various ways, *hyparchon* ("subsisting") and *harpagmon* ("robbery"), and one deserving of further comment, *phroneite* (have . . . attitude). *Hyparchon* is made from *hypo*, "under," and *arche*, "the beginning" (or "the first"), and means (as a noun) one who commands under another, a lieutenant; or, as a verb it can mean to begin doing something, or to arise and be ready, or to lie under (this is where the "subsist" comes from) in the sense of being taken for granted (or being the ground of), or to belong to or to be devoted to, or to be sufficient. If we put all this together, perhaps we may say that Christ Jesus feels that he belongs to and is devoted to God, who is the ground of his being, and therefore he must arise and be ready to begin doing what God commands, since he is in the position of lieutenant.

Harpagmon comes from *harpazo*, which means to ravish away, to carry off, to grasp hastily, to snatch up, to seize. The noun therefore means something that is seized, booty, plunder. There are several possibilities here. Either Jesus did not reach out to seize divinity, or he did not consider that it was taking something to which he had no right. Or it could mean that he did not insist on clinging to (grasping) the divinity that was his. I will use this last interpretation for application to the incarnation in the cosmos. But there is still another interesting possibility. *Harpazo* can also mean to grasp with the mind. The effect would then be that Jesus did not consider being equal with God to be something that was to be grasped only with the mind but something that was to be put into practice. And at this point the sense of *phroneite* comes in, for *phronesis* is a kind of wisdom, the kind often called "prudence," a practical wisdom, wisdom put into practice. And the kind of *phronesis* Jesus practiced is well expressed in the exhortation "Let each of you look to the interests of each other." (This, by the way, is a characteristically Jewish ideal, expressed also as the pious person's attitude of "What is mine is yours and what is yours is yours.")[6]

---

6. This ideal was exemplified in the life of Hillel the Elder. See Yitzhak Buxbaum, *The Life and Teachings of Hillel* (Northvale, N.J.: Aronson, 1994) 170, citing *Pirke Avot* 5:13.

The self-emptying can be seen as having two stages—or "effusions," if we borrow Walsh's word, or "ecstasies," if we use mine. The first is the ecstatic movement from divinity to humanity (in the text), which I choose to expand to the whole of the cosmic reality. The lieutenant commander, who is rightfully in the "form of God"—which we now understand to be formlessness, infinitude—does not cling to that but pours himself out in ecstasy and takes on form, finitude as such. To be finite is to be a slave, a *doulos,* one who is in bondage or is subject to another. Finite beings are all subject to the laws and conditions of their existence, limited by their natures, and many of them subject to one another in various ways.

The second ecstatic movement is the one urged by the Pauline text, seconding Jesus and the usual Jewish teaching: pour yourselves out for one another. Give yourselves without stint, without limitation. Here we have already a hint of how the circle will be closed, the Infinite becoming finite and the finite—in the very terms of its finitude—becoming infinite.

We can also see in the *phronesis,* the practical adoption of the divine ecstasy, the interaction that I have proposed as essential to the dynamic Godhead. It is agape, it is energy-sharing, it is systemic, it makes oneness, wholeness. As the dynamic of the cosmos, it will take different forms (including some that are apparently not seeking the interest of the other at all).

The second text I find applicable is John 1:18:

> No one has ever seen God. The only-begotten God *(monogenes theos),* the one being in the bosom *(kolpon)* of the Father, That One exegeted *(exegesato).*

Here "God" refers to the Infinite Ground, the invisible Father, the First, the Archon. The only-begotten God may be (more or less the same as) the *Hyparchon.* The *Hyparchon* is in the *kolpon,* the "hollow," of the Father, having his being in the ultimate Ground of the Father to whom he is devoted. This *Hyparchon* is the One who "exegetes." To exegete is to manage, direct, govern, to go first, lead the way, guide, to teach, to expound, interpret, to describe or devise. It is also to be one who opens up the meaning of the sacred. I choose to see such exegesis as a kind of ecstasy. It "unpacks" and externalizes the reality hidden in the unity of the *kolpon,* in the "emptiness" of the invisible and ineffable. And it does so by "devising," that is, giving form.

These two, the *Archon* and the *Hyparchon,* the Invisible One and the Exegete, dwell within each other. What is enfolded (enstatic) in the Invisible is unfolded (ecstatic) in the Exegete. What is hidden in the formlessness of the First is displayed in the differentiated forms of the Second. If the exegesis is seen as Incarnation and the Incarnation as referring to the entire Cosmos, then the Cosmos can be regarded metaphorically as the interior of the Hidden One exteriorized, turned inside out. And the incarnate Exegete will manifest the interactivity that is the dynamic within the Person-Community of the Ground. The Cosmos will be built of interactivity and this interactivity will be a kind of eucharist, cross-feeding and energy-sharing.

The Theocosmic Exegete and the Nature of Finitude

The Exegete, like agape itself, does two things: it establishes distinction, or "severalization," and it unites by interactivity; it makes different, and it makes one. This is how a finite world is constructed. The Theocosmic Exegete, God exegeting Godself by making the world, does the characteristic Godlike thing: being many who are one. Both the "unpacking," the spreading out in variety of the unlimited potentialities of Being, and the gathering together so as to make still more different kinds of things, and gathering them yet again and again in assemblies of assemblies—both the scattering and the gathering are acts of the Exegete.

The diverse beings of the universe exist in terms of one another, in terms of their relations to one another, of their interactions with one another. They constitute mutual support systems and systems of such systems. Each one is able to be what it is only in the context of what it is doing for the others to which it is related. Self-being and for-others-being arise together.[7] In the natural world, there are many activities

---

7. Keiji Nishitani, in *Religion and Nothingness,* trans. Jan Van Bragt (Berkeley: University of California, 1982) has an interesting discussion of what he calls "circuminsessional interpenetration" in the context of the Kyoto School's understanding of *Shunyata* (Emptiness) and Heidegger's concept *Dasein* (lit., "there-being," in the sense of the facticity of existence): "all things are master and servant to one another. . . . To say that a certain thing is . . . servant to every other thing means that . . . it is a constitutive element in the being of every other thing, making it to be what it is and thus to be situated in a position of autonomy as master of itself" [148]; ". . . self-centeredness only comes about at one with other-centeredness, and other-centeredness at one with self-centeredness. And this is quite

and processes. But it is the *inter*actions,[8] the relations of several processes to one another, that make the universe-process, that build up the structure and the operation of the various levels of wholes that the cosmos is. These processes "mutually indwell" one another, so dependent are they upon all the others in order to be themselves. But this is just the way enstasis and ecstasis are related and united in the Trinity.

Just as in the Trinity there is no such thing as a single Person, so in the universe there is no such thing as a single being. All beings exist in co-acting communities, or systems of many beings. And it is from the collective, cooperative, interactions of the beings in the systems that whole new levels of being emerge.[9] This fundamental feature of the natural universe is significant for the view I am proposing of the cosmos as a kind of "incarnation" of the Trinity. It cannot be done by any single cosmic being. It can be done only by the whole cosmos, in its multitude of ordered and creative interactions. It can be done only by scattering and gathering, or severing and clumping.

To begin to get a sense for this, consider a figure drawn on a sheet of paper, any sort of figure, a closed curve. The figure has a boundary. The boundary defines it, separates the inside of the figure from the outside. The closed boundary makes the figure contain its insideness. This is the beginning of selfhood in the finite order. Also, we might think of the boundary as drawing the space together inside itself; it makes a spot, a body, a corpuscle, in the space. There is a togetherness inside the boundary that there is not outside. The figure is discrete, set off, separated. When you have drawn several ("severed") discrete bodies, you can relate them to one another in various clumping patterns. The discrete bodies, and the discrete clumps of discrete bodies, will be "different" from one another in various ways, initially just by being severed from one another, but then by being in different clump patterns. And then there will be clumps of clumps and patterns of clumps of clumps and patterns of patterns of clumps of clumps. We

---

natural and as it should be" [264]. I believe this is congenial with my sense of the enstatic/ecstatic relation (see note 5 above).

8. See, e.g., John H. Holland, *Hidden Order: How Adaptation Builds Complexity* (Menlo Park: Helix, 1995) 3, for examples of the importance of interaction in the immune system and the central nervous system.

9. See Stuart Kauffman, *At Home in the Universe: The Search for the Laws of Self-Organization and Complexity* (New York: Oxford, 1995) 24, on the emergence of new levels of reality as wholes.

may notice that there is more unity in a patterned clump than there is in a single bounded figure. And more unity even than there was on the unmarked paper before the severing line was drawn. This is the exegesis of the invisible in terms of finitude.

In the natural world, beings will have relations of mutual reference, of position and motion in space and time, motions that affect clumping, patterning, and renewed severing, which in turn will limit the kinds of motions. Motions and patterns take place in terms of natural law, restricted according to the values of the cosmic parameters. From the motions, the patterns, the interactions, new wholes emerge with their own characteristic patterns, motions, patterned motions, with their own natural laws.

The emergent wholes are now the individuals for further unions. Each new level emergent exists precisely as the group of interacting individuals. It is not their product as something separate from them; it is themselves, interacting. The emergent cannot be divided, taken apart, and still be itself, still be present. It has its own definition, boundary, and selfhood. A great change may have taken place, as when non-living molecules by their interactions compose a living cell. These interactions are eucharistic sharings. Their emergents are analogical christic bodies. As the compounding goes forward, the exegesis unfolds.

Patterned clumping and behavior according to natural law means that some behaviors will be possible, others impossible. Wood will burn in air, which contains oxygen, but not under water, which is composed in part of oxygen. The clumping interactions, forming emergents, have opened up new interactions and blocked others. And most interesting of all, they have made some developments—under appropriate conditions—inevitable. Once there are clumping and patterning (combinations and permutations), possibility and impossibility (probability and branching development), in limited populations, certain things will spontaneously happen. Some of these will come right out of the nature of finitude itself.

Emergents will form when the conditions for them are right, but they need the conditions to continue. The first needs are for multiplicity and diversity, repeated copies of the same thing and many different kinds of things. A great deal of diversity is required in order to have a high chance of getting useful interactions. But diversity is available. And here is one way we can see inevitability. Notice that the number of ways of putting pieces together is always much greater than the number of pieces themselves. And when patterning is included, the diversity is much greater still. If, for these pieces, there is a certain probability of a particular interaction occurring, and if there are sufficient multiplicity and diversity, the probability of that interaction actually happening a significant number of times will approach inevitability, even if the probability in any single encounter is quite low. The chance may be one in a million, but if you have a million, then you should get one. And since there may be more than one way of obtaining a given effect, the diversity will improve the chances in this way as well. This has a great deal to do with formation of molecules, shuffling of genes, and filling of niches in the biological world.

Finally, finitude and the need of organized beings to have the conditions for their existence continually met, result in issues of scarcity of resources, competition, cooperation, trickiness of various sorts (deceptions, dominations, cheating), predation, parasitism, enslavement, failure, death, and destruction. The drive to be and to be more, pressured by the limitations of the environment will bring forth also sensitivity (gaining information about the environment), intelligence (processing and applying the information), social organization, language, consciousness.

All of these are exegesis of the Invisible in the forms of finitude. Being tends to be more and to be in every possible way. It expresses as Being-communicating, interactive and holistic. Finite being has difference and change. These will be possible and necessary because it can be said of a finite being (as it cannot of the infinite) what it is *not*. "Notbeing" will play a major role in everything about finite being, whereas infinite being is the "fullness of Being" and nothing can be denied of it. Finite being will be severed and interactive and novelty-creating.

Nobody "causes" these things to happen. There is no "choice" about whether this will be done. Nor does the Infinite "design" the forms of the finite. The forms of the finite arise from fundamental necessary relations in finitude itself. But those "necessary relations" include chance, spontaneous order, historical accidents, natural selection acting on complex adaptive systems, learned behaviors, and conscious choices by those beings capable of such acts. The amazing thing about the finite is that out of very simple entities and rules there come, stage by compounding stage, life and self-awareness, and morality and science and art. The Infinite is exegeted in the forms of finitude and then that finitude so knits itself up into more and more complex organizations that eventually it becomes capable of knowing itself as the exegesis of the Infinite and revering the Infinite in Itself and in Its finite expression. All a eucharistic feast of splendor.

To and From the Stars: Pre-Biotic Energy-Sharing

It seems that stars are the crucial things in getting this universe well started. If stars can be made, then the rest will very likely follow. If stars cannot be made, nothing of what we know will follow. But how are stars made? Stars are formed by the clumping of matter with large distances in between. And where did the matter and the large distances come from? They are both accounted for by something called "the inflation scenario." It is a modification of the Big Bang schema for the origin of our particular universe, unproved but widely accepted.

The observed Hubble expansion—clusters of galaxies moving away from each other—and the detection of the cosmic background radiation lead to the conclusion that our observable universe originated in hot thermal communication. There was a time, about fifteen billion years ago, when all the matter we now see was close enough together that collisions could average out the temperature. The matter was close enough together because the universe was very small in the first tiny fractions of its existence, and all the matter was created together at that time. It came out of a field of potential energy, the "inflaton," which converted to what is called "rest mass" of matter. The potential was actualized simultaneously with the space expanding very rapidly for a very brief period. What made it expand? Negative gravity. The energy of the negative gravity balanced the positive energy of the appearing matter. Perhaps we may think of it more or less correctly as being like steam compressed in a small container, then suddenly released in a large space. The expansion causes the temperature to drop and so the steam condenses into liquid water. The space seems to sweat water throughout its volume. A phase change has occurred.[10] (For a fuller explanation, please read note 10 now.)

10. Inflation runs from time 10^{-35} second (from "the beginning") to 10^{-32} second; the size of the universe, much smaller than a proton, increases by a factor of 10^{50}. According to Heisenberg uncertainty relation between time and energy (when the time interval is known, the energy is unknown: energy may appear and disappear within the interval), "empty" space can produce energy as matter/antimatter "virtual" particles, coming into being and annihilating again. By Einstein's $E=mc^2$, energy is equivalent to mass and thus is subject to the gravitational force. The force is figured in terms of density and pressure. Mass can also be thought of as inertia,

What is of interest for our cosmic incarnational approach is the analogy to the Invisible/Exegete union of John 1:18. The negative energy of the repulsive gravity and the positive energy of the appearing matter and radiation are not two separate entities or forces or operations. They are two sides of the same reality. The potential energy of the field (negative) causes the gravitational pressure to be negative, so the space expands. Expansion causes the potential energy to convert to actual, so matter and radiation appear. Given that the original field is full of potential energy, this is a perfectly natural event. The Being-pressure of agape in the God-Community makes it perfectly natural that it should express itself in creation, in the exegetical cosmos. Another level of analogy suggests that the primary analogate may be the enstatic/ecstatic relations among the Persons. Because the nature of

---

the force required to initiate motion or to change speed or direction of motion, at rest inertia and moving inertia. Density measures at rest inertia and pressure measures moving inertia. The gravitational force is proportional to the density plus three times the pressure (for three dimensions). If the pressure term is high, the gravitational force will be controlled by the pressure term. The pressure term is a combination of positive kinetic energy and negative potential energy. The inflaton is almost entirely potential energy, so the pressure term will be negative and will be dominant in calculating the gravitational force. This means that the gravity will be negative, or repulsive. This is what produces the rapid expansion (this replaces, for its duration, the regular Hubble expansion). The expansion reduces the temperature (probability of a particle colliding—exchanging energy—with another particle), so the virtual particles that have come out of the energy field do not find partners for annihilation and thus they remain. The potential of the inflaton converts to actual energy in the form of matter and radiation. When the potential is exhausted, the negative pressure ceases. Positive density again rules gravity and the universe resumes Hubble expansion.

See Jeremy Bernstein, *An Introduction to Cosmology* (Englewood Cliffs, N.J.: Prentice Hall, 1995) for a technical exposition, and John D. Barrow, *The Origin of the Universe* (New York: Basic, 1994) for a popular presentation.

The rapid expansion accounts for the fact that matter and radiation now too far apart to be in communication by any transmission at the speed of light were formerly close enough together to reach thermal equilibrium; and it solves some other Big Bang puzzles. But one of the consequences of the inflation scenario is that it requires that the density of the observable universe be exactly the critical density needed to keep the universe on the edge between fly-away expansion and crunching recollapse. All the baryonic matter (protons and neutrons are baryons) that we are so far able to observe adds up to only about 10% at most of the required density. So, if inflation's mathematics are right, there must be some other kind of matter out there. See Michael Riordan and David N. Schramm, *The Shadows of Creation: Dark Matter and the Structure of the Universe* (New York: Freeman, 1991).

Being is agape, these are two aspects of the same reality. In the same way, the Invisible Father and the unitarily generated Exegete are one reality.

Energy-sharing continues in the early universe as the elementary particles are formed. The original particles from the matter condensation of the inflaton are X mesons and anti-X mesons. They decay into quarks (and anti-quarks) which unite to form protons and neutrons (and anti-protons and anti-neutrons).The decay rates of the X and the anti-X are different, so slightly more quarks are formed than antiquarks, and consequently more protons than anti-protons. When the mutually anti-particles have finished annihilating one another, what is left is a matter, rather than an anti-matter, universe. The annihilations produced photons (radiation particles), one photon for every particle annihilated, so the universe is also full of light. The matter particles now interact with one another and reheat the universe.

Some of the photons turn into electron/positron pairs, and the pairs annihilate back into photons. But the (Hubble) expanding universe continues to reduce the temperature, and at time one second the photons no longer have the energy to turn into pairs. The existing pairs annihilate, but again, for every billion pairs, there is one electron left over. So there are as many electrons as protons.

Originally there were as many neutrons as protons. But while protons are stable, neutrons decay in a matter of minutes. However, while the temperature was high enough, protons and electrons could unite to replace them. But when no more electrons were being made from photons, neutron production fell off so that we now have only two neutrons to every ten protons—which is why the universe has more hydrogen (just protons) than any other element.

The next milestone is at one minute, when atomic nuclei begin to assemble: one proton, one proton plus one neutron, plus another proton, plus another neutron equals helium. There matters rest, about 75 percent hydrogen and 25 percent helium, for the next three hundred thousand years. By that time the temperature has fallen enough that energetic photons can no longer bump electrons from their attachment to nuclei. Nuclei pick up an electron for every proton and matter becomes electrically neutral. And since the photons are no longer bumping into electrons, they are able to travel reasonable distances in straight lines, and the universe becomes transparent to light.

This decoupling of matter and radiation opened the way to the formation of stars. Stars have to form under the influence of gravity, weakest of the four natural forces, and there had been too much competition from the other interactions up till now. Now matter begins to clump together as stars and galaxies and clusters of galaxies and superclusters. This process goes slowly, but by one billion years, galaxies are forming.[11]

The galactic cloud fragments into hundreds of billions of small clouds as it collapses under self-gravity, and the small clouds concentrate in the same way. They are spheres of hydrogen and helium. As they become denser (more than 160 times as dense as water), the temperature in their interiors goes up tens of millions of degrees. High temperature means vigorous collisions, energy-sharing. Both the strong and the weak nuclear forces are at work. The weak force enables some of the protons to emit positrons and thus turn into neutrons; and the strong force enables the protons and the new neutrons to stick together. Two protons and two neutrons make helium-4 and a lot of extra energy as radiation. One by one the stars are turning on.

The first nuclear synthesis is of helium from hydrogen. When a star's hydrogen is used up, it no longer has enough pressure from inside to resist gravitational collapse, and it begins to contract and grow denser and again hotter. At this stage it welds helium into carbon. Nitrogen and oxygen are spin-offs of this process.[12] Hydrogen, oxygen, carbon: the makings of hydrocarbons, foundation of life. If the star is massive enough (at least four solar masses), the synthesis of still heavier elements can follow: sodium, magnesium, silicon, sulfur—components of the land masses of planets. A further stage of synthesis leads to element number 26, iron, most stable of all. Central star-reactions stop here but heavier elements can be made in its outer atmosphere where neutrons emitted from the core can be captured by synthesized nuclei. Captured neutrons may decay into protons by emitting electrons and thus turn the nucleus into one of higher atomic number.

11. Joseph Silk, *Cosmic Enigmas* (Woodbury, N.J.: American Institute of Physics, 1994) is mostly about galaxy formation. Riordan and Schramm, 115–53, covers this stage of the evolution, with helpful illustrations.

12. See Barrow, 124–5, for the extraordinary coincidence by which carbon fits an energy level—a "resonance"—greater than the sum of the energies of the helium and beryllium nuclei, so that it is very easy for a lot of carbon to be synthesized. But once made, the carbon could easily have been converted into oxygen by union with helium, except that this reaction just fails to be resonant, and therefore, although plenty of oxygen is made, the carbon survives in equal quantity. P. W. Atkins, *The Periodic Kingdom: A Journey into the Land of the Chemical Elements* (New York: Basic, 1995) traces the formation of other natural nuclei.

Having reached its "iron age," the star may contract its outer regions and then explode them out again, scattering the heavy elements. Second generation stars in formation can sweep these up, gaining a headstart on their own synthesis operations. Heavy elements not taken by stars are subject to collisions in the interstellar medium, and in this way intermediate number elements not synthesized in stars can be formed. By the time we have passed through three generations of stars, we may have a little of all the ninety-two natural elements.

The time is now about ten and a half billion years. There may have been more than three generations of stars. Some burn out quickly, others last a long time with a steady production of light and warmth. In the interstellar medium there are molecules as well as atoms. They are on dust grains, bits of silicon, oxygen, magnesium, and iron, covered by a thin layer of water ice. Radio telescopes have found about a hundred different kinds of molecules with up to as many as thirteen atoms per molecule. Among these are carbon monoxide, water, methane, and ammonia. The most numerous combinations are of carbon, hydrogen, oxygen, and nitrogen, the very elements that make up almost all of living bodies.

Symbiotic Catalysis: The Origin and Nature of Life

I like to use the word "symbiotic" in a much broader sense than the "mutualism" of biology. I use it to describe any kind of sharing in which each party does something important for the other, in which both benefit, and indeed in which the interaction between the two (or more) constitutes a new unit of reality in some way. In this sense it is closely related to "self-organizing," which means a process in which relatively simple units are linked by their own natures to compose a higher level unit with its own rules of order and relationship.

After the formation of atoms and molecules, the next place we look for this exegetical incarnation of trinitarian life is in the complex interactions of biomolecules. Sugars are formed based on carbon rings of shared electrons—so thoroughly shared that they are called "delocalized," no longer identified as belonging to their atoms of origin but to the molecule as a whole, their collective charge spread continuously over the entire assemblage. Hydrogens and oxygens being added, we have a proper carbohydrate. A sugar of special interest is ribose, because it is the foundation of ribonucleic acid, RNA, one of the coding molecules (together with DNA) for making the other molecules of which living bodies are composed.

To the ribose molecule are added a phosphoric acid group, which will handle energy storing and releasing as well as chaining, and a nitrogen base group, which will handle the coding. With these additions, we have a molecule called a "nucleotide." When a number of these are chained together, we speak of RNA. Life seems to have started with RNA; we will come to DNA later. RNA chains can self-assemble because the phosphate groups can link to one another. But RNA can also do another thing: it can replicate. The nitrogen base groups are rather like pieces of a jigsaw puzzle and certain matching ones can fit together: adenosine pairing with uracil, and guanine with cytosine. This enables a length of RNA chain to attract the nucleotides to form a complementary chain. If the double strand then splits, each single strand will attract complements, and they will have succeeded in replicating each other.

But a molecule that can copy itself this way will soon make many copies, using available atoms or small molecules in its environment. If various RNAs, with different sequences, share an environment, they will be in competition with one another for these raw materials, and any advantage that any sequencing pattern can show in relation to obtaining materials and copying at speed will enable it to make more copies and constitute a larger portion of the population. This can be demonstrated in the laboratory.[13] Variants can arise from copying errors and take over a population. This is darwinian selection acting on a self-replicating molecule, the first "gene."

What might give an RNA such an advantage? Finding a catalyst to make its reactions go faster. Among the early RNA sequences there must have been some that linked amino acids to their ribose sections. This brought the amino acids close enough together that they could make their customary peptide bonds. Some of the resulting peptides could act as enzymes and catalyze certain reactions. If among those

13. See, e.g., Nigel Calder, *The Life Game* (New York: Viking, 1973) 80, description of an experiment in which a portion of genetic material (plus an enzyme and appropriate food) is allowed to replicate in a test tube. Then poison is introduced. Replication stops for a short while, but within minutes mutant versions of the genetic strand appear and replication resumes. See also Bryan Bunch, "Self-Replicating Molecules That Are Not Alive," *The Henry Holt Handbook of Current Science and Technology* (New York: Holt, 1992) 166–7, and Christian de Duve, *Vital Dust: Life As a Cosmic Imperative* (New York: Basic, 1995) 61.

reactions was the replication of the RNA sequence that had helped assemble the peptide, then a powerful catalytic cycle had been formed.

The RNA, being in a certain sequence, would force the amino acids to assemble in a certain sequence, and that sequence would define the peptide. A particular RNA makes a particular peptide, which helps make the same RNA again. Natural selection would then work on both the peptides and the RNAs and their combinations. One of the results of this winnowing was that the peptides concerned became limited to proteins, made of a select group of twenty left-handed amino acids.[14]

This is clearly a symbiotic relationship. But we will now see it compounded. One kind of RNA making one kind of protein is one cycle. If this protein, in addition to catalyzing the assembly of its own RNA, facilitates another RNA, perhaps by helping with some portion of its translation into protein, and that protein in turn helps the first RNA with a part of its work, then the two cycles are helping each other. Adding yet more simple cycles, each doing something different to help what is now becoming a community effort, we have what Manfred Eigen called a "hypercycle."[15] This is our best explanation so far of the transition from the non-living to the living. When we have a hypercycle enclosed in a cell membrane, we will have the magic moment when life began.

William Loomis believes that although each step in achieving the hypercycle may have been rare, the diversity and supply of chemicals was so great and hindrances so few that in a few million years there could easily have been hypercycles all over the planet. And this new method of creating proteins increased the diversity of materials and thus the likelihood of successful hypercycles forming. "By directing the polymerization of [only] four different amino acids in peptides

14. C. de Duve (previous note), p. 63. The difference between a "peptide" and a "protein" is that a peptide is any chainlike assemblage of any amino acids, whereas a protein is a special class of peptide, made of a large number of amino acids but limited to a set of twenty specific L-amino acids (from Latin *leavus*, left-handed).

15. Manfred Eigen and Peter Schuster, *The Hypercycle: A Principle of Natural Self-Organization*. See Calder, 78, for photo, and surrounding pages for popular exposition of how the hypercycle works. See William F. Loomis, *Four Billion Years: An Essay on the Evolution of Genes and Organisms* (Sunderland, Mass.: Sinauer, 1988) 22–7, for technical explanation, including the "hairpin" turn of RNA that exposes the three-base "codon" which specifies an amino acid, and calculations of how many subcycles are needed for a fully functioning hypercycle.

up to fifteen amino acids long, nucleic acids could specify millions of different peptides."[16] This is a natural principle that shows again and again: a very few different items, because of the huge numbers of their combinations and permutations, can give rise to enormous numbers of interactive communities of various sorts.

This is the proposed cosmic eucharistic sharing that makes a christic body in image of the trinitarian unity. Each new level of being manifests properties not possessed by its components, but properties that emerge from what constitutes the compound union itself, namely the *interaction* of the constituents. The new properties are the properties of the integrated dynamic of the assemblage.

Community Life

The new hypercycles soon improved their lot by enclosing themselves and a good supply of building materials (food) within lipid bilayers, cell membranes equipped with ports for entry and exit of desired and undesired products. At some point these primitive cells could be styled "bacteria," carrying the code for making themselves in a new and improved nucleic acid, the double-stranded DNA, deoxyribonucleic acid ("deoxy-" because the sugar has lost one oxygen atom). DNA has very stable double strands, using base-pair bonding, which RNA does not, and so it is preferred for long-term storage of the information. It does not do any "work," leaving that to RNA, which actually guides the assembly of the proteins, but like a queen bee in the middle of a hive, it is tended by enzymes and opened for transcription, its directions being carried out by the multitude of workers who comprise the other tenants of the cell.

Like all cells, bacteria treasure their DNA, but they are also very generous with it. Gene-swapping goes on all the time among the different strains of bacteria, by a variety of means.[17] Bits of DNA—"small replicons"—pass through openings in cell membranes or through conjugation tubes or by being encased in capsules with tube-tails that can attach to other cells and deliver replicons down their chutes. Sorin Sonea and Maurice Panisset declared in their *New Bacteriology* that "in nature any bacterium has access to most, and possibly to all, genes

16. Loomis, 27.
17. See Sorin Sonea and Maurice Panisset, *A New Bacteriology* (Boston: Jones Bartlett, 1983) 41.

belonging to other bacterial strains." The bacteria therefore constitute "a planetary bacterial entity." This entity undergoes "evolution as one individual or as a communicating society, just as mankind undergoes cultural and technical evolution."[18]

The next example of community living is the formation of the eukaryotic cell from a symbiosis of bacteria. This origin of the large cell with another membrane inside to protect its DNA and a number of specialized bodies whose behaviors benefit one another, was proposed by Lynn Margulis. It seems to have been a creative response to the great oxygen poisoning (free oxygen released by the photosynthesis practiced by cyanobacteria) about two billion years ago that killed 90 percent of living things. Some bacteria had become tolerant of the oxygen by growing protective membranes, and some others had become able to use the oxygen. These latter, the aerobes, invaded the protective anaerobes and somehow neither destroyed them nor were destroyed by them. The host cell was able to use the energy-rich products of the aerobe's efficient metabolism, and the small aerobic partners benefited by living in the rich soup of the host's fermentation wastes.[19] All the rest of Earth's creatures (other than the bacteria) are descended from this symbiosis.

Multicelled organisms now appear and their differentiated organs and tissues form another kind of community. A very sophisticated expression process turns on certain genes for certain purposes and turns them off again. Cells develop one way or another depending on what their neighbors are doing, where they are located in the body, and what stage of development they have reached.[20] All the various organs and organ systems work together, united by the DNA carried in each of their cells, and the body as a whole is a single individual. Individuals live in the context of their environment and those who succeed in earning a living there leave progeny to carry on their genes. Genes for making bodies that adapt well to the environ-

---

18. Ibid., 112.

19. Lynn Margulis, *Symbiosis in Cell Evolution* (San Francisco: Freeman, 1981). Margulis does not think that the nucleus itself resulted from symbiosis, but she does believe that the other organelles (bodies within the cell which function analogously to organs) in the eukaryote arose through symbiosis. The aerobic bacteria concerned, for instance, became what we call *mitochondria*, which all of us (eukaryotic types) have in our cells.

20. Lewis Wolpert, *The Triumph of the Embryo* (New York: Oxford, 1992).

ment and are more prolific in offspring will crowd out alternative genomes. There is a lot of competition among variants. Variations in the genome come from mutations at the molecular level, from copying errors, and from several devices for gene shuffling. Prominent among these, of course, is sex, with its meiotic crossover and recombination of genes. But another interesting process is the rearrangement of genes within a single genome by modular assembly.

This is a method used on several levels by nature. It takes advantage of history, using combinations already worked out in the past. This was the method used to string together polymers, such as RNA and proteins, mixing the four bases of the nucleic acids in the one case and the twenty amino acids in the other. A few units combined in many different ways. Genes can be put together by a similar method from minigenes.[21] The advantage is this: a basic portion of a gene that has proved to be very successful can be conserved unchanged, while remaining portions can be varied for application to particular situations.[22] The proteins made from these modularly assembled genes will also be put together from modular units called "domains." This avoids having to start from scratch each time. The domain that repeats a basic function can be coded for by the conserved minigene; only the variable functions of the protein will need new minigenes. Even the variable domains may be assembled from ready made sub-units in this way, allowing new combinations to appear quickly.

Further reflection on modular assembly shows that the development of life is a highly probable affair, for at each advance the modular units will already have been tested and selected. The number of combinations of these units, although large, is not so large that it cannot be exhaustively explored, all combinations being submitted to natural selection before proceeding to the next level of assembly. Christian de Duve, who holds that life and consciousness are bound to emerge from the step by step modular assembly, says that "as evolution proceeds in a given direction, the range of available

---

21. Not all of DNA codes. Stretches of coding DNA, called "exons" because they "express" as proteins, are interrupted by stretches of non-coding DNA, called "introns." Enzymes can cut out the introns and splice the exons together when it is time to copy them. At this point the modular units can be assembled in various ways. See de Duve, 75–8, 222–6.

22. The conserved portion, which will be the same in all these varied genes, even across species lines, is called a "homeobox." See de Duve, 197.

choices narrows, and its commitment becomes increasingly focused and irreversible."[23]

Competition and Cooperation

All lesser group involvements take place in the grand community of the ecological region. Here non-living features, such as land, water, climate, make significant contributions as well as the bacteria, the plants, and the animals. The relationships can be quite intricate. Bacteria have mutual assistance programs with the roots of plants; they also live in the guts of termites and in the digestive tracts of ruminants. The methane they produce affects the atmosphere, keeping it from collecting too much oxygen and setting the forests on fire. Tiny polyps in the oceans form coral reefs which become homes to many other species. The oceans themselves moderate climates, opening up niches for life. Flowing between islands, they promote speciation by isolating kin groups. Diversity increases. Food chains develop. Predators and prey evolve better senses, abilities, protective devices. Social organizations develop.

At this point we need to remember that trinitarian life, when expressed in terms of finitude, requires both "scattering" and "gathering," both severing and uniting. This means that each living creature must act to preserve its own existence and to promote the copying of its genes. If it does not do this, there will not be multiplicity, diversity, evolution, and therefore no exegesis in terms of incarnation. So a great deal of what we call "selfishness" and looking to one's own interests is needed. On the other hand, out of this self-interest drive various forms of cooperation have emerged, gradually—as intelligence grew— showing as empathy, until true morality appeared.

Predator-prey relationships bring out two interesting points. The first is that "good" and "evil" are historically point-of-view judgments. What is good for the predator is inevitably evil for the prey. This relation has persevered to the human era and the cultural institution of warfare: what is good for the victor is evil for the conquered. Victors believe that God has been on their side; conquered peoples, who have frequently sustained heavy losses in families, territory, means of livelihood, culture, puzzle over why God abandoned them and try to invent new theologies to cover their hurt. Sometimes the

---

23. Ibid., 77; see also 86 and 226.

conquest is largely economic or cultural, but the point-of-view judgment is the same: the economic policy or religious/social form that prevails believes itself right and the destruction of its competitor justified.

The other interesting point is that out of predator-prey relationships all sorts of progressive variations arise. Keener senses was a first development: smell, hearing, sight. But that had to be integrated into a complex feedback process in a nervous system that could couple the detection of items in the environment to appropriate actions. Eventually the formation of internal models of the environment and of the possible interactions of the animal with the environment gave great advantage; alternative courses of action could be played out internally without wasting time and energy actually doing them. Intelligence evolved. Not wasting energy has been a consideration from the beginning. That was a strong reason for using modular assembly; taking up ready-made modules saved making them from still smaller units. This is the foundation of eating, ingesting molecules already assembled by some other body's expenditure of energy. The same "reasoning" applies to letting some other animal kill a prey, then running that animal off and eating the prey oneself, and even to tricking someone else into raising your children for you, as cuckoos do.

Trickery, cheating, taking advantage of others usually pays off handsomely, and a great deal of it is done. Butterflies, for instance, imitate the colors and patterns of other butterflies that predators have learned are poisonous or bad-tasting. This protects the cheats for a while, until the predators discover the subterfuge and start eating both models and mimics, whereupon the models' variants begin to show in larger proportions and their mutation prevails. Many predators have learned how to disguise themselves and lie in ambush, just as many prey species have gradually shaped to resemble twigs or leaves or shadows in the grass. More intelligent animals will sometimes play deliberate tricks on their fellows, giving false alarms to distract others while they themselves consume the special treat. The insistence on looking out for one's own genes leads to destruction of another male's cubs and the forced production of one's own. The prevalence of rape among our species and the higher incidence of child abuse on the part of step-parents (and unlicensed companions of parents) are the behavioral descendants of a long line of ancestors.[24] This, of course, is in no

---

24. Many examples of this sort of behavior can be found in Lyall Watson, *Dark Nature: A Natural History of Evil* (New York: HarperCollins, 1995).

way an excuse or justification for behaviors that we clearly identify as wrong, but it does show where they come from and why.

On the other hand, cooperation has also risen through the ranks, beginning with the structural symbioses we have already mentioned. Colonies, mating pairs with offspring, hiving insects, herds, and packs all share life-protective and life-promotive functions in their groups. Altruism, as the willingness to deprive oneself for another, appears in proportion to the fraction of genes shared with a close relative, and very gradually is extended beyond close genetic relationship, to others of one's species and to other species. Gestures of friendship have developed, food and grooming sharing stabilize bonds, rituals of conciliation and peace-making grow up, grieving for others' pain or loss or death has its beginnings in the beasts with larger brains. Human goodness, as well as human sinfulness, has antecedents.[25]

The Human Brain

Modular assembly and complex interactions, with their emergents in compounded organized order, are again in evidence when we look at the human brain. Even a single neuron is a very complicated affair, operating by electrical polarization (collecting a charge) and depolarization to pass a message from one end of the cell to the other, and by highly specialized chemistry to pass it on to the next cell.

The neuron's input end is a forest of dendritic fibers, branching and subbranching, and receiving chemical signals through its thousands of synapses from other neurons. As all this information is funneled toward the cell body, a number of factors act to process it: whether the original inputs were stimulating or inhibitory; whether their relay was delayed (or blocked) at junctions where subbranches join major branches; whether an impulse was passed by an OR gate (either one of the subbranches would do) or by an AND gate (both branches needed); additional information coming in from synapses located closer to the cell body. The decision the cell needs to make—

---

25. See Robert Jay Russell, *The Lemurs' Legacy: The Evolution of Power, Sex, and Love* (New York: Putnam, 1993); Frans de Waal, *Peacemaking among Primates* (Cambridge, Mass: Harvard, 1989), and *Good Natured: The Origins of Right and Wrong in Humans and Other Animals* (Cambridge: Harvard, 1996); Alfie Kohn, *The Brighter Side of Human Nature: Altruism and Empathy in Everyday Life* (New York: Basic, 1990).

either "remain polarized" or "depolarize"—is passed along the cell membrane from one patch to another, each ion channel in the membrane opening or closing as stimulated by the one before it. But there are also synapses on the cell body, and the "decision" is subject to change. At the farther end, the axon is covered (in patches) with insulation, but the uncovered spots can still receive last minute corrections to the debatable decision, which is eventually settled and transmitted through the axon's branches to its synapses with all the further cells with which it communicates.

These single cells (of which there are about two hundred billion in the whole brain, thirty billion in the cerebral cortex), complicated as they are individually, next link in sequences and in assemblies and in sequences of assemblies, and in assemblies of assemblies, until they are a global network. Each level of organization has its own output product, from a simple reflex to a perception, to concepts and organizations of concepts and reflections on concepts. Probably these arrangements are actively *constructed* by the brain itself and winnowed by a selection system of the same type as that operating among the genes. This would include making copies of the neuron patterns, having competitions between the patterns, having modular units of patterns form larger patterns, and being capable not only of producing variants by copying error but of constructing variants by changing one or more modular units without necessarily changing all the rest. Especially valuable core modules might be repeated again and again in many different variants, a kind of embedded grammar.[26]

And what about the chemical aspect of this communication net? The molecules that stimulate the receptors at the synapses are neurotransmitters; there are dozens of them known so far. Some of these are excitatory, others inhibitory. The amount of chemical released into the synaptic cleft can vary. The number of post-synaptic receptors sensitive to a given transmitter can vary. When the transmitter has been released and has stimulated its receptor to start an impulse in the next cell, the transmitter will usually be reabsorbed by the "button" from

---

26. Alwyn Scott, *Stairway to the Mind: The Controversial New Science of Consciousness* (New York: Springer-Verlag, 1995) 80–94. The cell assembly idea originated with Donald Hebb, *The Organization of Behavior* (New York: Wiley, 1949). See also William H. Calvin, *How Brains Think* (New York: Basic, 1996) and William H. Calvin and George A. Ojemann, *Conversations with Neil's Brain: The Neural Nature of Thought and Language* (Reading, Mass.: Addison-Wesley, 1994).

which it was released and recycled; this recycling time can be varied. In a general way, synapses change strength with use: the more they are used, the more transmitter is released, and the stronger the synapse is. All this adjustability is what enables the brain to learn, to remember, to create. Without it, the living circuitry would be as rigid as our electronic machinery's.

Recently discoveries have been made indicating that brain neurotransmitters may reach other parts of the body and be received and have effects there. Not only that, but these other tissues—especially immune cells—may also be able to synthesize transmitter molecules and send them out. On the other hand, hormones—thought to be produced only by glands—are being produced and stored in the brain. Exciting work has been done by Candace Pert and her colleagues at the NIMH, showing that there is a family of peptides (about sixty to seventy of them) that interact among three major systems: the nervous system, the endocrine system, and the immune system. The endocrine system, through its hormones, regulates and integrates various functions; for instance, there are numerous different growth-promoting hormones, some of which stimulate division in a wide variety of cells, others being more specific. The immune system (spleen, bone marrow, lymph nodes, and several types of immune cells in circulation) not only defends the body against invaders but is responsible for tissue repair and wound healing and for "tissue integrity" and maybe even the body's "molecular identity" (by the lymphocytes regulating the number of cells and their molecular constituents).

These peptides include neurotransmitters, hormones, endorphins, growth factors, and other special molecules that attach to a multitude of specific receptors on the surfaces of all body cells. Remembering the important contribution of the hormones to our emotional experiences, as well as the cognitive activity of the brain, we can say that we have here a genuine "psychosomatic" network of unifying interactivity for the entire body. This is how the body keeps in touch with itself, shares its news and its assistance, and accounts itself one single unified being.[27]

27. Fritjof Capra, *The Web of Life: A New Scientific Understanding of Living Systems* (New York: Anchor, 1996) 280–5. Pert is quoted as saying, "I can no longer make a strong distinction between the brain and the body" (Boston, Elmwood Symposium, 1989, unpublished). Capra points out that peptides influence mood and behavior, and that all bodily functions are emotionally colored (e.g., the entire

Human Consciousness

But does this wonderful human brain-body explain human consciousness? With human consciousness we come to a situation we have not faced in any of the other levels of the cosmic organization. We experience our own consciousness *subjectively*, as subjects, from the inside. All the other levels of organization we had observed from the outside, objectively, seeing them as objects of our cognition. But in the case of our own consciousness, we do something more than and quite different from knowing it as an object for our cognition. We know it by being it. We ourselves are the cognizer.

It is also true that we can reflect on the facts of our consciousness and can observe that some subjective experiences can be correlated in a rough way with certain objective observables: various interactions with the environment match pleasure or pain, blows to the head can knock you unconscious, anesthetics can put you to sleep and keep you from remembering, intoxicants can loose you to strange perceptions and regrettable behavior, even psychosocial incidents can terrify you, make you angry, depress you or exalt you. We can trace perception through certain areas of the brain; we can identify language areas and motor areas; and we can relieve certain illnesses by brain surgery.

But can consciousness—not the behavior of our bodies, objectively observable, but our subjective experience of being aware, of being conscious of being conscious, of being ourselves—can this be exhaustively explained and accounted for in terms of the objective observables alone? Some neuroscientists claim Yes, others insist No. A strong example of the first school is Francis Crick, who believes that he himself, his joys and sorrows, his sense of being "I," his personal identity and experience of free will, "are in fact no more than the behavior of a vast assembly of nerve cells and their associated molecules."[28] In other words, nature has evolved a combination of molecules so artfully working with one another as to produce a creature which experiences itself as transcendent of the molecules, but which also discovers

---

intestine is lined with peptide receptors). For detail see Candace Pert, *Molecules of Emotion: Why You Feel the Way You Feel* (Los Angeles: Simon & Schuster, 1977).

28. Scott 138, citing Crick, *The Astonishing Hypothesis: The Scientific Search for the Soul* (New York: Simon and Schuster, 1994).

that this is an illusion and its sense of being a "self" is not true. The creature knows that it isn't there.

Examples of the other view are Erwin Schroedinger and Eugene Wigner. Schroedinger argues that we exclude subjective experience from the world-picture we are willing to take seriously and then claim that we have discovered that there is no such thing there. But, Schroedinger asks, who has framed the picture and determined its contents? We ourselves; our conscious self is the picture-maker. Wigner says something similar, that the starting point in physics is not actually the position of a particle but the knowledge of the observer concerning the position of the particle. Therefore it is "unreasonable to describe the basic concept—the content of the consciousness of the observer—in terms of the derived one . . . the concept of the positions of atoms."[29]

Most recently, David Chalmers has set aside the "easy problems" of showing how some particular brain behaviors result in certain observable effects, and has directed attention to "the hard problem" of understanding the nature of our interior, subjective experience of consciousness. This cannot be done by the old-fashioned materialistic reductionist methods, or even by contemporary nonreductionist materialist methods. A whole new approach is needed. It is no use trying to "explain" consciousness in terms of "structure and functions." It is not that kind of problem. It doesn't exist in that context. You cannot account for subjectivity in terms of objectivity.[30]

I propose to make my contribution to this question in these terms: What does it mean to "explain" something? Presumably it means to give an account of something less well known in terms of something better known. Explanations are either of the axiomatic type—tracing back to axioms and definitions and ultimately to undefined terms—or of the dictionary type—going round in a circle, every word of any explanation having to be explained elsewhere in the explanation-network. In practice, we feel that we have an adequate explanation when we are no longer motivated to ask for one. But that satisfaction depends on the context of all our thoughts about what we think we understand and what constitutes "understanding." This con-

29. Ibid., 115–6. The Wigner quote is from "Are We Machines?" *Proceedings of the American Philosophical Society,* 113:95-101, 1969.

30. David J. Chalmers, *The Conscious Mind: In Search of a Fundamental Theory* (New York: Oxford, 1996).

text is shaped by collective and social consensus, often accompanied by explicit criteria, such as conformity to some authority (living or written), or measurability or repeatability or other standard of public shared judgment. An interesting question is whether "explanation" so restricted always results in "understanding."

The definition of what constitutes an acceptable explanation, therefore, may have built into it certain exclusions that prevent certain things from being "explained." In the present case, only explanations in terms of the behavior patterns of matter are acceptable in the scientific community. I cannot help being amused by the way all these researchers into consciousness and its relations with nervous systems (and other systems), are terrified of being thought "mystical" by their peers. Their works invariably contain a disclaimer to this effect somewhere, usually in the form "There is nothing mystical in this." I wonder what they think "mystical" means—probably psychic or occult or superstitious or to be taken on faith without question—in any case inaccessible to the agreed upon criteria of what an explanation is allowed to be. But our own experience of being conscious is a very difficult case, as Chalmers has pointed out, for it does not seem to be readily handled by the acceptable explanation schemes.

I propose therefore to revert to the rather simple definition of explanation as accounting for the less known in terms of the better known, and to ask, What is better known to us than our own consciousness? And why should we not face the fact that an explanation of a subjective experience cannot be had by excluding the subjectivity and admitting only a postulated objective arrangement as what is really there, the experience we have notwithstanding. I suggest that we acknowledge consciousness as a primary reality, a ground reality, something that cannot be explained in terms of something else because there is nothing else prior to it or simpler than it or better known than it in terms of which such explanation might be couched. This is, I would urge, our actual lived experience. We do not experience our consciousness as a composition or an effect. We experience it as that which experiences all the things that we do experience. We experience it as the prior on which all else depends, as the knower of the known. It is what we start with and what we end with in our explorations of reality.

There are some interesting derivatives from this view. If our subjectively experienced consciousness is a primary datum, then it is not exhaustively accounted for as an emergent from bodily interactivities, even though some of its modifications can be correlated with some of the latter's. It must always be included in its own right as an independent ingredient. But if this is the case, then there would not seem to be any ground for excluding it from any level of cosmic organization. It must run all the way back.

This is reminiscent, of course, of Teilhard de Chardin's *dedans* and *dehors*, the within and the without, or consciousness and complexity, the twin aspects of any reality. "Within-ness," like "without-ness," is here a cosmically generalized term, showing in appropriately specific ways according to the various levels of organization in the universe. We have been able to identify and describe the levels of the *dehors* because we have comparable access to all of them. We do not have comparable access to the various levels of the *dedans*. Our access to our own within is unique. So we cannot give directly experienced phenomenological accounts of the "consciousness" of cats, fish, bumblebees, pansies, bacteria, etc. But we can allow for the possibility that it is there in that level's own way.

And we can do something more. We can pull the whole thing together by remembering the model of the Incarnation and regarding the within and the without as two dimensions of a single fundamental reality. We can use the basic concepts of Daniel Walsh and Teilhard here as names for the most general form of "interaction," having both subjective and objective aspects. Walsh said that the starting point is all important and that the starting point is *agape*. Teilhard said that what links all beings without exception is "the affinity of being for being," his definition of "love." Every level of organization is simply this affinity, showing in more and more complex (compounded) and more conscious ways.[31] The *dehors* and *dedans* are two dimensions of a single reality. Teilhard's "affinity," Walsh's *agape*, are indicators of a ground-level reality, a universally generalized reality.

It is important not to be distracted by Walsh and Teilhard calling this ground-reality "love." This word, much cheapened in our culture, makes us think of human emotional experience as the primary analogate. This is incorrect. The primary analogate is the interactivity— whatever that is—of the Trinity. This is then exegeted in the cosmos in terms of the two dimensions of material substances and the various forms of unifying interiority for which we do not have a proper termi-

31. Pierre Teilhard de Chardin, *The Phenomenon of Man* (New York: Harper & Row, 1961) 264 (Torchbook edition).

nology except at our own level, where we are reflexively aware of it as our conscious selfhood. Both of these dimensions exhibit the differentiating and unifying interaction of the Ground indicated by the term *agape*.

Just as at the top of our complexity/consciousness scheme there is nothing more suitable in terms of which to explain our *within* experience of consciousness, so at the reductionistic bottom of the *without* explanation chain we have the Laws of Nature, the cosmic parameters, and the four fundamental forces. What explains them?[32] We do not explain them. We start with them. They explain other things. But are they not instances of "affinity of being for being"? So we have two dimensions. For us, from our standpoint, the unexplained is at the "top" for the within and at the "bottom" for the without. But both are clearly interactive being-sharing to form unions. This is what I call using the model of the Incarnation. And it is this same reality that I have been calling here the eucharistic sharing of being. It is the trinitarian being-by-union.

I consider that trinitarian eucharist is a good term for what is going on. Eucharist is what forms the Church. Church is the living body of people who are united by sharing *agape*. If they do not share *agape*,[33] no amount of church membership or believing or even reception of sacraments—external signs of the reality which is divine *agape*—will constitute them Church. Church is the *corpus Christi quod est ecclesia*. Church is the Body of the Exegesis of the Trinity. Eucharist is the sharing in both dimensions, the without and the within, the interactivity, the cross-feeding of each with all, giving every aspect of one's being ("body, blood, soul, and divinity") as nourishment for all the rest. Incarnation is perhaps the structural name for What Is, but Eucharist is the dynamic name for What Is Going On.

Conclusions for Spirituality

I see several applications of this proposed view for our everyday spirituality. The first probably is to see that the traditional ideas and terms and beliefs are not uncongenial to contemporary understanding of the natural world. On the contrary, they seem to me to cast

32. On this question, see Paul Davies, *The Mind of God* (New York: Simon Schuster, 1992).
33. Consider John 13:34-35 and I Corinthians 13:2.

very helpful light on it. And at the same time, our natural knowledge helps us to see that the traditional doctrines have further layers of significance which we may not have mined as yet. This has the consequence of making us feel more comfortable in our contemporary world. We can hold it all together, we do not have to set aspects of it at odds with one another. We ourselves can feel "at home in the universe," as Stuart Kauffman puts it. We are kin to everything else. Everything else is kin to us. If we find divinity in ourselves, there is divinity all the way through. The whole thing is a divine expression, an exegesis, an incarnation.

A further ramification from this would be that we can study the sciences, we can work in the world, we can believe in the cosmic enterprise, we can see our efforts, though small, as definitely contributing to the over-all expression. We can put the untoward events of a finite world—shaping itself up by trial and error, accomplishments along with side effects, point-of-view good and evil—in perspective. We can exert ourselves to increase the good for all without making an unsolvable theological problem and mystery out of the means by which all this is happening. We can remember that all events are significant on their own proper levels. We can give up expecting moral or personal relationship meanings in natural biological or physical events.

We can stand amazed at the creativity of the world's expression of its Creator, who has "given birth to" a world which has evolved to the place where it can "give birth to" God. The universe is a gigantic Theotokos Project. That is what is going on. How it is going on is according to the necessities of finitude and the creative possibilities of combining them. That is, by being many and one together like the Trinity, by being a within joined with a without like the Incarnation, and by being sharing of Being like the Eucharist.

We can devote ourselves to practicing what the sacrament of the eucharist means. It is not, therefore, primarily a ceremony in a building set apart for religion. It is primarily the building up of the Body of Christ, as St. Paul said. The Messiah—bringer of peace, justice, and loving-kindness—"comes" as this Body grows. It is not a single magical individual; it is a whole community, whose limits are not known. The Body grows as the members feed one another with their lives, with trinitarian interaction, *agape.*

For Thomas Merton, I believe, this would have social, political, economic, and interreligious application, and I agree with this. Full

Eucharist means sharing on every level of our reality. I like to talk about "Jesus' Suppers"[34] as celebrations and sharings that may actually have taken place in Galilee and as multilevel sharings that could take place now. I see them as starting with ordinary food sharing, expanding to other material goods such as shelter, clothing, medicine, tools. On a next level there would be energy sharing, working with/for one another, also sharing emotional energies, being supportive. Sharing of mental goods would come next, news, personal stories, memories, ideas, what makes us feel that we are a community; also, we can teach one another and clearly this is what Merton felt he had to do. Above this is the sharing of the deep and precious insights and revelations that have shaped our lives; I imagine Jesus telling the story of his baptismal realization of the universality of the divine filiation, on which all the rest of his ministry was based. And as others tell their secret stories of God's favor to them, devotion and joy and happiness emerge and are shared by all.

There is no particular membership requirement for participating in such a eucharist. Life-sharing with anyone in any way becomes an "element" for eucharist. Anyone participating in the life-sharing becomes thereby a member of Church, of the Messianic—peace-bringing—Body. We can therefore address ourselves to furthering, deepening, our social/political, economic, religious sharing as eucharist-practicing. And if we are to have purely ceremonial eucharists, let us devise them so that they can be inclusive rather than exclusive, so that they can say clearly what the cosmic Eucharist is, One Body.

34. See Bruce Chilton, "Origins of the Eucharist," *Bible Review* (Dec. 1994) 39, and B. Bruteau, "Jesus' Suppers," *The Roll* (Sept. 1996).

Thomas Merton's
Poetic Incarnation of Emptiness

Alan Altany

I. Introduction: A Heaven of Naked Air

Thomas Merton's later poetry is an emblem of his transcending his previous desire for explanatory, propositional, theological demarcations, a geography of the "unknowing" and "emptiness" of the sacred. Thus, the progression of Merton's poetic work can be seen as a poetics of disappearance: the disappearance of an old, corrupt world in favor of a vision of a kenotic, new world; the disappearance of the false self or empirical ego in favor of discovering the true self in and inseparable from God; the disappearance of traditional religious imagery in favor of spontaneous imagination and antipoetry; the disappearance of an exclusively supernatural category of the sacred in favor of a humanized and intimate experience of the sacred in the center of the profane. Merton was a man and poet of transformation. This article seeks to interpret the topography of that transformation in Merton's poetry of the 1960s and especially within *Emblems of a Season of Fury*.

In his early monastic years the sacred for Merton tended towards a super-essential conception of a divine reality beyond the immanent boundaries of this world. His poetry of the 1940s and 1950s is filled with images of a theological dualism between the natural and the supernatural, between the profane and the sacred. It looks mainly towards the future for consummation:

> And every burning morning is a prophecy of Christ
> Coming to raise and vindicate
> Even our sorry flesh.[1]

> "The Trappist Cemetery—Gethsemani,"
> *A Man in the Divided Sea*, 1946

---

1. *The Collected Poems of Thomas Merton* (New York: New Directions, 1977) 118.

Merton tended to condemn the profane and praise the sacred without acknowledging any need of the one for the other, any coincidence of opposites.

The early Merton believed mystical experience directed him towards silence, but the poetic vision compelled him to speak: "Words and silence, standing face to face / Weigh life and death. . . ." ("A Responsory").[2] Sr. Therese Lentfoehr would later use the phrase, "Words and silence," as the title for her book on Merton's poetry. The spoken, the unspoken, the unspeakable will become the pillars of Merton's necessary paradox:

> We must receive new seeds from an old harvest
> Old truths out of a time newborn. . .
>
> "A Responsory"[3]

The view of a re-created, primal paradise as the goal would be displaced by a view of the sacred in a process of intimate interaction with the profane towards the union of these nonopposite opposites. By the late 1950s the transformed sense of the sacred was changing Merton's anthropology. In Christ Merton found both the sacred and the profane. The sacred was emptied and thereby the profane disclosed the sacred.

One of the discernments for an authentic mystical life has always been a growth in love in any yielding to the sacred. Even in the darkness the mystic loves. In "A Psalm" Merton writes:

> The Spirit sings: the bottom drops out of my soul
> And from the center of my cellar, Love, louder than
>   thunder
> Opens a heaven of naked air.[4]

It is "naked" precisely because it is empty of ego configurations. Merton's poetics of disappearance reimagined his vision of love which in turn led to a further incorporation of an "incarnation of emptiness." Merton's sacred became more paradoxical the more simply empty it became. In later years he began to risk more spiritual and psychological nakedness than ever before and it was leading him to places the younger Merton would not have been very capable of imagining.

---

2. Ibid., 672.
3. Ibid., 678.
4. Ibid., 220.

What follows is a sketch of the historical, poetical, and spiritual trajectories of Merton's imaginative quest for compassion through a strange and unpredictable incarnation of emptiness.

II. An Incarnational Transformation

The continued transformation of Merton's mystical vision moved away from the danger of becoming extremely individualistic and disembodied and towards a new sense of responsibility for human involvement, even if from behind the monastic enclosure. The boundaries of his experience merged with the experience of others as more of his religious conceptual idols evaporated or were smashed. The twentieth century had lost touch with meaningful symbolism and its spiritual power. In his poem "The Lion" Merton addresses this loss of symbolism, imagination, enchantment and the sacred:

All classic shapes have vanished
From alien heavens
Where there are no fabled beasts
No friendly histories
And passion has no heraldry.

I have nothing left to translate
Into the figures of night
Or the pale geometry
of the fire-birds.
If I once had a wagon of lights to ride in
The axle is broken
The horses are shot.[5]

Are purely individual myths and symbols really myths and symbols at all?

Merton's poetry in the 1960s was a continual experimentation with forms and content. Some of it has been called antipoetry because it seems to defy the traditional view of what poetry should be. He included prose in the poetry, "found poems," surrealistic imagery that moved swiftly from one impression to another, Zen paradox and metaphysical lyrics. Little of this kind of work was original with Merton as he tried poetic approaches that had been used decades earlier in American poetry. But his mystical perspective and the monastic

5. Ibid., 643.

rhythm of life gave his work a unique point of view. He would have agreed with Henry Rago that "the true poet is willing to give up poetry in order to find poetry."[6] The poem may end in silence, the contemplative goal of the aesthetic work. Merton "in one of his taped lectures . . . took the view that a good poem was 50 percent silence and what was not said in a literary work was just as important as what was made explicit, if not more important."[7] What he tried to do in his later work was to give words to his experience of love in the darkness and unknowing for "Only in the Void / Are all ways one. . . ," ("The Night of Destiny").[8]

Deeply important to further understanding the mystical insights and the forms of the later poetry and the changing form of the sacred for Merton is an awareness that his theology became profoundly incarnational *and* apophatic. In the traditional mystical literature the image of "ascent" is used to describe the movement from the self to union with Ultimate Reality. Neoplatonic sources are evident in such a scheme that passes through the stages of purification, illumination, and union. It would be more accurate in Merton's case to portray his development as a spiraling inward and outward simultaneously where the contemplative, or liturgical experience of God was the ground for the experience of God horizontally in the world. In his Christ-mysticism Merton believed God is found in the center of the self.

This view of Christ as the human face of God and the divine face of humanity expanded Merton's poetic vision to encompass the totality of human experience. He believed that in Christ God emptied himself and took on the weakness and ordinariness of a human being, but "not only 'this' man, but also, in a broader and more mystical sense, yet no less truly, 'everyman.'"[9] Even more directly, he said that "if we believe in the Incarnation of the Son of God, there should be no one on earth in whom we are not prepared to see, in mystery, the presence of Christ."[10] In a prose poem, "Hagia Sophia," Merton speaks of

6. Nathan Scott, *Adversity and Grace* (Chicago: University of Chicago Press, 1968) 248.

7. Ross Labrie, *The Art of Thomas Merton* (Fort Worth, Texas: Texas Christian University Press, 1979) 21.

8. *Collected Poems*, 635.

9. Thomas Merton, *New Seeds of Contemplation* (New York: New Directions, 1962) 294–5.

10. Ibid., 296.

Sophia (Wisdom, Mother of all) crowning the *Logos* with his human nature, thus

> She crowns Him not with what is glorious, but with what is greater than glory: the one thing greater than glory is weakness, nothingness, poverty.[11]

For Merton Christ disappeared and disappears into humanity as the ultimate *mythos*, the sacred empties itself of itself and becomes as nothing, with the mission to love unto death. The poem concludes with an image of this incarnational hiddenness in humanity:

> The shadows fall. The stars appear. The birds begin to sleep. Night embraces the silent half of the earth. A vagrant, destitute wanderer with dusty feet, finds his way down a new road. A homeless God, lost in the night, without papers, without identification, without even a number, a frail expendable exile lies down in desolation under the sweet stars of the world and entrusts Himself to sleep.[12]

The image of Jesus for Merton had ranged from the Son of God, the King, the cosmic Logos and Pantocrater to the universal man and hidden center of human existence. The eschatological, universal work of Christ was to be found in the historicity of humanity and the history of human persons. The incarnation was seen more as a present involvement of God in the world and not only as a one-time historical engagement. Merton believed that religion has a share in the responsibility for the destructive isolation of Christ from the existential nexus of life in the world.

A disincarnate theology became for Merton a flagrant absurdity that obscured experience of authentic human life and the sacred. It was such conventional theology that helped pave the way for the rise of atheism and agnosticism in the modern world. Regarding such an accepted conflation of supernaturalism, power and will, Kilcourse says "Merton goes on to diagnose the Christian fault in imaging Christ as Prometheus. This image had justified war, pogroms, crusades, Auschwitz, the atomic bomb."[13] It is one reason Merton felt a special bond with those atheists who refused to accept the image or idea of a God that seemed to deny the full integrity of human life.

11. *Collected Poems,* 363.
12. Ibid., 370–1.
13. George Kilcourse, *Ace of Freedoms: Thomas Merton's Christ* (Notre Dame, Ind.: University of Notre Dame Press, 1993) 200.

Merton wrote a number of essays on the work and thought of Albert Camus and sensed a closeness with the French atheist because of Camus' fierce desire to seek truth. Camus dismissed the idea of God "as irrelevant because it is *inaccessible* to the mind and experience of so many modern people."[14] Merton believed Camus failed to realize that love for God and love for people were the same love, that love of God did not negate the value or dignity of human life. Merton focused upon Camus' novels and upon his depiction of the mythical figure of Sisyphus. Camus had said that for moderns the only real philosophical question is whether or not to commit suicide. Camus' Sisyphus, the "hero of the absurd," faces an impossible task symbolized in his being condemned to roll the stone up the hill over and over again because it rolls back down just as he reaches the top. Merton sees in Camus' *Myth of Sisyphus* a statement against suicide as an authentic response to the absurd. Sisyphus faces his impossible situation and "having finally elected to give it meaning by freely embracing its absurdity, he has overcome absurdity."[15] Merton admired Camus' courage and commitment to facing the absurd and death in the name of freely deciding to live his life. For Merton, life as absurd was a more genuine response than theological idols that both trivialized God and debased being human.

An awful sense of being a victim of love, especially when all seems absurd, is welcomed by the mystic for as Merton said, "love is the epiphany of God in our poverty."[16] The old ideas/idols are to be abandoned as one travels the darkness of faith (i.e., dark to the discursive understanding towards God). Merton saw that darkness as the agony of truth gradually being disclosed in the ancient sense of *a-letheia*, or un-hiddenness. In *Conjectures of a Guilty Bystander* he wrote, "it is precisely anguish and inner crisis that compel us to seek truth, because it is these things that make clear to us that we are sunk in the hell of our own untruth."[17]

Kilcourse has added to Woodcock's characterization of Merton's poetry as "poetry of the choir" and "poetry of the desert" by examin-

14. Patrick Hart, ed., *The Literary Essays of Thomas Merton* (New York: New Directions, 1981) "Terror and the Absurd: Violence and Nonviolence in Albert Camus," 248.

15. Ibid., "Three Saviors in Camus: Lucidity and the Absurd," 286.

16. "As Man to Man," *Cistercian Studies* IV (1969) 93.

17. *Conjectures of a Guilty Bystander* (Garden City, N.Y.: Doubleday, 1965) 183.

ing the "poetry of paradise consciousness" and "poetry of the forest." A lost, forgotten (but not totally unremembered) unity is dissolved, for Merton, in a profane(d) life lived in the isolation of the empirical (false) self. The contemplative "return to paradise" is both psychological and ontological. The sin is to forget, neglect or reject one's true self or nature. Kilcourse explains that "what becomes crucial is Merton's appreciation of sin as an ontological lapse, not merely a moral lapse. Sin violates the person's very *being*."[18] by making being itself banal. Therefore, Merton's incarnational vision of reality is a path of reconceptualization and reincorporation of the sacred in relation to human consciousness and identity. His poetry then becomes an emblem of the metaphor of metaphor-making within contemplative awareness of the paradox of a "paradise" regained that was never actually lost.

What is this "paradise consciousness" for Merton? It is the true self come to realize that it never has and never could exist except in a unity with the sacred. This is a universal and unique trauma of the human heart that helps connect Merton to his readers.

> Much of the power of Merton's appeal to readers revolves around his autobiographical wrestling with the superficiality of an external persona, a seductive "false self" that paralyzes the authentic power of love and communion. The "true self" is easily chased into hiding or appears wearing a disguise.[19]

This kind of disguise is to Merton the persona of a veritable hell.

III. Emblems for a Pilgrim

A key collection of poetry for this study is *Emblems of a Season of Fury* (1963). The Second Vatican Council was in its second session. Merton was still Master of Novices. Late that year President John Kennedy was assassinated. *Emblems* is a varied collection of poems of social protest and poems clearly influenced by Merton's study of Zen. The previous year Merton had been ordered by his superiors not to publish anything further on the issues of war and peace. The conflict within him about his desire for more solitude continued. In 1960 a building was constructed on the monastic grounds which Merton was allowed to use alone for a few hours each day. His abbot discouraged

18. Kilcourse, 53.
19. Ibid., 76–7.

Merton's ideas about joining another, more eremitic, order such as the Carthusians or the Camaldoli.

Merton's apophatic contemplation continued, but a long-suppressed openness to the world had begun in the late 1950s and can be found in the social protest poems in *Emblems*. The very word "fury" is not too strong for the emotions now released within Merton. He not only protested war and racism, but his own illusions. It was a time of crisis. His inner dark night was not only about solitude and contemplation, but about love. He had felt that he could never really, fully love because he was not worthy of love. The paradox is that the more solitude he was to have, the greater became his passion for the state of the world and his compassion for others. As his theology became more incarnational, his poetry became more simply paradoxical.

In a 1963 letter Merton constructed the image people had of him and how distorted it was. Fr. M. Louis Merton, O.C.S.O., was not the serene and detached monk and mystic of light that the early image may have projected. He would always struggle with and against the image manifested by the popularity of *The Seven Storey Mountain*. He said that those who believe in such an image

> do not know how unwilling I would be to have anyone repeat in his own life the miseries of mine. That would be flatly, a mortal sin against charity. I thought I have never done anything to obscure the lack of anything that a monk might conceive to be a desirable quality. Surely this lack is public knowledge, and anyone who imitates me does so at his own risk. I can promise him some fine moments of naked despair.[20]

"Naked despair" is an appropriate way to describe the mystic night where knowledge seems to have been lost and love is more dreadful, demanding and "awful" than consoling, more an incarnational experience of emptiness than of fullness.

Poetry marks Merton's inner longing for only that which will suffice. This explains, as Kilcourse describes, Merton's interest in the German poet, Rainer Maria Rilke, who "grew more and more important in Merton's understanding of poetry. He described him as the poet of *Innerlichkeit*, inwardness or interiority."[21] Merton's other interests in-

20. Michael Mott, *The Seven Mountains of Thomas Merton* (Boston, Houghton-Mifflin Co., 1984) 393.
21. Kilcourse, 53.

cluded Pasternak, Suzuki, Weil, Russian mystics, Central and South American poets, Sufis as well as nuclear war, racial equality, Asian religions, modern monaticism and fourteenth century mystics. In 1961 he wrote

> I am still a 14th century man: the century of Eckhart, Ruysbroeck, Tauler, the English recluses, the author of "The Cloud," Langland and Chaucer—more an independent and a hermit than a community man, by no means an ascetic, interested in psychology, a lover of the dark Cloud in which God is found by love. This is what I am: I must consent to be it and not be ashamed that I am not something more fashionable.[22]

As his poetry became more simple, "flattened," freer of traditional meter, poetic diction and imagery, he worked to allow the words, the semantic associations, to speak for themselves. Sometimes the result was more didactic than poetic vision, but *Emblems* is a collection that tries to hold together Merton's far-reaching sides. It is the emergence of Merton's dialectical synthesis of mystical and social, monastic and worldly, poetic and religious, sacred and profane. *Emblems* "proved a watershed in Merton's transformation as a poet . . . (he) wrestles openly with spiritual crisis. The poems open to a more universal experience."[23] His incarnational mythopoetics unites the unique with the universal.

Emblems of a Season of Fury opens with "Why Some Look Up to Planets and Heroes." For Merton the real voyage is into the fathomless reaches of the true self where God is found, not simply into the space-time continuum. He sees a "hero" as one willing to "travel" into the void of God in order to experience God *and* one's true self. His critical attitude towards the use of technology sees it as a modern pseudo-religion where ". . . the computers are convinced / Fed full of numbers by the True Believers."[24] One can only speculate on what Merton's thought would have become in today's artificial intelligence, Information Processing System, technophiliac, virtual reality age. Just as he saw the use of drugs as a futile attempt at an infantile, instant mysticism, so too he saw the idolizing of technology as a modern form of magic that seeks a mechanical solution to spiritual questions. Merton did not

22. Mott, 362.
23. Kilcourse, 62.
24. *Collected Poems*, 307.

live to see humans land on the moon in 1969, but he tended to see space as symbolic of the mystic's darkness, cold and forbidding, but also beautiful, revealing and compelling. Space was more a theological and poetic reality for Merton than a scientific one and to ignore the inner chaos led to great danger because in such a world "Your own ill-will / . . . Peoples the world with specters" ("Macarius and the Pony").[25]

The incarnation of Christ meant for Merton a progressive incarnating of the sacred in the profane where each was transformed. As the sacred was described in terms of silence or darkness or emptiness, it lost its previous conceptual limitations. Thus, the night was an essential "sickness" prior to union with the divine. Merton also believed Zen could enliven the heart of the Christian faith which for him was not "doctrinal formulas, juridical order and ritual exactitude . . . (but) a *living experience* of unity in Christ which far transcends all conceptual formulations."[26]

"Song for Nobody" is a brief poem where a flower is a concrete image for existence itself, where words cannot say what the flower "says" simply being what it is. One is reminded of Eckhart saying that if one understood something as simple as a flower and how it has its existence in God, one would know more than the world. By not turning the flower into a "thing" as in Tennyson's "Flower in a Crannied Wall" where the flower is picked, objectified and thus killed, Merton sees that the flower is empty of the ego-attachment which is a millstone and albatross to human awareness.

> A yellow flower
> (Light and spirit)
> Sings by itself
> For nobody. . .
>
> (No light, no gold, no name, no color
> And no thought;
> O, wide awake!)
>
> A golden heaven
> Sings by itself
> A song to nobody.[27]

25. Ibid., 318.

26. Thomas Merton, *Zen and the Birds of Appetite* (New York: New Directions, 1968) 39.

27. *Collected Poems*, 337, 338.

The flower is a symbol for the sacred and the way the sacred is more than any possible idea of the sacred. The Zen influence is apparent. A little flower can lead to insight or enlightenment as much as anything else for "the ordinary experience of everyday life is the 'place' where enlightenment is to be sought."[28] Quoting D. T. Suzuki, Merton emphasized the need for the little flower to be left alone by the grasping mind and simply to be seen as, of all things, a little flower:

> Zen always aims at grasping the central fact of life, which can never be brought to the dissecting table of the intellect. To grasp the central fact of life, Zen is forced to propose a series of negations. Mere negation however is not the spirit of Zen. . . When the spirit of Zen is grasped in its purity, it will be seen what a real thing that (in this case a flower) is. For here is no negation, no affirmation, but a plain fact, a pure experience, the very foundation of our being and thought. All the quietness and emptiness one might desire in the midst of most active meditation lies therein. . . Zen must be seized with bare hands, with no gloves on.[29]

The flower is to be seen in its suchness, in its original innocence with the "bare hands" of pure consciousness in the immediate moment, with what Christian contemplative tradition calls "purity of heart." As Kilcourse says, "the flower's wakeful presence to the inner self depends on the absence of all other identities. . ."[30]

In this poem and others such as "Song: If You Seek. . . ," "O Sweet Irrational Worship," "Night Flowering Cactus," "Love Winter When the Plant Says Nothing," and "The Fall," Merton is both disclosing a Zen influence upon him and reacting against a centuries-long tradition in the West that went from medieval universalism to modern nihilism to reductionistic relativism to an ontological, psychological sense of absolute autonomy. G. K. Chesterton had said that if God or the sacred is lost or forgotten, it is not that people will believe in nothing, but that they will believe in anything. The sociologist of religion, Peter Berger, agrees with this view when he calls our time an "Age of Credulity" where no ideas or practice, no matter how implausible or destructive, can not find its followers. The medieval cosmos was a living vine of symbolic truths about God and reality. By the twentieth

---

28. Thomas Merton, *Mystics and Zen Masters* (New York: Dell, 1969) 223.

29. D. T. Suzuki, *Introduction to Zen Buddhism* (London, 1960), cited in *Mystics and Zen Masters*, 49.

30. Kilcourse, 65.

century the shared meanings had dissipated and writers, artists and poets were careening to create their own symbol systems and mythic patterns, or else abandoning the need for such ancient truth-telling vehicles altogether.

Where was the place for the divine in such a scheme of things? Initially it had seemed like a great liberation, but the loss of the power of the symbol (and an incarnational, sacramental vision) came at high cost. Eric Heller in "The Hazard of Modern Poetry" portrays the change this way:

> Reality, freed from its commitments to the symbol, became more really real than before. The hand of man, reaching out for his reality, was no longer unsteadied by the awe and fear of the symbolic mystery. He acquired the surgeon's hygienic dexterity. And reality, pressed the mechanic way, yielded ample nourishment real, if not divine. As reality became more real, so the symbol became more symbolic and art more artistic. . .
>
> But there were also signs of uneasiness. They mounted to a climax of tension in the seventeenth century. What was first felt to be a liberation appeared more and more as a robbery. Robbed of its real significance, what did the symbol signify? Robbed of its symbolic meaning, what did reality mean? What was the State on earth? A Leviathan. What was God? More and more a *deus absconditus*, an infinitely remote and impenetrable veiled God.[31]

An inevitable Enlightenment, rational utopia in a machinomorphic cosmos beckoned.

In the nineteenth century the biological theories of evolution were also transposed into cultural and sociological theories of a momentum of momentous "progress." Thomas Huxley coined the term "agnosticism." For the first time in human history, theoretical atheism was not only the view of a growing number of people, but it was hailed as more moral and intellectually honest than theism. By the twentieth century logical positivism and analytic philosophy were saying that the traditional questions of religion and philosophy, such as whether there is a God or spirit, refer to nothing real, i.e., "verifiable" by empirical investigation. They were deceptive, even illusory language games and thus, "non-sense." This was the atmospheric impetus for Merton's subsequent antipoetry, "to give the world back its language, to

---

31. Giles Gunn, ed., *Literature and Religion* (New York: Harper & Row, 1971) 172–3.

rescue us from the tyranny of logical positivism's absurdities. . ."[32] A brief look at Merton's antipoetry will conclude this examination.

A societal focus upon facticity and technology did not bring the psychological, moral and spiritual "progress" as had been expected. Merton recognized this and sought a way to return poetry to its truth-telling capacities as the mother tongue of humanity and the vision quest. It was in the Zen poems that he expressed an alternative to the trivialization of metaphysics through the experience of darkness, emptiness and the void. As a Christian, Merton found that "God Himself, the personal God, is the *deepest center* of consciousness and unification,"[33] but that God was No-thing, not an object as other objects that exist. God was empty and void of "God," God was dark to the intellect. Merton came to echo Eckhart's words that "there is something in the soul so closely akin to God that is already one with him and need never be united to him."[34] In the incarnational experience there is no-where to go since one has been found already by whom one seeks. An emblem of this vision is a spiraling circle going nowhere and, thus, everywhere. Dogen, a foundational figure in Zen, said that "if you can't find the truth right where you are, where else do you think you will find it."[35]

Zen greatly helped Merton to a deeper understanding and experience of the sacred by pointing him towards direct, unitive experience empty of abstractions and corrective of his tendency towards wordiness. In both Zen and mysticism in general the paradox is that "emptiness *is* the fullness, the fullness the emptiness; the darkness *is* the light, the light the darkness."[36] Suzuki says that "as Buddhists would say, the realization of Emptiness is no more, no less than seeing into the nonexistence of the thingish ego-substance. . . (and that) to be absolutely nothing is to be everything"[37] for to seize upon something as an object is to limit the experience of all else. For Suzuki the void or zero is a creative womb and source of all good which he puts this way: zero = infinity, and infinity = zero. Merton accepted the saying that "Zen is your everyday

32. Kilcourse, 171.

33. *Zen and the Birds of Appetite*, 69.

34. Raymond Blakney, trans., *Meister Eckhart* (New York: Harper & Brothers, 1941) 205.

35. Stephen Mitchell, ed., *The Enlightened Mind* (New York: Harper Collins, 1993) 101.

36. Walter Stace, *The Teaching of the Mystics* (New York: New American Library, 1956) 237.

37. *Zen and the Birds of Appetite*, 109.

mind" where enlightenment, or what Merton called "metaphysical intuition of the ground of being," is to be "found" in the midst of concepts and contradictions, anywhere and everywhere, because "you cannot find it anywhere at all, because in fact it is nowhere in the first place."[38]

In "Song: If You Seek. . ." solitude is portrayed as the teacher who leads into emptiness, "Opening the windows / Of your innermost apartment." It is the "now" that "cuts / Time like a blade" and is the silence beyond distinctions which enables God to be heard. If solitude is followed, it will lead to "golden-haired suns, / Logos and music, blameless joys, / Innocent of questions / And beyond answers. . ." The closing lines identify the solitude as the person's true self where nothingness and all are one. Silence has the final word because it encompasses all that is and is not:

> For I, Solitude, am thine own self:
> I, Nothingness, am thy All.
> I, Silence, am thy Amen![39]

"O Sweet Irrational Worship" shows the change from Merton's early analogical dualism between the natural and the supernatural. As far back as *The Ascent to Truth* (1951) Merton was saying that "in mystical experience, God is 'apprehended' as unknown. . . He becomes present not in a finite concept but in His infinite reality which overflows every analogical notion we can utter of Him."[40] In the poem Merton speaks of a union of the self with nature:

> By ceasing to question the sun
> I have become light,
>
> Bird and wind.
>
> My leaves sing.
>
> I am earth, earth.

The world becomes more real in the union of natural and supernatural. It is no longer simply analogous of the sacred, but is the sacred in its profane identity. Thus, Merton proclaims

---

38. Ibid., 33.

39. *Collected Poems*, 341.

40. Thomas Merton, *The Ascent to Truth* (New York: Harcourt Brace Jovanovich, 1981) 83.

My heart's love
bursts with hay and flowers.
I am a lake of blue air
In which my own appointed place
Field and valley
Stand reflected.

I am earth, earth.

The transformation of the self which is so key to Merton's incarnational idea of the sacred is given mystical expression in "Night-Flowering Cactus." The usually thorny, thus perilous, cactus blooms suddenly during the night. Just as mystical experience is often characterized as momentary and ineffable, so too is this flowering: "I know my time, which is obscure, silent and brief / For I am present without warning one night only."[41] In the dark the real flowering appears, a symbol for the true self which is empty of all the ego-serpents of the daylight, or discursive consciousness. The flowering is "my timeless moment of void" which Lentfoehr sees as reflecting both Zen consciousness and

> the Eckhartian concept of "perfect poverty" that occurs only when there is no self left as a "place" for God to act in, and hence He acts purely in Himself. It is only then that one comes to his true "self" or, in the Zen terms, the "no-self," in which one achieves his true identity which consists in "the birth of Christ in us."[42]

The transformed self is innocent and "As a white cavern without explanation" that speaks with a silent voice:

> When I open once for all my impeccable bell
> No one questions my silence:
> The all-knowing bird of night flies out of my mouth.

The mystic vision not only startles, but starts a change in all who experience it:

> You live forever in its echo:
> You will never be the same again.

41. *Collected Poems*, 351.
42. Sr. Thérèse Lentfoehr, *Words and Silence: On the Poetry of Thomas Merton* (New York: New Directions, 1979) 61.

"Love Winter When the Plant Says Nothing" is about the emptiness and creative darkness of spiritual experience. The scene is winter. There seems to be no life, no words to speak. Yet, there is something here that is full of life though it is hidden by the snow and barrenness. The seeming death is an image of the dark night which Merton interpreted as "the necessary condition of the soul prior to union with God."[43] It is a matter of "waiting upon God in darkness."[44] Inside of nature and more pointedly, inside the human spirit, Merton finds the fire of the sacred at "a burly infant spot," and calls upon silence to "love this growth." The self grows in the fertile darkness of the sacred which is likened to "golden zero / unsetting sun." What seems to all appearances to be purely profane is in reality a womb for the sacred teeming with unlimited life. The poem ends with "Love winter when the plant says nothing."[45] The cold and dark winter is the mystical darkness which Merton sees as the fire that destroys false persona so that the true self can fulfill its destiny.

In "Grace's House" Merton writes about the drawing of a house on a hill by a four-year old girl. He sees her world as "O paradise, O child's world!" which is separated from our world by an uncrossed river, a "crystal / Water between our ignorance and her truth."[46] It is a picture of the house as the sacred center of the child's world, on the holy mountain as in some transformed world where the sacred and the profane have become one:

> No blade of grass is not blessed
> On this archetypal hill,
> This womb of mysteries.

But as Lentfoehr emphsizes, the leitmotif of the poem is that

> There is no path to the summit—
> No path drawn
> To Grace's house. . .

> Alas, there is no road to Grace's house!

---

43. John Teahan, "A Dark and Empty Way: Thomas Merton and the Apophatic Tradition," *The Journal of Religion*, vol. 58, no. 3 (July 1978) 271.

44. Thomas Merton, *What is Contemplation?* (Holy Cross, Ind.: St. Mary's College, 1948) 24.

45. *Collected Poems*, 353.

46. Ibid., 331.

The house itself is the geography to travel, it is both the path or road and the map of the path. As Merton writes in "The Fall,"

> This is the paradise tree. It must remain unseen
> until worlds end and arguments are silent.[47]

IV. The Pilgrimage Goes Public and Profane

Merton came to see that the aesthetic and the mystical were to serve each other in acting against what was to him the murderous anesthetic, necrophobic mentality of the age. His poetry loses its detachment and becomes "flattened," the theological imagery replaced by realistic reporting. There are several poems in *Emblems* that illustrate this low-toned approach to what Merton sees as evil.

"Chant to be Used in Processions Around a Site with Furnaces" is a droning poem spoken by the commander of a Nazi death camp. The matter-of-fact tone, the quotations, the obsessions with cleanliness amidst the killing of children, women and men, the mechanical recitation of events, the grotesque euphemisms are powerful:

> How we perfectly cleaned up the people and worked a big heater

> I was the commander I made improvements and installed a guaranteed system taking account of human weakness I purified and I remained decent. . .

> I made cleaning appointments and then I made the travellers sleep and after I made soap. . .

> When trains arrived the soiled passengers received appointments for fun in the bathroom they did not guess. . .

> Another improvement I made was I built the chambers for two thousand invitations at a time the naked votaries were disinfected with Zyklon B. . .

> I guaranteed the chamber and it was sealed you could see through portholes. . .

> How I could tell by their cries that love came to a full stop I found the ones I had made clean after about a half hour. . .

> How I commanded and made soap 12 lbs fat 10 quarts water 8 oz to a lb of caustic soda but it was hard to find any fat. . .

---

47. Ibid., 355.

You smile at my career but you would do as I did if you knew yourself and dared

In my day we worked hard we saw what we did our self-sacrifice was conscientious and complete our work was faultless and detailed. . .[48]

For Merton this view is the result of a world without the sense of the sacred to disclose the value of the profane. All becomes mechanistic and death-bound, a brutal compound of necrophobia and necrophilia. The murderers seem so sane in many ways, they can appreciate music, love their families and dogs and then go to work where they commit genocide all in a day's labor.

The more Merton's incarnational transformation continued, the more his image of Christ embodied the sufferings of people. Dietrich Bonhoeffer had a view of God as suffering with people:

God lets himself be pushed out of the world on to the cross. He is weak and powerless in the world, and that is precisely the way, the only way, in which he is with us and helps us. . . The Bible directs man to God's powerlessness and suffering; only the suffering God can help.[49]

Bonhoeffer wants to take the world and human suffering in all seriousness.

Nearly twenty years after Bonhoeffer's death Merton was himself engaged in a dialectical process with the world. In a letter to Czeslaw Milosz in 1959 Merton talked about Christ being "profaned" in the suffering of the death camps:

Whatever the mystery of Providence may be I think it is more direct and brutal in a way. But that is never evident as long as we think God apart from the people in the concentration camp, "permitting them to be there for their own good" (time out while I vomit). Actually it is God Himself who is in the concentration camp. That is, of course, it is Christ. Not in the collective sense, but especially in the defilement and destruction of each individual soul, there is a renewal of the Crucifixion. . .[50]

48. Ibid., 345–9.

49. Eberhard Bethge, ed., *Letters and Papers from Prison* (New York: Macmillian, 1953) 360–1. This passage is from July 16, 1944.

50. Merton to Czeslaw Milosz, May 21, 1959, as cited in Mott's *Seven Mountains*, 358–9.

Merton emphasizes that it is in the self that Christ is found, the self that lives in the world, even the hellish world of the camps, not in the disincarnate empirical ego that is without any world because it is totally and only with and for itself. This all meant for Merton an acceptance of the profane as both real and necessary for the *kenosis* or emptying of the true self and the sacred. He wrote that God was not a working hypothesis or stop-gap for holes in the scientific worldview, but present in the self and world.[51] Kilcourse calls this Merton's kenotic and incarnational Christology where

> the Christ of kenosis subverts for Merton any complacency in his own spirituality. He discovers the epiphany of Christ in the human experience of poverty, in historical discontinuities, at the margins of Christendom, and in the rejection and vulnerability of the world's scarred victims and despised outcasts.[52]

In 1963 four black children were killed in Birmingham by a bomb during Sunday school. Merton's response is found in "Picture of a Black Child with a White Doll."[53] The bombing was for Merton both an indictment of personal and societal evil and a horrible manifestation of the need of love: "(Yet how deep the wound and the need / And how far down our hell. . .)." The poem is addressed to one of the little girls murdered, Carole Denise McNair, a victim of those she was so far beyond because she knew the need for a love ". . . without malice / And by a better instinct. . . ." For Merton a disembodied compassion is an oxymoron, an impossible delusion. His Christocentric, incarnational, contemplative theology led him to see individual and collective egoism as unabashedly evil.

Emblems of a Season of Fury was a pivotal work written at a pivotal time in Merton's life. His own dark night had begun to find some initial dawning. The Indian poet, Tagore somewhere calls a mystic a "bird of dawn" and Merton was such a bird. The dark dawn disclosed a conscious union with a God who was more radically incarnational than ever before to Merton and a union with the experiences of people all over the world, past and present. He came to see that the sacred was to be found in the center of history, historical consciousness and the profane. In his theology of kenotic compassion the furies of the dark night became strange

51. *Conjectures*, 320.
52. Kilcourse, 43.
53. *Collected Poems*, 626–7.

emblems of an awful and necessary season of the true self's emptiness into Christ. Besides, for Merton there were few emblems of anything.

Although a detailed discussion is beyond the scope of this paper, the attitudes that created *Emblems* and were created by it issued in the anti-poetry of Merton's final major volumes of poetry, *Cables to the Ace* (1968) and *The Geography of Lograire* (1968).

Cables to the Ace chronicles the incarnation of the sacred in its prosaic disguises. In this volume Merton continues his life-long theme of union with God, cables to "the ace of freedoms." Christ is mentioned only late in the poem. This meditation is an attempt, an experiment, to experience the sacred in an age that seems to have abandoned even the memory of the sacred. The poem is political, social, anthropological, eschatological and mystical.

Near the close of the poem Merton mentions the "ace" for the first time:

> I am about to make my home
> In the bell's summit
> Set my mind a thousand feet high
> On the ace of songs. . .[54]

While the manipulative and anti-communicative world burns itself out, the image of free-flying birds is used to intimate inner freedom:

> But birds fly uncorrected across burnt lands
> The surest home is pointless:
> We learn by the cables of orioles.

The ground for this freedom is the "ace of freedoms" which is Merton's way of speaking of God and of union with God "in the bell's summit." In the swarm of spiritual numbness that Merton has talked about in much of the poem he is able to find the still point that transforms the entire world for the self by mystical oneness with God. Merton's inner geography had expanded to include everyone's geography. The "cables" are as the support for a bridge to the summit. Is it strange to see this whole book as a love poem? Lentfoehr does:

> This message to the age, an ironic and witty variously structured
> antipoem, rich in allusion and aimed at a technological

---

54. Ibid., 453.

society that dehumanizes man, can have its genesis only in a heart permeated with God's love and love for all human-kind.[55]

The poem is an antipoetry poetics of incarnated love.

Cables did not fully succeed and suffers from what many modern poets have found in trying to create a work without culturally and religiously formed symbols and imagery, namely, a subjectivist expression that sometimes eludes the reader's understanding. But what Merton began in *Cables*, he developed more fully, and more successfully, in his final major poem, *The Geography of Lograire*.

The poem remained unfinished at the time of Merton's death. In the preface he said that it was "only a beginning of patterns, the first opening of the dream. . . (the) struggle of love and death." It is a vision of the fundamental unity of humanity with Merton, as narrator, serving as the hub for the various times, places, cultures, events. Through "found poetry" and by a continuation and expansion of the mosaic kind of collage begun in *Cables*, Merton developed what he called a surrealistic meditation. By contrasting primitive kinds of cultures with the modern, he implies that much is to be gained by a renewal of contact with the unconscious forces and symbolic vitality of the old ways. With alternations of prose and poetry based upon extensive readings in the hermitage at Gethsemani, the poem attempts to manifest the worth of all people. Merton called it his offbeat anthropology. It sees history as a contemporaneous whole in the experience of each person. In the Prologue to the North canto, Merton feels the unity of human geography:

> Explain the air of all
> Feel it under (me)
> Stand
> Stand in the unspoken
> A cool street
> An air of legs
> An air of visions
>
> *Geography.*
> *I am all (here)*
> *There!*

55. Lentfoehr, 45.

The whole work ends in despair. There is no appended theological caveat which rescues the situation from its tragic reality. *Geography* is Merton's geography of the way to realize that the sacred has no meaning in the modern world apart from an intimate knowledge of its incarnation in the midst of human idols, hells, worldliness. Thus, to hold that a monastic life was a retreat and escape from the "world," as the young Brother Louis did in the 1940s, was an insult against the world, the monastic life and the sacred. Merton's paradise became less a nostalgic look at a primal unity and more an embrace of the bloody, beautiful world where Ranters, Cargo cults, Artic expeditions, sterile technological flights and tragic Indian ghost dances were all part of the flesh and spirit of that world.

Merton's incarnational vision combined with the influence of Zen to yield for him a sacred season of love and death where, as he stated in connection with his mystical experience at the Buddhist shrine at Polonnaruwa in Sri Lanka shortly before his death, "everything is emptiness and everything is compassion." Electrically burned in death, Merton in life had burned for a union with his God and with all peoples. His poetry incorporates the intellect and the furies of the unconscious as it integrates contemplation with social concern, aesthetic with religious meaning. It helps to restore to poetry its truth-telling, myth-sharing, shamanistic, prophetic role by disclosing the incarnated experience of the sacred. The mystical and the worldly unite in his idea of the sacred.

> Midnight!
> Kissed with flame!
>
> See! See!
> My love is darkness!
>
> Only in the Void
> Are all ways one:
>
> Only in the night
> Are all the lost
> Found.
>
> In my ending is my meaning.
>
> ("The Night of Destiny")[56]

56. *Collected Poems*, 634–5.

"Abundant, Multiple, Restless": Levertov and Merton in the 1960s

Emily Archer

Conversations Here and Now

"Denise Levertov was here today," and it was "a good visit together," Thomas Merton begins a letter dated December 10, 1967, exactly one year before his death.[1] Among other things, Levertov and Merton discussed "the merits of self-immolation as a way of protesting the war in Vietnam" that day while Ralph Eugene Meatyard took a series of photos collected in *Father Louie*.[2] Levertov's "good visit" was still on Merton's mind the next day: "Denise Levertov was here yesterday," he begins a letter to an inquiring student, and continues:

> What poets do I like? . . . . I do like Bill Williams but I find I don't read a great deal of him. Pound I respect and don't read. Duncan I like. Oppen I have quoted some. Creeley etc. ok. I wouldn't say any of these had influenced me. Denise Levertov I respond to very much as a poet and a person.[3]

While meetings between the two poets appear to be few, many places in their poems and prose meet and converse about a mutual concern

1. Thomas Merton, *The School of Charity: The Letters of Thomas Merton on Religious Renewal and Spiritual Direction*, ed. Brother Patrick Hart (New York: Farrar, Straus, Giroux, 1990) 355.

2. Meatyard, Ralph Eugene, *Father Louie: Photographs of Thomas Merton*, ed. Barry Magid, with an essay by Guy Davenport (New York: Timken Publishers, 1991) 92–3.

3. Thomas Merton, *The Road to Joy: The Letters of Thomas Merton to New and Old Friends*, ed. Robert E. Daggy (New York: Farrar, Straus, Giroux, 1989) 361.

for language and words, as both respond to the urgencies and crises of the sixties.

The following essay looks to some of the reasons Merton might have "responded very much" during the sixties to Denise Levertov, whose importance as an American poet of great spiritual depth and clarity has continued to grow. One can imagine the dialogues that might have continued between the two had Merton not died one year after that "good visit," especially conversations on poetry, prophecy, tradition, and political engagement. As poets and guardians of the word, both shared an abiding concern for the renewal of language in what Merton calls an age of destruction, and Levertov, an age of terror. Merton and Levertov's lives as artists moved both of them closer to the pulses of war and racial unrest in the sixties and, at the same time, to a keener critique of language, a surer understanding of the efficacy of poetry, and of the poet's necessary pre-position, "in the world."[4]

Even though he gets her book title wrong, Merton enthusiastically writes about Levertov in another letter:

> One new poet I am very happy about is Denise Levertov. New Directions has done a book of hers, *With Eyes in the Backs of Their Heads*. I think it is very fine, very spiritual in a broad, Jungian sort of way. She is not Catholic as far as I know, or may be.[5]

Merton's letters suggest that he had been reading Levertov's work at least since the publication of *With Eyes at the Back of Our Heads* (1960), for in 1961 he advises Mark Van Doren that New Directions (publisher of all of his poetry) "has published a poet called Denise Levertov I think you would like. Have you seen her book? It starts with a wonderful version of a Toltec poem about what an artist ought to do . . .":[6]

> *The artist: disciple, abundant, multiple, restless.*
> *The true artist: capable, practicing, skillful;*
> *maintains dialogue with his heart, meets things with his*
>   *mind.*[7]

4. The phrase is key to Levertov's aesthetic ethic, and comes from her first volume of collected essays, *The Poet in the World* (New York: New Directions, 1973).

5. *The Road to Joy*, 239. The title is *With Eyes at the Back of Our Heads*.

6. Ibid., 43.

7. Denise Levertov, *Collected Earlier Poems, 1940–1960* (New York: New Directions, 1979) 84.

Merton and Levertov both responded to the political and social crises of the sixties with changes in their own ways of being artists, demonstrating their own multiplicity and restlessness, their unwillingness to subscribe to dogmas or roles, either aesthetic or religious, which would silence the necessary dialogue between poet and heart, poet and history.

Both poets struggled before the sixties with a dialectic Merton called "poetry and contemplation"[8] and Levertov's work implicitly called "poetry and subjectivity." Merton's desire to reconcile what he once perceived to be mutually exclusive activities is the basis of his 1958 reappraisal of "Poetry and the Contemplative Life," an essay that originally appeared in *Commonweal* in 1948. During the sixties Merton begins living into his new sense that

> true contemplation is inseparable from life and from the dynamism of life—which includes work, creation, production, fruitfulness, and above all love. Contemplation is not to be thought of as a separate department of life, cut off from all man's other interests and superseding them. It is the very fullness of a fully integrated life.[9]

Merton's exile in the early fifties from aesthetic reflection and the language of poetry was nearly over by the time he issued his praise of Levertov's work. No longer could he ignore his own "condition of being a poet" and of having to respond to the demand poetry and language were making on his vocation. Having to make a choice between the contemplative and the artistic life had clearly been a false dichotomy for Merton.

Psalmists in the World

As Merton settled into the monastic life in the 1940s, Levertov was also occupied with her own decisive changes, both geographically and aesthetically: from England to New York, and from the influence of British neo-romanticism that prevails in *The Double Image* (1946) to the actualities of American culture, politics, and speech. Among her

8. See Merton's revision of these terms in "Poetry and Contemplation: A Reappraisal," *The Literary Essays of Thomas Merton*, ed. Brother Patrick Hart (New York: New Directions, 1981) 338–54.

9. Merton, "Poetry and Contemplation," 339.

influences are William Carlos Williams, H. D., Charles Olson, Robert Creeley, and Robert Duncan, all of whom rejected the well-wrought urns of formalist poetry for image-controlled, breath-driven "high energy constructs." But even before she left England, Levertov's restlessness with neo-romanticism and its subjectivity was clear. Written during a brief sojourn in Sicily in 1948, "Too Easy to Write of Miracles" contrasts the language of the "easy" lament—disembodied, self-circumscribed—with the language of the lived life. It is "Easy like the willow to lament, / rant in trampled roads where pools / are red with sorrowful fires," but

> difficult to write
> of the real image, real hand, the heart
> of day or autumn beating steadily . . .
> 　　　　　. . . and achieve
> the unhaunted country of the final poem.[10]

Moving beyond the self as subject of the poem also meant moving from passive watching to active witnessing:

> Some are too much at home in the role of wanderer,
> watcher, listener; who, by lamplit doors
> that open only to another's knock,
> commune with shadows and are happier
> with ghosts than living guests in a warm house. . . .[11]

Being integrated, taking root in life—these are tasks for the poet whose relationship to the world speaks "I-Thou," whose art is not self-referential and appropriating, but dialogic and other-directed, a relation both Merton and Levertov believe is founded upon imagination and love.

　　By the early sixties, Levertov was articulating, in both poetry and prose, an aesthetic which was at once avant-garde and quite ancient. Her practice of "organic form" forges new relationships between form and content, even as it honors the origins of certain words and older practices of language. And "contemplation" is a key term in this recursive poetics. She echoes Merton in her description of contemplation as inseparable from creative dynamism, and especially from the creation of a poem. "The condition of being a poet," Levertov asserts in 1965, is a matter of fulfilling a demand that history and experience

---

10. Levertov, *Collected Earlier Poems*, 10.
11. Ibid., 7.

awakens, and "the beginning of the fulfillment of this demand is to contemplate."[12] What Levertov means by contemplation is lodged within the origin of the word. "To contemplate," she says,

> comes from *"templum,* temple, a place a space for observation, marked out by the augur." It means, not simply to observe, to re-gard, but to do these things in the presence of a god. And to med-itate is "to keep the mind in a state of contemplation"; its synonym is "to muse," and to muse comes from a word meaning "to stand with open mouth"—not so comical if we think of "inspiration"—to breathe in.
>
> So—as the poet stands openmouthed in the temple of life, contemplating his experience, there come to him the first words of the poem: the words which are to be his way in to the poem, if there is to be a poem.[13]

Like Merton, Levertov was challenged with tasks of integration. Bringing her "double images" into dialogue lay not entirely, but sig-nificantly, in her desire to write poems with a "line still taut"[14] to the dancing Jewish Hasids and Christian mystics of her ancestry. From ghostly subjectivities to mysterious actualities—that is one way of de-scribing Levertov's evolution toward becoming a "poet in the world," aided profoundly by the implicit "conversation" between Jew and Christian that has continued to shape her work. It is an ancient and on-tological conversation, and concerned above all with language and presence. Merton mused in the letter above, whether Levertov "may be" Catholic. The spirituality he recognizes in Levertov's work in the early sixties is incipient and broad, indeed—catholic perhaps, but not yet Catholic.[15] There is everywhere "the presence of a god" in Levertov's work, from the earliest poems to the most recent, but the turnings from "god" to "God" have been gradual. The air she breathed as a child was inescapably religious, filled with the cadences of Anglican liturgy and the characters of biblical and Hasidic legend. Levertov affirms her syncretic spiritual heritage in a number of poems,

12. Levertov, *The Poet in the World,* 8–9.
13. Ibid., 8.
14. Levertov, "Illustrious Ancestors," *Collected Earlier Poems,* 77.
15. Even when she does "convert" to Catholicism, she remains, as Merton became, ecumenical in thought and practice. Levertov's comments on her move-ment "to a position of Christian belief" are found in "A Poet's View," *New and Selected Essays* (New York: New Directions, 1992) 239–46.

foremost the well-known "Illustrious Ancestors," which tells how Rabbi Schneour Zalman, the legendary eighteenth century Hasidic "Rav of Northern White Russia" "'prayed / with the bench and the floor.' He used / what was at hand." "As did / Angel Jones of Mold," she continues, the Christian mystic-tailor "whose meditations / were sewn into coats and britches."[16] In a later poem, as Levertov tells of her own parents' spiritual identity, she reveals much of her own:

> As a devout Christian, my father
> took delight and pride in being
> (like Christ and the Apostles)
> a Jew.
> > It was
> > Hasidic lore, his heritage,
> > he drew on to know
> > the Holy Spirit as Shekinah.
>
> My Gentile mother, Welsh through and through,
> and like my father, sustained
> by deep faith, cherished
> all her long life the words
> of Israel Zangwill, who told her,
> 'You have a Jewish soul.'
>
> I their daughter ('flesh of their flesh,
> > bone of their bone') . . .[17]

It can also be said that Denise Levertov, "bone of their bone," has "a Jewish soul," and a Hebraic way of being "in the world" alongside the Christian one. Furthermore, it is neither simply with the mystic in her maternal Welsh tradition nor with the Hasid in her paternal heritage that she keeps a "line still taut," but with earlier Christian mystics such as Julian of Norwich [18] (whom Merton also came to love), and particularly with the ancient Hebrew psalmist. This line to the psalmist is cast in a number of different streams and depths throughout the decades of her poetry and her statements on poetics, but most importantly in her relationship to language.

16. Levertov, "Illustrious Ancestors," *Collected Earlier Poems*, 77.
17. Levertov, "Perhaps No Poem But All I Can Say and I Cannot Be Silent," *Oblique Prayers* (New York: New Directions, 1984) 35.
18. See "On a Theme from Julian's Chapter XX" and "The Showings, 1–6" in Denise Levertov, *Breathing the Water* (New York: New Directions, 1987) 68, 75.

Levertov's poems return to Hebraic origins in their implicit practice of the word as *dabar,* or "word" in Hebrew, which concretely and immediately unites word and deed. Wilson Baroody explains that "biblical writers understand words as concrete, even physical objects in contrast to the typical modern, dualistic conception of them as having little or no physical reality."[19] Walter Brueggemann, Susan Handelman, Isaac Rabinowitz, and Edith Wyschogrod, among others, explore the biblical texts in the original Hebrew and find that the apprehension of language embodied in *dabar* is fundamentally constitutive and efficacious. Its power is primarily relational, performative, and ethical.[20]

Levertov's convictions about the constitutive and ethical nature of language begin with elements as small as the letters of the alphabet. In the worded world of the Hebrews, no part of language is insignificant. All letters, syllables, and words constitute the vast tissue of creation. And of the poem, Levertov says "I believe every space and comma is a living part of the poem and has its function, just as every muscle and pore of the body has its function."[21] To use the title of one of her most important sequences, Levertov's whole poetic corpus can be seen as a vast "relearning the alphabet." And "the necessity" is foremost the redemption of words:

> . . .
>
> each part
> of speech a spark
> awaiting redemption, each
> a virtue, a power . . .[22]

In Levertov's aesthetic ethic, it is not just the poet who must take responsibility for words, but the teacher, the critic, and the reader, for

19. Wilson G. Baroody, "Biblical Mysticism: Hearing and Speaking God's Word," *Studia Mystica* 14:4 (1991) 9.

20. See Walter Brueggemann, *Israel's Praise: Doxology Against Idolatry and Ideology* (Philadelphia: Fortress Press, 1988); Susan Handelman, *The Slayers of Moses: The Emergence of Rabbinic Interpretation in Modern Literary Theory* (Albany: State University of New York Press, 1982); Isaac Rabinowitz, "'Word' and Literature in Ancient Israel," *New Literary History,* vols. 3, 4 (Charlottesville: The University of Virginia, 1973) 118–39; and Edith Wyschogrod, "Works That 'Faith': The Grammar of Ethics in Judaism," *Cross Currents* 40.2 (Summer 1990) 176-93.

21. Levertov, *The Poet in the World,* 3.

22. Levertov, *"The Necessity," Poems 1960–1967* (New York: New Directions, 1983) 58.

"when words penetrate deep into us they change the chemistry of the soul, of the imagination. We have no right to do that to people if we don't share the consequences."[23] In the Hebrew language, the consequence of every utterance is folded into the very act of speaking. The effect of one word is simultaneous with its utterance; its power is immediate. In Hebrew experience "speech act" is a redundancy. Speech *is* act. In the utterance of the word—*dabar*—things happen.

Merton was also preoccupied in many of his writings with the spiritual efficacy of words, especially the contrast between the language of the Word, born in silence and charity, and what Augustine calls the "wrangling of tongues" that characterizes the language of Babel, words cursed with division and darkness.[24] The "political" speaker of Merton's poem "Tower of Babel" concedes that words are "the makers of our only reality,"[25] but that emptied of their "essential meaning," words have no connection with a vertical or spiritual dimension. They then become merely a

> . . . means of locomotion
> From backward to forward
> Along an infinite horizontal plane . . .[26]

"The most obvious characteristic of our age is destructiveness," Merton begins the essay "Theology of Creativity." No discussion of creativity "which is supposed, in the end, to be theological," he argues, will make sense unless we first examine how the word "creativity" itself has been severed from its origins and "essential meaning."[27]

Merton's lament over our misuse of this word points to his fundamental and continual concern over the misuse of language, which for him, as for Levertov, has profound aesthetic, ethical, ontological, and theological implications. Merton believes, no less than Levertov, that words have constitutive power, but that it is "characteristic of our age" to destroy the covenant between word and truth, word and world. Words must be restored to their original connection and reverenced as a reality-making power, he insists. Instead of renewing con-

23. Levertov, *The Poet in the World*, 114.

24. Thomas Merton, *Bread in the Wilderness* (Collegeville: The Liturgical Press, 1971) 159–60.

25. Thomas Merton, *Collected Poems* (New York: New Directions, 1977) 22.

26. Levertov, *Collected Earlier Poems*, 22.

27. Merton, *Literary Essays*, 355.

versations with the Creator, current uses of the word "creativity" reduce it to cliché or caricature, or worse, a justification, he argues, for the "creation" of violent tools and art.[28] Only when such words are returned to the City of God will their healing power be restored. The Psalms belong to the City of God, explains Merton, where "there is only one language spoken . . . . [and] that language is charity."[29]

Levertov moves closer both to the world and to the "City of God" as she learns not only to lament authentically (not just "rant in trampled roads"), but to praise, with the power of words that seek their source in *caritas*. In his study of the "sociological question of the Psalms," Walter Brueggemann adopts a Jewish attitude toward language and identifies Israel's praise as "the duty and delight, the ultimate vocation of the human community; indeed of all creation. . . . Praise is not only a human requirement and a human need, it is also a human delight. We have a resilient hunger to move beyond self."[30] Brueggemann believes that praise is more than a response to God's power, even more than a risky alignment with the divine Other. Praise is "also *constitutive* of theological reality" and of the world in which it is spoken:

> To be sure, praise is addressed to heaven. That is central to Barth and the tradition to which I refer. But it is equally true that praise is spoken by human voices on earth. The address to God indicates that praise is a theological act of profound dramatic importance. Praise is spoken on earth. Inevitably then, praise is not a pure, unmitigated impingement on heaven. The act also impinges on earth. That is, praise is not only a religious vocation, but it is also a social gesture that effects the shape and character of human life and human community.[31]

This argument for the efficacy of praise is congruent with the nature of the Hebrew word itself, the *dabar*. The word is a world-maker and the act of praise is a sacred doing, a *mitzvah*. To the Hebrew, the consequences of an utterance do not merely follow the act of speaking, but "are folded into it so that the speech act includes at least some consequences."[32] The language of praise makes a radical claim for presence,

---

28. Ibid., 355–56.
29. Merton, *Bread in the Wilderness*, 160.
30. Brueggemann, 1.
31. Ibid., 3.
32. Wyschogrod, 178.

and in doing so, is responsible "on earth" for its power. A psalm of praise, explains Brueggemann, "is not a response to a world already fixed and settled, but it is a responsive and obedient participation in a world yet to be decreed and in process of being decreed through this liturgical act."[33] Psalms are responses to the "multiple, restless" world by poets who are themselves "multiple, restless." The poet of praise is a poet decisively *in* the world. Merton echoes this understanding of the psalmist as a poet "in the world" and the Psalms as constitutive praise in *Conjectures of a Guilty Bystander:*

> The universe of the Old Testament is a praising universe, of which man is a living and essential part, standing shoulder to shoulder with the angelic hosts who praise Yahweh: and praise is the surest manifestation of true life. The characteristic of Sheol, the realm of the dead, is that there is no praise in it. The Psalms then are the purest expression of the essence of life in this universe: Yahweh is present to Hs people when the Psalms are sung with triumphant vigor and jubilation (not just muttered and meditated in the individual beard). This presence and communion, this *coming into being* in the act of praise, is the heart of Old Testament worship as it is also of monastic choral praise.[34]

From *The Double Image* (1946) to *Relearning the Alphabet* (1970), Denise Levertov's earlier work is occupied with learning to be "a poet in the world" which, like the world of the ancient Hebrews, is far from being fixed or settled. Like Thomas Merton, Levertov reverences language as a living power and perceives no hiatus between thought and word, word and action. Language *is* enactment. In a 1968 interview, Levertov describes the effect of her political activities on her art: "I feel that it is poetry that led me into political action and not political action which has caused me to write poems more overtly engaged than those I used to write."[35] More than twenty years later, when asked to talk about the relationship of faith and art, she feels "a fraud . . . sitting down to write about faith that works!" and speaks instead of "Work

---

33. Brueggemann, 11.

34. Thomas Merton, *Conjectures of a Guilty Bystander* (New York: Image Books, 1966) 135.

35. Quoted in Kerry Driscoll, "A Sense of Unremitting Emergency: Politics in the Early Work of Denise Levertov," *Critical Essays on Denise Levertov,* ed., Linda Wagner-Martin (Boston: G. K. Hall & Co., 1991) 148.

That Enfaiths."[36] Once again, language leads the way. When she began writing *Mass for the Day of St. Thomas Didymus* (in *Candles in Babylon*), Levertov conceived it only "as an experiment in structure."[37] But by the time she had arrived at the *Agnus Dei,* I discovered myself to be in a different relationship to the material and to the liturgical form from that in which I had begun. The experience of writing the poem—that long swim through waters of unknown depth—had been also a conversion process, if you will.[38] The words of the *Mass* do not merely represent reality, they constitute a new reality. Levertov's poetic comes from a practice of language that is relational, revelatory, and performative—all hallmarks of the Hebraic attitude toward the word. Instead of a "hiatus between seeing and saying," the poet's reception and expression are synchronous, says Levertov: "The poet does not see and then begin to search for words . . . he begins to see and at once begins to say or to sing, and *only in the action of verbalization does he see further.*"[39]

Levertov believes that it is the poet's task to take responsibility for this living power and the consequences of its work in the world. Poetry has "kinetic force": in both writing and reading the poem, something otherwise dormant or stagnant may be moved, may "come into play."[40] "Poetry *can* matter," Levertov's work implicitly answers Dana Gioia's recent question.[41] Language has efficacy. It has alchemical force and dynamic consequences because it is more than the "dress" of thought. The convictions that poetry does matter and that language has efficacy lie at the heart of Levertov's aesthetic ethics, an ethics with which Merton was in accord.

36. Denise Levertov, *New and Selected Essays* (New York: New Directions, 1992) 247.

37. Ibid., 249.

38. Ibid., 250.

39. Levertov, *The Poet in the World,* 73.

40. Ibid., 6.

41. In a critique of the role of contemporary poetry in American culture, Gioia asks outright, "Can poetry matter?" In an article and later book by that name, Gioia explores "the decline of poetry's cultural importance" and its increasing confinement to a subculture which ironically "demeans its own art" through clubby committee work. Gioia believes poetry does matter, assenting with Pound that "If a nation's literature declines, the nation atrophies and decays," and lamenting with William Carlos Williams that "It is difficult / to get the news from poems / yet men die miserably every day / for lack / of what is found there." See *Can Poetry Matter? Essays on Poetry and American Culture* (St. Paul: Graywolf Press, 1992) 2–8, 20.

While it is the language of poetry and the act of writing the poem that leads (over years) to Levertov's "enfaithment," for several years Merton found language to be an impediment to the contemplative life, and was thus engaged in the early nineteen-fifties in working out his understanding of silence, even as he investigated the power of words. Merton's "Tower of Babel" (the longer morality play) was written, says David Cooper, "from the perspective of a man who still believed in the efficacy of separateness," the separateness of the earthly city and the heavenly city.[42] If language belongs to the earthly city and silence to the heavenly city, one must question seriously the efficacy of poetry as an aid to the holy life. Merton's separation of the two cities undergirds his "Theory of Prayer":

> Not in the streets, not in the white streets
> Nor in the crowded porticoes
> Shall we catch You in our words . . .[43]

Language has power, but human beings have appropriated it as a tool for their own gain and destruction:

> . . . the singers are suddenly killed,
> Slain by the blades of their own song—
> The words that clash like razors in the throat
> Severing the tender strings.

> For the things that we utter turn and betray us,
> Writing the names of our sins on flesh and bone
> In lights as hard as diamonds.[44]

Before Merton reappraised poetry and contemplation, his God seemed to dwell not in a world noisy with human speech, but in "those soundless fathoms" of the "armed ocean of peace."[45] Not until Father Louis makes peace with poetry again in the late fifties will he begin to grieve for language in a way that brings him closer to the world. And then in his own way he finds, as Levertov did, that it was language that led him into political action and a more integrated social conscience, not vice versa. A maturing Merton witnesses the world at that pivotal turn

---

42. David Cooper, *Thomas Merton's Art of Denial: The Evolution of a Radical Humanist* (Athens: The University of Georgia Press, 1989) 152.

43. Merton, *Collected Poems,* 179.

44. Ibid., 179, 180.

45. Ibid., 180, 179.

of decade with a new way of seeing: "This morning, before Prime, in the early morning sky, three antiquated monoplanes flew over the monastery with much noise, followed by a great heron."[46]

Levertov's "A Letter to William Kinter of Muhlenberg," offers its gratitude to a "Zaddik" who taught her a way of seeing that contemplates and celebrates those sorts of redeemed juxtapositions:

From the bus, Zaddik,
going home to New York,

I saw a new world
for a while—it was

the gold light on a rocky slope,
the road-constructors talking to each other,

bear-brown of winter woods, and later
lights of New Jersey factories and the vast

December moon.[47]

Like the Hasidim in her heritage, Levertov sees holiness and beauty in whatever is "at hand," making no sharp distinctions between "sacred" and "profane." The Hasidim teach that lodged within the most mundane are "sparks" of the divine, and the task of the human is to redeem those sparks.[48] In "Stepping Westward" the woman in pilgrimage recognizes the chiaroscuro of this "sense of wonder," the "shadow" that keeps that sense pure but not naive, an act of attention, not an indulgence in sentimentality. She is "glad to be"

. . . who, myself,
I am, a shadow
that grows longer as the sun
moves, drawn out

on a thread of wonder.[49]

Shadows and burdens, life's necessary "evils" are transformed along the "thread of wonder," and "begin to be remembered / as gifts,

---

46. Merton, *Conjectures of a Guilty Bystander*, 15.

47. Levertov, *Poems 1960–67*, 46–7.

48. See Ronald Younkins, "Denise Levertov and the Hasidic Tradition," *Descant* 19.1 (Fall 1974) 40–8. The "legend of the sparks" is central to Hasidic ethics.

49. Levertov, *Poems 1960–67*, 165–6.

goods." This is the language of a Hasidic commitment to transformation, of finding the sacred in the profane, and good in evil.

In 1974, Ronald Younkins "eulogizes" the Hasidic influence in Levertov's work as one of those aesthetic forces that declined in the 1960s "as new forces emerged."[50] Younkins believed that ultimately Levertov's Hasidic-like commitment to transformation became harder to maintain in the face of the "stubborn, insistent reality" of the later sixties and her preoccupation with "the burning flesh" of children in Vietnam. Along with several others, Younkins had praised the growth of Levertov's orphic consciousness in her earlier work and her transformative remembrance of burdens as "gifts, goods," but was dismayed by Levertov's later poetic confession in "Advent, 1966" that

> There is a cataract filming over
> my inner eyes. Or else a monstrous insect
> has entered my head, and looks out from my sockets with mul-
>   tiple vision,
>
> seeing not the unique Holy Infant
> burning sublimely, an imagination of redemption,
> furnace in which souls are wrought into new life,
> but, as off a beltline, more, more senseless figures aflame.[51]

Yet unlike several critics, such as Alvin Rosenfeld,[52] Younkins is not willing to pronounce the changes of that time as an aesthetic or ontological failure. He grants her, instead, a necessary restlessness, understanding that her

> search for a proper understanding of the poet's role is not completed. In response to a rapidly changing world Levertov will very likely continue to examine and, if necessary, redefine her function and obligations within the community.[53]

Younkins's understanding of Hasidism's "declining influence" is partial. While Levertov's poems are, in fact, barely visited by *zaddiks*, sparks, and excerpts from Buber's *Tales* after the late sixties, the spiritual

50. Ronald Younkins, "Denise Levertov and the Hasidic Tradition," *Descant* 19.1 (Fall 1974) 40.

51. Denise Levertov, *Poems 1968–1972* (New York: New Directions, 1987) 124.

52. See Alvin H. Rosenfeld, "'The Being of Language and the Language of Being': Heidegger and Modern Poetics," *Boundary 2* 4 (1976) 535–53.

53. Younkins, 47.

and ethical influence of Judaism is by no means lost, but rather absorbed into the larger motifs of her ethics and aesthetics, even into the design of her political engagement. When Hasidism's larger context—Hebraism—is considered, those so-called "tremendous changes" throughout the sixties fall much more congruently into what Levertov continues to believe about her own artistic temperament and habit of working.

A recognition of this larger spiritual ground also puts Levertov's apparently "tremendous changes" in the sixties and seventies into another perspective. Against the larger background of Hebraism, Levertov's decisive alternations of praise and lament resemble the pattern of the ancient Hebrew psalmist. In the Bible it is common to find a psalm of great lyrical beauty, tranquillity, and assurance juxtaposed without explanation or warning by one of nearly unrelieved lamentation, rage, abandonment, or petition for revenge. The celebration and wonder of Levertov's early poetry yields for a time to anger and near despair, as we see in poems from *The Sorrow Dance* (1967) well into *Footprints* (1972), which reveal a Jewish capacity for raw lamentation and rage as Levertov responds to the pressures of history.

Merton's engagement with Hebrew poetry extends beyond the reflections in *Bread in the Wilderness,* his first book about the Psalms, into his own psalming poetry, some of them his own renderings of the originals. "The Captives—a Psalm" brings the lamenting Psalm 137 into the twentieth century with the raw regret, revenge, and grief of the original voice still intact:

> The children of God have died, O Babylon,
> Of thy wild algebra. . . .
>
> Our bodies are greyer than mud.
> There, butterflies are born to be dancers
> And fly in black and blue along the drunken river
> Where, in the willow trees, Assyria lynched our song!
>
> May my bones burn and ravens eat my flesh
> If I forget thee, contemplation!
> May language perish from my tongue
> If I do not remember thee, O Sion, city of vision,
> Whose heights have windows finer than the firmament . . . .[54]

This poem represents the trend of most contemporary poetic "translations" of the Psalms. Rather than a scholarly concern for each word's

---

54. Merton, *Collected Poems,* 212.

archaeology, it employs what George Steiner calls in *After Babel* "understanding as translation," a realization of the "complete semantic event" of the original.[55] While not a translation in the technical sense, Merton's psalm is a trans-lation, in the etymological sense; it *carries* meaning *across* one century and culture to another.

Levertov's and Merton's participation, in their own ways, as poets of political protest is also characteristic of the ancient psalmist's commitment to *communitas*, to the tribe or cult. Theirs is a much older aesthetic than the one which asks, "Can a political poem be poetry?" That question, Levertov explains,

> seems to me a wholly modern one. The Romantic image of the poet was above all one which emphasized his individuality—his difference from other people rather than the ways in which he resembled them; and this led to the elevation of the lyric mode as the type or exemplar of poetry, because it was the most *personal* mode. . . . The Romantic period accelerated the isolation of the poet from the community . . . by seeing the artist as endowed with a special sort of temperament which was not only operative during *the making* of works of art, not only when the poet donned the Bardic mantle, and was actually writing, but which made him at all times supersensitive.[56]

It is in *the making* that the poet as poet is revealed, Levertov has always insisted, not in some sort of "Bohemian style of life." Merton also looks to the origin of *poet—poiein*, "to make, create"—to reappraise the dialogue between poet and contemplative:

> To the true Christian poet, the whole world and all the incidents of life tend to be sacraments—signs of God, signs of His love working in the world. However, the mere fact of having this contemplative vision of God in the world around us does not necessarily make a man a great poet. One must be not a "seer" but also and especially a "creator"—a "maker."[57]

The contemplation required to make a poem that will "sing being" to another does require a certain degree of solitude, Levertov insists, but

55. George Steiner, *After Babel: Aspects of Language and Translation* (London: Oxford University Press, 1975) 7.

56. Denise Levertov, *Light Up the Cave* (New York: New Directions, 1981) 116–118.

57. Merton, *Literary Essays*, 345.

solitude is not to be confused with insulation. This is a solitude that leads one to, not away from, the Other, as she learned from Rilke: "I came to see solitude, and the individual development for which it is a condition, as the only valid ground on which communion of the many, the plural Other of brother-and-sisterhood, can take place."[58] Levertov believes the Romantic era in English poetry bestowed an unfortunate focus on poetic *temperament* rather than poetic *working*:

> It was an easy ego-trip. The public, predictably, began to think of [poets] as undependable fellows, at best whimsical and capricious, at worst, dangerous madmen, and in any case not responsible citizens. The madness of the poet, as seen by the bourgeois, is not the divine madness of the shaman poets of ancient or primitive societies, but a quotidian foolishness and tendency to exaggerate, not worthy to be taken seriously.[59]

The psalmist provides the counter-model in a return to the earliest, most "essential meaning" of *poet:* responsible to the community, focused on the making, the creating, the working. In the original language of the Psalms "the terms for 'meditation' *(higgayôn, sîhâ, hagîg)* are focused on the process of poetic composition itself."[60] In contrast to its usual Christian-Hellenic associations with silence, stillness, and withdrawal, Hebraic "meditation" and poetry take place dynamically, in time, aware of history and also reflexively aware of their own processes. To claim David and Asaph as prototypes of the Romantic poet is simply not defensible. In Harold Fisch's view, the Psalms' apparent subjectivity is actually quite limited, for they are "insistently" dialogic:

> the encounter between the "I" and the "Thou" is the signal for a change not merely in the inner realms of consciousness but in the

---

58. Levertov, *Light Up the Cave,* 286. Levertov is not blind to Rilke's failure in this regard. She continues parenthetically: "(Rilke himself, of course, shunned the many in practice, and can scarcely be claimed as democratic in theory either; yet there are letters of his written in the revolutionary Munich of 1918 which show him to have been too open-hearted, apolitical and aristocratic though he was, to have been altogether irresponsive to that stir of new possibility, even if he soon became disillusioned with it.)"

59. Ibid., 117.

60. Harold Fisch, "Psalms: The Limits of Subjectivity," *Poetry with a Purpose: Biblical Poetics and Interpretation* (Bloomington: Indiana University Press, 1988) 107–8.

realm of outer events. . . . we are emphatically in the realm of political and historical experience. . . . for the God who meets us in
the interior drama of the soul is the same God who acts mightily
in history.[61]

"My own probably unattainable goal," Levertov writes, as poet and
political dissident in 1975, "is to attain to such osmosis of the personal
and the public, of assertion and of song, that no one would be able to
divide our poems into categories. The didactic would be lyrical, the
lyrical would be didactic."[62] These are the words of a contemporary
psalmist and pilgrim who dwells richly in the inner zone, but does not
remain there, who is not afraid to sing the hard songs of history.

By the mid-sixties, Merton was also sure that the new heaven
and earth would be characterized by multiplicity and admixtures of
the kind to which Levertov aspires, not separate cities dividing earth
from heaven, poetry from contemplation: "Eschatology is not an invitation to escape into a private heaven: it is a call to transfigure the evil
and stricken world."[63] What is called for, Merton believes, are meaningful acts of language, "raids on the unspeakable," words uttered and
grounded in Christian hope "where every other hope stands frozen
stiff before the face of the Unspeakable," which he defines in terms of
language and absence:

> It is the void we encounter, you and I, underlying the announced
> programs, the good intentions, the unexampled and universal as-
> pirations for the best of all possible worlds. It is the void that con-
> tradicts everything that is spoken even before the words are said;
> the void that gets into the language of public and official declara-
> tions at the very moment when they are pronounced, and makes
> them ring dead with the hollowness of the abyss.[64]

Heidegger answers the question "What are poets for in a destitute
time?" in part by describing the shepherd-poet who both endures and
reaches into that abyss carved by absence:

61. Ibid., 108–110.
62. Levertov, *Light Up the Cave*, 128.
63. Thomas Merton, *Raids on the Unspeakable* (New York: New Directions,
1966) 5.
64. Ibid., 4.

> In the age of the world's night, the abyss of the world must be ex-
> perienced and endured. But for this it is necessary that there be
> those who reach into the abyss. . . . Mortals, when we think of
> their nature, remain closer to that absence because they are
> touched by presence . . .[65]

The poet's task is to attend to what the abyss "remarks," that is, a fugitive presence that leaves traces that the poet must follow.[66] Thus, "to be
a poet in a destitute time means," Heidegger says, "to attend, *singing,*
to the trace of the fugitive gods. This is why the poet in the time of the
world's night utters the holy."[67]

Heidegger's psalmic image of the poet as a singing "shepherd
of being" is closely related to Denise Levertov's own sense of the
poet's task and its musical relation:

> The *being* of things has inscape, has melody, which the poet picks
> up as one voice picks up, and sings, a song from another, and
> transmits, transposes it, into tones others can hear. And *in his doing
> so* lies the inscape and melody of the poet's *own* being.[68]

In Levertov's aesthetic ethic, the music of inscape is never sung to oneself, for oneself. She is impatient with much "confessional" poetry and
its "miasmic subjectivities."[69] She agrees with Cid Corman that poetry
gives us "not experience thrown as a personal problem on others but
experience as an order that will sing to others."[70] Levertov's poems
preserve the psalmic tradition of moving fluidly between person and
community, idiolect and dialect. The I-we explorations of a Levertov
poem speak of witness, not confession.

The Psalms illustrate the difference, observes Kathleen Norris
in *The Cloister Walk,* "between what the poet Galway Kinnell has
termed the 'merely personal,' or individual, and the 'truly personal,'
which is individual experience reflected back into community and tradition."[71] It is one of the paradoxes of the psalms to be both "an indi-

65. Martin Heidegger, "What are Poets For?" *Poetry, Language, Thought,*
trans. Albert Hofstadter (New York: Harper & Row, 1971) 92–3.

66. Ibid, 94.

67. Ibid. Emphasis mine.

68. Levertov, *The Poet in the World,* 17.

69. Ibid., 46.

70. Ibid., 47.

71. Kathleen Norris, *The Cloister Walk* (New York: Riverhead Books, 1996)
100.

vidual cry and a collective affirmation, a spontaneous overflow of feeling and a formula speaking to us of what we have always known."[72]
This movement from 'I' to 'we' was familiar to the ancient Hebrew,
whose understanding of 'individual' and 'self' is largely alien to contemporary American culture. In her experience as an oblate in a
Dakotan Benedictine monastery, Norris finds that "praying the psalms
is often disconcerting for contemporary people who encounter
Benedictine life: raised in a culture that idolizes individual experience,
they find it difficult to recite a lament when they're in a good mood, or
to sing a hymn of praise when they're in pain."[73] The Benedictines preserve the Jewishness of the psalms, sung daily in a communal setting,
Norris continues, "restoring to our mouths words that have been
snatched from our tongues and relegated to the page, words that have
been privatized and effectively silenced. It counters our tendency to
see individual experience as sufficient for formulating a vision of the
world."[74] Merton observes the communal nature of the Psalms when
he stresses "the importance of the Choral recitation of the Divine
Office": "We all differ, we all have our own problems and troubles, and
yet we all sing together: 'Hear my cry, hearken to my prayer . . .' The
very syntax makes us one."[75]

On the other hand, Levertov argues, the other extreme is also
problematic, and a poem which has ignored the inner experience in
favor of documentation and political polemics will be similarly poor:
"The dangerous contrasting assumption by partisan poets and their
constituencies [is] that the subject matter carries so strong an emotive
charge in itself" that intrinsic beauty and music is rendered unnecessary. A political poetry which is truly poetry will remember its "roots
in song, magic, and the high craft that makes itself felt as exhilarating
beauty even when the content voices rage or utters a grim warning."[76]

Whether Levertov herself is always able to embody such an aesthetic in her politically engaged poetry is matter for much critical comment. Her few "unmusical" or quasi-lyrical lamentations of the sixties
drew much criticism and shaped (practically divided) critical attention
to her work from then on. But the raw lamentation of "Advent 1966"

72. Fisch, 118.
73. Norris, 101.
74. Ibid., 100.
75. Merton, *Bread in the Wilderness*, 119.
76. Levertov, *Light Up the Cave*, 126.

is clearly a distant relative to Psalm 79, Psalm 88, and Psalm 137 in its anguish, its alienation from the spiritual homeland, its reflexive aware-ness of poetic "failure": "How could we sing the Lord's song in a for-eign land?" (Ps. 137:4). Yet, like the psalmist's, Levertov's lamentations are, in fact, shaped by a commitment to transformation, one that must be forged both in the darkest halls of inner being and the cruelest cells of history.

Younkins's understanding of history and poetry is apparently not Jewish enough when he concludes that "a preoccupation with so-cial and political struggle has made transformation impossible" in Levertov's war-era poetry. Levertov keeps a line taut with her Hebraic ancestors precisely *because* she remains in the dark waiting room Advent is meant to be, "seeing *not* the unique Holy Infant / burning sublimely, an imagination of redemption" (emphasis mine). She resembles her Jewish ancestors in attending to the raw facts of history without grasping prematurely for messianic transformation. "There is a cataract filming over / my inner eyes," she psalmically confessed, knowing that the very utterance of that *dabar* in itself stirred some change in both person and history, and that "the poem has a social ef-fect of some kind whether or not the poet wills that it have."[77] The poet of "Advent 1966" resembles the psalmist in a shared capacity to rage and lament for God's apparent absence and abandonment. A mon-strous many-eyed insect shapes sight where transformative divine vi-sion should be.

There is no evidence that Denise Levertov has ever consciously worked to make "redemption" an agenda or force in her art. Rather, "inner colloquy" is what she believes necessary: "what the poet is called on to clarify is not answers but the existence and nature of ques-tions; and his likelihood of so clarifying them for others is made pos-sible only through dialogue with himself."[78] "The true artist / maintains dialogue with his heart" and in so doing, fulfills the task of the poet articulated by Ibsen: "to make clear to himself, and thereby to others, the temporal and eternal questions. . . ."[79] Taken out of con-text, Merton's words in 1958 seem to point to the same aesthetic con-viction, that the poet's "necessity" involves an outering or uttering of inner conversation or contemplation:

77. Levertov, *The Poet in the World*, 6.
78. Ibid., 45.
79. Ibid., 44.

> If the intuition of the poet naturally leads him into the inner sanc-
> tuary of his soul, it is for a special purpose in the natural order:
> when the poet enters into himself, it is in order to reflect upon his
> inspiration and to clothe it with a special and splendid form and
> then return to *display it to those outside.*[80]

But Merton reveals right away that this is a "danger" for one who also seeks to "lose himself in the mystery and secrecy and infinite, tran-scendent reality of God."[81] The only way to reconcile the artist and mystic, Merton concludes, is not "the application of some abstract, *a priori* principle, but purely by a practically practical appeal to the will of God"; one who is called to be a poet (a "Christian" poet, for Merton) will be engaged in both "contemplation" and "declaration."[82] It is in this final point that Merton and Levertov meet; although their paths of arrival are quite different.

In 1964 Levertov admonishes the editors of *things* magazine:

> Therefore if our poetry is to seek truth—and it must, for that is a con-
> dition of its viability, breath to its lungs—then it cannot confine itself
> to what you, the editors of *things,* in your prospectus, have called di-
> rect statement, but must allow for all the dazzle, shadow, bafflement,
> leaps of conjecture, prayers, and dream-substance of that quest. . . .
> We need a poetry not of *direct statement* but of *direct evocation:* a po-
> etry of hieroglyphics, of embodiment, incarnation. . . . [83]

At the root of the word *statement* is *stand;* at the root of *evocation* is a *calling forth* or *out.* From one comes *statue,* from the other a summons to waking, hearing, looking, seeking. Levertov's poetics reject statuary in favor of the contours of the fluid word—what is called out can leap, dazzle, and baffle. What is evoked is called forth, suggesting the pres-ence of something that has lain hidden or sleeping,

> what's not found
> at once, but lies
>
> within something of another nature,
> in repose, distinct.
> Gull feathers of glass . . . [84]

80. Merton, *Literary Essays,* 350.
81. Ibid.
82. Ibid., 353–4.
83. Levertov, *The Poet in the World,* 58, 61.
84. Levertov, "Pleasures," *Collected Earlier Poems,* 90.

Levertov's grammar of presence closely matches what Owen Barfield observes of Hebrew language and theology: like the psalmist, she insists on the creative, creating reality of what lies *within:*

> . . . idolatry is the effective tendency to abstract the sense-content from the whole representation and seek that for its own sake, transmuting the admired image into a desired object. . . . The idols, their Psalmist insisted, were not filled with anything. They were mere hollow pretences of life. They had no "within."[85]

The commandment to not "make for yourself an idol" is not simply an injunction against polytheism on the part of a jealous Jahweh. It has everything to do with language, warning against the comfort of worshipping a name that will stand still with the certainty and authority of *statement*. It is quite a different matter to follow a God whose name declares no such certainty. I AM WHO I AM is a God of Being-in-Becoming whose grammar is so infinite that it allows any "skidding of meaning," any elusive showing of presence, any action in history. The Hebraic divine name is neither purely noun or verb, but a mysterious, dynamic union of both.

Like the psalmist, Denise Levertov expresses no desire to be original, rather to be "originary," to reach back in acts of naming to words which still bear some imprint of that dynamic union. Her practice of language is etymological. "Etymology" comes from the Greek *etumos*, which means the "truest sense." The poet, says Levertov, rejects the "merely cosmetic" in the process of writing the poem with words which reveal the truest sense, "in favor of the attempt to reach back and down to the origins of each image."[86] Merton also demonstrates this "etymological" poetic. When the exiles in Merton's morality play "Tower of Babel" long for work, freedom, and peace, the answer lies in a renewal of words, a re-formation of language that depends upon a will to "relearn the alphabet" in the truest sense. Through Christ's mercy, proclaims the prophet of Merton's poem, "All our words become true":

THE ANCIENT: Ah, yes, I have heard in the past that words could be true.

RAPHAEL: They are meant to bind minds together in the joy of truth.

85. Owen Barfield, *Saving the Appearances: A Study in Idolatry* (New York: Harcourt and Brace, 1965) 110.
86. Levertov, *New and Selected Essays*, 241.

> THOMAS: You must discover new words reborn out of an old
>   time
>   Like seeds from an old harvest.[87]

Merton and Levertov grow as "poets in the world" as they turn their attention to history and their compassion to the Other, a "conversion" or turning parallel with a growing attention to the history of words, the otherness of language, and a vocation as guardians of that living power. Thus, the truth-value of words lies largely in re-membering and caring for the bodies of words no less than for the body politic.

Besides being reverent acts of etymology, Levertov's poems are acts of *midrash,* imaginative interpretations of what her attention to the world's text yields. She composes *midrash*-poems, "not desiring apocrypha / but true revelation," as her Jewish ancestors might say.[88] A midrashic relationship with language is a matter not of rounding off, but opening out:

> Midrash, like the white fire of revelation, is indeed the negative
> space "formed" by the shapes of the letters we write in our effort
> to know God's will. The identity of the pieces says each of us con-
> tains all the elements, and it is always a matter of turbulent,
> though delicate balance. The detachable element suggests a dy-
> namic, not fixed relationship between all the parts.[89]

Notes of a scale, threads, tesserae—are images Levertov uses for the openness and incompletions of the pilgrim way. While each implies the potential of something whole and complete—the melody, the weaving, the mosaic—the task at hand for Levertov is much like the "idea" E. M. Forster says "the novelist must cling to. Not completion. Not rounding off, but opening out."[90] Not answers; questions. Not a major (or even minor) scale whose leading tones seek resolution, but a whole tone scale whose harmonics can lead anywhere, whose direction is penultimacy itself. Merton recognizes this same principle of midrashic incompletion both in the Psalms and in Gregorian chant,

---

87. Merton, *Collected Poems,* 266.

88. Levertov, "At the Edge," *Collected Earlier Poems,* 115.

89. Milgrom, Jo. "At the Altar of Decision: A Workshop in Handmade Midrash," *Parabola* 18:3 (August 1993) 90.

90. E. M. Forster, *Aspects of the Novel* (New York: Harcourt, Brace & World, 1927) 169.

and such an insight looks forward to developments both in his poetry and in Levertov's developing aesthetic:

> The beauty of God is best praised by the men who *reach and realize their limit* knowing that their praise cannot attain to God. It is then that the inarticulate, long *jubilus* takes over in Gregorian chant: some of the extended melismatic developments of the alleluia in the Easter Liturgy, particularly those of the seventh tone. Gregorian chant has a special grace for bringing out this experience of praise that reaches its limit, fails, and yet continues in a new dimension.[91]

"Nothing in [the Baal-Shem] is eschatological, nothing in him presses the claim to be something final, conclusive," says Martin Buber of Hasidism's legendary founder; therefore "his hour is not the hour of redemption, but of a renewal . . . he only seeks to help the redemption, to prepare for it."[92] The poet's necessity is to take words back to their origins, where their light and salt can be restored:

> From love one takes
> **petal** to **rock** and **bléssed**
> away towards
> **descend** . . . .
>
> for love and
> or if in fear knowing
> the risk, knowing
> what one is touching, one does it . . . .[93]

The poet doesn't *accomplish* the redemption of language, suggests Levertov. She cares for the divinity and the ethical power of each word. The language of illusion (*pace* idolatry) is a language which has stopped living in unknowing, has stopped the difficult but necessary "awaiting" and has instead forged its own solutions and finalities.

The Psalms represent the kind of music and language Merton prescribes for an age of destruction: "They are the songs of God in this world. Singing them, we become more fully incorporated into the mystery of God's action in human history."[94] Likewise, the kind of

91. Merton, *Conjectures of a Guilty Bystander,* 136, 137.

92. Martin Buber, *The Origin and Meaning of Hasidism,* ed. and trans. Maurice Friedman (New York: Horizon Press, 1960) 39–40.

93. Levertov, *Poems 1960–67,* 58.

94. Merton, *Bread in the Wilderness,* 59.

"singing" to which a Levertov poem aspires is neither background music nor aesthetic decoration. It is a regard for a fundamental, cosmic *melos*, a counter to the "ill wind" we breathe, "a beating of gongs, efficacious / to drive away devils."[95] It is a power of the most primitive kind of strength and efficacy because it comes from a particular relationship with language itself:

> The poet's task is to hold in trust the knowledge that language, as Robert Duncan has declared, is not a set of counters to be manipulated, but a Power. And only in this knowledge does he arrive at music, at that quality of song within speech which is not the result of manipulations of euphonious parts but of an attention.[96]

Journeys to the Fire's Core

Levertov's "During the Eichmann Trial" takes us into the moral heart of one of the worst crimes of modern history and to the heart of Merton's and Levertov's critique of language. With this poem "the abyss has opened" and Levertov begins to proceed from many of the same common presuppositions as the Hasidim. In Buber's articulation of it,

> . . . it is not for any man to live any longer as though evil did not exist. One cannot serve God merely by avoiding evil; one must engage oneself with it . . . . The sparks of God's light, in their deepest exile that we call evil, yearn for liberation. . . . Their appearance signifies an appearance of God in the things that are seemingly farthest from Him.[97]

Levertov's poem's grammar of ethics begins with an epigraph by Robert Duncan: "When we look up each from his being . . . ." Levertov's three-part poem then "completes" Duncan's clause, not with a solution, but with the troubling question, **"Here is a mystery, / a person, an / other, an I?"**[98] Adolf Eichmann stands before the poet and the world

> isolate in a bulletproof
> witness-stand of glass,

95. Ibid., 33.
96. Levertov, *The Poet in the World*, 54.
97. Buber, *The Origin and Meaning of Hasidism*, 53–4.
98. Levertov, *Poems 1960–67*, 63.

a cage where we may view
ourselves, an apparition

telling us something he
does not know: we are members

one of another.[99]

The world of which Eichmann is part fails to see or hear the Other, and can hold no true conversation, only monologues. The "Unspeakable" has infected both language and relation. L. S. Dembo explores the contrasts between the monological and dialogical life and finds his model for the dialogical Jew, not surprisingly, in Martin Buber, who "sees the Other as an intimate, takes communality as the ideal for human behavior."[100] Dembo finds the "monological" opposite in those who live in an "atomized totality . . . as Sartre depicted it in his pre-Marxist days":

> Whether Jew or gentile, the monologist lives in the I-It relation
> . . . . [and] renouncing monotheism, finds himself in a state ap-
> proaching "nausea" as he beholds the randomness or gratuity into
> which things and language have fallen. . . . hearing only his own
> voice, each finds not the meaning for all carried by Logos but only
> the private meaning he determines for himself. Committed only to
> words and performance or manipulation, not to communication,
> the Monological Jew is an exile in all facets of his life—a self-
> absorbed loner compelled to endure *distance from*, never *relation to*,
> others. That is to say, he inhabits not only a literal Diaspora but a
> psychological and moral one as well.[101]

Dembo then suggests that a relation between monologism and idola-try has an aesthetic counterpart:

> That the Mosaic injunction against graven images could in any
> way be relevant to life in this secular age seems most improbable,
> unless, that is, there is such a thing as aesthetic idolatry, the idolatry

99. Ibid., 65.
100. L. S. Dembo, *The Monological Jew: A Literary Study* (Madison: The University of Wisconsin Press, 1988) 5.
101. Ibid., 5–6. Dembo's own note to this comment tells us he is "para-phrasing the Heraclitean fragment well-known to readers of both Buber and T. S. Eliot: 'Although the Word is common to all, most men act as if each had a private vision of his own'" (175).

inherent in image-making and in the praise of objects or persons that we find in certain kinds of poetry.[102]

In contrast, a dialogical poetry will enact the "I-Thou" relation in the belief that "language is a thoroughly social phenomenon" and the "use" of language therefore "involves one's coming to an understanding with others about situations, not just naming objects."[103]

Adolf Eichmann's crime was at its foundation a profound failure of the imagination, a failure to "look up from his being" and recognize the being of another. "Every man must know 'I am one of countless shards of clay'"—that is the problematic knowledge required; yet it is the knowledge Eichmann lacks. "We are members / one of another" has no meaning for him. Levertov's poem bears the insistent message of Hasidism and of her aesthetic ethic—Everyman means precisely Every Man. No one is beyond the reach of the original "holy sparks." At the same time, no one is exempt from making the inner response to other beings that translates, with outward care, into *caritas*.

The Eichmann trial also provoked a response from Thomas Merton, in the form of "A Devout Meditation in Memory of Adolf Eichmann," an ironic essay in *Raids on the Unspeakable* (1966). The "Author's Advice to His Book" declares, "*Raids*, I think I love you more than the rest," in part because "You have considered the critical challenge of the hour, that of dehumanization, and have dealt with it as you could, with poetry and irony rather than tragic declamation or confessional formulas."[104] Levertov engages the crisis with poetry, Merton with irony, but neither with declamations or confessionals. For Levertov, the crux of the problem is a matter of language and relation, a failure of the dialogical imagination. Merton's concern for language is similar to that in "Theology of Creativity." Here, he explores the semantic dissolution of the word *sane:* "One of the most disturbing facts that came out in the Eichmann trial was that a psychiatrist examined him and pronounced him *perfectly sane*."[105]

---

102. Ibid., 6–7.
103. Ibid., 28–9. Dembo makes a useful connection here with M. M. Bakhtin's theory in *The Dialogical Imagination*.
104. Thomas Merton, *Raids on the Unspeakable* (New York: New Directions, 1966) 2–3.
105. Merton, *Conjectures of a Guilty Bystander*, 45.

David Cooper points to Merton's extensive reading and interest in Erich Fromm's theories of social pathology as the foundation of the Eichmann essay and its critique of *sanity*.[106] But language abuse is deeply embedded in dehumanization and social pathology, so the essay is also about "word sickness," the severance of *sane* from its roots in a healthy, Christian humanism. *Sane* is a word whose origin—Latin *sanus*—means "whole," "healthy." Where language has decayed and become merely representational or instrumental, terms of excess and absolutism abound: *"perfectly* sane," *"totally* sane," *"too* sane." Merton's humanizing corrective brings back the language of indirections, doubt, and penultimacy as he speaks for the future of "modern man": "If he were a little less sane, a little more doubtful, a little more aware of his absurdities and contradictions, perhaps there might be a possibility of his survival."[107] And the truest conversations with God are not perfectly uttered and pure, but may be, in Denise Levertov's words, "oblique prayers."

The need for the poet to be a "custodian" of language in the absurd and contradictory world gained even sharper focus in the poems of Levertov's *The Sorrow Dance* (1967). In the earlier sixties, Levertov firmly set the foundation for the poet's task, exploring the contours of the self, its limits and its powers in service to the poem, its need to make clear the "questions," not to propose answers or solutions. Now at the threshold of new crises in the world's body, Levertov responds with images of the body's knowledge. What we know by "looking up" from our being also has a personal dimension. It is quite natural that Levertov, a poet grounded in the processes of perception, would turn to the body, the very ground of perception. While this body-knowledge and its relationship to language flowers fully in the seventies and early eighties, one can find its beginnings in *O Taste and See* (1964) and *The Sorrow Dance*. Denise Levertov's "originary" relationship with language not only takes her back to the body, where words are grounded in their physical production, sound, and duration; it also leads her to the body of words, to their own beginnings and transformations.

Many of Levertov's poems during these years lament the misuse, erosion, or silencing of language. In exchange for the creative *dabar* are "Those groans men use / passing a woman on the street . . . ."

---

106. David Cooper, *Thomas Merton's Art of Denial: The Evolution of a Radical Humanist* (Athens: The University of Georgia Press, 1989) 244–5.
107. Merton, *Conjectures of a Guilty Bystander*, 49.

> It's a word
>
> in grief-language, nothing to do with
> primitive, not an ur-language;
> language stricken, sickened, cast down . . .[108]

Where once the world disclosed itself, a readable, singable text, it is now "filling up fast with / unintelligible / signs . . . ."[109] Trying to continue the "lived life" in such a world seems nearly impossible. The soul "dwindles sometimes to an ant / rapid upon a cracked surface," or is swallowed up in a numbing grief that prevents the word from creating the necessary knowing:

> Biafra, Biafra, Biafra.
> Hammering the word against my breast:
> trying to make room for more knowledge
> in my bonemarrow:
> And all I see
> is coarse faces grinning, painted by Bosch
> on TV screen as Humphrey
> gets nominated . . .[110]

Language appears to have become a "series of counters to be manipulated," a system of random squeaks and grunts emptied of meaning save its immediate appropriation. Levertov observes that words unmoored from their sacred origin and power can be made to mean anything. It happens in the seemingly innocent exchanges of children:

> Do you want some gum?'
> 'Yes!' 'Well yes means no,
> so you can't have any.'

But "Yes" also "means no" in the language of military logic:

> "It became necessary
> to destroy the town to save it,"
> a United States major said today.
> He was talking about the decision
> by allied commanders to bomb and shell the town
> regardless of civilian casualties
> to rout the Vietcong' . . .[111]

108. Levertov, "The Mutes," *Poems 1960–67*, 196.
109. Ibid., 198.
110. Levertov, "Biafra," *Poems 1968–72*, 16.

Levertov is certainly one of those poets to whom Merton could be referring when he argues that "poets are perhaps the ones who, at the present moment, are most sensitive to the sickness of language."[112] In his essay "War and the Crisis of Language," Merton recognizes that rampant "word sickness" infects not only military, but also religious establishments. His experiments with "anti-poetry" and his reflections about language naturally lead him to "observe that religion too has reacted to the same spastic upheaval of language" and curiously enough, he says, in a "revival of *glossolalia*—'speaking in tongues'":[113]

> . . . there is here a significant implication that ordinary language is not good enough, and that there is something else which is at once more real and less comprehensible. Has ordinary language somehow failed? . . . He who speaks in an unknown tongue can safely speak without fear of contradiction. His utterance is definitive in the sense that it forecloses all dialogue.[114]

Both Levertov and Merton are acutely aware of the rise of a tongue which "forecloses all dialogue," which gnostically secures meaning for the few who know the shibboleth. The "word sickness"[115] of the late sixties is, in effect, a rampant monology. There is an "utter finality" to monological speech that is totally alien to the poet's relationship with language, especially to a poet whose Hebraic ancestry assumed that the word is constantly, unendingly, in conversation. Merton uses precisely the same example as Levertov of military *glossolalia* and monologism: the words of the major who shelled the South Vietnamese town of Bentre, reducing "bombing" and "saving" to synonyms:

---

111. Ibid., 20–1.

112. Merton, "War and the Crisis of Language," *The Critique of War: Contemporary Philosophical Explorations,* ed. Robert Ginsberg (Chicago: Henry Regnery Co., 1969) 99.

113. Ibid., 101.

114. Ibid., 102–3.

115. Ibid., 99. Merton explains the origin of the term "word sickness": "Long before George Steiner pointed out that the German language was one of the casualties of nazism and World War II, Brice Parain in France had studied the 'word sickness' of 1940, the moral illness of journalese and political prose that accompanied the collapse of France. In proportion as the country itself accepted the denatured prose of Vichy—in which peace meant aggression and liberty meant oppression—it lost its identity and its capacity for valid action. It succumbed to 'a full armed language without practical application.' This, Parain reflected, had al-

> A classic example of the contamination of reason and speech . . .
> an insatiable appetite for the tautological, the definitive, the *final*.
> It is the same kind of language and logic that Hitler used for his
> notorious "final solution." The symbol of this perfect finality is the
> circle. An argument turns upon itself, and the beginning and end
> get lost: it just goes round and round its own circumference . . . .
> They were thought to be Vietcong and were therefore destroyed.
> By being destroyed they became Vietcong for keeps; they entered
> "history" definitively as our enemies, because we wanted to be on
> the "safe side," and "save American lives"—as well as Vietnam.[116]

Language ceases to be dialogical when it is no longer perceived to be
a living thing; when it is an instrument, not an organism. It is an "It,"
not a "Thou," an object that can become appropriated for any use.
Emptied of its constitutive power, language becomes merely a tool,
and the original covenant between word and world is broken. Now it
can only represent, can only be an abstraction or shadow of something
else. In Levertov's aesthetic logic, the poet is the "instrument" of the
word; the word is not the instrument of the poet or of anyone else.[117]

Both Thomas Merton's and Denise Levertov's political protest
is clearly a protest of language abuse. They believe, in Levertov's
words, that language is "a *power*, something held in sacred trust,"[118]
and that "One should speak words," as the Hasid does, "as if the heavens were opened in them, and as if it were not so that you take the
word in your mouth, but rather as if you entered into the word."[119]
Levertov's sequence, "Relearning the Alphabet," the title poem of a
volume (1970) Merton would not live to read, is testimony to this continued relationship with language, of a need to re-enter the "ur-language" and serve it in acts of renewal. It speaks clearly of her
Hebrew-like commitment to the covenant between word and world.
As though it had been inspired by the Jewish mystics, this sequence
embodies "a theory of letters . . . which dealt with [each letter] as with
the elements of the world and with their intermixture as with the in-

---

ready happened before, in World War I, when words meant one thing in the
trenches and another behind the lines."

116. Ibid., 105–6.

117. Levertov, *The Poet in the World*, 4.

118. Ibid.

119. Martin Buber, *The Legend of the Baal-Shem*, trans. Maurice Friedman
(New York: Schocken Books, 1969) 39.

wardness of reality."[120] Against the backdrop of an unintelligible "world of terror," Levertov composes her own psalm which seeks to return to an ur-language and the ground of being, "to find 'I-who-I am' again."[121] The language Levertov seeks is not one she must create; it will not be "original." Rather, one must take the title's verb seriously: the process is "re-learning" a language antecedent to her own utterance of it.

The twenty-six parts of the sequence are headed by letters of the alphabet, recalling Psalm 119, an alphabetical acrostic beginning with *aleph*, the first letter of the Hebrew alphabet. While the Levertov poem is obviously not structured as formally as the Hebrew acrostic, it shares with its psalmic ancestor a supreme awareness of its own textuality. Words, phrases, and images from previous poems return to participate in the "faring // forth into the grace of transformed continuance."[122] The poet turns, for example, "from the unbridged rush of waters towards / 'Imagination's holy forest'" much the way she did from her sister Olga's alien inscape, where "everything flows."[123] "Wanting the Moon" is revisited in the 'M' poem: "Honest man, I wanted / the moon and went out to sea to touch the moon . . ."[124] With kinetics recalling "With Eyes at the Back of Our Heads," with the etymological force of "Joy," and with the place of destination prefiguring "An Interim: Part I," the poet re-learns the inward reality of 'I' and 'J':

> I go stumbling
>   (head turned)
>   back to my origins:
>   (if that's where I'm going)
>   to joy, my Jerusalem.[125]

The kind of grief Levertov risked denying after Olga's death is translated into the basic elements of language in poem 'F': "The *vowels of affliction*, of unhealed / *not to feel it.*" Yet Levertov speaks as though she had been directly inspired by the psalmist or the Zaddik when she

---

120. Ibid.
121. Levertov, *Poems 1968–72*, 92.
122. Ibid., 92.
123. Levertov, "Olga Poems," *Poems 1960–67*, 204–5.
124. Levertov, *Poems 1968–72*, 94.
125. Ibid., 92.

declares that, "uttered," those unhealed vowels are "transformed in utterance / to song."[126]

The very first line of "Relearning the Alphabet" recalls the journey back to the origin of "joy" in the sequence "Joy" from *The Sorrow Dance:*

A

Joy—a beginning. Anguish, ardor.
To relearn the ah! of knowing in unthinking
joy . . .[127]

"Ah!" is that echoic *"iu"* she discovered earlier as "joy's" origin. In the semantic scheme suggested by Levertov's "organic" acrostic, "ah!" mingles "joy" and "anguish" and purifies them by fire through "ardor," a word for passion which itself suggests fire. The poem takes "joy" itself, a word with a history in both her text and in a larger context, as "a beginning." *"A"* beginning, not *"the"* beginning—the indefinite article is given enormous semantic weight as the first word of the letter—A—in question. That indefiniteness is consonant with the spirit of *midrash,* to which so much of Levertov's aesthetic belongs. There is no definite beginning of the alphabet any more than there is a finality of the Word. The Hebraic encounter with the Text/text is everlastingly indeterminate. In "Relearning the Alphabet" we have an apt enactment of Levertov's midrashic poetic. Unlike the monologies she has been lamenting, these utterances declare nothing final; their destination is the "fire's core," an image Paul Lacey calls Levertov's "signature for the contrarieties of joy."[128] The word *is* the pilgrim path:

All utterance
takes me step by hesitant step towards

T

—yes, to continuance: into
that life beyond the dead-end where
. . . . I was lost.[129]

126. Ibid., 91.
127. Levertov, *Poems 1968–72,* 90.
128. Paul Lacey, "A Poetry of Exploration," *The Inner War: Forms and Themes in Recent American Poetry* (Philadelphia: Fortress Press, 1972) 130.
129. Levertov, *Poems 1968–72,* 98.

Being "lost," in this poem, is the opposite of being in pilgrimage. The condition of being lost is the result of nurturing "something in me that wants to cling / to *never*" and other absolutes, of a "looking for" instead of a "looking up," of seeking solutions instead of living in questions:

> Lost in the alphabet
> I was looking for
> the word I can't now say
>
> (love)
>
> and am called forth
> unto the twelfth letter
> by the love in a question.[130]

This poem is less a matter of calling upon the alphabet than of being "called forth" by the letters themselves, of being summoned by language to the mysterious inscape of *caritas:*

> The forest is holy.
> The sacred paths are of stone.
> A clearing.
> The altars are shifting deposits of pineneedles,
>   hidden waters,
>   streets of choirwood,
> not what the will
> thinks to construct for its testimonies.[131]

The construction of "testimonies" involves a way of seeing alien to the pilgrim poet who sees the world "only as / looked-up-into out of earth," and whose way of traveling is open to the leading of imagination:

> V
>
> Vision sets out
> journeying somewhere,
> walking the dreamwaters:
> arrives
> not on the far shore but upriver,
> a place not evoked, discovered.[132]

The poet's journey to the "fire's core" has transformed utterance from the dead-level speech of monologue to dialogue and trust in the

130. Ibid., 94.
131. Ibid., 99.
132. Ibid., 99–100.

power of the Other, inseparable with in-sight and with the power of language:

S

. . . .
The door I flung my weight against
was constructed to open   out
                                                 towards me.
In-seeing
to candleflame's
blue ice-cavern, measureless,

may not be forced by sharp
desire. . . .[133]

On the eve of her most intense revolutionary activity, the "anguish" and "ardor" of political protest, Levertov learns, paradoxically, that "Transmutation is not under the will's rule." To put it in terms of a holy grammar, relearning the alphabet is a matter of dwelling in prepositions, not in the objects of transitive verbs that the will designs or dictates:

Y

Vision will not be used.
Yearning will not be used.
Wisdom will not be used.
Only the vain will
strives to use and be used,
comes not to fire's core
but cinder.[134]

The "vain" will attempts to call forth "presence" only to name it and secure it. But the poet whose path is language finds that "Absence has not become/a presence." By the time the poet reaches 'Z', the blaze from the fire's core

        addresses
a different darkness:
absence has not become

133. Ibid., 97.
134. Ibid., 100.

the transformed presence the will
looked for,
but other: the present,

that which was poised already in the ah! of praise.[135]

The sounds with which Levertov ends her "organic" acrostic
bring A and Z, *aleph* and *tav,* Alpha and Omega, full circle. But it is not
a closed circle; it is more akin to the "clearing" in the holy forest, full
of "shifting pineneedles." To re-learn the alphabet at this stage of pilgrimage does not mean to establish the letters, by magic or by faith.
The conversation depends instead on the discovery, by indirections, of
the *present* that lies hidden and poised within elusive *presence.*

Merton urges the reader of *Raids on the Unspeakable* to consider
"the critical challenge of the hour" in large part as a crisis of words.
Levertov takes up such a challenge in "Relearning the Alphabet" by returning to the "fire's core" of language. Merton "dealt with it as [he]
could" in the poetry of *Cables to the Ace* (1968), an experimental book
that critiques language in our age as "familiar liturgies of misunderstanding," words that have strayed as far as possible from their "fire's
core," words infected by the emptiness of advertising and officialese,
by the garbled grammar of the Unspeakable. *Cables to the Ace* is perhaps Merton's most ironic "raid on the unspeakable." There he holds
up portraits of language tutored by Mammon, Moloch, and Belial, as
he advises the Reader, "My attitudes are common and my ironies are
no less usual than the bright pages of your favorite magazine."[136]
Those ironies are alive, for example, in his parody of Yeats' "The Lake
Isle of Innisfree":

> I will get up and go to Marble country
> Where deadly smokes grow out of moderate heat
> And all the cowboys look for fortunate slogans
> Among horses' asses.[137]

The line once taut to the Word seems to be nearly severed, he warns:
"the sayings of the saints are put away in air-conditioned archives";
your "Words replaced by moods," and "your confessions are filed /

135. Ibid.
136. Thomas Merton, "Prologue," *Cables to the Ace,* in *The Collected Poems of
Thomas Merton* (New York: New Directions, 1977) 395.
137. Ibid., #61, 434.

In the dialect / Of bureaux and electrons."[138] "In holy ways there is never so much must," the "comic" poet of Merton's Lograire speaks,[139] but in the land of the Unspeakable, the cables are stretched taut to "must," to the grim requirements of appointments, strategies, circuits, and vectors:

> And each must know the number of his key
> With a key in his eye and an eye for numbers
> A number of appointments
> A truly legal score:
> And each must find his logical apartment.[140]

Poetry dwells in quite a different place, where "must" implies sacred possibility:

> I think poetry must
> I think it must
> Stay open all night
> In beautiful cellars.[141]

And the poet does, too, as he "walk[s] away from this poem"—"I am about to make my home / In the bell's summit" and "learn by the cables of orioles," keeping a line taut to a very different source of words:

> I will call the deep protectors out of the ground
> The givers of wine
> The writers of peace and waste
> And sundown riddles.[142]

In Tension Toward the New

The poets of both *Cables to the Ace* and *Relearning the Alphabet* turn a prophet's ear to language, fulfilling what Merton himself says of prophecy in "A Message to Poets":

> To prophesy is not to predict, but to seize upon reality in its moment of highest expectation and tension toward the new. This ten-

---

138. Ibid., #2, 396; #3, 397; #5, 398.
139. Merton, *Collected Poems*, 459.
140. Merton, *Cables to the Ace*, #52, 431.
141. Ibid., #53, 431.
142. Ibid, #87, 453.

sion is discovered not in hypnotic elation but in the light of every-day existence. Poetry is innocent of prediction because it is itself the fulfillment of all the momentous predictions hidden in every-day life.[143]

Levertov's own terms for the role of the prophet in poetry are con-tained in the 1981 essay "Poetry, Prophecy, Survival," where she makes clear the connections between poet and prophet which are often em-bodied in "Staying Alive" and other politically engaged poems. Hers is an essentially Hebraic understanding of the "vatic" role that keeps her grounded "in the world," and writing out of the "light of everyday existence." Sir Philip Sidney praised the psalmist David for "handling his prophecy" like a poet, an exemplary *Vates*,[144] and Levertov returns, like Sidney, to an older, essentially Hebraic understanding of the vatic and prophetic. Her attention to time, her witness of history, her explo-ration of a language that disturbs conventions and powers—all resemble the Hebrew prophet, the *nabi*, whose role was not limited to prediction of the future.

The *nabi*-prophet has a crucial role to play in the relationships among word, human being, and divine Being. First of all, as Buber ex-plains, the *nabi* is not a translator or interpreter of an antecedent lan-guage, something already spoken:

> the *nabi* does not convey a finished speech that has already be-come audible; rather he shapes to sound a secret, soundless speech, in the human sense, pre-verbal, in the divine, primordially verbal, as the mouth of a person shapes to sound the secret, soundless speech of his innermost being. . . . For the prophetic word of the Bible, in contrast to that of the Delphic oracle, means that the originating speech and the finished speech are Biblically identical, whereas in the Hellenic an ecstatic babbling must first be transmitted into ordered speech.[145]

Second, the Hebrew *nabi* works not merely in one direction, "from above to below," but as a mediator *between* God and man. The role of the *nabi* is to aid the dialogue between human and divine, not merely

143. Thomas Merton, *Raids on the Unspeakable*, 159.

144. Philip Sidney, *An Apology for Poetry. The Golden Hind: An Anthology of Elizabethan Prose and Poetry*, eds. Roy Lamson and Hallett Smith, revised ed. (New York: W. W. Norton & Co., 1956) 274.

145. Buber, *The Origin and Meaning of Hasidism*, 156–7.

to bear a proclamation or announcement: "The *nabi* only exists in the relation between deity and humanity, as the mediator of the speech, the 'bearer of the word in the vertical plan.'"[146] And third, unlike the Greek prophet, who serves as a "mouthpiece" for the gods, the *nabi* is not appropriated in part, in *piece*, for divine purposes. Instead, Buber explains, "It is decisively important to observe that God does not say here that he wants to use the human mouth as His own: *the whole human person* shall be as a mouth to him. That the Greek prophet is not and cannot be. His mouth 'speaks forth,' not his person."[147] God and human retain their otherness and consequently, their wholeness, their *sanity*, as "the Biblical distance between God and man is still preserved."[148]

The similarities of the *nabi's* language to Denise Levertov's organic poetics as well as to Merton's aesthetic in the sixties are important. "Form is never more than a revelation of content" Levertov has said. The things of the world speak in their own inherent forms, and it is up to the poet to unveil, discover, or reveal them, not to find or invent forms to contain them. Received forms, poetic or otherwise, are often incapable, in Levertov's view, of revealing the "strawness of a straw,"[149] the divine spark she believes present in all created things and beings. When the poet attends to the world with discipline, intensity, and reverence, form arises in consort with content, in revelations of *quidditas*. The relationship of form to content, moreover, can only be discovered "in the work, not before it," Levertov asserts.[150] The *nabi*, the prophet poet delivers a language "in the grasp of a hand," raw, not received. Merton's "message to poets" is nearly synonymous in its understanding of prophecy and the poem's origin. "We who are poets," he says,

> know that the reason for a poem is not discovered until the poem itself exists. The reason for a living act is realized only in the act itself. This meeting is a spontaneous explosion of hopes. That is why it is a venture in prophetic poverty.[151]

146. Ibid., 155.
147. Ibid., 156–7.
148. Ibid., 156.
149. Levertov, *The Poet in the World*, 51.
150. Ibid., 9.
151. Merton, *Raids on the Unspeakable*, 155.

In her review of *Relearning the Alphabet,* Sr. Bernetta Quinn calls Levertov a "prophet in the Flannery O'Connor sense."[152] Among the many intersections of Levertov's and O'Connor's aesthetics, including the practice of organic form,[153] is their shared belief that "ordinary speech no longer suffices" in our day, as Levertov puts it.[154] In "Poetry, Prophecy, Survival," Levertov says,

> In this dangerous, extraordinary time we can't, I feel, rely solely on the subtle and delicate possibilities of change implicit in the giving and receiving of all art; we also need direct images in our art that will waken, warn, stir their hearers to action; images that will both appall and empower.[155]

Levertov was criticized by many for recording appalling, "unpoetic" scenes of war:

> . . . the scheduled breaking open of breasts whose milk
> runs out over the entrails of still-alive babies,
> transformation of witnessing eyes to pulp-fragments,
> implosion of skinned penises into carcass-gulleys.[156]

Abraham Heschel explains that it is not simply the prophet's words that are "enlarged," but that the prophet herself feels and perceives events and experiences as much larger, more consequential, than the ordinary person. There is no hiatus between eye and tongue:

> Indeed, the sort of crimes and even the amount of delinquency that fill the prophets of Israel with dismay do not go beyond that which we regard as normal, as typical ingredients of social dynamics. To us a single act of injustice—cheating in business, exploitation of the poor—is slight; to the prophets, a disaster. To us injustice is injurious to the welfare of the people; to the prophets it

152. Sister Bernetta Quinn, O.S.F, "Review of *Relearning the Alphabet,*" *Denise Levertov: Selected Criticism,* ed. Albert Gelpi (Ann Arbor: The University of Michigan Press, 1993) 29.

153. Flannery O'Connor, *Mystery and Manners: Occasional Prose,* eds. Sally and Robert Fitzgerald (New York: Farrar, Straus & Giroux, 1969). "Art requires," says O'Connor, "a delicate adjustment of the outer and inner worlds in such a way that, without changing their nature, they can be seen through each other" (34–5).

154. Levertov, *New and Selected Essays,* 149.

155. Ibid.

156. Levertov, "Life at War," *Poems 1968–72,* 122.

is a deathblow to existence: to us, an episode; to them, a catastrophe, a threat to the world. . . .[157]

Neither Merton nor Levertov is "thinking too exclusively of the *predictive* sense of the word *prophecy*"[158] when they consider the vatic role of the poet in the world. Merton identifies the "Christian poet" as "the successor to David and the Prophets; he contemplates what was announced by the poets of the Old Testament; he should be, as they were, a mystic, full of divine fire."[159] Levertov also looks to the ancient Hebrew prophets for her model, finding several roles for their utterance: threat, promise, reproach, admonition. But to those she adds her own: "above all . . . the prophets provide words of witness."[160] It is within the role of witness that Levertov's prophet sings in consort with the psalmist. She insists that, along with lamentations for "the whole flesh of the still unburned," "a poetry of praise is equally necessary" in a time of dearth, "that we not be overcome by despair but have the constant incentive of envisioned positive possibility—and because praise is an irresistible impulse of the soul."[161]

The praise essential to poetry and prophecy has nothing to do with the anesthetic verse of the "insensitively cheerful"; authentic praise, "that profound impulse . . . is trivialized if its manifestations do not in some way acknowledge their context of icy shadows."[162] This praise, as Levertov defines it, is not an "escape—not instead of but as well as developing our consciousness of what Man is doing to the world and how we as individuals are implicated" and it takes all the power of the imagination, she continues, to "create works that celebrate" goodness and beauty under the shadow of Babel.[163] When Levertov looks at the ancient Jewish psalmist-prophets and their efficacy she sees that "what they had to say had to be said *powerfully*, with imagination and linguistic resourcefulness" in order to do more than re-present; rather, the call is to transform:

157. Abraham Heschel, "What Manner of Man is the Prophet?" *Parabola: Prophets and Prophecy* 21.1 (February 1996) 6.

158. Levertov, *New and Selected Essays,* 147.

159. Merton, *Literary Essays,* 344.

160. Levertov, *New and Selected Essays,* 148.

161. Ibid., 146.

162. Ibid.

163. Ibid., 144.

prophetic utterance, like poetic utterance, transforms experience and moves the receiver to new attitudes. . . . they are "inspired," they breathe in revelation and breathe out new words; and by so doing they transfer over to the listener or reader a parallel experience, a parallel intensity, which impels that person into new attitudes and new actions.[164]

Levertov's comments in "Poetry, Prophecy, Survival" indicate an affinity with her Jewish ancestors that not only directs her *making* (poems "hard as the floor"), but her role in the service of art and society. Levertov's poetry consistently moves from 'I' to 'we'; her art has a social function that is fundamental to the utterance of both psalmist and prophet. To witness like a prophet is to praise and lament like a psalmist.

Merton's "Message to Poets," originally delivered in 1964 in Mexico City to a group of new Latin-American poets[165] concludes not with the familiar liturgies of secular aesthetics, but with a credo and liturgy both ancient and modern, clothed in a contemporary psalmist-prophet's imperatives for language:

Word-magic is an impurity of language and of spirit in which words, deliberately reduced to unintelligibility, appeal mindlessly to the vulnerable will. *Let us* deride and parody this magic with other variants of the unintelligible, if we want to. But it is better to prophesy than to deride. . . . *Let us* obey life, and the Spirit of Life that calls us to be poets, and we shall harvest many new fruits for which the world hungers . . . . *Let us* be proud of the words that are given to us for nothing; not to teach anyone, not to confute anyone, not to prove anyone absurd, but to point beyond all objects into the silence where nothing can be said. We are not persuaders. We are children of the Unknown. [166]

The direction Merton's own poetic and aesthetic journey appeared to be taking in the late nineteen-sixties pointed him, like Levertov, beyond all wordiness to the Word. Guy Davenport finds it tempting "to see a visual commentary on the conversation" between Merton and Levertov in the Meatyard photos that document their visit that December day in 1967 at Gethsemani.[167] He sees their

164. Ibid., 148.
165. Merton, *Raids on the Unspeakable*, 159.
166. Ibid., 159, 160.
167. Meatyard, 93.

conversation about self-immolation re-imaged by Meatyard's camera in fiery forms:

> Levertov is seated in front of an active fireplace. The vivid wood grain of the cedar altar over the hearth opening recalls flames. Another image of the altar is superimposed in that of the gas heater. . . . A second image of the altar candle hovers under a thermometer, which blends together with an altar icon. (93)

What both Denise Levertov and Thomas Merton may have shared that day together, but certainly in their parallel journeys as poets in the 1960s, was a conviction about language that took words back to the "fire's core" where the purifying heat and light of the Word could be restored in the world.

It is also tempting to speculate about the various parallels and divergences that might have existed in the 1990s between the poetic vocations of Denise Levertov and Father Louis. Levertov continues to be a vital poet in the world, harvesting "new fruits for which the world hungers" in the recent poems of volumes such as *Evening Train* (1992) and *Sands of the Well* (1996). Nearly twenty-five years after Merton's death, Levertov remembers "one of the tapes of informal lectures Merton gave at Gethsemani in the 1960's," and the fruit of her memory is a poem, "On a Theme by Thomas Merton." Its lines imagine the suffering of a God whose call goes unanswered, whose effort at conversation is unmet:

> 'Adam, where are you?'
> > God's hands
> palpate darkness, the void
> that is Adam's inattention,
> his confused attention to everything,
> impassioned by multiplicity, his despair.[168]

God gropes for a "Fragmented Adam" who dizzies himself "like a child / at a barbaric fairgrounds," absent both to himself and to the God who "suffers the void that is his absence."[169] The multiplicity that leads to despair is the chaotic shape-shifting of a culture and an age which has lost its mooring in the covenantal *dabar*, the Word in the world.

168. Levertov, *Evening Train* (New York: New Directions, 1992) 113.
169. Levertov, *Evening Train*, 113.

The "true artist" of the Toltec poem to which both Merton and Levertov responded is "multiple" in a radically different way: fluid in unfolding, restless as a pilgrim is restless, "faring / forth into the grace of transformed / continuance."[170] Both Levertov and Merton became "poets in the world" during the decade of the sixties in ways which took them forever out of the "logical apartments" of dogma, either aesthetic or ecclesiastical, and into the geography of the *oikoumenikos*, "the whole inhabited world," the open house of God, which is where they once met, and where the conversation continues:

> "No, God's in the wilderness next door
> —that huge tundra room, no walls and a sky roof . . ."[171]

170. Levertov, *Poems 1968–72*, 92.
171. Levertov, *Oblique Prayers*, 78.

Thomas Merton and James Laughlin:
Two Literary Lives in Letters

David D. Cooper

IN MEMORY OF J. LAUGHLIN, 1914–1997

I.

Your letters are quite the most stimulating that I receive.
—James Laughlin to Thomas Merton, 11 August 1959[1]

If making close friends is part of the hard work of becoming a whole person, the friendship of Thomas Merton and James Laughlin reveals a remarkable labor of mutual self-completion. The story of their friendship begins in the early 1940s when Laughlin inaugurated his New Directions publishing enterprise in Greenwich Village and Merton forsook all worldly enterprise for monastic life at the Abbey of Gethsemani, a Trappist monastery hidden in rural Kentucky's knob country. Merton and Laughlin continued to write each other's lives in letters until Merton's death in 1968.

During their twenty three-year friendship and literary collaboration, Merton and Laughlin, in addition to meeting annually at Gethsemani, exchanged 739 letters: 403 letters from Merton to Laughlin (dated 28 September 1945 through 28 November 1968) and 336 from Laughlin (14 May 1945 to 4 December 1968). Thomas Merton's letters to James Laughlin are preserved at the New Directions

---

1. The Thomas Merton Studies Center Archives. Bellarmine College, Louisville, Kentucky.

Archive in the basement of Laughlin's home in Norfolk, Connecticut. Those original letters will eventually be deposited, along with the entire New Directions Archive, in Harvard University's Houghton Library. In the early 1960s Thomas Merton began making single carbons of his letters to Laughlin. Ninety carbons (dated 29 January 1960 to 19 July 1968) are collected in the Thomas Merton Studies Center at Bellarmine College, Louisville, Kentucky. The Bellarmine collection also includes 201 original Laughlin letters to Merton, dated 15 March 1949 to 4 December 1968. The balance of Laughlin's letters are filled out by carbons and photocopies from the Norfolk archives.

Drawing on the entire extant correspondence, I edited *Thomas Merton and James Laughlin: Selected Letters*, published by W. W. Norton in 1997 as the sixth volume of James Laughlin's correspondence with principal New Directions writers, including William Carlos Williams, Delmore Schwartz, Ezra Pound, Kenneth Rexroth, and Henry Miller. For that edition, I chose 176 Merton letters and 40 letters from Laughlin. I included one letter from Merton to Robert M. MacGregor, long-time managing editor at New Directions, and a letter from Laughlin to a special friend of Thomas Merton's written after Merton's death and included as an Epilogue. In addition to respecting Mr. Laughlin's desire that the volume include many more Merton letters than his own, I also cut and abridged material from the extant correspondence that pertains to banal business detail, routine copyediting matters, dead-end projects, or extreme marginalia. In selecting letters for the Norton edition, I linked certain narrative lines in Merton and Laughlin's long and fulsome correspondence that shed light on the following: (1) their personal and professional relationship, especially the bearing Merton's strong sense of moral imperative as a writer had on Laughlin's vision of social purpose and ethical accountability as a publisher; (2) the role that Laughlin played in facilitating Merton's development as a poet and writer, including discussions of books Laughlin frequently posted to Gethsemani, the writers he encouraged Merton to read, and the visits Laughlin arranged for Merton with other New Directions authors; (3) critical incidents in their private lives balanced by renderings of their ordinary routines, especially Merton's at the monastery; (4) their comments and reflections on important public events—literary, social, and political; and (5) the genesis and evolution of Merton's books published by New Directions. I tried to make selections that forge these narrative lines together into a coherent story of two literary lives told in letters.

II.

*The little paperback anthology celebrating your [New Directions] an-
niversary sounds good. Twenty fifth! I got in pretty near the ground
floor, didn't I? It makes me feel good to realize that I have been with you
all the way since the first little man and the funny horse appeared on
your letterheads. In fact long before Mark [Van Doren] sent you my
poems I had sent you some from St. Bonaventure in 1940 or 41.*

Thomas Merton to James Laughlin, 5 April 1961[2]

Son of New Zealand-born watercolorist Owen Merton and
American art student Ruth Calvert Jenkins, Thomas Merton, born in
1915, never knew the emotional stability or financial security that
cushioned James Laughlin's childhood. Laughlin's father, Henry
Hughart Laughlin—whose grandfather, along with five uncles,
founded the prominent Jones and Laughlin Steel Corporation in 1856,
a bulwark of Pittsburgh's booming Gilded Age steel business—sent
his son to the finest schools. From his birth in 1914 James Laughlin
rode a predictable American trajectory of upper-class status and success. He first attended the private Arnold School in Pittsburgh. In an
effort to spare their sons the unpleasantness of the Depression in
America, Laughlin's parents sent James and his brother to the exclusive boarding school Le Rosey near Geneva, Switzerland, where his
classmate, Muhammad Reva Pahlavi, future Shah of Iran, was
whisked off by his bodyguards every Saturday night for amusement in
Geneva. Next came terms spent at the Eaglebrook School in Deerfield,
Massachusetts. Laughlin's admittance into Harvard University in 1932
was virtually guaranteed by his prep school tenure at the famous
Choate School in Wallingford, Connecticut (not far from his wealthy
aunt's country estate near Norfolk), where his teacher Dudley Fitts
first introduced Laughlin to as yet uncelebrated contemporary authors
and poets like Ezra Pound and Gertrude Stein.

Thomas Merton's boyhood is a study in contrasts. On the opening page of *The Seven Storey Mountain* (1948), his best-selling autobiography, Merton chronicled the year of his birth in the chilling and stark
imagery of a world war convulsing the French landscape a few hundred kilometers north of his birthplace in Prades, the South of France.
He noted the corpses of soldiers strewn among rotting horse carcasses

2. David D. Cooper, ed., *Thomas Merton and James Laughlin: Selected Letters*
(New York: W. W. Norton & Co., 1997) 157.

along the river Marne and the French forests denuded by artillery barrages. Faced with chronic money problems and the uncertainties of a violent war being waged in Europe, the Mertons moved to America, launching a long period of geographic instability, financial insecurity, and emotional disruption that would affect Thomas Merton's early years. After his mother died when he was only six years old, his father set out on a restless quest for artistic inspiration. On occasion Merton would accompany Owen on painting trips to Bermuda, Provincetown, and back to the South of France. Most of the time the boy was left with maternal grandparents on Long Island or with family friends in France or an uncle and aunt in England.

Merton's boyhood, in a word, was rudderless, without fixed horizon. His early education was frequently and unpredictably disrupted. He bounced from public grade schools on Long Island to a local school on Bermuda where he often skipped class, to a French lycee in Montauban where the French boys ruthlessly picked on him because of his big ears, and back to middling boarding schools in England. By the time Merton was seventeen, the last of the weak blocks of familial security had been knocked from beneath him by his father's particularly debilitating death from a malignant brain tumor. "As an orphan," he later confessed poignantly, "I went through the business of being passed around from family to family, and being a 'ward,' and an 'object of charitable concern,' etc. etc. I know how inhuman and frustrating that can be—being treated as a thing and not as a person. And reacting against it with dreams that were sometimes shattered in a most inhuman way."[3]

By 1933, when Thomas Merton entered Clare College to begin a short-lived university career at Cambridge, James Laughlin, nineteen years old and in mild rebellion against the commercial ethos of his wealthy family, took a leave of absence from Harvard. He traveled to Rapallo, Italy where, in August 1933, he met and later studied with Ezra Pound. Pound dashed Laughlin's desire to join the fledgling modernist literary movement when he unceremoniously dismissed Laughlin's poems and told him that he'd never make it as a poet. Instead, Pound encouraged Laughlin to use his family's means to good end and become a publisher. "I thought to myself," Laughlin

---

3. William H. Shannon, ed., *The Hidden Ground of Love: The Letters of Thomas Merton on Religious Experience and Social Concerns* (New York: Farrar, Straus & Giroux, 1985) 605.

later reflected calmly, "that if I couldn't be a writer, maybe as a publisher I could hang around with writers and have a good time."[4] While the young student was no doubt shaken by Pound's snub, the incident at the "Ezuversity" is often overstated. Nevertheless, as Kenneth Rexroth concluded, "Laughlin worked day after day, often till far into the night, himself, and hard, to publish writers who often were far less good than himself, year after year, for little thanks. He is an excellent and original poet, and might have been writing his own poems."[5]

In any event, Laughlin listened to Pound's advice. With financial backing from his aunt, Mrs. Leila Carlisle, who also provided an unused stable on her Norfolk estate that housed New Directions' first offices, and a $100,000 graduation present from Henry Hughart Laughlin (which the young graduate promptly used to purchase a ski lodge in Alta, Utah, that would reap enough return on investment to bankroll his publishing company for many years), Laughlin launched the New Directions Publishing Corporation. From the very beginning he published the poets who would spur the modernist literary revolution in America and form a stable of new writers Laughlin would publish for many years to come, which included Pound, William Carlos Williams, Kay Boyle, Dylan Thomas, Djuna Barnes, Henry Miller, and Merton.

While Pound counseled Laughlin in Rapallo on how to spend his money, Thomas Merton, emotionally anguished by the cruel death of his father, set out on his own journey to Italy that, like Laughlin's, would have a lasting impact on his future life course. Merton made a solitary sojourn to Rome in the summer of 1933, where he underwent a wrenching psychotic break in a lonely hotel room one night that he later characterized as a religious conversion experience. Cut to the quick by an intense, sudden, and painful insight into the corruption of his own soul, mysteriously linked to a deep interior peace inspired by the religious art of Rome, that he had never felt before, the episode became the benchmark of Thomas Merton's religious life. The summer in Rome set Merton upon a course that would establish him as one of the twentieth century's most significant religious personalities and place him among its most prolific writers and poets.

4. James Laughlin, "For the Record: On New Directions and Others," *American Poetry* 1.3 (Spring 1984) 56.
5. Kenneth Rexroth, ed., *American Poetry in the Twentieth Century* (New York: Herder and Herder, 1971) 126.

In Italy, in the summer of 1933, Thomas Merton and James Laughlin—unknown to each other at the time and separated by what may seem an unbridgeable chasm of class, family background, education, spiritual bearings, social privilege, and promise—began what to both of them would be their life work in which each would play formative and prominent roles for the other.

But first, for Merton at least, there would be more searching and more trial. Returning from Rome, he entered Clare College at Cambridge University. Shortly afterwards, he was invited to leave under threat of a palimony suit. The spiritual malaise and moral searching that began in Rome continued to agitate deeply within him. After being received into the Roman Catholic Church in 1938 and not long after graduating Columbia University with a master's degree in English Literature the following year, Merton awakened to a calling to priesthood and the monastic life. He visited a Trappist monastery for the first time on the day after Japan bombed Pearl Harbor. As the world inched toward another conflagration, Thomas Merton had finally arrived home. He imagined a future far different than his past. "[T]here will be no more future," he reflected enthusiastically, "not in the world, not in geography, not in travel, not in change, not in variety, conversations, new work, new problems in writing, new friends—none of that, but a far better progress, all interior and quiet!!!"[6]

III.

I don't exactly know what to think or say about your idea of giving up writing poetry. Most poets with your gift just wouldn't be able to stop if they wanted to. . . . [I]t really just seems to me impossible that you won't write poems later on. A faculty like that is just part of your being, and I don't see how any amount of will power can cut it off. . . .

James Laughlin to Thomas Merton, 6 April 1949[7]

On December 13, 1941, Merton, twenty-six years old, was officially accepted into Gethsemani and given the robes of a Cistercian oblate. He met the abbot, Dom Frederic Dunne, who gave Thomas Merton his new name in religious life—"Louis"—thereby completing a transformation from poet and would-be novelist, English professor,

---

6. Thomas Merton, *Run to the Mountain: The Story of a Vocation*, ed. Patrick Hart (New York: HarperSanFrancisco, 1995) 458.

7. Cooper, *Thomas Merton and James Laughlin*, 51.

erstwhile fellow traveler, and jazz aficionado into a potential contemplative aching for silence, solitude, wordlessness, and freedom from human suffering and worldly folly. Dom Frederic, the gentle abbot who received Merton as a postulant and later presided over Frater Louis's profession of simple and solemn vows, quickly became Thomas Merton's Ezra Pound, guiding and encouraging his literary pursuits. This was a quiet but formative irony that Merton and Laughlin would never fully appreciate in spite of its critical importance to a personal friendship that spanned a quarter century, a literary relationship that spawned more than twenty books, and a commercial partnership that would reap the sort of profits that made it possible for New Directions to publish important but notoriously unprofitable poets.

Merton was less prepared to accept the insistent urgings of Dom Frederic, however, than Laughlin had been to follow Pound's career counseling. Convinced that his literary instincts could only disrupt a life of prayer, Merton's misgivings and ambivalence over his identity as a poet and writer grew intense and divisive upon entering the monastery, a motif that surfaces in both Merton and Laughlin's letters during the 1940s and early 1950s. Dom Frederic's warm support and determined encouragement of Merton's literary talents—cresting early with the phenomenally successful autobiography *The Seven Storey Mountain*—provided emotional shelter from Merton's storms of self-doubt. When Dom Frederic died in 1948, Merton lost an important mentor whose wise guidance helped to quiet the turmoil of Merton's inner divisions. This support was critical during Merton's early years in the monastery, when he was not only wracked by persistent conflict between his literary instincts and his new identity as a monk but had to adjust as well to the formidable rigors of monastic life in the 1940s, a communal life of extreme hardship, sacrifice, and asceticism. Even though the Cistercians are a communitarian or "cenobitic" monastic order, the monks lived in strict silence before the reforms set in motion by the Second Vatican Council in the 1960s. Their lives were punctuated daily by communal prayers, meals and minimal sleep, reflective study and spiritual reading, and plenty of manual labor in the monastery fields.

Fortunately, James Laughlin stepped into the breach after Dom Frederic's death. From the moment Mark Van Doren, Merton's Columbia University professor, mentor, and thesis adviser, sent Laughlin an uneven collection of Merton's first poems, published as

Thirty Poems in 1944, New Directions issued a virtual *carte blanche* to publish just about anything and everything the young monk/poet submitted. It is no exaggeration to say, in fact, that James Laughlin and New Directions *made* Thomas Merton as a poet, and—along with Robert Giroux and Merton's literary agent, Naomi Burton Stone—contributed considerable impetus to Merton's still-swelling reputation as a writer, social critic, autobiographer, ecumenist, spiritual guide, and commentator on our life and times. Laughlin and his staff, for example, routinely brokered Merton's poems to leading literary magazines like the *Saturday Review, The New Yorker,* and *Poetry.* They underwrote some of Merton's most controversial political writing—notably, *Breakthrough to Peace* (1962), whose difficult road to publication is mapped in Merton and Laughlin's letters of 1961 and 1962, and the trenchant *Raids on the Unspeakable* (1966). The New Directions office also organized a *samizdat* of influential figures, including W. H. Ferry of the Center for the Study of Democratic Institutions, to read Merton's mimeographed essays on peace, nuclear weapons disarmament, and social justice issues during the civil rights movement and the Vietnam War after Merton's Trappist superiors flatly ordered him to stop writing about faith and social witness as they bore directly on the political turbulence and social unrest roiling an anxious and troubled era. Laughlin even made it possible for Merton to set out on his ill-fated Asian trip in 1968 by arranging for his American Express card and traveler's checks and coaching Merton on the fine arts of foreign travel.

IV.

[T]he thing is to be heard. And everything is perfectly soundproof and thought proof. We are all doped right up to the eyes. And words have become useless, no matter how true they may be. But when it comes to action, then I am more helpless than anyone: except within my own very limited sphere of prayer, with which I have no quarrel at all. That is perhaps the last great power that can do anything: and the less said about it the better.

—Thomas Merton to James Laughlin, 18 August 1961[8]

Viewed strictly from a literary vantage point, it may seem odd that Thomas Merton became one of James Laughlin's most favorite

8. Ibid., 166.

New Directions poets. Given his philosophy of publishing, it is even surprising that Laughlin pressed ahead so quickly and unequivocally in publishing Merton's early work. Laughlin frankly admitted that "Merton's early religious poems, except for their color and vigor of imagery, do not particularly interest me. There is something facile about them."[9] Merton's pious early verse ran radically counter to the hallmarks of literary modernism that Laughlin actively sought in the hard-edged, experimental writing of early New Directions poets like Pound, William Carlos Williams, Henri Michaux, George Oppen—and Gertrude Stein, whose *Three Lives,* reprinted by New Directions in 1941, makes Merton's *Thirty Poems* (1944) seem, in comparison, too glib indeed.

As a publisher Laughlin was instinctively drawn to experimental poetry that fulfilled the critical injunctions of the new literary modernism: mold-breaking innovations in literary forms and cut-to-the-quick, bare knuckles social commentary leavened with lassitude and angst. He sought out poets who rebelled against "the standardization of language," poets who searched "with all . . . ingenuity for a solvent to"[10] conventional literary forms. This gave the early New Directions list an obvious house style and an unmistakable feel: unconventional, iconoclastic, nonconformist. Aesthetic experimentation merged with Laughlin's sense of place in literary history to produce a publishing philosophy he summed up in the preface to *New Directions 15:* "The theory was simply this: Literature, a whole culture in fact, goes dead when there is no experiment, no reaching out, no counterattack on accepted values. Even if the experiment is a failure, it must exist as a force and be given a showing place."[11]

The religious poetry that dominated Thomas Merton's earliest work, up to and including *The Tears of the Blind Lions,* published by New Directions in 1949, hardly fit the new style, to say the least. The early Merton was fundamentally a psalmodist. For stylistic inspiration he looked backward to biblical and liturgical prototypes such as the aubade, the canticle, and the hymn. While the social commentary of Merton's religious verse counter-punched accepted values, it was a conservative and reactionary criticism, decidedly retrograde when compared to the social critiques launched by other New Directions

---

9. James Laughlin, *Random Essays* (Mt. Kisco, N.Y.: Moyer Bell, 1989) 8.
10. Ibid., 78.
11. James Laughlin, "Preface," *New Directions in Prose and Poetry* 15 (1955) ii.

authors at the time. Expressing a disdain for worldly living undoubtedly connected to his bohemian youth, tempered by a theological le-
galism Merton embraced upon entering the monastery, his early
poems lashed out at the godlessness and apostasy that he uncritically
associated with secular America, making for, quite frankly, some
forced and clumsy poetry characterized by severe vacillations between
sentimentality, sarcasm, righteousness, and rage.

In addition, there was a moral angle to consider in the publishing relationship. By the early 1950s, as Merton explained in an unpublished letter to his agent, he began considering "a moral question
which would confront me if I were found to be actively cooperating in
the production of books by other people ([Laughlin's] protégés) who
write what might be considered as morally undesirable material."[12]
Merton had a good point. At a time when New Directions published
the poems of a cloistered religious, it was also publishing Djuna Barnes
and Arthur Rimbaud and issuing titles from Henry Miller, whose
books were headed to the Supreme Court in a landmark pornography
case. The second edition of Kenneth Patchen's *The Journal of Albion
Moonlight* appeared under the New Directions imprint the same year
Laughlin published Merton's own first volume of poetry. Patchen's
journal—a descent, the jacket blurb boasted, into "the far boundaries
of love and murder, madness and sex"—flaunted the traditional
Christian moral concerns central to Merton's early work.

Nonetheless, Merton remained steadfastly loyal to Laughlin. As
their letters indicate, they rarely broached any moral qualms that
Merton might have harbored privately over other books New
Directions published. Writing to Laughlin on June 26, 1950, for example, Merton skirts potentially serious questions of moral propriety
by camouflaging them as matters of "monastery diplomacy."[13] Merton
and Laughlin's literary as well as personal relationship never broke
stride over the issue of art and Christian morality. Merton and Henry
Miller, largely at Laughlin's instigation, even became fast friends and
mutual admirers of each other's writing.

For his part, although Laughlin privately faulted Merton's early
poems for lacking range and technical severity, he still found something extremely likable and approachable in Merton's verse from the

12. Thomas Merton to Naomi Burton Stone, 27 January 1951. Thomas
Merton Studies Center.

13. Cooper, *Thomas Merton and James Laughlin*, 69.

very beginning, even if the monk's early poems had little resonance in the New Directions canon. Laughlin stuck with him. It is a testament to Laughlin's devotion to Merton and his sharp instincts as an editor that he continued encouraging Merton to write poems even during a fallow period in the early 1950s when the monk swore off poetry writing. It is also a testament to Laughlin's prescience as a reader that Merton, beginning with the publication of *The Strange Islands* in 1957, would blossom into one of New Directions' *most* experimental poets. From the drafts of new poems Merton began sending him in 1956, Laughlin sensed an important new direction in the writing, the beginning of what he considered the secularization of Merton's poetry. Laughlin applauded, he writes in *Random Essays,* "the new verbal tone, a mixture of satire and irony, fused into black humor, and a structure of depersonalization . . . in which the speaker is much withdrawn from the content of the poem"[14] that began to energize the new poems, cresting in the deadpan prose poem *Original Child Bomb* (1962) and the chilling "Chant To Be Used in Processions Around a Site With Furnaces" (1961), which Laughlin considered Merton's most remarkable poem. Suddenly freed from restraint, Merton combusted into an experimental poet *par excellence.* He "wrote" found poems. He translated contemporary and ancient poetry from the Greek, Spanish, Portuguese, French, and Chinese. He began exploring the possibilities of an "anti-poetry" based on the mass culture criticism of the leftist critic and philosopher Herbert Marcuse and the Chilean poet Nicanor Parra. Other new modes of writing breached from the depths of Merton's creative unconscious: satire and pseudo-comedy, prose poetry, long poems, collage, surrealistic word play, mosaic, ethnographic verse, parody, and pseudo-myth. It took a horrible accident in Bangkok to shut off the faucet, leaving behind two volumes of fascinating and multi-layered poetry—*Cables to the Ace* (1968) and *The Geography of Lograire* (1969)—for a new generation of literary critics and Merton scholars to sort out.

V.

I am really excited about all this. All sorts of really dizzying prospects are opening up. Maybe get invited into Bhutan . . . etc. Wow.

---

14. Laughlin, *Random Essays,* 11.

If I just die of amebic dysentery on the banks of the Ganges, that in itself would be superb. Though doubtless unpleasant.

—Thomas Merton to James Laughlin, 5 September 1968[15]

Part of the reason for James Laughlin's continued devotion to Merton-the-poet was Laughlin's extraordinary affection for Merton-the-person. Considering the often difficult, frequently volatile, and sometimes outright nasty episodes Laughlin suffered at the hands of other New Directions writers, Thomas Merton must have seemed a saint. Even the gentle pediatrician could be a pain. Hugh Witemeyer reports in his Introduction to *William Carlos Williams and James Laughlin: Selected Letters* that certain tensions trailed through the long relationship between Laughlin and Williams. Frustrated by Laughlin's frequent travels abroad and his domestic ski trips, Witemeyer writes, "the workaholic doctor sometimes envied and resented the globe-trotting . . . jaunts and bachelor freedoms of his wealthy young friend,"[16] a resentment that came to a head in 1950 when Williams turned to Random House to publish his poems. Although he eventually returned to the New Directions fold, Laughlin was hurt by what he considered Williams' betrayal, and their relationship became awkward and strained for many years. It is painfully clear from *Delmore Schwartz and James Laughlin: Selected Letters* (1993) that Schwartz also resented Laughlin's frequent absences from the Greenwich Village office and his laid-back lifestyle. He even accused Laughlin of conspiring with Nelson Rockefeller to have an affair with Schwartz's second wife. Unhinged from reality, Schwartz's letters, according to Robert Phillips, "developed into dark and obsessive harangues. . . . He accused Laughlin of disaffection, even of cheating him on his royalty statements. . . . [I]t must have been extremely painful to Laughlin to receive such attacks."[17] The mercurial Kenneth Rexroth (whose letters to Laughlin were edited by Rexroth's biographer Lee Bartlett and published in 1991), populist to the core, often pounded Laughlin with invective during fits of impatience, and on occasion he accused Laughlin of being a puppet for New York literati. Henry Miller—chronically broke—habitually complained about his contracts, accusing Laughlin,

15. Cooper, *Thomas Merton and James Laughlin*, 335.
16. Hugh Witemeyer, ed., *William Carlos Williams and James Laughlin: Selected Letters* (New York: W. W. Norton & Co., 1989) xi.
17. Robert Phillips, ed., *Delmore Schwartz and James Laughlin: Selected Letters* (New York: W. W. Norton & Co., 1993) xv.

as George Wickes recounts in his Introduction to *Henry Miller and James Laughlin: Selected Letters* (1996), of taking "unfair advantage of him."[18] And, of course, the deeply complicated Ezra Pound, to whom Laughlin remained steadfastly devoted even while weathering Pound's storms of political rage, forced Laughlin to take strong public stands against the poet's anti-Semitism and pro-Fascist diatribes.

For Laughlin it must have felt like an interpersonal retreat of sorts from the bruising relationships with other New Directions writers when he flew down to Louisville and rented a car for the hour long ride south to Bardstown for annual visits with Thomas Merton at Gethsemani. Laughlin recounts those trips with simple affection in his essay about Merton. That Laughlin selected the piece to lead off *Random Essays* says something about his esteem of and affection for Thomas Merton.

There is perhaps no greater testament to Laughlin's personal affection for Merton and his commitment to Merton's vision and continuing message as a writer than the long and painstaking labor Laughlin devoted to the posthumously published *Asian Journal of Thomas Merton*. When the fragmentary notebooks and journals Merton kept during his Asian travels in 1968—often consisting only of nouns and verbs strung together into lists or cryptic shorthand reminders for entries Merton clearly intended to flesh out for later publication—fell into Laughlin's hands after Merton died, Laughlin was determined to make a book out of them despite a daunting editorial task that would take him the better part of two years. With the help of Naomi Burton Stone and Gethsemani's Br. Patrick Hart, Laughlin pieced together into a seamless narrative the disjointed prose fragments Merton recorded in three separate notebooks. He tracked down the names and addresses of the many people Merton talked to during his two-month travels. He traced arduous bibliographic leads in order to identify exact sources of quotations from Buddhist and Hindu spiritual texts that Merton randomly strewed throughout his notebooks. Laughlin even skillfully and tediously transcribed a poem Merton wrote, in a jiggly hand, into a small pocket notebook amid plane timetables and phone numbers while riding on a train; and he included "Kandy Express" in an eighty-page section of uncollected works he appended to the massive *Collected Poems of Thomas Merton*, issued by New

18. George Wickes, ed., *Henry Miller and James Laughlin: Selected Letters* (New York: W. W. Norton & Co., 1996) xxi.

Directions in 1977. Due largely to a combination of Laughlin's editorial pertinacity and his continued devotion to a writer/friend, *The Asian Journal* nearly rivaled the critical attention and popular appeal of Merton's first chapter in a long autobiographical opus, the run-away bestseller *The Seven Storey Mountain*. Looking back over six productive and ambitious decades in the book business, Laughlin didn't hesitate to rank *The Asian Journal*, as he noted in a letter to me, "one of the most important things I did in publishing."

VI.

We are going through the grey, cold days that come just before Christmas, which seem empty but are really very wonderful. You miss their emptiness there, where you have stores all over the place. Here there are no shop windows, only the bare trees, and a marvelous silence, and the rain.

Thomas Merton to James Laughlin, 21 December 1953[19]

Throughout their nearly thirty-year friendship, Laughlin and Merton's relationship never strayed from intimacy and mutual understanding, respect and tolerance. From the beginning they shared a search for integrity as writers and as midwives to the voices of others along with a common desire to live meaningfully and fully in a world that often seemed to defy authentic living and real purpose. On a journey of very different life courses, Merton and Laughlin met on the commons of their frequent letters. More so than any other New Directions author with the possible exception of William Carlos Williams, Laughlin always made it a point to go out of his way to visit Merton personally at his remote monastery. Meanwhile, through their letters they invited each other into their moral struggles. They fed each other's moral aspirations. As important, they shared the simple rhythms of their felt worlds. Along the way, Merton nourished Laughlin's nascent spirituality,[20] deepened his ethical commitments as a publisher, and inspired a compassion for social justice in the Harvard-educated son of a wealthy Pittsburgh socialite. For his part, Laughlin, who longed from an early age to be the poet that his mentor, Ezra Pound, discouraged him to become, was instrumental in helping

19. Cooper, *Thomas Merton and James Laughlin*, 93-4.
20. See esp. Letters 11, 12, 13, and 19 in Ibid.

Merton becoming the poet he never really wanted to be. Merton had the incredible good fortune, as Robert Coles, a friend of both men, has perceptively written in the inaugural number of the literary journal *Conjunctions,* dedicated to Laughlin, "to work with, to have the continual personal support of a very special person—someone who, maybe it can be said, finds satisfaction in enabling others to have their say . . . someone who . . . has been graced in a most special way, so that his own pride is that of the pastoral person—the one who is forever attentive to the needs of others."[21]

With the literary insight of a good editor, the insistence of a trusted friend, and the savvy of a successful publisher, Laughlin made it possible for Merton to look back later in life over his vocation as a writer and reflect disconcertedly in the Preface to the 1966 Japanese translation of *The Seven Storey Mountain:* "It is possible to doubt whether I have become a monk (a doubt I have to live with), but it is not possible to doubt that I am a writer, that I was born one and will most probably die as one."

---

21. Robert Coles, "A Struggle for Humility," *Conjunctions* 1 (1981) 245.

Cultural Resistance and Literary Identity: Merton's Reading Notebooks

Claire Hoertz Badaracco

This is my place and yet I have never felt so strongly that I have "no place" as I have felt here since becoming fully reconciled to this as "my place." My place is in reality no place, and I hesitate to act as if I were anything but a stranger anywhere, but especially here. I am alien to everything, even contemplation, even writing.[1]

Examining Merton as a reader, not just as a writer, contributes to a better understanding of the ways in which his work anticipated later debates among deconstructionists, post-structuralists, as well as neo-feminists and critical theorists engaged in weighing the aesthetic values of the Western Christian literary tradition and its impact on culture.[2] The many critical perspectives of the late capitalist era question not only the authority of books generally, but, more profoundly, debate the reader's relationship to the Author of sacred books. Interestingly, Merton's working notebook entries about his spirituality of reading anticipate this development. His approach to language was existential, and presupposed the central problem of modernism: that readers' "identity" is the chief source for imposing meaning not originally intended by an author. In a philosophy of reading developed by neo-feminist writers, philosophers and theologians, one finds a similar critical approach. It is therefore valuable to regard Merton within the

1. Thomas Merton, *The Courage for Truth: Letters to Writers*, ed. Christine Bochen, (New York: Harcourt Brace, 1993) 29, Letter from Thomas Merton to Jacques Maritain, February 22, 1960.

2. David Lyle Jeffrey, *People of the Book: Christian Identity and Literary Culture* (Grand Rapids: Eerdmans, 1996).

mainstream of the Western Christian literary tradition, in the context of the American literary canon, and within the macro-story that forms the basis for many late-twentieth-century narrative strategies articulated by critical theorists.

Two streams of argument in postmodern criticism exist about the truth of biblical books: one is logocentric, or fundamentalist, while the other is event-centered or gnostic.[3] The major contribution, however, has come from women, who argue that the meta-narrative which constitutes the Western Christian literary tradition is androcentric, or male-centered, and therefore culturally determined. Among neo-feminists in the Judeo-Christian and Islamic traditions, contemporary writers are reassessing the meaning of sacred books associated with patriarchal culture, including the Old Testament, Koran and Torah.[4] Whereas earlier waves of feminism discussed how culture undermines the Feminine principle in the world, the current trend is to restore ancestral texts through their reinterpretation. While "classical" feminism concerned itself with freeing the human spirit and gaining civil rights, the modern media persisted in its construction of a female prototype rooted in material consumption and in images of the body, distorting the spirituality of self-determinism, individuality and cultural transcendence that linked feminism historically with other utopian ideologies of the modern and postmodern era.[5]

In addition to critical theories, new typologies have emerged from the language of social science: "mediated" texts possess cultural "agency," words are regarded not as truth but as facts; they have a "social life." The quality of a text as cultural agent, whether it is oppres-

3. Jeffrey, 140-7.

4. Ursula King, ed. *Feminist Theology from the Third World*. (London: SPCK/Orbis Press, 1994); *Religion and Gender* (Oxford & Cambridge, Blackwell, 1995).

5. Claire Badaracco, "Utopian on Main Street," in *Rethinking Religion, Media and Culture* (Sage: 1997); Alicia Ostriker, *Feminist Revision and the Bible* (London: Blackwell, 1993).

The most recent development of this trend in literature may be judged the third or fourth wave of feminism in the twentieth century. Among the classic literature that the movement produced are such benchmarks as Elizabeth Cady Stanton's *Women's Bible* (1895), Betty Friedan's *The Feminine Mystique* (1963), Kate Millett's *Sexual Politics* (1970), Doris Lessing's *Golden Notebook* (1962), and Alice Walker's *The Color Purple* (1982) among many others. All challenged the literary "canon" as androcentric, and positioned feminism squarely within mainstream modernism.

sive or liberating, is not a quality inherent in the language itself, but in the interactive power that exists between the text and its reception by a reader. Communication scholars offer propositions of a "reception theory," that all public texts—and that could apply to scripture contained in ancient, sacred printed books, or scripts for the secular media—are "enacted," able to silence, corrupt, free or transform, to the degree they are able to engage believers.[6] Without readers, texts have no life, no meaning and no power. Agency in language is pivotal to the problem of resistance and identity in Merton's notebooks. Entries about his reading anticipate later articulation of the same principles by several later critical schools, few of which are Christian in philosophy. In Merton's framework, on one extreme stands the principle of "selfhood and identity" and on the other is the principle of "alterity" or discernment, where the self could be "the outsider" or Merton's "no one." In a reading notebook for 1963, he observed,

> Rain batting down on the tin roof. Cornpicker far over there roaring in the rain (no comment!). Two pine trees, among many cedars, on top of the rise across the hollow. Red sage grass & pale greyish yellow mud. Suppose nobody were here to see it. Perhaps nobody is. To realize that the "I" who sees is no one, & that there is "no one" here. or rather: "No one" is here! The one who reads this will be no one. Or if it is "someone," then what he reads is entirely different from what is written. He reads what he himself would have written. - whoever he may be! But if he is no one then he can read what I have written [.] As if emptiness could be a possession![7]

Popular success in the genre of spiritual autobiography lies less in how an individual escapes the trap of culture, than in how an individual articulates a universal self, striking chords in the cultural memory or imagination in the collective identity. Throughout Merton's life, his resistance to what he termed the "collapse of culture" and his alienation from the destructiveness synonymous with post-war modernity explains why the monk's confessional autobiography and spiritual journalism became an American publishing *best-selling* phenomenon.

6. J. Martin-Barbero, *Communication, Culture and Hegemony: From Media to Mediations* (London: Sage, 1993); Seyla Benhabib and Judith Butler, et al. "Feminism and Postmodernism: Subjectivity, Historiography, and Politics," in *Feminist Contentions: A Philosophical Exchange* (New York: Routledge, 1995) 17–34, 107–26.

7. Reading Notebook #13, n.p. [12] Merton Archives, Thomas Merton Studies Center, Bellarmine College.

In his literary essays and poetry, Merton defined alienation in modern literature as inseparable "from culture . . . from life in society."

> Alienation begins when culture divides me against myself, puts a mask on me, gives me a role I may or may not want to play. Alienation is complete when I become completely identified with my mask, totally satisfied with my role, and convince myself that any other identity or role is inconceivable. The man who sweats under his mask, whose role makes him itch with discomfort, who hates the division in himself, is already beginning to be free.[8]

Merton's ability to capture and express the temper of his times also suggests why so many men returning from World War II sought another peace in the swelling ranks of the Trappist monasteries between 1946 and the mid-1950s.

Alienation is integral to Thomas Merton's theology of creativity: in deconstructing the false self, he uncovered his likeness to the image of God, the source of his true freedom.[9] As Merton resisted the conformist expectations of the material culture of the fifties by entering monastic life, he resisted spiritual domination by his religious superiors in the monastery:

> I have renounced 12th century France. That is I have given up accepting the 12th century spiritual climate as a practical reality for myself & for my community. Certainly I love it & am at home in it. . . . but I remain in the 20th century with a special obligation to my contemporaries - & to myself as "contemporary."[10]

He lived long enough to rethink his infatuation with the political resistance movements of the sixties, saying that "the peace movement is exactly the sort of thing I am protesting against.—the rationalistic & utilitarian spirit." In his reading notebook for 1966, Merton admitted that he saw his job as "to get loose from the mental tangle I got in by wanting too much to identify myself with a particular movement & with groups in it."[11]

---

8. Thomas Merton, *Literary Essays,* ed. Brother Patrick Hart, "Why Alienation is for Everybody" (New York: New Directions, 1981) 381.

9. *The Literary Essays,* 368.

10. Reading Notebook #13, 13. Merton Archives, Thomas Merton Studies Center, Bellarmine College.

11. Reading Notebook #17, 37. Merton Archives, Thomas Merton Studies Center, Bellarmine College.

Since the time of Merton's death, postmodern critical themes have been sharply articulated by women who use both the autobiographical and confessional modes associated with the Western Christian literary tradition to express resistance both to the material secular culture that commodifies them, and to the patriarchal religious culture that turns their biblical identity into a political problem. To throw out the inheritance of sacred books, though, is to compound the errors of the patriarchy, according to womens' arguments. Ample evidence exists that the contemporary restoration of ancestral or sacred texts, and their reinterpretation through exegesis is occurring in all religions and in undeveloped regions as well as in first world countries. This can be attributed to global democratization and increased economic power among even the world's poorest women. Further, women's resistance to patriarchal culture is rooted in their interpretation of the failure of postmodern material culture to offer them a significant alternative reality. A philosophy of reading as a political act emerges from the syncretic drive that the poet Alicia Ostriker attributes to women alone, yet it would seem also to apply to Merton:

> Instead of Image we possess Word. An alternative beauty bursts into existence, through the language of the stutterer Moses. It is a triumph of Language . . . for are we not commanded by the text itself to interrogate, to engage in dialogue with each other, with the text, with God?[12]

The integration of the Feminine principle in Merton's spirituality also proved an important counter to the cultural masks modernism imposed. In a world which overadulated strength by force, monastics sang psalms to the Virgin Mary to express the sweetness they imagined as their own spiritual identity, which the world denied in its reality. From Merton's deliberate separation from culture, his resistance even to the imposed spiritual regulations in the monastery, emerged his spirituality of alternating resistance and submission. "The only genuine spiritual life is generated here by reactions against this spirit [of enforced stability and immobility]. . . ."[13] Reading played a large part in that pattern of resistance and submission. The text was the conversion process through which he captured whom he might become, in nature and in Christ.

12. Ostriker, 50.
13. Reading notebook #17, 51. Merton Archives, Thomas Merton Studies Center, Bellarmine College.

As Merton's seventy (plus) working notebooks demonstrate, his reading ultimately transformed his alienation, integrating it as part of the surface of the text, while his writing led him into a further resistance to the cultural masks that the identity of a writer imposed. His reading notebooks between 1959 and 1966 record that he read some classics of monasticism, but more often books published within the year. In 1959, for example he read Norman O. Brown's *Life Against Death* (1958), Marie-Dominique Chenu's *La Theologie au douzieme siecle* (1958), a 1957 biography of Martin Heidegger, Rollo May's *Existence* (1958), Henry Bars, *Maritain en Notre Temps* (1959), Giulio Basetti-Sani, *Mohammed et Saint François* (1959), Victor Frankl's *From Death Camp to Existentialism* (1959), Abraham Heschel's *Between God and Man* (1959), as well as earlier imprints by Suzuki on Buddhism, and Ananda Coomarasawmy. The notebook dated 1959 also indicates he read Lewis Mumford's *The City in History* (1961), Gerhard Von Rad's *Old Testament Theology* (1962), Walter Millis and James Real's *The Abolition of War* (1963). His reading notes at the end of 1965 and beginning of 1966 indicate a broadening taste for the classics and a diminishing intensity to keep up with recent releases, though he read the W. W. Norton contemporary translations of Rainer Maria Rilke (1962) within two years of publication. All this indicates not only the intellectual appetite of the reader, but explains how the cloistered writer was able to articulate the temper of the times. In addition to his many friendships with writers, Merton kept up with what the creative world was saying, despite his protest against the other destructive essence of modern culture.

For Merton, reading was close to meditation and remained part of an interior life. In his notebook he confessed,

> Perhaps I write to slow down my reading & reflect more. . . . In the hermitage I read much more slowly, take more time, cover less ground. In the morning, with two & a half hours of reading, I still read very little, & the time is gone like a half hour. There is no quantitative estimate of this time. It is simply a "period of reading" with its own quality.[14]

The popularity of Merton's writing—including those works commissioned as promotional tracts for the monastic life—served as another source of temptation, to build a "false self" in need of decon-

---

14. Reading notebook #17, 51. Merton Archives, Thomas Merton Studies Center, Bellarmine College.

struction. "I am still publishing far too much of everything. I am hoping that this will be the last "three book" year," he wrote in a letter to Mark Van Doren.[15] In contrast to his guilt and estrangement from the publicity machinery that turned his personal revelations into popular public texts and made him a well-known author, Merton's reading led him beyond preoccupation with his identity as a monk and as a writer.

Among the contemporary writers who have contributed to the emerging body of literature about women's identity and alienation from material and from patriarchal culture, even the landscape can participate in a transcendental conversation with the reader. This can lead the self out of the morass of identity or culture, as several contemporary writers, including Annie Dillard, Kathleen Norris, Patricia Hampl and other "spiritual journalists" demonstrate, citing Merton often in their respective works.[16]

Three main principles—"selfhood," "agency" and "alterity"— form the basis of the neo-feminist critical approach. First, the principle of "selfhood" or identity suggests that a reader looks into a text for an aspect of the self otherwise unavailable in reality; rather, personal identity is found in the mimetic power of the word. Secondly, the transformative power of a text takes shape in the principle of its "agency:" that is, words constitute a reality beyond personal identity imposed by ideas of a false self in culture—they are a way out. The "agency" of a literary text lies in its power to draw the reader in, as well as to lead the reader out, to discover a new identity within the culture of an imaginative world. Thirdly, the principle of "alterity" explores the vantage point of the writer as an outsider. In this way, the creative writer tries to put into words the reality of what is not the self, ultimately disengaging from both word and culture a balance that the critical voice strives to achieve. In "alterity" is embeded the idea of reading as an interactive performance with a text. More concretely, the values of religious scripture are performed in worship, reading or preaching. These acts give life to subgenres, including "testimony," "witness," "call" "homiletic" and "journey."[17] The spirituality of writers

15. Thomas Merton to Mark Van Doren, February 24, 1966, Columbia University Archive.

16. Claire Badaracco, "Animated Outsiders," *Merton Annual* 8, 1996, 150-61; see also "Utopian on Main Street."

17. M. Fulkerson, *Changing the Subject: Women's Discourses and Feminist Theology* (Minneapolis: Fortress, 1994); Wolff, J, *Resident Aliens: Feminist Cultural Criticism* (New Haven: Yale, 1995).

tends to be "intensified" rather than "dissipated by independence from dogma," and the spiritual freedom to re-imagine the Feminine at the center rather than on the periphery of a sacred drama, drives a "syncretism" rather than a separatism from traditional textual interpretation and its inherent moral lessons.[18]

Following three decades of theological arguments for the restoration of women's presence in biblical history by Elizabeth Fiorenza, Elaine Pagels and many other theologians in the past decade, a global philosophy of resistance among religious women of many faiths and ethnic groups has developed. Rebecca Goldstein, for example, reads Lot's wife, Irit, as an allegory about obedience to God's will and "the demands of transcendence and the backward pull of love and accidental attachment." What motivated Lot's wife to look back? Goldstein speculates that it wasn't voyeurism, nostalgia or disobedience, but a desire to be united with her children. Lot's wife looked back because she wanted to see if her daughters were following, and was so grief-striken at their fate, she desired to join them. God's act, in her view, was an act of mercy, not retribution.[19]

For the writers Cynthia Ozick, Marcia Falk, and Margaret Ann Doody, the Old Testament figure of Hannah is not about maternity, but about conformity, self-assertion and identity. Hannah moved civilization forward by "inventing" inward prayer, according to Ozick. She reads the exchange between Hannah and her husband Elkanah who questions her, "Why weepest thou?" when he sees her lips moving in Temple and thinks her drunk, as the "first principle of feminism," that every human being should be treated as an end rather than a means, and in Hannah is the transcendence of assigned roles by religious authorities. Marcia Falk's reading of Hannah is consistent with Ozick's, though she reads Hannah as a prototype for changing inaudible, invisible prayer into a communal voice that included everyone, a "truly inclusive, spiritual community," and a "community of equals." Hannah's triumph, according to Falk's reading, is not in bearing successfully the son she longs for, but in resisting cultural barriers to internalizing her prayer. Margaret Ann Doody's reading of Hannah also

18. Sheila Briggs, "Buried With Christ," The Politics of Identity and the Poverty of Interpretation," in *The Book and the Text: The Bible and Literary Theory*, ed. Regina Schwartz (New York: Blackwell, 1990).

19. Rebecca Goldstein, "Looking Back at Lot's Wife," in C. Buchman & C. Spiegel (Eds.), *Out of the Garden: Women Writers on the Bible* (New York: Fawcett, 1994) 3–12.

explores the classic nature of the text and its connection to the "lost child recovered" theme in Greek drama. Because Hannah lives up to her promise to give Samuel back to God through service to the temple, he is a man, according to Doody, "cut off from the feminine" and is condemned to regard all other women as substitute mothers for the one he lost. As a child of the temple, he is burdened by becoming the ultimate insider who thinks holiness unremarkable; he has been raised to think it routine, his right. He exists, Doody imagines, in a "state of superb latency," having been raised "Peter-Pan like, without parents." Samuel sits in the heart of the sacred shrine but lives without feelings of dread, awe or excitement about his privilege. He never has experienced a state of "alterity," being on the perimeter, in exile, excluded.[20]

The social role of the spiritual outsider, estranged from culture, is the spiritual formation for the critic. (Did any critical intelligence in Christian literary history ever emerge from one who "belonged"?) Poet Kathleen Norris reads the book of Psalms as a celebration of "alterity," of living on alien soil, because it leads to a deepening of spiritual life. In an off-Broadway production, the dramatist Elizabeth Swados styled Job as a clown, the ultimate outsider, the loser. Patricia Hampl read the story of Jonah as a lesson in the consequences of human separation, from one another, and from God. Jonah, according to Hampl, told his fellow sailors that he worships Yahweh, but he "talks to God as if he were a rival author, part of the competition, ever a book ahead of him."[21] The heart of the Western Christian literary tradition is the struggle to throw off the ideological implications in the religious imagination, and to reimagine and reinterpret with each reading the individual reader's relationship to the Word. Like Merton, therefore contemporary women writers seek to discover a language within the "mediated" material culture (one that results from the pervasive influence of celluloid and digitized images) that has the potential to be common and utopian, global and particular, relevant to secular society and to sacred scripture.

20. Cynthia Ozick, "Hannah and Elkanah: Torah the Matrix for Feminism," 88–93 and Marcia Falk, "Reflections on Hannah's Prayer" 94–102 and Margaret Ann Doody, "Infant Piety and the Infant Samuel," 103–22, in *Out of the Garden: Women Writers on the Bible* (New York: Fawcett, 1994).

21. Kathleen Norris, "The Paradox of the Psalms," 221–233 and Patricia Hampl, "In the Belly of the Whale," 289–300, in C. Buchman & C. Spiegel (Eds.), *Out of the Garden: Women Writers on the Bible* (New York: Fawcett, 1994).

Resistance, then, is central to reading as an active spiritual endeavor, for Merton in his time, and for neo-feminist writers today. If identity is a spiritual construction rather than a political or psychological one, the connections between generations of believers, and even within the "selves" of one individual writer, become increasingly the work of the religious imagination, individualized by each writer. This realization gives a power to the text that is transformative and conversational, which possesses respectively the power of agency, to pull together a community of outsiders, who share an understanding that whatever else they might not be, they have in common a distance from the world.

Merton's observation in his reading notebook for 1965 demonstrates his immersion in the values of the televisual age despite his distance from the world, and his sacralization of the imagination's ability to soar beyond its earth-bound limits, to reinterpret the possibilities of alterity, and in doing so revolutionize the identity of the modern self. He wrote,

> Liturgy of the space age—participation of everyone in space flights by tv. seeing the man hanging around moving like a fish in the void[.] I am excluded from all this, & I am not sure that it is so wonderful to merely "not see" & not be with it. It is a kind of poverty, perhaps senseless, perhaps useful. We get newspaper pictures of it on the bulletin board. From the beginning man has wanted to fly. See Eliadi on Shamanism. The ascension. The flight of Mohammed. Now [is] this fabulous achievement wasteful? The highest expression of liturgy is waste—sacrifice[.] There has to be this waste & this display (but don't go & condemn the splendor of Cluny etc—which was more justified on the same grounds!)[22]

Merton in his time accomplished what contemporary neo-feminists seek to accomplish today—not to find their identity in a text, but to associate with the images evoked in their imagination of their absence from the text, or to imagine their transcendence of the world of the text as a means of being, in their own place and time, their existence part of their larger "task or *auftrag*," as Merton phrased it, of the "suffering that informs the moral imperative of life."[23]

---

22. Reading Notebook #16, 51. Merton Archives, Thomas Merton Studies Center, Bellarmine College.

23. Reading Notebook #16, 51. Merton Archives, Thomas Merton Studies Center, Bellarmine College.

Women readers seem to ask, "What good is suffering if it does not lead to response to suffering?" Merton would have argued that "Without resistance to what is, there is neither purpose nor task in suffering, but only a passivity." Undoubtedly, contemporary critical theorists also would argue against any passive reception of texts by a reader, because to do something other than resist or talk back to the text would be to deny the readers' automony and authority.

Not only does current critical theory imply an active spiritual resistance to all norms and unexamined beliefs that have been inherited as part of culture, but it also suggests that one must throw off alienation itself as cultural baggage. Whatever distance between readers' belief and the text that is implied by the concept of alienation must somehow be replaced: rejection and resistance are not synonymous. Merton commented in his reading notebook,

> "I think my writing is split in two categories as regards this question. "The world" seen in terms of nature, of manual work, of literature, culture, Asian philosophy etc etc is fully *accepted*. Also "man" in his historic reality. What is not accepted—the "world" in its contemporary confusions. I have not faced technological society & the crises of maladjusted man in a culture which develops too fast for him. I tend to reject it & curse it. To foresee nothing but doom for it. There may be some truth in my pessimism, but the pessimism itself has an evil root, & instead of getting the root out I have been cultivating it in the name of "spirituality" or what you will. This is no longer honest. My task is to come to terms *completely* with the world in which I love & of which I am a part, because this is the world redeemed by Christ—even the world of Auschwitz. But how "come to terms" with Auschwitz, Hiroshima, the American South? Surely there can be no compromise with them. Yet they too must be "redeemed." The great task of redemption is in America which imagines itself Christian ! That is why I am here, & must stay here.[24]

The philosophical problem that Merton and contemporary women writers have in common is not alienation from the surrounding materialism of "the world," but how to love the world, to be in it but not of it, ready to change it through the power of words. The writer Allegra Goodman observed that, "The prophets do not speak in a vacuum:

---

24. Reading Notebook #16, 53. Merton Archives, Thomas Merton Studies Center, Bellarmine College.

they raise their voices in a specific culture, and like all artistic expression, their language is grounded in particular social circumstances." Elizabeth Rosen concludes similarly that reading has instructed her in the "extent to which the era in which one lives determines what one sees in a biblical text and how that is further modified by who does the reading."[25]

So all reading of sacred texts filters historical, political, and cultural analysis to determine meaning. The Bible is not a newspaper. The book is a collection of stories about events, not facts. If God is in the events, their "revelation" or larger meaning in each culture is the task for the reader, not the journalist, critic or historian. Each reader's response to the Word is another spiritual autobiography, another confession. The post-modern critical theorist would argue that all texts endure across cultures and over time: words have lives of their own. The power of words, or their "agency" lies in how readers activate the meaning inherent in the stories: how they aspire to change their own identity, or to change church, society, material culture, the world, the Other from which they stand alone and apart because they picked up a book, read it, and found in it something sacred.*

25. Allegra Goodman, "Prophecy and Poetry," 301–9 and Elizabeth Rosen, "Rebekah and Isaac: A Marriage Made in Heaven" 13–26, in C. Buchman & C. Spiegel (eds.), *Out of the Garden: Women Writers on the Bible* (New York: Fawcett, 1994).

*This article is based on a talk at Gethsemani Abbey, the Merton Scholars' Retreat, February 1996, and has been expanded in response to the suggestions of the scholars attending that conference, particularly George Kilcourse and Robert Daggy.

Metaphors and Allusions: The Theopolitical Essays of Thomas Merton

Bradford T. Stull

A dream: the old television show "To Tell the Truth" is on. Sitting before the celebrity panel are three male contestants. Balding, dressed in the black and white robes of the Trappist monk, each pretends to be the same person, Thomas Merton. At the end of the show, the celebrities secretly write down their picks: they try to guess the identity of the real Thomas Merton. The host then asks the famous question: "Will the real Thomas Merton please stand up?"

Sadly, the dream ends before the true Thomas Merton rises. Perhaps it so ends because there is no real Thomas Merton. Like the Zen koans he admires, perhaps Merton is, finally, a twentieth-century model of the postmodern paradox, a man who is, at once, the author of the devout, nearly xenophobic *The Seven Storey Mountain* and the author of the extraordinary, sometimes impenetrable long poem, *The Geography of Lograire*. Still, the desire to see the end of the dream compels this essay, generates a desire to construct an end albeit tentatively, temporarily. Who is the Thomas Merton that rises? None other than the author of theopolitical essays, essays that weave together the discourses of religious reflection and political commentary in order to address social concerns. Among other strategies, these essays deploy metaphor and allusion to suggest the possibility of a faithful, countercultural awakening, an awakening desperately needed in an age marked by the presence of the bureaucratization of death, of bureaucratic killers.

Faithful Awakening

In a decidedly provocative strategy for a Roman Catholic monastic, Merton metaphorically alludes to the early Marx in order to explore what the faithful awakening might mean. He asks in the Preface to *Faith and Violence,* a collection of theopolitical essays, this: "Is faith a narcotic dream in a world of heavily-armed robbers, or is it an awakening?"[1] Merton's allusion makes clear what any reader of the early Marx knows: while hardly a defender of faith in God, Marx discusses faith within the context of peasant and working-class suffering, suffering caused by oppressor classes. For the early Marx, faith is not simply an opiate, but one that helps people survive the brutality of a world gone awry.

Merton's allusion also makes clear that he himself had Marxist sympathies. The metaphor "heavily armed robbers" is not only the paraphrased voice of Marx: it is, in fact, the melded voice of both Marx and Merton. The essays collected in *Faith and Violence* make clear that Merton understood faithful people to live amongst, between, within, armed camps, armed camps that rob, maim, murder. Merton had, by the 1960s, fully embraced the terrifying reality of a world where, as Frances Quéré suggests, "fascism and Auschwitz haunt our nights," where "cocktails of bacteria and neutrons will perhaps be the last cups from which we drink."[2]

It is needless to say that Merton did not opt fully for the early Marx. While Merton understands the world's powers and principalities to be oppressive, he nonetheless articulates the meaning of faith in a way that allows it to be something other than a narcotic, something other than an opiate which mercifully allows people to suffer more easily, more painlessly, than they would otherwise. For Merton, faith is an awakening. However, faith is not an awakening in the way some Merton aficionados might think. Merton is often understood to be a devoted monk who can help people discover, rediscover, kindle, rekindle, dip into or deepen their Christian practice and devotion, thereby awakening them to the reality of a loving and salvific God. Laity and professional theologians and religious alike have tended to see Merton as one who offers a profound vision of Christian practice, as Roman Catholic spiritual master *par excellence,* as nuanced avatar of Christ.

1. Thomas Merton, Preface, *Faith and Violence: Christian Teaching and Social Practice* (Notre Dame: University of Notre Dame Press, 1968) x.
2. Frances Quéré, Introduction, *The Book of Christian Martyrs,* Chenu, Bruno, et al., trans. John Bowden (New York: Crossroad, 1990) 13.

Such a reading of Merton was conspicuously present at the 1995 International Thomas Merton Society (ITMS) meeting at St. Bonaventure University. At the opening banquet, for instance, conversation at one table spun around this question and its corollaries: "When did you meet Merton and what has he done for you?" The most eloquent testimony at the table came from an elderly Colombian woman. A devout lay Roman Catholic, she finds in Merton not only her spiritual director, but a holy man who, as she understands it, wrote out of the driven necessity to glorify God.

Other, even more devoted stories swirled constantly at the conference. One woman suggested that Merton's corpse should be exhumed in order to determine whether or not it has begun to decompose; she thinks Merton is a good candidate for beatification. Another person claimed that the smudged entry in Merton's St. Bonaventure Journal, where Merton writes of deciding to join Gethsemani, was caused by Merton's passionate tears, tears falling as he decided to commit to God. At times, the ITMS meeting resembled what one could imagine to be the beginning of the redaction of the Gospels, or the formation of a saint's cult.

This particularly reverent reading of Merton also is manifest among professional scholars. For instance, E. Glenn Hinson, a professor of Church History writing in the field of ecumenical affairs, draws on Merton as a model for ecumenism. He writes that "What we can learn from Thomas Merton, then, has something to do with the preparation for ecumenical encounter. . . . Unless we discover, as Merton did, the cosmic Christ who precedes us in our encounters with one another, we will remain hopelessly tied to our parochial perceptions."[3] Hinson clearly looks to Merton as a Christian master of Christological discernment whom we should read in order to help us experience Jesus Christ as a "cosmic" figure of salvation.

This is not an illegitimate approach to Merton. After all, the answer to the question, "Who is the real Thomas Merton?" has yet to be answered fully. Merton is a moving figure for a host of complex reasons, only one of which is the academic desire to understand his work, to place it in intellectual perspective. In fact, the academic reading of Merton, juxtaposed to the Colombian woman and her

---

3. E. Glenn Hinson, "Expansive Catholicism: Ecumenical Perceptions of Thomas Merton," *The Message of Thomas Merton,* ed. Br. Patrick Hart. (Kalamazoo: Cistercian, 1981) 69.

eloquent testimony of spiritual growth, sounds somewhat dreary, even unimportant.

Nonetheless, these readings of Merton are dangerously close to expressing what Lawrence Cunningham has called "those pieties that one so often identifies with Christian writing."[4] Many readers tend not to find Merton to be a sharp counter-cultural critic, but rather a sweet guide to the Lord Jesus Christ. Cunningham's deliciously sarcastic tone—"those pieties"—is well founded in Merton himself. In a letter to the then-rising feminist theologian Rosemary Ruether, Merton acidly wrote that "I love all the nice well-meaning good people who go to mass and want things to get better and so on, but I understand Zen Buddhists better than I do them."[5] This sentiment arises from a time in Merton's life when *The Seven Storey Mountain*—that zealous autobiography of the world-weary new monk—could be characterized as the "early Merton." At a time when Merton immersed himself in conversation with a wide range of figures, few of whom populate a local parish, he more and more found the reverent religious practice of church Catholicism troubling.

In a 24 March 1967 letter to Ruether, Merton writes that he hadn't "even been reading about monasticism, or monastic literature at all." Instead, he had been delving into Faulkner and Camus, and thus "sneaking out the back door of the Church."[6] This is not to suggest that Merton did not remain a committed priest and monk, even though a common myth suggests that he was on the verge of leaving the church during this period. Merton remained a committed Catholic, but his Catholicism was not that of the Baltimore Catechism, of the local parish priest. Rather, it became the Catholicism of a counter-cultural, even counter-Church monk who, not incidentally, had devoted his life to language. He was not reading Faulkner and Camus by accident or happenstance. With Cunningham,[7] I see Merton more as a writer, less as a theologian; more as a rhetorician, less as a guide to piety. Merton himself admits to Ruether that "I am not a pro at anything except writing: I am no theologian."[8] It is here that one can, perhaps, begin to examine the truth.

4. Lawrence Cunningham, "Thomas Merton: The Monk as a Critic of Culture," *Merton Annual* 3 (1990) 198.

5. *At Home in the World: The Letters of Thomas Merton and Rosemary Radford Ruether*, ed. Mary Tardiff, O.P. (Maryknoll, N.Y.: Orbis, 1995) 17.

6. Ibid., 50.

7. Cunningham, 187

8. *At Home*, 50.

Theopolitical Essays

While Merton is often best known for his meditative, autobio-graphical, and even devotional nonfiction, he came to write, during the 1960s, "theopolitical essays" that join the rhetorics of religious dis-course and political commentary in order to speak to the great prob-lems of the social order. I use the term "theopolitical essay" to distinguish a certain sort of nonfiction that intentionally, even seam-lessly, weaves together the discourses of religion and political com-mentary. I do not mean nonfictional theology that speaks to the political order, like that of Johann Baptist Metz, Jon Sobrino, Rosemary Ruether or other political, liberation, or feminist theologians. Nor do I mean nonfictional political commentary that dips into religious dis-course at times, like that of the conservative Catholic newspaper columnist Cal Thomas. Theopolitical nonfiction is not religious reflec-tion on the political order. Nor is it political reflection that borrows from religion in order to make its point. Within the work of the "theopolitical essay," religious and political discourse fully inform each the other.

An excellent example of such nonfiction is Martin Luther King, Jr.'s famous "I Have a Dream" speech, delivered at the 28 August 1963 March on Washington. John Patton, in an illuminating essay, holds that the speech is a "significant example of theo-political rhetoric" "devel-oped in the fashion of a theological proclamation."[9] As such, it melds "the messages of agape-love, non-violence, hope for the future, and the dream of a just society."[10] Furthermore, the speech is generated and unified by what Martha Solomon calls a "matrix metaphor": "the Declaration of Independence and the Constitution as a covenant."[11] King's speech is not primarily religious discourse that comments upon politics, nor is it political commentary that borrows from religious discourses. Rather, "I Have a Dream" weaves the discourses of religion

---

9. John H. Patton, "'I Have a Dream': The Performance of Theology Fused with the Power of Orality," *Martin Luther King, Jr., and the Sermonic Power of Public Discourse*, ed. Carolyn Calloway-Thomas and John Louis Lucaites (Tuscaloosa: The University of Alabama Press, 1993) 104, 105.

10. Ibid., 126.

11. Martha Solomon, "Covenanted Rights: The Metaphoric Matrix of 'I Have a Dream,'" *Martin Luther King, Jr., and the Sermonic Power of Public Discourse*, ed. Carolyn Calloway-Thomas and John Louis Lucaites (Tuscaloosa: The University of Alabama Press, 1993) 69.

and the political world into a form of nonfiction that is properly called theopolitical. It lives, at once, in the political and religious worlds. So too Merton, an older contemporary of King, turned to theopolitical nonfiction as a way to speak to the crises of his age. Neither purely theological nor political, Merton's theopolitical essays show that his self-description is apt: he was not a professional at anything but writing.

Professor Cunningham insightfully has begun to explore this dimension of Merton. As Cunningham suggests, "Any careful reader of Merton soon realizes that his serious writing needs a good deal of 'unpacking' both because Merton was a poet who understood the polyvalence of language and because he had absorbed so much reading in his contemplative years in the monastery."[12] Cunningham rightly finds in Merton not the pious tones of a "Christian writer" but the complex brilliance of a writer who was a Trappist monk, a Trappist monk who was a writer. Anyone acquainted with Merton's life knows that this particular monk was not particularly silent, not particularly disengaged from the world, or focused on the adoration of the icons. Rather, Merton spent his years at Gethsemani reading voluminously, writing copiously. What emerged, as Cunningham writes, was polyvalent language dense with the presence of other texts.

This Thomas Merton rises boldly, strongly, in a number of places. Consider for, instance, the lead essay in *Faith and Violence,* "Toward a Theology of Resistance." This theopolitical essay explores the possibility of faithful awakening through the use of polyvalent language (metaphor) and allusions to others (the reading to which Cunningham refers). These rhetorical techniques, playful as they are, lead Merton's serious readers into counter-cultural and intertextual worlds that can awaken them, in the fashion of Zen rhetoric, to the reality of violence as a way to counter the destructiveness of humanity.

Metaphorical Play

As Kenneth Burke argues in *Process and Change,* central to human being is the ability to abstract; further, metaphors are the way that humans accomplish the act of abstraction.[13] Metaphors allow hu-

---

12. Cunningham, 198.
13. Kenneth Burke, *Permanence and Change: An Anatomy of Purpose,* 3rd Ed. (Berkeley: University of California Press, 1984) 103–6.

mans to move from one class of thing to another class, thus illuminating, even systematizing, the meaning of experience.

Elena Malits has already suggested that such as understanding of metaphor was central to Merton's work, work that was, perhaps not incidentally, contemporaneous with much of Burke's. Malits writes that "Merton appreciated that metaphor represents a conceptual leap which takes us into new intellectual territory. But he also would have insisted that metaphors have something to do with the very form, the existential shape, of one's life."[14] For Merton, as for Burke, metaphors allow humans to cross boundaries, to break down the lines of demarcation that might, at first or even second glance, seem permanent. Yet for Merton, again as was true for Burke, metaphor is more than an intellectual game to be played by language dilettantes. Rather, metaphor is central to human being. As Malits holds, "metaphors have something to do with the very form, the existential shape, of one's life." In Merton's "Toward a Theology of Resistance," central to this the existential shape is the awakening of faith.

To join the awakening is to move metaphorically, to make a conceptual leap beyond and across borders of existence. To unpack the essay, as Cunningham claims that Merton readers must do, is to realize that metaphor does "have something to do with the very form, the existential shape, of one's life." Merton, through his use of metaphor, invites his readers into a counter-culture awakening that challenges the foundations of American life itself. Merton asks his readers to leap conceptually in order to reshape existence.

Consider these counterposed metaphors from "Toward a Theology of Resistance":[15]

> [our antiquated theology] shudders at the phantasm of muggings and killings where a mess is made on our own doorstep
>
> and
>
> [our antiquated theology] blesses and canonizes the antiseptic violence of corporately organized murder because it is respectable, efficient, clean, and above all profitable.

With the metaphors that inform the first of these sentences and give it its energy, Merton suggests that theology—and culture—is

14. Elena Malits, C.S.C., "Thomas Merton and the Possibilities of Religious Imagination," *The Message of Thomas Merton,* ed. Br. Patrick Hart (Kalamazoo: Cistercian, 1981) 52.

15. Merton, "Towards," 7.

deluded. The verb "shudders" metaphorically personifies the subject of the sentence, "theology," giving this abstract practice bodily weight and presence. Theology shudders, within this world Merton linguistically constructs, not at muggings and killings, but at the "phantasm" of muggings and killings. Unless one lives in world where specters literally haunt one's nights, surely "phantasm" metaphorizes the muggings and killings. The metaphorization of those actions is both positive and negative. Positively, it reinforces our primal fears: muggers and killers are specters, people who violate the codes of civilization, thus calling civilization into question. This phantasm evokes terror because this violence, while distant in most American lives, is rooted in the tangible, the visible. Muggings and killings do sometimes strike in our homes, in our neighborhoods. Negatively, "phantasm" calls into question the legitimacy of the "shudder" theology experiences when it thinks of these muggings and killings. "Phantasm," after all, implies imaginative activity, the sense that these are not real fears, merely the nightmares of a child who thinks monsters live under the bed. Read this way, the metaphors suggest that theology shudders at the imaginative creation of its own mind.

Conversely, the metaphors of the second sentence turn the subject "theology" into a member of the church hierarchy, a priest who can exercise canonical authority. This theology, the very same theology that shuddered at the phantasms of muggings and killings, is able to view other sorts of "messes" much differently. It blesses and even canonizes what Merton suggests is corporately organized murder. Of course, at one level, this language is literal. One need only think of a certain cardinal who blessed the troops on their way to Vietnam. As Merton writes in another essay, a Catholic Bishop in the United States assured President Johnson that "the war in Vietnam is a 'sad and heavy obligation imposed by the mandate of love.'"[16] Protestants, in an ecumenical spirit, are not exempt. Merton tells his readers that "Billy Graham declared that the war in Vietnam was a 'spiritual war between good and evil.'"[17]

At another level, the quotation is also metaphorical. This level of interpretation depends on the word "murder." It is one thing to

16. Thomas Merton, "Vietnam—An Overwhelming Atrocity," *Thomas Merton: The Nonviolent Alternative*, ed. Gordon C. Zahn (New York: Farrar, Straus, Giroux, 1971) 91.
17. Ibid.

bless "killing." "Killing," finally, tends to indicate a human action within the bounds of civilized conduct: one kills a deer; one does not murder it. Killing might be justified, defensible, even blessable in certain situations. Murder never is because murder is violation of law. Merton, with the use of the word "murder," metaphorically charges this sentences, suggesting that theology, as a priestly subject, clerically condones and supports that violation of a fundamental human taboo. The U.S. government and businesses with corporate concerns in Vietnam would not have called the killing in Vietnam murder. Neither would have the U.S. clergy that patted the troops on their way to the war. In fact, these clergy provided the veneer of blessing, claiming that Vietnam was a holy war to be waged by God's troops. That the killing fields were murderous fields was inconceivable to these parties. Murder, after all, is immoral. Rather, Vietnam resided on the plane of war and, thus, was sanitized, made culturally and religiously acceptable: it was killing, not murder. Merton, however, metaphorizes the sorts of corporate violence we have come to condone or at least ignore, as murder. He asks one to leap conceptually, to explore the possibility that the killings justified by state and Church are both illegal and immoral.

The counter-cultural energy of this sentence also depends on the metaphorical phrase "antiseptic violence." The killing fields of Cambodia and Vietnam, drinking blood as Merton wrote, were hardly clean. "Antisepsis," the root of the adjective "antiseptic," indicates destruction of the microorganisms that cause septic disease. Septic disease, most graphically, involves the invasion of a body by bacteria, and often involves pus, rotting pus. The clerics then, the personification of "theology," bless corporate violence because it is that tool that wards off the sepsis, the invasive rotting of the body. Merton, it goes without saying, finds this posture laughable. The metaphorical power of this phrase is finally ironic, a rhetorical trope Merton returns to again and again in his work. The irony is immediately revealed at the head of the sentence: this theology that blesses and canonizes is "antiquated." It offers both the wrong diagnoses and prescription; it identifies the patient as the microorganism and kills it with the treatment.

The play of these metaphors about antiquated theology are aided by the following set:[18]

---

18. Merton, "Towards," 6.

> The violence we want to see restrained is the violence of the hood
> waiting for us in the subway or the elevator
>   and
> Violence today is white-collar violence, the systematically orga-
> nized and bureaucratic and technological destruction of man.

In the first quotation, Merton invokes what is for us in the late nineteen nineties a dated metaphor—the hood. We would speak of gangbangers, but the import is clear. Merton imagines, and asks his readers to do so as well, violence personified in the mythic boogie man who lurks on our street corners, ready to prey. Merton admits that our fear of the hood is "reasonable": after all, there are "hoods" who do prey on people. The problem, however, is that violence as the hood becomes an inflated metaphor: we come to associate all violence in our lives with that particular image. As Merton writes, in an effort to unpack this metaphor and thus decrease its power, the "violence of a few desperate teen-agers in a slum" does not warrant the attention given to it.[19] Rather, we would do better to focus on the larger picture: global, institutionalized violence that is produced and managed by what he calls the white collars.

This is the importance of the second quotation in the set. "Violence" as the subject of the sentence is metaphorized adjectivally and thus becomes associated with a class: it is "white-collar" violence. This is an old cry, dating at least to Marx. Not incidentally, Merton's readers again realize that a marxist analysis of social problems was not foreign to his world view. Merton suggests, with this metaphor, that those whom our own counter-cultural youth call "the suits" manage a global system of violence that threatens human being itself. Merton implicitly sides with the "blue-collar," those who labor but don't direct. In order to explore the violence of human life, he names it with a class marker, providing the image of planners, desk-workers, whose trade in violence arises from their offices, their files, their appointment books. What the white-collar workers offer to violence is the power of the modern state: bureaucratized technology. Americans should fear the street violence of the hood less than the white-collar violence of the bureaucrat because, finally, the white-collar violence is globally organized: the extraordinary organizational power of the modern state is turned over to the "destruction of man."

19. Ibid., 7.

For Merton this white-collar violence is found, among other places, in Vietnam and American inner-cities. *Faith and Violence,* after all, emerges when the smell of Napalm and Watts was in the air. White-collar violence is also found, according to Merton, in Auschwitz, or at least in Auschwitz as it stands metaphorically for the entire Shoah. In "Toward a Theology of Resistance," Merton quickly, briefly, even cryptically offers a single example of the white-collar murder machine: Adolf Eichmann. After discussing the "meticulous efficiency" of white-collar violence, Merton writes that "Adolf Eichmann and others like him felt no guilt for their share in the extermination of the Jews" in part because the extermination, at least at Eichmann's level, took place on paper: the Jews became numbers and thus erasable.[20]

With this name "Eichmann," Merton moves out of the world of metaphorical play into the world of realism. Drawing from recent world history, he suggests that his metaphors are not pure fantasia, the feverish dreams of a left-wing monk. Rather, Eichmann stands, plain and simple, as the classic, real, example of the sociopolitical, white-collar elite that corporately organizes murder. The Nazi organization of the Shoah was, sadly, a model of efficient bureaucracy. How else can 6 million be killed in a few years, short of nuclear and biological weapons? And, of course, these sorts of weapons aren't as clean.

Eichmann, to complicate the essay even further, serves a dual function. At one level, he is a literal example of the white-collar murder machine metaphor. At another level, he is also metaphoric. Merton uses Eichmann as a way to step out of metaphoric play and also as a way to return to it. It is not only Eichmann who is an example of the murder machine. It is "Adolf Eichmann and others like him." Eichmann implicitly serves as metaphor for the U.S. suits, among others, who are pursuing "modern technological mass murder."[21] After reading Merton's essay, one might look at a suit who heads an armament concern and think, "Eichmann."

In all, Merton uses metaphor as a way to bring his readers into a faithful awakening that is more than a trip into the triune God, more than a journey of adoration to the divine. It may include this triune trip, this journey of adoration—again, after all, Merton was a priest— but he plays these metaphors off each other in order to move his readers to see the reality of violence. This reality is not the hood. It is, rather,

20. Ibid., 6.
21. Ibid., 7

the respected white collar. The white collar, moreover, is Adolf Eichmann. If one stands by, blinded by the metaphor of the hood on the corner, one will again witness the destruction of an innocent people of God.

Allusive Wandering

"Eichmann" also serves as an allusive marker, an intertextual connection, as will be discussed in more detail below. For now, let it suffice to highlight this: in the brief discussion of Eichmann, Merton presumes a great deal of knowledge about World War II, about the Nazis, about the Shoah. So too Merton suggests connective possibilities: to unpack me, he seems to be saying, one needs to unpack Eichmann.

Just as he uses metaphor, Merton uses allusion to invite his readers into a faithful awakening that would have them see the reality of violence in order to counter the destructiveness of a world gone awry. As Cunningham suggests, one cannot read Merton with sophistication unless one reads him with an eye toward unpacking his suitcase full of other writers and figures to whom he alludes. To read Merton's theopolitical essays is to become an intertextual creature, to embrace a decidedly counter-cultural, theopolitical faith that involves wandering through words.

Merton's allusive, intertextual play is common among theopolitical figures, as it is among most members of the literary class. The phrase "allusive, intertextual play" means more than what Julia Kristeva calls the "banal sense of 'study of sources'" and something other than what she calls "transposition."[22] Rather, "allusive, intertextual play" points to a demand placed upon Merton's readers. "Toward a Theology of Resistance," for instance, requires its readers to enter into worlds beyond the bounds of the essay itself. The essay cannot be read fully, even fruitfully, unless one moves with Merton through what the rhetorical theorist Patricia Bizzell has called "cultural archives," through what E. D. Hirsch, in his famous, or infamous, *Cultural Literacy* has called the cultural background presumed by the text.[23]

22. Bradford T. Stull, *Religious Dialectics of Pain and Imagination* (Albany: State University of New York Press, 1994) 180, note 5.

23. Patricia Bizzell, "The Function of Cultural Archives in Persuasion: The Examples of Frederick Douglass and William Apess." Paper presented at the Conference on College Composition and Communication, Milwaukee, March 1996;

Merton did not spend a quarter of a century in the monastery prayerfully silent, contemplatively absorbed in the mysteries of the incarnation. Merton, as Cunningham reminds us, read, and read widely.

Consider again Merton's invocation of Adolf Eichmann as a realistic example of the white-collar murder machine metaphor and as the metaphorical representative of all white-collar murderers. Merton does not "unpack" Eichmann. Rather, he lets Eichmann stand as a brief metaphorical flash, an illuminating moment within the discussion about white-collar violence. Merton presumes either that the reader knows Eichmann and the world of suffering that Eichmann represents or will be willing to delve into this world.

This presents a wonderfully rich complexity for readers, but it also necessarily presents some difficulties. For instance, I once taught "Toward a Theology of Resistance" to a class of lower-division undergraduates. They well recognized the intertextual, allusive demands that Merton makes. As they put it, "why doesn't Merton write so that we can understand him?" What they meant was this: to confront Eichmann as a representative name was to confront a world of texts with which Merton was intimately familiar, for which he had the greatest respect, to which he demands his reader go.

Unfortunately, for most of my students, Eichmann was an unknown entity. At first read, they could not move with Merton because they could not move with Merton into the texts that are imbedded in "Eichmann." To read Merton, to enter into the possibility of his faithful awakening, my students had to be led into the intertextual world that Eichmann represents. After they were, the allusive density of Merton's text became more manageable, more meaningful.

Not surprisingly, Merton himself provides an intertextual connection, a way into Eichmann. Were "Toward a Theology of Resistance," and his other theopolitical essays, coded into the hypertext markup language (html) now available for the World Wide Web, the word "Eichmann" would appear highlighted, indicating that it serves as a link to other sites on the WWW. One such site would be Merton's "A Devout Meditation in Memory of Adolf Eichmann." Published in 1966 as part of *Raids on the Unspeakable* and reprinted in *Thomas Merton: The Nonviolent Alternative,* this theopolitical essay at once ironically explores

---

E. D. Hirsch, *Cultural Literacy: What Every American Needs to Know* (New York: Vintage, 1988).

Eichmann in more detail and ironically alludes, as part of this discussion, to the white collar murder machine discussed in "Toward a Theology of Resistance." Consider, for instance, the following quotation, presented at length:

> No, Eichmann was sane. The generals and the fighters on both sides, in World War II, the ones who carried out the total destruction of entire cities, these were the sane ones. Those who invented and developed atomic bombs, thermonuclear bombs, missiles; who have planned the strategy of the next war; who have evaluated the various possibilities of using bacterial and chemical agents; these are not the crazy people, they are the *sane* people. The ones who coolly estimate how many millions of victims can be considered expendable in a nuclear war, I presume they do all right with the Rorschach ink blots too.[24]

While realistic, this entire passage is one of ironic amazement. By the standards of society, Merton suggests, Eichmann and the corporate planners of murder are sane. Yet, he finds this difficult to grasp. The repetition of the word "sane" suggests a dumbfounded tone; Merton keeps repeating the phrase, apparently hoping that it will become sensible as he does so, but of course it cannot. The sanity of these people is juxtaposed with the markers of corporately organized death, calling into question their sanity. The suggestion is implicit, but clear: ones who develop thermonuclear bombs and calmly plan the destruction of millions cannot be sane.

However, Merton admits to the possibility that his own sarcastic reading of modern sanity might be flawed. Perhaps sanity is not what it seems, perhaps it does appropriately and accurately describe corporate murderers. In this reading, Merton claims that the faithful would do well to be a "little less sane, a little more doubtful, a little more aware of his absurdities and contradictions."[25] Merton suggests that if white-collar murder is sanity, then sanity is not a desirable state. Rather, the "less-than-sane" is more appropriate, more true to a world gone awry.

Interestingly, the further we move in time away from the direct of experience of Eichmann's world, the more allusively intertextual

24. Thomas Merton, "A Devout Meditation in Memory of Adolf Eichmann," *Thomas Merton: The Nonviolent Alternative*, ed. Gordon C. Zahn (New York: Farrar, Straus, Giroux, 1971) 161–2.

25. Ibid., 162.

"Eichmann," and thus Merton's text, will become. It may be the case that elder citizens who lived through the revelations of Eichmann's actions in Nazi Germany could read Merton's invocation of Eichmann with the ability to move with Merton. For our youngest citizens, Eichmann and the Shoah are textual worlds that can be entered only through textual wandering. If one's faithful awakening involves Eichmann, one's faithful awakening now, and even more so in the future, will depend upon one's ability, inclination, even monastic desire, to live in a textual world.

Yet, the move into Eichmann can take one through Eichmann into a world beyond text. To awaken to Eichmann and what he represents is to awaken to the suffering of others. To move allusively with Merton is to become awakened to the analogical connection that Merton makes: Eichmann is to the Jews as the U.S. white-collar murder machine is to the Vietnamese, or to oppressed third-world workers struggling under corporate neo-colonialism.

The faithful awakening for Merton is, finally, an encounter with the suffering other.[26] Merton directs us to begin a pilgrimage not to a holy place, not to Eden desired, for that holy place, that Eden, is a chimera, an illusion. Paradise, be it the holy city or the pristine garden, does not exist. Rather, Merton claims that the new form of pilgrimage is a journey to the other who has suffered under the advance of the crusading peoples across the globe. Eichmann, then, is an allusive way to make this pilgrimage, to travel to the effects that violence has had on the suffering other.

An examination of Merton's allusive use of John XXIII in "Toward a Theology of Resistance" only strengthens this point and provides it with a particularly Catholic twist.[27] Merton first refers to John XXIII as one who quotes Augustine, thus beautifully demonstrating Cunningham's argument. To enter into Merton's faithful awakening is to enter into intertextual play. To read Merton is to read John XXIII is to read Augustine.

Merton writes with reference to *Pacem in terris* and its allusion to Augustine: "'what are kingdoms without justice but large bands of robbers?'" Merton thus demonstrates that he is a citizen of the church as well as the world. With Eichmann, Merton shows that a cloistered monk can move intertextually—and ask his readers to do likewise—

26. Stull, *Religious Dialectics*, 64–5.
27. Merton, "Toward," 4–6.

through the world at large, through the complexities of global violence. With John XXIII and Augustine, Merton anchors his allusive, intertextual play in the church itself. To read Merton's theopolitical essays is not simply to read the global culture. It is, as well, to read the culture of the church, particularly the church of Vatican II. This allusion to *Pacem in terris* also demonstrates that metaphor and allusion are not strictly separable. To read John XXIII is to read Augustine is to read a metaphorization of the world. The intertextual becomes the metaphorical. Modern nation states become kingdoms which, without justice, become ruled not by governments but by criminals, by groups of thieves.

Following his allusion to John XXIII and Augustine, Merton asserts that "The problem of violence today must be traced to its roots: not the small-time murderers but the massively organized bands of murderers whose operations are global."[28] With this, Merton allusively and firmly anchors his claims regarding the problem of violence in the Catholic tradition. To see the reality of violence—that is, to discern the real nature of violence and thus be able to counter it—requires not only a metaphorical play, an oppositional encounter of symbols that will lead to awakening. To see the reality of violence requires not only allusive wandering through the texts of the world, in one case those represented by Eichmann. To see the reality of violence also requires allusive wandering through the theopolitical texts of the church. John XXIII and Augustine lead Merton and thus readers into the world of corporately organized murder, of globally sanctioned death. The texts of the Church, we must understand, are not simply about salvation through Christ Jesus. Rather, they are complex indictments, rooted in Christian practice, of the white-collar murder machine—whatever its century.

Metaphor, Allusion, the Hint of Zen

Merton's theopolitical essays are rooted firmly in the Christian tradition, but because they demand conceptual leaps and studious journeys through intertextual reality, one might well begin to look at them as Merton's attempt to practice his understanding of Zen language theory. In effect, the theopolitical essays, with their use of metaphor and allusion, might be understood as aids to Zen contemplation.

28. Ibid., 4.

In this way, the real Thomas Merton might be standing before his readers not in the robes of a Trappist monk, but a Zen practitioner.

Anne Carr claims in her insightful study of Merton that Zen has developed rhetorical strategies that call language about reality into question. These strategies are not meant to call into question reality, however. Rather, they are used to bring about ontological awareness, to help practitioners understand the nature of reality itself.[29] As Merton understands this Zen rhetorical process, language can help open world views, help dislodge misconceptions about the nature of the world.[30]

Thus, one might begin to think about the metaphorical play and allusive wandering demanded by Merton's theopolitical essays as Zen rhetoric. The metaphorical juxtapositions, for instance, are meant to upset accepted notions about violence and the causes of violence. The connections that link the hood, the white-collar managers and the Eichmann are outlandish, but that is the point. The metaphors attempt to disrupt "business as usual" in order to move readers to see the reality of violence as it is. So too allusive wandering requires diligent, dedicated readers to move beyond preconceived understandings of reality into wider, more complex, less graspable visions. One might understand Catholicism as an organization that supports the civic order in which it finds itself. To wander with John XXIII and Augustine, however, is to wander into a counter-cultural world. This counter-cultural world disrupts any understanding of Catholicism and culture that permits the blessing of soldiers who labor for the governments and corporations which organize murder.

The metaphorical play and allusive, intertextual wandering of Merton's theopolitical essays lead the reader into the possibility that the world is not as it appears that, in fact, nothing is as it is. It is in this frame of disrupted perceptions that the real Thomas Merton stands, or so it seems.

---

29. Anne E. Carr, *A Search for Wisdom and Spirit: Thomas Merton's Theology of Self* (Notre Dame: University of Notre Dame Press, 1988) 78–9, 81–6.

30. Thomas Merton, *Zen and the Birds of Appetite* (New York: New Directions, 1968) 49.

Merton and Camus on Christian Dialogue with a Postmodern World

David Joseph Belcastro

I start from where I am, not in the twelfth century but in the twentieth. It happens that I have just been reading a very interesting essay of Camus, "Le Desert." From a certain viewpoint Camus, in this essay, is totally anti-Christian and absolutely anti-monastic. But strangely enough his conclusions are very close indeed to monastic conclusions, so close, indeed, that I am tempted to write a study of them from a monastic viewpoint.[1]

Thomas Merton wrote a series of seven essays on the literary work of Albert Camus with the intention of eventually publishing a book.[2] The first phase of these essays[3] was specifically written in response to Camus' criticism of the Church as a collaborator with the state in the violent oppression of people around the world. Merton heard in Camus a prophetic voice challenging him to examine critically the Christian faith he professed and the monastic life he lived.[4]

1. Thomas Merton, *Contemplation in a World of Action* (New York: Doubleday, 1973) 240.
2. Thomas Merton, *The Hidden Ground of Love; The Letters of Thomas Merton on Religious Experience and Social Concerns,* ed. William H. Shannon (New York: Farrar, Straus and Giroux, 1985) 430.
3. While Merton, in response to Czeslaw Milosz's advice, began reading Camus during the late 1950's, he did not begin work on the essays until the summer of 1966. His essays on Camus were written in three phases: summer through autumn of 1966, spring through midsummer of 1967, and the early months of 1968.
4. Camus presented a paper at the Dominican Monastery of Latour-Maubourg in 1948 in which he sought to establish common ground with the monks and to encourage them to join with him and others in the resistance to all forms of

While Merton believed that Camus did not fully understand the Christian message,[5] he accepted Camus' criticism of the Church as valid, believing that the Church contributes to the violence that is in the world whenever the Church fails to communicate openly and honestly with those who are outside the Christian community. Merton, therefore, responded to Camus' criticism and he did so with the hope of discovering in dialogue[6] with Camus conditions under which communication between Christians and people of other traditions, both religious and secular, may conceivably be more authentic and creative.

In this article, I will sort out those conditions for communication presented in Merton's first phase of essays on Camus. Furthermore, I will note the manner in which Merton entered into conversation with Camus in these essays and find there additional insights into his unfolding line of thought on Christian dialogue with a postmodern world. As we shall see, Merton anticipated, in theory and in practice, our day when Christians could no longer enter conversations with people of other traditions from a position of supposed superiority.[7] He knew that the postmodern era would require Christians to find new ways not only of talking with, but relating to, the diverse cultures of the world; ways which would inevitably change the manner in which the Church understands itself and the Gospel it proclaims.

---

human violence. Merton considers this address at length in his essay "Camus and the Church." It clearly established the framework in which Merton approached Camus' work. See "The Unbeliever and Christians" in *Resistance, Rebellion, and Death,* trans. Justin O'Brien (New York: Alfred A. Knopf, 1961) 69–74.

5. Camus was not unfamiliar with Christian theology. He wrote a dissertation on Augustine. While he relied heavily on the interpretations of others, for example Etienne Gilson, this early work reflects religious themes that would occupy Camus's thinking. For further discussion, see Patrick McCarthy's *Camus* (New York: Random House, 1982) 71ff.

6. While Merton never met Camus nor corresponded with him, it is appropriate to describe Merton's study of Camus as a dialogue. It was Merton's habit to correspond with authors he was reading. Because of Camus death in 1960, this was not possible. The tone of Merton's essays on Camus, however, is nonetheless one of an engaging dialogue. Furthermore, one can hear something of this dialogue via a third person, i.e., Czelaw Milosz who introduced Merton to Camus and with whom Merton corresponded regarding his reading of Camus.

7. See David D. Cooper's *Thomas Merton's Art of Denial; The Evolution of a Radical Humanist* (University of Georgia Press, 1989) where the author traces Merton's development as a post-Christian humanist who embraced all the peoples of the world and the major issues that confronted them as they entered their uncertain future together.

Merton's first phase of writing began the summer of 1966 and ended the autumn of the same year. During these months, Merton wrote four of his seven essays: "Terror and the Absurd: Violence and Nonviolence in Albert Camus," "Three Saviors in Camus: Lucidity and the Absurd," "Camus and the Church," and "Prophetic Ambiguities: Milton and Camus." This phase focused on four concerns which framed Merton's thought on Christian dialogue with others: the problem of nihilism in the modern world, the need to develop a language for peacemaking, the significance of Camus to this effort, and the Church's responsibility to participate in this effort in a cooperative manner.

"Terror and the Absurd: Violence and Nonviolence in Albert Camus" was written in August. It sympathetically examined the features of an ethic developed by Camus in *The Rebel: An Essay on Man in Revolt* which worked out a synthesis between violence and nonviolence.[8] In contrast to the revolutionary who will use violence to overthrow a totalitarian government to construct an equally abstract notion of the State and in contrast to the pacifist who will respond to the oppression of a totalitarian State with nonviolent resignation, Camus developed the Rebel. The Rebel protests in the name of humanity, on behalf of each and every individual man, woman, and child, and for the sake of persons who are alive here and now, against the philosophical and socio-economic abstractions constructed by reactionaries and revolutionaries alike who seek to establish and justify their ideologies and institutions of authority and power over people. Consequently, the Rebel is also a person who refuses to be resigned to the oppressive powers of a totalitarian State or to be silent with regard to abstractions on which that power is constructed or to be passive in the face of the violence that power may exercise without respect for the liberty of all persons. The Rebel, however, is unable to take up arms with the executioners of a violent revolution nor is the Rebel able to join hands with victims who choose nonviolent resignation in the face of violent oppression. The Rebel chooses to stand midway between the extremes of revolution and resignation, demanding open and inclusive dialogue, believing that words are the only effective way for

---

8. For further discussion on Camus' synthesis of violence and nonviolence, see his "Neither Vi Nor Executioners," trans. Dwight Macdonald, with an Introduction by R. Scott Kennedy and Peter Klotz-Chamberlin entitled "An Ethic Superior to Murder" (Philadelphia: New Society Publishers, 1986).

building a world in which humankind can again discover reasons for living that value and nurture life.[9]

Merton saw in Camus' Rebel an acceptable model for postmodern Christians; a viable alternative to violent revolution and passive resignation, both of which Merton believed to be unreconcilable to the Gospel. It was obvious to Merton that violent revolution was not an alternative for a person committed to following the example of Jesus. While a related objection is less obvious, nonviolent resignation was no less acceptable to Merton. He agreed with Camus' criticism of nonviolent resignation for two reasons. Nonviolence can result in the illusion that a person who takes up this position is innocent of any participation in the human problem of violence; a participation that both Camus and Merton saw as unavoidable and an innocence that both believed to be impossible. Furthermore, they believed that a position of nonviolence can lead to the equally illusive opinion that a person can be exempt from the obligation to defend oneself and others from injustice and violence; an exemption that is rooted in a denial of the human condition and practical reality; a passivity that inevitably contributes to the violence that it tries to deny. For these two reasons, Merton believed that the Christian cannot retreat into the silence of nonviolent resignation. Rather than understanding the Christian as a person who is ultimately concerned with creating a beautiful soul, Merton was now of the opinion that the ultimate concern of the Christian was in, with, and for the world. Merton came to believe that Camus' ethic of the Rebel, while basically atheistic, was nonetheless in accord with the Gospel and offered possibilities too often neglected by Christians, in particular, the option of actively participating in open and inclusive dialogue with all peoples which focuses on human life rather than abstract ideologies, whether they are religious, political or otherwise.[10]

9. For further discussion on this point, see Camus' "The Wager of Our Generation" in *Resistance, Rebellion, and Death*, 237–48.

10. While Merton agreed with Camus that a position of innocence cannot be held in this world and while he accepted Camus' criticism of the Church as sometimes preaching resignation in the face of oppression and violence in order to maintain an illusion of innocence, he believed that Camus was wrong in assuming that this is what the Gospel requires of Christians. Camus argued that the nonviolent position is constructed on two premises he personally found to be unacceptable: there is a God and those who suffer oppression in this world do so believing that God will reward them with a future life. Merton believed that Camus had not suf-

During September, Merton wrote "Three Saviors in Camus: Lucidity and the Absurd." This essay focuses on the problem of nihilism and the need to develop a language that protects humankind against its tendency toward self-destruction. It begins with a summary of Camus' thought on the ultimate absurdity of life and our futile attempts to make sense of it. This need to make sense of the Absurd emerges from the fear of death and the belief that death can be overcome by the construction of an ideal social order based on intellectual abstractions. Because death cannot be overcome, all attempts are counterproductive, resulting not in life affirming societies but societies which embody death in their abstractions, in the words that are used to construct those abstractions and in the institutions those abstractions undergird. In other words, humankind's struggle against death is in reality an embrace of death. This embrace of death is manifested in the institutionalization of murder in economic poverty, political oppression, capital punishment, holy crusades and war.[11] Language, consequently, is distorted in this service to death. It is used to deceive and manipulate humankind to believe that war is peace, poverty is prosperity, oppression is justice and death is life. Camus believed that the only hope for humankind against modern nihilism is in the restitution of language in the service of truth, that is in the lucid consciousness of death and the Absurd. In this way, humankind would be able to protect itself from its tendency toward self-destruction.

Merton was in full agreement on Camus' analysis of the modern world and he recognized in Camus' novels, short stories, and plays artistic expressions of this analysis which had serious implications for the Church. In "Three Saviors in Camus: Lucidity and the Absurd," Merton reviews three of Camus' works: "The Renegade," "The Misunderstanding" and "The Growing Stone." In the first two works, efforts at communication, because essentially deceptive, result in violence. The third work, offers an alternative.

"The Renegade" is a satire on a kind of Christian triumphalism which distorts the Gospel by its hidden resentment of others and its love of power. Consequently, the language of the Church, while proclaiming salvation, in reality prepares the way for a totalitarianism[12]

---

ficiently come to terms with the problem of God nor had he understood that non-violence can be a form of active resistance rather than passive resignation.

11. See Thomas Merton's "The Root of War is Fear" in *New Seeds of Contemplation* (New York: New Directions, 1961) 112–20.

12. Merton, in a lecture delivered to the novices at the Abbey of Gethsemani, explains that Joseph Hromadka, a Czech protestant theologian, was of the opinion

which institutionalizes hatred, violence and injustice. In this story, a nameless missionary is sent from Europe to proclaim the Word of God to a primitive tribe of savages for whom he has no respect and only disgust. It is he, however, who is converted by the pagans, discovering within himself an "immortal soul of hatred." The story begins with the missionary, tongue cut out and mind in violent turmoil, waiting to murder the next missionary who is coming to take his place, to settle with him, his teachers and with the whole of Europe for having deceived him. It was the sword and the sword that now alone ruled his life. But as we listen to the missionary's soliloquy, we discover that the sword of brutal power and not the Gospel of peace has always been the tool of his trade. His language, the language of the Church he served, as well as, the language of the continent from which he came, is committed, not to life, but to death.[13]

The second work is a play.[14] In "The Misunderstanding," Jan, a Christian, returns home to a village in Central Europe from North Africa with his new wife. He has come home to announce to his mother and sister that he has made his fortune and wants to take them away to a place where they can be happy. Because he wants to surprise them, he tries to construct an elaborate plan whereby he might enter the inn managed by his mother and sister as a stranger. His wife, to no avail, tries to persuade him to simply present himself without disguise as their son and brother. Merton tells us:

> Jan is a savior who observes those he wishes to save, analyses them, studies them as their superior, and without consulting them arranges everything to suit his abstract plan for their salvation. He decides to manipulate their lives (whether they like it or not) and surprise them with the gift of happiness.[15]

---

that Christianity prepared the way for Communism. It is not certain from the context whether Merton was in complete agreement with Hromadka. It is clear, however, that Merton was at least open to this thesis. "Communism vs. Capitalism," cassette AA2235, Credence, 1988.

13. Albert Camus, "The Renegade," in *Exile and the Kingdom* (New York: Vintage Books, 1958) 34–61.

14. Albert Camus, "The Misunderstanding," in *Caligula and Three Other Plays* (New York: Vintage Books, 1958) 77–134.

15. Thomas Merton, "Three Saviors in Camus: Lucidity and the Absurd," in *The Literary Essays of Thomas Merton*, ed. Patrick Hart (New York: New Directions, 1981) 283.

Unknown to Jan his mother and sister have been robbing and murdering their guests in order to steal a small fortune and escape from their dreary existence to a far away country of sea and sunshine.[16] While he is trying to find the right words with which to reveal himself and his surprise, his mother and sister kill him. The root of this tragedy, Merton tells us, is in Jan, in two fatal flaws, his distrust of love and his veneration of abstract reason. Regardless of his good intentions, Jan's assumed position of superiority results in violence and death.

While "The Renegade" and "The Misunderstanding" focus our attention on the nihilistic nature of the Church's use of language, "The Growing Stone"[17] is an effort by Camus to work out an alternative to the Church's approach to communication with the world which may be more effective in building an authentic community between the old established European civilization and the cultures of what was then the emerging Third World; a community in which there is open communication, honest dialogue and clear language.

D'Arrast, a French engineer, travels to South America where he finds himself participating in a local church procession which requires him to move a ceremonial stone. Rather than taking the stone to the designated place in the town's cathedral, D'Arrast, unexpectedly and without explanation, carries the stone deep into the woods of the bordering forest, away from the Church and into the natural environment of the indigenous people. Here, the native people, not fully understanding the meaning of this act, say to him, "Sit down with us." These concluding words suggested to Merton that Camus was implying that where there is openness, humility and the willingness to accept human limitations, to accept the other person as s/he is, to be oneself without pretensions, communication, though never absolutely perfect, may become possible and may lead to the building of authentic community where human life and freedom might flourish.

Reflecting on "The Renegade," "The Misunderstanding" and "The Growing Stone" at the end of "Three Saviors in Camus: Lucidity and the Absurd," Merton concluded:

> Here, although Camus is expressly non-Christian we must admit
> that in practice his ethic seems to tend in the direction pointed out

16. This situation was not apparently uncommon in Europe. Czeslaw Milosz tells about secluded inns with conniving innkeepers who used "the guillotine," a bed whose canopy fell at night, to kill unsuspecting travelers. *The Issa Valley* (New York: Noonday Press, 1981) 67.

17. Albert Camus, "The Growing Stone," in *Exile and the Kingdom,* 159–213.

by authentic Christian charity. Though Camus failed to understand the full import of the Christian message, the failure is for many reasons understandable, and once again it suggests that even for the Christian the moral aspirations of a Camus retain a definite importance. They bear witness to the plight of man in the world with which the Christian still seeks to communicate, and suggests conditions under which the communication may conceivably be more valid.[18]

The concluding essays in the first phase of Merton's work on Camus continue where this one ends. "Camus and the Church" and "Prophetic Ambiguities: Milton and Camus," both written in October, emphasize the importance of Camus as a prophetic voice in the modern world. Camus, like Milton, was a poetic thinker who created myths in which are embodied his own struggles to come to terms with the fundamental questions of life. He is to be understood as prophetic in the sense that he anticipated in his solitude[19] the struggles and general consciousness of later generations, in particular the modern world's tension between action and contemplation, its feelings of ambiguity and ambivalence, and its tendency toward nihilism.

Merton sets Camus before the Church as a prophetic voice challenging Christians to examine their participation in modern nihilism, that is, their support of the state in acts of violence against humankind. In "Camus and the Church" the dialogue between a priest and a prisoner at the end of Camus' *The Stranger* is presented for consideration on this point. The priest is attempting to prepare Meursault, a prisoner, for his execution by the state. Meursault, refuses to call the priest "Father," refuses to accept the priest's consolations and, thereby, refuses to willingly participate in the crime of capital punishment[20] constructed by the state and supported by the Church. Of such a priest, Camus will later write: "When a Spanish bishop blesses political executions, he ceases to be a bishop or a Christian or even a man; he is a dog just like the one who, backed by an ideology, orders that execution

18. Merton, "Three Saviors," 291.

19. Merton recognized in Camus the development of an asceticism and contemplative life which was very much in line with his own understanding of monastic traditions. He referred to Camus in "Day of a Stranger" as that "Algerian cenobite."

20. Camus was opposed to capital punishment. He saw it as a manifestation of nihilism. See his "Reflections on the Guillotine" in *Resistance, Rebellion, and Death*, 175–234.

without doing the dirty work himself."[21] Merton accepted as valid Camus' criticism of the Church for not speaking out clearly and without ambiguity against nihilism in the modern world, and, consequently, for becoming a collaborator with the state in the institutionalization of violence by preaching resignation, passivity and conformity. While Merton believes that this is a misunderstanding of the Gospel, he places the responsibility for this misunderstanding on the Church for distorting the Christian message by either preaching resignation to the oppressed peoples of the world or failing to encourage them with the Gospel to resist the injustices imposed upon them.

While Merton presents Camus as a prophet who brings judgment to bear upon the Church, he also sees him as a prophet who opens new ways of being in the world that promise new life for the Church. Now that we have reviewed the first phase of Merton's work on Camus, we are in a position to summarize the primary points and thereby clarify some of these new methods for authentic dialogue.

First, it is clear that Merton accepted Camus' criticism of the Church as a collaborator with the state in the violent oppression of people. The Church collaborates with the State whenever she, like the priest in *The Stranger*, preaches resignation and conformity in the face of oppression. The Church contributes to the violence that is in the world whenever she, like Jan in "Misunderstanding," distrusting love and acting from a position of superiority, constructs intellectual abstractions to manipulate people, regardless of intentions, however good one might believe them to be. The Church inevitably commits violence whenever she, like the missionary in "The Renegade," fails to come to terms with her love of power and her hidden resentment of people outside of her control. Merton believed that Camus' prophetic voice was rightfully challenging the Church to face her participation in the nihilism of the modern world by examining herself in light of the above accusations. The willingness to examine oneself, to be oneself and not what one pretends to be, is the first step in preparing for dialogue. In 1948, Camus had called the Dominican monks of Latour-Maubourg to this task.[22] In 1966, Merton reissued this appeal to the Church.[23]

---

21. "The Unbeliever and Christians" in *Resistance, Rebellion, and Death*, 71–2.
22. Ibid., 69–74.
23. "Camus and the Church" originally published in the December 1966, *The Catholic Worker*.

It is also clear that Merton believed Camus had suggested viable conditions under which communication may conceivably be more authentic and potentially creative. He accepted Camus' notion of revolt against death and the Absurd in contrast to violent political revolution or passive resignation as a position valid for Christians seeking to bring about change in the world. This position of revolt requires three things: lucidity, solidarity, and resistance. That is to say, the Christian, as a kind of Camusian Rebel, must maintain a clear mind on the problem of nihilism and be willing to join with others in continuous resistance to any and all acts of violence against humankind and intellectual abstractions on which those acts are based. As Camus suggested in the "Growing Stone," the Church's willingness to find common ground with people from other traditions will eventually present the possibility for open and honest dialogue. In order to "sit down" with others, however, the Church, like D'Arrast, must be open to the traditions valued by other peoples. This is not to say that the Church is to abandon the Christian faith. On the contrary, as Camus explained to the Dominican monks of Latour-Maubourg:

> . . . what I feel like telling you today is that the world needs real dialogue, that falsehood is just as much the opposite of dialogue as is silence, and that the only possible dialogue is the kind between people who remain what they are and speak their minds. This is tantamount to saying that the world of today needs Christians who remain Christians.[24]

It is to say, however, that the Church must think and speak in terms of real human life rather than in theological abstractions which often leave people confused and the problems they face unresolved:

> What the world expects of Christians is that Christians should speak out, loud and clear, and that they should voice their condemnation in such a way that never a doubt, never the slightest doubt, could rise in the heart of the simplest man. That they should get away from abstraction and confront the blood-stained face history has taken on today.[25]

It is in this resistance to the common problem of death and self-destruction, that the different traditions of the world, including

---

24. "The Unbeliever and Christians" in *Resistance, Rebellion, and Death*, 70.
25. Ibid., 71.

Christianity, can find solidarity. And, it is from this common ground, this solidarity, that a shared language can emerge that will facilitate peace and justice; a language in service to human life, not abstract ideologies.

While Merton accepted Camus' criticism of the Church and his conditions for authentic dialogue, he consistently maintained one reservation with regard to Camus. Repeatedly, Merton states that Camus failed to understand fully the Christian message. He does not fault Camus for this failure, but rather the Church for failing to communicate the Gospel clearly. But whatever the cause or nature of the misunderstanding, it is at this point Merton and Camus part ways. Even though Merton became a Rebel with Camus, he did so on very different grounds. For Camus, the position of revolt taken by the Rebel is grounded in humankind's resistance to death.[26] For Merton, it is humankind's response to the hidden ground of Love.[27]

It should be noted, that this difference is not articulated by Merton until he has given undivided attention to what Camus is saying. Throughout Merton's seven essays on Camus, the reader will find the following pattern: a statement of respect for Camus, an affirmation of Camus' general message, and, then, and only then, a comment by Merton on Camus' ideas in light of the Gospel.[28] Furthermore, as we have repeatedly observed, Merton never holds Camus responsible for misunderstanding the Christian message but always accepts responsibility, as a representative of the Church, for the misunderstanding. Consequently, Merton continually rethinks what he has to say as a Christian monk in the context of the ever widening circle of men and women interested in gathering with others to discover a common ground for people from diverse traditions. Respect for the other person, affirmation of what they have to share, and the willingness to struggle with his own message in light of the other person's thought, became characteristic of the way in which Merton entered into dialogue with the postmodern world in which he lived.

26. Camus' later thought moves beyond the Absurd and the Rebel. Consequently, any discussion of his grounding must be done in light of this change. While his death prevented him from fully developing his thought on this matter, the recent publication of an unfinished novel, *The First Man* (New York: Alfred A. Knopf, 1995), provides an opportunity to reconsider this subject.

27. Merton, *Hidden Ground of Love*, 115.

28. We find a similar pattern in Clement of Alexandria's interaction with Stoic philosophy. Because of Merton's work on Clement, a comparative study could be of value.

Merton's "True Self" and the Fundamental Option

Mark O'Keefe, O.S.B.

An important development in contemporary Catholic theology is the effort to attend to spirituality as a source for theological reflection. Without denying the importance of the Scriptures or established doctrine, a number of Catholic theologians have argued that spiritual experience—and the theological reflection of contemplatives and mystics on their spiritual experience—is also a valid source for theological reflection.[1] This is no less true in moral theology than in doctrinal theology. In fact, I have argued elsewhere that moral theology and spirituality are intimately interrelated and ought to be understood as mutually enriching.[2]

The work of Thomas Merton offers a particularly rich source for revealing the power of spirituality and of spiritual experience to illuminate moral reflection and, of course, for moral theology to illuminate spiritual reflection. In this article, we will look at Merton's distinction between the true self and the false self as it sheds light on the somewhat controversial discussion of the fundamental option in contemporary Catholic moral theology. Bringing Merton's insights together with fundamental option theory will help to shed greater light on both and will further illuminate an authentic understanding of the Christian life as dynamic and holistic.

1. See, for example, William M. Thompson, *Spirituality and Christology* (New York: Crossroad, 1991).
2. Mark O'Keefe, *Becoming Good, Becoming Holy: On the Relationship of Christian Ethics and Spirituality* (Mahwah, N.J.: Paulist, 1995). See also Dennis J. Billy and Donna Lynn Orsuto, eds., *Spirituality and Morality: Integrating Prayer and Action* (Mahwah, N.J.: Paulist, 1996).

Our reflection will proceed in the following manner: first, we will sketch, in summary fashion, an understanding of the fundamental option, noting an important line of criticism that has been raised in response to it. Second, we will examine Merton's discussion of true self and false self, looking briefly at the relationship between the false self and sin. This will allow us, thirdly, to examine the relationship between Merton's insights and fundamental option theory as they mutually enrich one another in illuminating the dynamic and holistic structure of the Christian life. Finally, we will suggest how Merton's discussion of the relationship of the self and society can help to offer a more broadly social perspective on the fundamental option.

The Fundamental Option

Moral theologians have pursued the discussion of the "fundamental option" largely as a corrective to pre-Vatican II explanations of sin.[3] The manuals of moral theology, the moral textbooks used in Catholic seminaries before the council, presented sin in a manner that came to be seen, in light of renewed biblical and theological studies, to be too act-centered, too individualistic, and too legalistic. Fundamental option theory has been used primarily to disclose how it is that sin is rooted at a level deeper than individual acts, that is, in a "fundamental option" against God.

The fundamental option theory has often been advanced by discussion of the biblical concept of the "heart" as the deepest core of the human person and by discussion of psychological insights into the deeper bases of human freedom.[4] Perhaps the most sustained discussion of the bases of the fundamental option relies on philosophical and theological reflections on freedom, associated especially with the work of theologian Karl Rahner. Rahner identifies two levels of freedom: the level of categorical freedom which involves the conscious ability to choose between individual objects (i.e., the level of "free choice") and the deeper level of transcendental freedom from which categorical freedom flows.[5] Transcendental freedom is the fundamental ability of

3. See, for example, Eugene Cooper, "The Notion of Sin in Light of the Theory of the Fundamental Option: The Fundamental Option Revisited," *Louvain Studies* 9 (Fall 1983) 363–82.

4. Bernard Häring, *Free and Faithful in Christ* (New York: Seabury, 1978) 1:164–222.

5. Karl Rahner, *Theological Investigations* (New York: Crossroad, 1982) 6:178–96; and *Foundations of Christian Faith* (New York: Crossroad, 1982) 90–115.

the human person to dispose himself or herself toward or away from God. It is realized in and influenced by categorical choices between discrete objects but cannot be simply equated with these choices. Moral theologian Josef Fuchs makes a similar distinction, speaking of freedom of choice and a deeper level of freedom which he calls "basic freedom."[6] Existing at this deep level of the person, the fundamental "option" is not a choice like any other, so that some moral theologians prefer to speak, not of "option" but of fundamental "stance." But, because the exercise of transcendental freedom is dynamic—that is, one's deepest self-disposing seeks an ever-deeper integration of the person's choices—it may be more accurate to speak of a fundamental "orientation" or fundamental "self-disposition."

For moral theologians influenced by Rahner and Fuchs, sin resides at the level of transcendental or basic freedom. True mortal sin involves a fundamental disposition of the person away from God, a life turned away from God. Sinful acts manifest this deeper reality of sin and sap the strength of a positive fundamental option, but sin cannot be simply equated with these acts.

Elsewhere, I have tried to demonstrate that fundamental option theory offers a valuable tool for understanding, not only sin, but the dynamism of the Christian life directed toward God—the life of grace, the journey toward holiness.[7] While moral theologians have been using fundamental option theory to speak of the deep and tragically dynamic growth of sin in the human person, the theory offers even richer possibilities for enlightening the dynamic growth and integration of the life fundamentally oriented and disposed toward God.

As Rahner has made clear, the exercise of transcendental freedom seeks the integration of the human person around his or her fundamental option. Tragically, for the sinner, this means that the negative fundamental option naturally tends toward the integration of further sinful choices into the sinner's disposition away from God—sin breeds sin. Happily, the human person cannot dispose himself or herself completely and finally in this life, always leaving hope therefore that God's grace may yet be effective in the sinner's lifetime. On the other hand, the positive fundamental option seeks the integration of all of one's choices, and ultimately all of one's desiring, into a self-disposing to-

6. Josef Fuchs, *Human Values and Christian Morality* (Dublin: Gill and Macmillan, 1970) 92–111.

7. O'Keefe, *Becoming Good, Becoming Holy*, 44–56.

ward God as the source and goal of all authentic human desire. This insight helps to explain the inherent dynamism, holism, and integration of the Christian life, authentically lived as empowered by grace. Overcoming sinful choices against God, growing in habitual dispositions (virtues) for the goods that can lead us to God, tutoring our desires (asceticism) can all be seen as part of the integrative dynamism of the positive fundamental option, the life directed toward God.

We are in a position, then, to see how the discussion of the dynamic integration of the positive fundamental option can illuminate—and be illuminated by—the Three Ways, a classic tool in the Christian spiritual tradition for understanding the growth of the Christian life. The concept of the Three Ways describes the growth of the Christian life from the battle against mortal sin at the earliest level of the *purgative* way, through the *illuminative* way of growth in virtue "illuminated" by charity, and finally to the *unitive* way in which the Christian life reaches its penultimate goal. In the same way, as we will see, fundamental option theory can illuminate and be illuminated by Merton's insight into the movement of the Christian life from the tyranny of the false self to the discovery and liberating of the true self.

Of course, fundamental option theory is not without its critics. Among these are Pope John Paul II himself who (without rejecting all forms of fundamental option theory) cautioned, in a 1984 apostolic exhortation,[8] against certain possible directions in fundamental option theory. His concern has been more recently and more systematically addressed in his 1993 encyclical *Veritatis splendor.*[9] The Pope's primary concern is to reaffirm the traditional Catholic teaching that the human person can sin in an individual act, a possibility called into question by locating sin at the level of transcendental freedom rather than in the exercise of categorical freedom in choosing between discrete options. The Pope's concern is shared by a number of moral theologians who have argued that the whole idea of two levels of freedom smacks of "dualism."[10] It is not my purpose here to attempt a defense of fundamental option theories of sin (though I suspect that a better nuancing of fundamental option discussions of sin might address the Pope's concern); but I would like to summarize the other theologians' charge

---

8. Pope John Paul II, *Reconciliation and Penance* (Washington: USCC, 1984) 56–64.

9. Pope John Paul II, *Veritatis splendor* (Washington: USCC, 1993) 98–108.

10. See, for example, articles in: William E. May, ed., *Principles of the Catholic Moral Life* (Chicago: Franciscan Herald Press, 1980).

of dualism, because it provides an instance of how the spiritual tradition and spiritual experience can illuminate a moral theological discussion.

For the critics of fundamental option theory, freedom is understood to entail the exercise of free choice guided by the conscience, for which we hold people morally responsible, whether as worthy of blame or of praise. It is certainly true, say the critics, that some choices are more complete and give greater direction or definition to one's life—for example, the decision to be baptized as an adult, to marry, to make a major career change, to enter professed religious life. We could speak of these as "fundamental options." The substantive objection arises when fundamental option theorists want to speak of the existence of some deeper level of freedom as the foundation of free choice. In fact, Rahner, and many who follow his thought, argue that the exercise of transcendental freedom is not fully available to consciousness. One cannot attain a reflexive knowledge of one's core freedom. It is manifested in our choices but not fully revealed in them. The critics, as mentioned above, argue that this theory of two levels of freedom, one of which is not available to reflexive consciousness, amounts to dualism, a split between the level of free choices and some mysterious deeper inner self that can be distinguished from the choosing self.

In my earlier work I suggested that the existence of an inner self, not fully available to reflexive consciousness, is a presupposition of traditional mystical literature. The human person encounters God, not only in a *manner* that cannot be described adequately in words but also at a *level* too deep for words (reflexive consciousness). The classic notion of a "dark night" of the soul describes an experience in which the person feels nothing, but in which God is, in reality, being encountered at a profoundly deeper level than human consciousness can grasp.

It is precisely at this point that we can usefully examine Merton's discussions of the true self, discussions that are entirely in line with the classic contemplative and mystical discussions of the depth of the human encounter with God in prayer. The present study began with the observation that theology can benefit from attending to the spiritual experience and theological reflection of contemplatives and mystics. In the exposition that follows, we will suggest that a discussion of fundamental option theory may be entered more profitably from the experience of a spiritual master like Merton than in reaction to an older theology of sin. At the same time, we will suggest that fundamental option theory, as briefly explicated here, can shed further light on Merton's less systematic theological discussions of self.

True Self—False Self

An important theme that runs through Merton's work is the distinction that he draws between the true self and the false self.[11] In various places, Merton uses a variety of terms to describe this distinction.[12] For the true self, he also uses the terms "real," "inner," "spiritual," and "deepest most hidden" self. He also speaks of the false self as an "external," "illusory," "smoke" or "superficial" self. In different contexts, these terms can have slightly different meanings and emphases. For our present purposes, we will take the various terms as synonymous, though it will be important to clarify what it means to speak of the "external" self as "false." Despite the variety of terms, and of real development in his thinking (as analyzed by Anne Carr), Merton's thought on this subject developed along sufficiently consistent lines to allow us to speak of a coherent, if not systematic understanding of the self.

For Merton, the "I" or "ego" of everyday consciousness and decisions is not the human person's true and deepest self. For Merton, Descartes' famous assertion of his *"Cogito ergo sum"* is quite profoundly wrong.[13] The human person's truest self is the inner and hidden self, the deepest reality of the human person where he or she is truly sustained by a most fundamental union with God as the Ground of being—where, if God were not continually present to us, we would simply cease to exist. For Merton, then, union with God is, in a real way, less "attained" than "discovered" or "awakened" and then accepted and nurtured. This awakening of the true self allows the

11. For more in-depth examinations of Merton's understanding of the self, see Anne E. Carr, *A Search for Wisdom and Spirit: Thomas Merton's Theology of the Self* (Notre Dame: University of Notre Dame Press, 1988); Thomas M. King, *Merton: Mystic at the Center of America* (Collegeville: The Liturgical Press, 1992) 1–36; and at least two works of William Shannon: "Thomas Merton and the Discovery of the Real Self," *Cistercian Studies* 13 (no. 4, 1978) 298–308 and "Thomas Merton and the Quest for Self-Identity," *Cistercian Studies* 22 (no. 2, 1987) 172–89. For a more popular discussion, see James Finley, *Merton's Palace of Nowhere: A Search for God Through Awareness of the True Self* (Notre Dame: Ave Maria, 1978).

12. See Shannon, "The Discovery of the Real Self," 301.

13. Thomas Merton, *New Seeds of Contemplation* (New York: Dimension Books, 1961) 7–9.

Christian to say with Saint Paul: "I live now, not I, but Christ lives in me" (Gal 2:20).

The "I" or "ego" of everyday consciousness is really an external or superficial self. At this level, it is certainly real enough, as it carries out the daily activities of human living and interactions. In fact, the external self is largely the self of everyday choices, good and bad, and of virtues and even of character. But, more deeply, the external self always retains an illusory character. It carries on the daily activities of life as if it encompasses the fullness of human existence; but, to the degree that it carries on these activities without cognizance of and conformity with the true self grounded in God, it remains cut off from a deeper reality.

Although it can be spoken of as a "false" self in the sense of being sinful; more basically, the false self is more superficial and illusory than essentially evil.[14] Although the illusion of the primacy and separate existence of the external self is the result of original sin, it is not sinful in itself but simply not ultimately or deeply real. Still, personal sin, for Merton, starts with this external or illusory self, as it seeks to construct an edifice of pleasure, honor, and power to shore up its illusory existence. The false self wants to exist as if it were autonomous, as if the human person's deepest identity were not the self grounded in and united with God. This search for an illusory existence is the root of real, personal sin.[15]

For Merton, the dynamic of the Christian life can be described as the movement from the illusory reign of the false self to the discovery and awakening of the true self. This awakening is possible only because Christ first reaches out to us, working to unite us with him.[16] Merton equates this life movement with the patristic and monastic understanding of the movement from image to likeness and with the effort to attain purity of heart, so much the goal of the monastic tradition.[17] Perhaps we might also equate it with the task of ongoing conversion that stands at the heart of the monastic and, more basically, of the Christian tradition. Our present study attempts to demonstrate that we may also helpfully speak of the movement from false to true

14. Ibid., 295–6.

15. Ibid., 33–5. See also Carr, *Search for Wisdom*, 13; Finley, *Palace of Nowhere*, 35.

16. Thomas Merton, *The New Man* (New York: Farrar, Straus, and Cudahy, 1961) 232.

17. Thomas Merton, *The Silent Life* (New York: Farrar, Straus, and Giroux, 1957) 1–26.

self as the ongoing integration of the Christian's positive fundamental option.

It is clear that, for Merton, the true or real self is not fully available to consciousness.[18] The real self cannot be examined like an object from outside. He speaks of the true self metaphorically as a "shy, wild animal" that can be glimpsed only in stillness and calm.[19] For the Christian, therefore, the real self represents his or her life "hidden with Christ in God"; it shares in the hiddenness of God. This explains why, for Merton, the true self is "awakened" or "discovered," not in active self-reflection but in contemplation. Further, the hiddenness of the true self also explains, in part, Merton's interest in Zen meditation as an approach to an experience of "pure awareness" of the true self.[20]

Fundamental Option and True Self

George Kilcourse has suggested a possible connection between Merton's discussion of the true self and fundamental option theory.[21] Our brief exposition of both will now allow us to explicate the connection, though it will require some further clarification of each.

For William Shannon, Merton's "real self" can be understood as the human person's openness to transcendence (Rahner) or as the human capacity for the divine (Dan Walsh).[22] Shannon concludes that the real self is "nothing other than the divine call at the core of our being to become one with God and in him with all others. It is the capacity for divinity, the openness to transcendence, that God creates in each one of us. It is the seed of God straining to burst the shell of the superficial self in order to actualize our capacity for the divine."[23] Similarly, Walter Conn, building on the thought of Bernard Lonergan equates the real self with the radical drive for self-transcendence.[24]

---

18. Merton, *New Seeds*, 7–8, 279–80. See also Carr, *Search for Wisdom*, 30–1; King, *Mystic at the Center*, 25–8; and Shannon, "The Quest for Self-Identity," 184–5.

19. Merton, "Inner Experience," 5.

20. Carr, *Search for Wisdom*, 41–5. See Thomas Merton, "The Inner Experience (I)," *Cistercian Studies* 18 (1983) 6–9.

21. George E. Kilcourse, *Ace of Freedoms: Thomas Merton's Christ* (Notre Dame: University of Notre Dame Press, 1993) 53.

22. Shannon, "The Discovery of the Real Self," 301.

23. Ibid., 308.

24. Walter E. Conn, "Merton's 'True Self': Moral Autonomy and Religious Conversion," *The Journal of Religion* 65 (October 1985) 524–5.

Transcendental freedom is the foundational ability of the human person to affirm his or her own truest purpose as a capacity for divinity precisely by saying "yes" to God. This exercise of transcendental freedom is a "yes" both to God and to our truest self, and the fundamental disposition of self for God is freedom's deepest purpose and the human person's most authentic fulfillment. The positive fundamental option, then, is the exercise of transcendental freedom by which the human person says "yes" to God and "yes" to one's truest self in God. The negative fundamental option is the self-contradictory exercise of fundamental option by which one says "no" to God and therefore "no" to one's truest self. It is to say "yes" instead to the illusory and sinful constructs of the external or false self.

The fundamental option shares in the hiddenness of the true self since it flows from the deepest core of the human person. Neither is available to conscious self-reflection. Rather, the fundamental option reveals itself in concrete exercises of free choice, most especially in the expressions of self-giving love that manifest a self disposed and surrendered to the God who is love.

Merton does not explicate, in any sustained or systematic way, the relationship between the true self and the external self. How is the everyday "I," the conscious self that makes decisions and even grows in virtue related to the deepest and truest reality of the human person? How can the conscious "I" truly be called "illusory" or "false"? Perhaps in recalling the somewhat ambiguous relationship between the transcendental and categorical levels of freedom, we can also shed light on the relationship between the true and the false selves—and vice versa.

The deepest and foundational level of human freedom is the level of transcendental freedom. The level of free choice, the categorical level, is the conscious realization of freedom in the world of discrete objects of choice. The categorical level, then, can be understood as an external manifestation or realization of freedom. It must be assumed that, because of human contingency and limit, not every individual choice is a complete realization of the human person's most fundamental self-disposing; but if human existence were not touched by sin, there would be at least a complete consistency between the two levels. Without sin, the deepest core of the human person and the deepest exercise of human freedom would find a consistent realization in individual free choices. Every individual choice would be in conformity with the authentic self-disposing of the person for God. But because of sin, there is not a complete consistency between the two levels, as the traditional category of venial sin has suggested—that is, there are sinful choices that are not consistent with, but not completely contradictory to, the heart that is more basically turned toward God.

From this perspective, the conscious "I" and the exercise of free choice are certainly real. The objects of choice are real, and the conscious exercise of freedom in relationship to these objects is real. In itself, the conscious "I" is neither sinful nor even illusory; however, at the level of actual, historical human existence and experience, there is always a split between the deepest core of the human person and this conscious "I." As Merton suggests, this split is the result of original sin.[25] The human person believes himself or herself to be an autonomous "I," a subject independent of God who, in reality, is the very ground of every human existence. The conscious "I," then, influenced by sin, becomes caught up in an illusion of autonomous existence. The exercise of free choice too becomes skewed, so that even the growth of virtue as a habitual disposing of freedom's choosing, good in itself, retains an element of the illusory as long as it is cut off from its deepest meaning in a life directed to God (or, in more traditional Thomistic terms, as long as the development of virtue is not illuminated by charity).

It cannot be said, as Merton sometimes seems to say, that the conscious "I" is in itself false, illusory, or sinful; but Merton is certainly correct that original sin, partnered with the sinfulness encountered in society and confirmed and strengthened by personal sin, leads to the construction of a false, illusory, and sinful self that cannot be fully separated from the conscious "I" in this life.

The movement from the false self to the true self is not a movement of eliminating the conscious "I" but rather of "getting behind" it to its authentic roots in a self, more hidden but more real. It is the recovery of a more authentic unity between the inner and the external selves—or, perhaps, more accurately, it is movement to a more authentic unity realized in the unity of the whole person with God attained in Christ. It is therefore the elimination of the illusion of an existence autonomous from God, and the discovery and the grateful acceptance of a deeper unity with God. The false self—that is, the sin-constructed illusion of an autonomous self—is destroyed. The human person surrenders to God, surrenders to his or her truest self which has its existence only in God.

25. Merton, *New Seeds*, 280.

Fundamental option theory shows how this movement from false to true self is the very dynamic structure of the Christian life. The fundamental option, of course, is not an "option" in the sense of a one-time accomplishment, a once-for-all attainment. It is rather a self-disposing, a dynamic orientation of life in which human persons seek the integration of all their choices, exercises of categorical freedom, into their fundamental self-disposing toward God. The dynamic integration of the fundamental option is none other than the movement toward an ever greater consistency between the person's most fundamental self-disposing and all of his or her discrete choices. It is therefore the ongoing de-construction of the edifice of the false self and the unifying of the conscious "I" with the person's deepest self. We can see, along with Merton, that this is fully in line with such traditional concepts as the attainment of purity of heart and the life of ongoing conversion.

True Self and Society

Although it is true that, for Merton, the true self is "discovered" or "awakened" in contemplation, it is no less true that the true self is encountered and realized in self-giving love. The true self discovered in contemplation is revealed to be a self whose fulfillment is realized in love. In fact, as Merton says: "Love is my true identity. Selflessness is my true self. Love is my true character. Love is my name."[26] Merton's concept, then, does not enshrine solitary contemplation as a goal in itself. As Merton says: "A man cannot enter into the deepest center of himself and pass through that center into God, unless he is able to pass entirely out of himself and empty himself and give himself to other people in the purity of selfless love."[27] The discovery of the true self is realized and authenticated in selfless loving. In this, Merton is consistent with his monastic tradition that sees the salvation of the monastic person to be worked out in the ongoing, daily life of bearing with the burdens and serving one's brothers (or sisters) in community. In fact, for reasons that will be explained below, Merton is in line with contemplatives whose communion with God have lead them to a greater, not lesser, commitment to the service of their brothers and sisters.[28]

26. Ibid., 60.
27. Thomas Merton, *Seeds of Contemplation* (New York: New Directions, 1949) 41.
28. See Terry Tastard, *The Spark in the Soul: Four Mystics on Justice* (Mahwah, N.J.: Paulist, 1989).

In fact, Merton's unfolding of the distinction between true self and false self can help to illuminate the social ramifications of fundamental option theory. In speaking of the fundamental option as the deep self-disposing of the human person, neither the inherently social dimension of the human person nor the Gospel imperative to act for justice is immediately evident. The fundamental option may seem to imply that the ideal of the Christian life is essentially individual or even private. In contrast, Merton's thought, mirrored in his own life, holds together a contemplative ideal and a strong social commitment. His broader discussion of the deeper unity of the true self with other persons and of the tragic social edifice of false selves helps to suggest a broader, social understanding of the fundamental option.

First, in relation to the negative fundamental option, we can see that, for Merton, the illusory edifice of the individual false self has social roots and social ramifications.[29] As we have already seen, the weaving of the illusion of an autonomous existence by the external self is the result of original sin. This truly false and sinful self is then the root of personal sin and is further promoted by personal sin. But the construction of the edifice of pleasure, honor, and power in which the individual false self seeks its security has strong social connections. The illusion of the human person autonomous from God is promoted by the sinful elements of society. The constructs of pleasure, honor, pride, and power are appropriated from the tragic and fearful striving of other false selves, spread throughout society and extended through history. The petty and illusory construct of the individual false self contributes to the falsity and illusion already present in society.

The person's fundamental option cannot remain unaffected by the sinful illusion present in society. Certainly, the negative fundamental option, the person turned away from God, promotes the construction of the false self's shell of illusion and sin. The human person turned away from God is a self-contradiction, and the radical insecurity of the false self seeking autonomy from God can only seek security in a world of objects whose protection is ultimately illusory. In a world of sin, the false self finds, not so much allies (for each is seeking for its own individual security alone) but collaborators. In such a world, even the person whose life is fundamentally disposed toward God, feels the attraction of the illusion since no person, after the Fall, is born without the split between the true self and the external self. The positive fun-

29. Carr, *Search for Wisdom*, 73–4.

damental option is always threatened by the world of illusion and falsity constructed over time and extended across society, though the progressive integration of the person's freedom into his or her fundamental disposing creates an ever stronger defense against the temptation to accept the illusory autonomy of the human from God.

Merton's reflections, then, offer valuable insights into a theology of social sin and its relationship to the fundamental option. No less does Merton's thought help us to see the hidden but powerful connection between the true self and every other human person, and therefore between the positive fundamental option and the human community.

The true self, says Merton, grounded and fundamentally united with God, is necessarily and essentially related to every other self. The God who is the ground and sustaining power (the "hidden ground of Love") of my truest and hidden self is no less the ground of every other true self. Human discord and the illusion of individual persons autonomous from God and from one another is part of the illusion of the false self. In reality, the more that men and women are in touch with their truest self, the more that they realize that they are inherently and necessarily related to every other human person in God. Authentic solitude, then, promotes not a spirit of isolation or individualism but of profound connectedness. It is possible for the solitary contemplative to realize his or her unity with other persons far more deeply than people who live in a world of crowds and superficial contacts. The cloistered monastic person can realize a more profound relationship with humanity than the person absorbed in the secular world.[30]

The positive fundamental option, then, as the disposing of the self toward God and therefore toward my truest self, draws the person more deeply into relationship with other persons. To dispose one's life toward God is to dispose one's life to those other persons whose lives are likewise grounded in God. To say "yes" to my truest self, as dependent on and in relationship with God, is to say "yes" to humanity, to other human persons, and to the human community. The positive fundamental option then is necessarily a commitment to social engagement and not an individual or private relationship with God. The person disposed toward God is disposed to the building up of the

---

30. See Thomas Merton, "Philosophy of Solitude," in *Disputed Questions* (New York: Farrar, Straus, and Giroux, 1953) 163–93; and "Inner Experience," 121–6.

community of all. Merton's famous contemplative insight, while on the corner of Louisville's Fourth and Walnut,[31] in which he suddenly realized his profound relationship with the people around him, can be understood in this light.

Conclusion

Catholic moral theology seems to be passing out of a period in which its principal concern focused on individual moral issues and the methodologies needed to address those issues. Surely, reflection of this type remains essential if the discipline of moral theology is to offer real guidance when difficult moral decisions must be made. At the same time, however, there seems to be a developing sense that moral theology must also offer a broader framework to give perspective to and to guide Christian living—the broader context in which individual moral decisions can be understood as integral to the person's entire life precisely as a Christian. It is dialogue with Christian spirituality that offers moral theology the language and framework for offering this more holistic and dynamic understanding of the Christian moral life.

One area of controversy in post-conciliar Catholic moral theology has been fundamental option theory which, though discussed principally to explain sin, offers one way in which the holistic dynamism of Christian living can be understood. Summarized above and discussed at greater length elsewhere, I have attempted to demonstrate that spirituality can shed light on certain areas of controversy about fundamental option theory, such as the hiddenness of the exercise of transcendental freedom. More specifically in this article, I have attempted to show that Thomas Merton's distinction between the false self and the true self helps to illuminate the two levels of freedom identified by Rahner as the basis for a good deal of fundamental option thinking. At the same time, moral theology can shed its own light on spirituality, and our discussion has tried to show that the dynamic integration of the Christian life, envisioned by fundamental option theory, can illuminate the movement from the false self to the awakening and liberation of the true self. Further, Merton's social perspective on both the false self and the true self helps us to place fundamental option theory into a broader social context.

31. Thomas Merton, *Conjectures of a Guilty Bystander* (New York: Doubleday, 1966) 158.

In conclusion, then, we can offer the following summary: the human person is created as a dynamic capacity for the divine and with a fundamental freedom given by God, most basically, so that we can say "yes" to God, to dispose one's self to God. This is our true self affirming, by the exercise of this basic freedom, its foundational union with God and therefore its own deepest and truest meaning. In a world and in lives without sin, this fundamental self-disposing would be manifest consistently in the choices to be made among the myriad of objects and options encountered in every human life. Each choice and action would be consistent with a deep experience of the communion between and among all people whose truest selves are deeply interrelated in the very Ground of their being.

But, of course, neither our world nor our own lives is ever experienced, in our present existence, as free from sin. Because of original sin, but promoted by social sin and strengthened by personal sin, every human person experiences a disjunction between the deepest reality of the true self grounded in God and the conscious "I" interacting with the external world of other persons, of objects, and of options. The external self quickly becomes a "false" and even a "sinful" self with the construction of edifices of power, success and material possessions that seek to promote an existence autonomous both from the true self and from its foundational union with God. Tragically, every individual false self is built up by the collaboration of other false selves; but, rather than promoting an authentic unity of persons, the interaction of false selves merely promotes an even greater individualism and masks the deeper unity of all persons (and indeed of all of creation) in God.

The task of Christian living (made possible only by grace) is to destroy the edifices of the false self so that the true self in God can be awakened and liberated and so that the foundational unity of all persons can be realized. Experienced most closely in contemplation, the true self is most clearly manifest in self-giving, self-transcending love. All of this is to say that the message of the Cross must become a reality in every Christian life: the false and sinful self that seeks an existence autonomous from God must die, and the true self must be born again in the self-giving love for God and others that is witnessed and made possible by Christ. The true self must be "born again" in Christ so that the Christian can say with St. Paul: "I live now, not I, but Christ lives in me" (Gal. 2:20).

Grounded in a dynamic capacity for the divine, the "yes" of the true self to God seeks an ever-greater integration of the person's choices and actions into this fundamental self-disposing to God. This is to say that the person's fundamental self-disposing seeks a new consistency and coherence between the true self and the external self of the conscious "I" so that all of the person's individual choices are authentic manifestations of the true self. We can say, then, that the fundamental option of the person, rooted in the true self, seeks an integration, integrity, and authenticity within the person and between the person's deepest reality and his or her external choices and actions. With Thomas Merton, we can describe this movement to greater integrity and authenticity as the movement from image to likeness, as the nurturing of true purity of heart, or as the life of ongoing conversion. The Christian life is the graced, integrating movement from the false self built up by sin to the triumph of the true self in Christ, lived out in daily existence in anticipation of our final communion with God in Christ.

Merton, Moore, and the Carthusian Temptation

Johan Seynnaeve

Dedicated to the memory of
Dom Raphael Diamond, O.Cart.

I just learned that Dom T. Verner Moore, the Benedictine who gave us the retreat two years ago, became a Carthusian in Spain. The dog! When I went to him with my problem, he told me "Oh no, you don't want to be a Carthusian!"[1]

Not that I am altogether surprised at Dom Moore's becoming a Carthusian. I remember him describing a Carthusian at work, pruning a fruit tree in his little garden and frequently pausing to pray. He spoke of Carthusians several times in his conferences and when he was receiving monks privately, all those with Carthusian temptations were buzzing around the door of Saint Gabriel's room like flies around a honey pot. I complained that I could not seem to get much more than three hours of private mental prayer a day here. Dom Moore said he thought that was quite enough and told me how the Carthusians had to say many extra vocal prayers and were always complaining that they had so little time for private mental prayer and contemplation. . . . And now, there he is, a Carthusian. And here I am.[2]

---

1. Thomas Merton, *Entering the Silence: Becoming a Monk & Writer*, ed. Jonathan Montaldo (New York: HarperCollins, 1995) 98.
2. Thomas Merton, *The Sign of Jonas* (New York: Harcourt, Brace and Company, 1953) 60–1. Hereafter referred to as *SJ*.

Thus writes Thomas Merton on the feast of the Assumption of Our Lady, 15 August 1947, in *The Sign of Jonas* and in "The Whale and the Ivy." When Merton closed the doors of Gethsemani behind him in December of 1941, it was relatively easy for him to forget the world. The solemn perpetual vows he made on the feast of St. Joseph, March 19, 1947, confirmed his decision to consecrate his life to God in the monastery. Yet, he writes in the introduction to Part One of *The Sign of Jonas*, "I often wondered if I should not go to some other monastery. This was what is known as a 'temptation'" (*SJ*, 13).

It is difficult to imagine a monastic journey that is at the same time so similar to and so different from that of Thomas Merton as that of Thomas Verner Moore. Like Merton, Moore was immensely gifted and full of energy and ideas; but also like Merton, he was full of restlessness and contradictory drives. Both men were prolific writers; both entered orders and became priests, and both were engaged in a lifelong struggle to reconcile action and contemplation. Yet Merton lived a life that is difficult to envision Moore living. Born in Prades near the Franco-Spanish border, and shifting places among France, England, and the United States, Merton converted to Catholicism and finally settled down at Gethsemani. Moore, born into a Catholic family in Louisville, Kentucky, spent most of his active life in the United States, but lived his last years as a monk in a Spanish charterhouse. When, after his conversion, Merton entered an order, it was that of the Trappists, whose tradition of silence, manual labor, and liturgical worship set it radically apart from Moore's Paulists, the most active of orders. Finally, while Merton eventually resolved the possibility of a Carthusian vocation by remaining faithful to his vow of stability to stay at Gethsemani, Moore, after several unsuccessful appeals for admission starting as early as 1916, was accepted by the Carthusians at the age of seventy.

This essay[3] is structured as follows: the first section highlights the episode in Merton's monastic journey during which he tried to dis-

3. I am greatly indebted to Fr. Benedict Neenan, O.S.B., for information on Thomas Verner Moore. He graciously shared his extensive Moore materials with me and gave me a copy of his 1996 dissertation on the life of Moore. I would also like to thank Dom Philip Dahl, O.Cart., of the Charterhouse of the Transfiguration and Dom Aidan Shea, O.S.B., abbot of St. Anselm's Abbey. This article originated as a lecture given at The Fourth Kansas Merton Conference on 10 November 1996. I am grateful for all the responses and encouragements I received from conference participants, in particular Sr. Noreen Hurter, O.S.B., and Sr. Johnette Putnam, O.S.B.

cern whether he should go to the Carthusians or stay at Gethsemani; the second section touches upon the essential facts of Father Moore's life; the decisive moments in Moore's Carthusian vocation are the subject of section three; and in the fourth and concluding section of this essay I speculate on the different ways in which Merton and Moore resolved the Carthusian temptation.

I. Merton and the Carthusians

In March 1941 Merton was getting ready for the Holy Week retreat at Gethsemani. Part of the preparations was a trip to the library where he came across the entries on the Carthusians in the *Catholic Encyclopaedia*. They made such an impression on him that he reflected:

> What I saw on those pages pierced me to the heart like a knife. What wonderful happiness there was, then, in the world! There were still men on this miserable, noisy, cruel earth, who tasted the marvelous joy of silence and solitude, who dwelt in forgotten mountain cells, in secluded monasteries, where the news and desires and appetites and conflicts of the world no longer reached them.[4]

Three weeks later, a fellow-retreatant at Gethsemani mentioned the Carthusians at Parkminster. He told Merton that "[t]here were no longer any pure hermits or anchorites in the world: but the Carthusians were the ones who had gone the farthest, climbed the highest on the mountain of isolation that lifted them above the world and concealed them in God" (*SSM*, 327). The encounter prompted Merton to make a comparison between the Cistercians and the Carthusians.

> We could see the Cistercians here going out to work in a long line with shovels tucked under their arms with a most quaint formality. But the Carthusian worked alone, in his cell, in his own garden or workshop, isolated. These monks slept in a common dormitory, the Carthusian slept in a hidden cell. These men ate together while someone read aloud to them in their refectory. The Carthusian ate alone, sitting in the window-alcove of his cell, with no one to speak to him but God. All day long and all night long the Cistercian was with his brothers. All day long and all night long,

4. Thomas Merton, *The Seven Storey Mountain* (New York: Harcourt, Brace and Company, 1948) 316. Hereafter referred to as *SSM*.

except for the offices in choir and other intervals, the Carthusian was with God alone. *O beata solitudo.* (*SSM*, 327)

The question of which order attracted him more was easily answered. The Carthusians came closer to the idea he had of a monastic vocation, but because there was no charterhouse in the United States in 1941 and the war made it impossible for him to cross the Atlantic and consider one of the Carthusian houses in Europe, he chose to enter Gethsemani. It was in a way his second choice and even though he threw himself into his new life as a Trappist with zeal and devotion, the Carthusian attraction remained in his thoughts.

All the time I was in the novitiate I had no temptation to leave the monastery. In fact, never since I have entered religion have I ever had the slightest desire to go back to the world. But when I was a novice I was not even bothered by the thought of leaving Gethsemani and going to any other Order. I say I was not *bothered* by the thought: I had it, but it never disturbed my peace because it was never anything but academic and speculative. (*SSM*, 383)

The period of relative peace he enjoyed during his first years at Gethsemani would come to an end on the eve of Merton's solemn profession as a monk. In the prologue to *The Sign of Jonas* he tells us:

for me, the vow of stability has been the belly of the whale. I have always felt a great attraction to the life of perfect solitude. It is an attraction I shall probably never entirely lose. During my years as a student at Gethsemani, I often wondered if this attraction was not a genuine vocation to some other religious Order. [. . .] Like the prophet Jonas, whom God ordered to go to Nineveh, I found myself with an almost uncontrollable desire to go in the opposite direction. God pointed one way and all my "ideals" pointed in the other. (*SJ*, 10)

He had made every possible effort to believe and obey those who told him he was supposed to be a Cistercian. But his efforts, he felt, had not produced the effect which they produce in those he saw around him. Without being exactly unhappy at Gethsemani, he had in fact been relying on concessions to lead a more solitary life than is the usual lot of the Cistercian. He was beginning to wonder whether he could continue in that way. Meanwhile the impediments to his becoming a Carthusian were for the most part removed: the war was over and it would be possible to go to Europe, and, more importantly, in December 1950 a Carthusian foundation was started in the United States. In a letter to Dom Humphrey Pawsey, the superior of the new foundation in Vermont, he argues his case as follows:

> My desires go out to the Charterhouse before anything else, first because if I had been able to become a Carthusian instead of a Trappist in 1941, I would certainly have done so. Secondly because I believe the Carthusian life is the safest and best way to find God in solitude—certainly safer than the business of being a hermit on my own, which nevertheless I will try if nothing else is possible. [. . .] The third reason why I want to be a Carthusian is that I am fairly sure you would discourage me from writing any more, and that is what I want.[5]

It is important to note that Merton wrote this letter while his abbot, Dom James Fox, was away at the General Chapter. Dom James was unyielding when it came to Merton's leaving Gethsemani for another Order. "The answer, his superiors and spiritual advisers told him over and over, was inner solitude, detachment, a hermitage of the heart: he needed no physical place of solitude."[6] But already in 1949 Dom James had allowed him to take some of his intervals in the rare book vault to work on manuscripts. At the height of his stability crisis, Dom James, anxious to resolve the question of Merton's need for extended periods of silence and solitude, offered him a vacant toolshed in the woods as a refuge for certain hours of the day. This part-time hermitage, which he named St. Anne's, brought him the needed tranquility and the following realization:

> I no longer need to travel. Half a mile away is the monastery with the landscape of hills which haunted me for 11 years with uncertainty. I knew I had come to stay but never really believed it, and the hills seemed to speak, at all times, of some other country. The quiet landscape of St. Anne's speaks of no other country. If they will let me, I am here to stay.[7]

5. Thomas Merton, *The School of Charity: The Letters of Thomas Merton on Religious Renewal and Spiritual Direction,* ed. Br. Patrick Hart, O.C.S.O. (New York: Farrar, Strauss & Giroux, 1990) 41.

6. Michael Mott, *The Seven Mountains of Thomas Merton* (Boston: Houghton Mifflin Company, 1984) 230.

7. Thomas Merton, *A Search for Solitude: Pursuing the Monk's True Life,* ed. Lawrence S. Cunningham (New York: HarperCollins, 1996) 32.

By the spring 1955, however, his hopes return to the Carthusians. On April 27, 1955, he writes to Dom Jean Leclercq that he has reached a point at which he thinks he cannot remain at Gethsemani and that he feels confident he would be allowed to go to the Carthusians. When, a few weeks later, a letter from Dom Jean-Baptiste Porion, the procurator general of the Carthusians in Rome, arrives discouraging him from this course, he consults Thomas Verner Moore at the Carthusian foundation in Vermont, who encourages him to transfer to the Camaldolese. His appeal for admission at Camaldoli makes it all the way to the Vatican, but again he receives no encouragement for a transfer.

It would last until the fall 1955 before Merton would finally be at peace with the idea of staying at Gethsemani. In a letter of October 18, 1955 to the abbot general, Dom Gabriel Sortais, he writes

> that it would be most imprudent for me to leave Gethsemani or at least the Order and that there would not be much to gain. So I am quite sure I know God's will on this point, and I accept it willingly with the most complete peace and without regrets. This gives me the opportunity to sacrifice an appeal, a dream, an ideal, to embrace God's will in faith. Now it is over, and I promise you I will not worry you any more with this business.[8]

Much later, shortly before his trip to Asia, when reading about the Carthusians in Vermont, Merton reflects

> Maybe I am no true solitary, and God knows I have certainly missed opportunities, made mistakes—and big ones too! Yet the road I am on is the right one for me and I hope I stay on it wisely— or that my luck holds.[9]

By 1955, then, Merton was no longer arguing with himself about the need to transfer to another order. His "Carthusian struggle"[10] had gone through three stages. From his entrance in the monastery in 1941 to the time he made his solemn vows in 1947 the Carthusian life evoked interest and admiration in him but the attraction never caused any con-

---

8. Thomas Merton, *The School of Charity: The Letters of Thomas Merton on Religious Renewal and Spiritual Direction*, ed. Br. Patrick Hart, O.C.S.O. (New York: Farrar, Strauss & Giroux, 1990) 92.

9. Quoted in Mott, 532 [from the Restricted Journals, August 5, 1968].

10. This term and the threefold distinction in Merton's struggle I borrow from William H. Shannon, *Silent Lamp: the Thomas Merton Story* (New York: Crossroad, 1992) 148.

fusion about his life as a Trappist. The second phase was a period of vacillation that lasted from 1947 to the fall 1955, during which Merton became unsure about staying at Gethsemani and seriously considered a transfer to the Carthusians where he would have more solitude. The third stage was "a period of relatively peaceful acquiescence, extending from October 1955 to August 1965, when he became a hermit on the grounds of Gethsemani."[11]

II. Thomas Verner Moore

To those who do not know him, Thomas Verner Moore is best introduced at the supreme moment of his public life, when in 1939, one month before his sixty-second birthday, he became prior of St. Anselm's, the Benedictine monastery he helped establish in Washington, D.C. His appointment coincided with the award of a large grant from the Rockefeller Foundation, which enabled him to expand the Child Guidance Center, a clinic specialized in treating nervous and mental diseases in children, whose founder and director he was. Earlier that year the board of trustees of The Catholic University of America, the educational institution the center was associated with, had readjusted the name of the department Moore headed from "Department of Psychology" to "Department of Psychology and Psychiatry" in accordance with the increased importance of the expanded facilities. These events are indicative of the many paradoxes we come across in Father Moore's rich and eventful life. He was a highly successful academic who combined a strong publication record with impressive teaching credentials. Thoroughly familiar, through long years of studying the works of his patron saint Thomas Aquinas, with the field of scholastic philosophy, he was also equally at home in the experimental laboratory and the techniques of psychological investigation. He managed to reconcile the demands of his scientific career with his duty as a medical doctor specialized in psychiatry. The foundation upon which his many accomplishments in research, teaching, and treatment of patients with mental problems rested was his monastic commitment. Not only had he conceived the idea of starting a community of Benedictine monks at The Catholic University of America where monastic practice could be blended in with scientific research, he was also a living example of its feasibility.

11. Ibid.

Thomas Verner Moore was born on 22 October 1877 in Louisville, Kentucky. He studied with the Jesuits at Fordham University and St. Francis Xavier College in New York. In December 1896 he entered the Paulist novitiate and was ordained a priest in December 1901. He took his Ph.D. in 1903 under Edward Pace, a pioneer of psychology at The Catholic University of America. A year after obtaining his doctorate in psychology he studied under Wilhelm Wundt at the University of Leipzig. Upon his return to the United States in 1906, Father Moore first served as chaplain to the Catholic students at the University of California in Berkeley, and, in 1910, joined the faculty of The Catholic University as instructor of psychology. He entered medical school at Georgetown University in 1911, and two years later received permission from his Paulist superiors to continue his medical and psychological studies at the University of Munich. He obtained his medical degree from Johns Hopkins University in 1915, returned to The Catholic University and opened his psychological clinic at Providence hospital in Washington, D.C. In the last year of World War I he took a leave of absence from the university to serve in the army medical corps in France. Shortly after his return from Europe, he replaced Pace as head of the department of Psychology. Dissatisfied with his life as a Paulist, a religious life without vows, he requested and obtained a transfer to the Benedictines. In September 1923 he took another leave of absence from the university and started his novitiate at St. Benedict's Abbey, Fort Augustus, Scotland. A year later he made solemn profession and returned to the United States to start the Benedictine community of St. Anselm's, under the jurisdiction of the abbot of Fort Augustus.

> The twenty-three years between Moore's return from Scotland in 1924 and his entrance into the Carthusian Order in 1947 constituted the most productive years of his career as a psychologist and psychiatrist, during which he guided the psychology department at The Catholic University, expanded his clinic into an important center for treatment, training, and research, founded a school for mentally disadvantaged girls, and published his most important works in psychology and psychiatry.[12]

12. Benedict Neenan, O.S.B., *The Life of Thomas Verner Moore: Psychiatrist, Educator and Monk* (Unpublished Ph.D. dissertation, The Catholic University of America, 1996) 201.

In 1946 he received an invitation to lecture for a semester at the University of Madrid in Spain. At the end of his visiting appointment he entered the Charterhouse of Miraflores near Burgos in June 1947. He was accepted as a Carthusian novice on the vigil of the Feast of St. Luke, 17 October 1947. On the Feast of St. Bruno, October 6, 1949 he made his solemn profession and received the name of Dom Pablo Maria. In the fall of 1950 he returned to the United States to help establish the first American charterhouse near Whitingham, Vermont. After almost a decade in Vermont Dom Pablo was recalled to his house of profession, where he died on June 5, 1969.

III. Moore and the Carthusians

Father Moore traces his interest in the Carthusians to a period rather early in life when he read a work on the Fathers of the Desert.

> Their example was an ideal that hovered before his mind ever afterwards, but which he could see no possibility of attaining. And though in the long tramps he took in the mountains in summer he saw from time to time an inviting cave, not far from a spring or clean running water, he could not see how, in the climate of the United States, he could live through the winter in one of these caves or supply himself or be supplied with the bare essentials of daily sustenance that even a hermit would require.[13]

In the summer of 1913, during his second period of study in Germany, he went to England during the intersemester break to work in the library of the British Museum. He recounts what happened that first week of September:

> The library closed for a week early in September, so I concluded that I would get in my annual retreat. I dropped in to a Jesuit house and asked where I could make my retreat. The good father replied: "You must go to our house at Manresa, or the Fathers of Charity or to various places; but if you want to make a retreat that you will remember to the day of your death, go to the Carthusians at Parkminster." I concluded that that was the kind of retreat I wanted to make and so arranged with the Prior for the privilege. It was truly a solitary retreat; and I was left entirely to my own resources.

13. A Carthusian of Miraflores [Thomas Verner Moore], "Carthusian life and its inner spirit," *Messenger of the Sacred Heart* 85 (1950) 19.

The guest master visited me daily about noon to ask if there was anything I wanted. I rose for Matins and Lauds every night which I heard in the gallery or tribune of the church. My schedule for mental prayer, spiritual reading and other exercises was approved by the guest master. Sometime during the retreat I spoke hesitantly about the possibility of my becoming a Carthusian, but received no encouragement. I was profoundly impressed with Carthusian life, but left without any formulated resolve to be a Carthusian.[14]

The first written request for admission arrived at Parkminster in the fall 1916. In his answer the guest master pointed out that he could not resolve the question of Moore's Carthusian vocation and recommended him "to follow the advice of his spiritual director, to pray, and to wait until the will of God manifests itself more clearly either as an interior attraction or through the events or circumstances."[15]

A second letter, written in the summer 1919, received a much clearer answer. The novice master at St. Hugh's Charterhouse told him that his mind seemed absolutely opposite to the Carthusian spirit and that he could do nothing better than to bury completely the idea of ever becoming a Carthusian monk. He did what he was told, put the Charterhouse out of his mind, and turned all his energy to Benedictine channels. Looking back upon his years as a Benedictine he would later say: "From the time I entered Fort Augustus in 1923 up to about the year 1933 it never occurred to me that I should ever be anything else but a Benedictine."[16]

In 1933, however, the Carthusian temptation rebounded with a vengeance. While on retreat that year he thought he heard a voice telling him to become a Trappist. When he informed his superior about his desire to transfer to the Trappists he was told that his leaving St. Anselm's at a crucial point in its development would deal the fledgling community a devastating blow, but that, when the time should come, he should consider the Carthusians rather than the Trappists. This re-opened the question of a Carthusian vocation.

14. Thomas Verner Moore, *My Carthusian Vocation,* unpublished manuscript, Archives of Trinity College, Washington, D.C.

15. "de suivre le conseil de votre Directeur, de prier et d'attendre que la Sainte Volonté de Dieu se manifeste plus clairement soit par l'attrait intérieur, soit par les évènements et les circonstances." Paul Joseph Deltour to Thomas Verner Moore, 1 October 1916, unpublished letter, St. Anselm's Abbey Archives.

16. Thomas Verner Moore, *My Carthusian Vocation,* unpublished manuscript, Archives of Trinity College, Washington, D.C.

From then on he would not rest until he was finally permitted to give it a try. According to Fr. Benedict Neenan, "there were ten significant appeals by Moore for admission to the Carthusians between 1933 and August 1946, when he was finally accepted."[17]

In the spring of 1935 he was allowed to make an extended retreat at Parkminster. This time around his second stay at the charterhouse impressed the Carthusians so much that the Parkminster prior wrote to the prior at St. Anselm's: "I must confess that after having a long talk with him the determination not to dream of accepting him has been very much weakened."[18] Moore interpreted the news as a sign that they were willing to let him try his vocation and wrote to his superior in Washington: "[i]t seems to be the opinion of both the Prior and the Novice Master that I should remain longer to try my vocation, and in all probability remain."[19] The prior at St. Anselm's ordered him to return immediately reminding him again of the upset his departure would create both at the monastery and at the university. The abbot at Fort Augustus agreed, writing to Moore: "it seems to me that your secession, at the present and in the near future, would be detrimental— if not fatal—to St. Anselm's."[20] Moore was only slightly discouraged and at regular intervals made further requests to his superiors or the prior at Parkminster. Finally, in 1946, a year before his retirement from the university, the abbot of Fort Augustus informed him he would be relieved from his priorship at St. Anselm's. The abbot also indicated he would be willing to release him to join the Carthusians. After contacting Parkminster again Moore learned from the Carthusian prior that despite his courageous perseverance and successful trial at their charterhouse he would not be accepted there. His chances to be accepted at another charterhouse in Europe were scant. The charterhouse of Farneta in Italy, where the prior was an Englishman, gave him no hope of being able to join there. Along with his final refusal, however, the prior at Parkminster, had hesitantly suggested

17. Benedict Neenan, O.S.B., *The Life of Thomas Verner Moore: Psychiatrist, Educator and Monk* (Unpublished Ph.D. dissertation, The Catholic University of America, 1996) 286.

18. Adrian Weld-Blundell to Wulstan Knowles, 5 September 1935, unpublished letter, St. Anselm's Abbey Archives.

19. Ibid.

20. Wulstan Knowles to Thomas Verner Moore, 3 December 1935, unpublished letter, St. Anselm's Abbey Archives.

perhaps the Fr. Prior of our House of Miraflores, Burgos, Spain, who is an ex-missionary Bishop, might be willing. He knows a certain amount of English and has a Father Procurator who speaks it, I think. You will have to put your case to him very strongly, if you are to succeed! May God grant it if it is His Will.[21]

Moore wrote to Miraflores and to his surprise received a letter from the novice master with an affirmative answer. He was rewarded for the long years of patient and courageous perseverance and realized his lifelong dream when he entered Santa Maria de Miraflores in June 1947. He took to his new life with the enthusiasm of a young novice. The hard plank bed, the long fast, the three-hour night office, the absence of any kind of heat in the church—these austerities did not seem to bother the seventy-year old monk. It was no small edification for the Spanish community to see this former prior, this scholar, become simply one of the monks. Dom Pablo was not destined, however, to enjoy the stability he had hoped Miraflores would provide him. A year after his solemn vows he was sent back to the United States to help establish the first Carthusian foundation there. A decade later, in the summer 1960, he returned to Miraflores. Father Moore had stoutly borne up under this rather lengthy trial and his Carthusian calling emerged from it stronger and truer. Now more than ever, in the twilight of his days, he experienced the purgings that contemplation entails. The prior of Miraflores characterizes Moore's final years thus:

> In his last years in Miraflores Dom Pablo showed signs of great virtue. He was always smiling and pleasant—full of goodness and humility. He had many things to suffer: a progressive blindness, difficulty in understanding Spanish, his difference of age with the rest of the community; but he never gave expression to any complaint. Until 1968 he was present at Matins every night; it must be kept in mind that in Miraflores, during two months of the year, the temperature in the Church drops to one or two degrees centigrade below the freezing point. He used to say: "The most beautiful part of the Carthusian day is Matins." Likewise he was present at the recreations, and although they were a penance for him, because he had so much difficulty understanding the others, he was always in good humor. During the last two years of his life he was not able to leave his cell due to arterio-sclerosis. He was not able to cele-

21. Hugh Weld to Thomas Verner Moore, 26 June 1946, unpublished letter, St. Anselm's Abbey Archives.

brate Mass during the very last year. Regardless of his pains he was always found smiling and optimistic. I used to ask him: "Dom Pablo, how are you?" He would smile and answer: "Oh, always very well." On June 1, 1969 he began to feel ill, and from that time on kept to his bed; little by little the light of his life waned and on the 5th, the feast of Corpus Christi, he passed away, at 6:00 in the evening. His countenance was resplendant with an expression of peace and serenity. In Miraflores everyone felt his death very much—he was very much loved by all because of his exceptional kindness and understanding.[22]

What strikes one about this account is that Dom Pablo's last years in Spain were a severe period of trial, but that they brought about the holiness he had at his death. During those years he practiced what he theoretically held as the one thing he lived for. In the words of Dom Raphael Diamond, the former prior of the Vermont Charterhouse: "The spiritual value of his life is an example of what God will do to a man who has had a brilliant career, but one who has not allowed for those purifications that are necessary for really a life with God."[23]

22. "Dom Pablo en los últimos años pasados en Miraflores, demostró una gran virtud. Siempre afable y sonriente. Siempre lleno de bondad y humildad. Tuvo que sufrir debido a su ceguera progresiva, a su dificultad para entender el castellano, a su diferencia de edad con el resto de la Comunidad, jamás se le notó ninguna queja. Hasta 1968 asi[s]tió a Maitines todas las noches. Téngase en cuenta que en Miraflores durante 2 meses la iglesia está a temperaturas de uno o dos grados centígrados bajo cero. Solía repetir: "Los Maitines es lo más hermoso del día cartujano". Igualmente asistía a recreaciones con muy buen humor siempre, aunque eran una penitencia para él, pues le costaba mucho entenderse con los demás. Los dos últimos años de su vida, debido a la arteriosclerosis, no podía salir de la celda. El último año, no pudo celebrar la Santa Misa. A pesar de sus dolencias, siempre se le encontraba sonriente y optimista. Le preguntaba yo: ¿Dom Pablo, cómo está Vd.? Sonreía y siempre me contestaba: ¡Oh, siempre muy bien! El día 1 de junio de 1969, se sintío indispuesto, ya no se volvió a levantar; poco a poco se fue apagando y el día 5, fiesta del Corpus Christi, a las 6 de la tarde murió. Su rostro resplandecía con una expresión de paz y serenidad. En Miraflores todos sentimos muchísimo su muerte pues era muy querido de todos, por su excepcional bondad y simpatía." Prior of Miraflores to Dom Raphael Diamond, 1 November 1973, unpublished letter, Charterhouse of the Transfiguration Archives, Arlington, Vermont. English translation by Dom Benedict Kossman, O.Cart.

23. Raphael Diamond, O.Cart., interview with Benedict Neenan, O.S.B., Charterhouse of the Transfiguration, Arlington, Vt., 24 February 1995, St. Anselm's Abbey Archives.

IV. Conclusion

What can we learn from these two stories about the attraction to Carthusian solitude? When trying to answer this question, we have to keep in mind that the quest for the vision of God—the core of the monastic vocation—is fundamentally a matter of divine grace, "a gratuitous gift which God accords us. We can neither attain it nor possess it by ourselves, but we can desire it."[24] Yet, at the same time, we cannot but notice the individual trials of these two monks, which arise from their longing for the life of solitude.

Father Moore's life gives testimony to an extraordinary consistency. Never impatient with himself and the circumstances of his life, he came to the realization that only gradually and through continuous application could he reach the ideal to which he aspired. He manifested an astonishing constancy in persevering so long in his desire for solitude, despite opposition from both his abbot and the Carthusian prior. We know the importance he laid on motives according to which he taught that one has to purify one's intentions and to decide one's actions.[25] One does not see why he could not have applied these criteria in his own case. His many different vocations, his intense activity and his wide interests reveal one and the same source: his intense and honest desire to seek the encounter with God.

In contrast to Moore, who sought a life that witnessed values he could not find within the Paulist or Benedictine tradition, Merton was able to rediscover the eremitical dimension that lay buried within the Cistercian tradition. Life in community, so characteristic of the monastic vocation of Merton before he took his solemn vows, seems to have become more and more a testing and training ground for the contemplative vocation which, he was convinced in the years following his solemn profession, could best be realized in the solitude of hermitage. The spiritual and institutional renewal Merton helped further within the structure of his own order gradually appeased his desire for a tran-

---

24. Thomas Merton, *Honorable Reader,* ed. Robert E. Daggy (New York: Crossroad, 1989) 21.

25. "Moore's life displays another driving force from within: the need to always strive for the highest possible level of attainment of which one is capable. It was a principle he instilled in his students, patients, monks, and retreatants. It was a principle he adopted in his own life, whether it has to do with a level of education, a level of professional achievement, or a level of the spiritual life." Neenan, *The Life of Thomas Verner Moore,* 4.

sit from the cenobitic life of the Trappists to the semi-eremitical life of the Carthusians. In the prefaces to the Japanese editions of *The Seven Storey Mountain* (August 1963) and *Seeds of Contemplation* (March 1965) Merton writes:

> I am still in the monastery, and intend to stay there. I have never had any doubt whatever of my monastic vocation. If I have ever had any desire for change, it has been for a more solitary, more "monastic" way.[26]

> And the author remains in the same monastery nearly twenty years later, still convinced of the reality of the way he seeks to travel, still seeking to understand better the illusions that are met within this way but not in order to abandon the way.[27]

In the opening quote preceding this essay Merton records his reaction to Moore's becoming a Carthusian and recalls that Moore dissuaded him from following the same path. The following anecdote related by two former students of Moore hints at the possible meaning of his discouragement:

> One day, while a student was tussling with a Monroe calculator, he suddenly said, "Never leave your community for a contemplative order!" In utter amazement she replied, "But I never had such a thought!" Years later, we who heard the remark, realized it was probably an expression of his own inner struggle.[28]

26. Merton, *Honorable Reader*, 65.

27. Ibid., 87.

28. Sr. M. Corde Lorang and Msgr. Timothy J. Gannon, "Thomas Verner Moore: 1877–1969," *Newsletter of the American Catholic Psychological Association* 19 (Autumn 1969) 6.

Pleading for Sanity: Cosmic Heart in a Sea of Fire

John Wu, Jr.

"There is an optimism which cheapens Christianity and makes it absurd, empties it. It is a silly, petty optimism which consists in being secure because one knows the right answers . . . I will multiply negatives in honor of the God of Job."

—Thomas Merton to Czeslaw Milosz, 6/5/61

"And a monk should wind himself up in a cocoon?"

—Thomas Merton to C. Waddell, 1/4/64

" . . . one fell in step with the dance of the universe, the liturgy of the stars."

—"The Sacred City," in *Preview of the Asian Journey*, 79

> They recken ill who leave me out;
> When me they fly, I am the wings;
> I am the doubter and the doubt,
> And I the hymn the Brahmin sings.

—"Brahma," R. W. Emerson

1. In the Sea of Fire

In "Honorable Reader," Thomas Merton wrote presciently,

The new world will not be built by the Russian perversion of the Marxist dialectic . . . (nor) by the destructive passions of

267

> Fascist militarism . . . (nor) the magic of imperialist technology.
> We cannot hope for anything more than deception and confusion
> in 'dollar diplomacy'.[1]

The monk's social and political critique lay in his ability to see through the thin facade of power politics, the phony subterfuges that lay in all the shallow schemes and apparent good will and accepted paradigms that drive the great powers. He idealized the then Third World, as he often did by locating the real future and hope of the planet in East Asia, Africa and, particularly—at least to this writer—in his first love, his beloved Latin America, which more than any other region of the world he appropriated to himself. The monk saw in their then pre-technologized and free-from-the-market-economy people and societies a purity long lost in the mechanized civilization of North America. He neither allowed himself to be taken in by the north's often unquestioned myths of progress nor to where that progress fatefully led. Whether he was objective with regard to the way he reflexively favored the south over the north, or the east over the west remains at best problematic.

However, what remains unquestioned, given both Merton's political orientation and native compassion for the underdog, was that he saw the major powers in opposition to the downtrodden and disenfranchised of the world. Further, he saw in both communist and capitalistic democratic societies, including his own adopted America, the unhealthy roots and festering wounds of alienation as well as the moral and spiritual brutalization of the human species acting dishonorably. Compassion for the beleaguered, the underdog, was Merton's natural bent and the Gospels its true fulfillment; this, despite early in his career, he was hardly in a position to predict both the starkness and the richness of that message and the existential price that would, in his own life, be exacted from living out the Gospels. In a relatively short time, the monk/writer was to experience not only a baptism of water but of *fire* as well.

In America, he saw this terrible sea of fire engulf his own society not so much by police tactics—though there were gross manifestations of that too in the struggle over civil rights and to end the war in Vietnam—but rather, to his mind, through a misguided technology which, the more successfully marketable it became, the more it ate away into man's inner freedom. As his basic temperament and per-

---

1. Thomas Merton, *Honorable Reader: Reflections on my Work*, edited with an introduction by Robert E. Daggy (New York: Crossroad, 1989) 42–3.

ception did not allow him to critique the world from a merely liberal political agenda, he came to see the programs of the major powers as morally corrosive forces tending to diminish both personal and communal freedoms. And, as artist and man of faith, he increasingly saw the curtailing of the diminishment of the inner person as his principle role, a task for which his readings and contemplative vocation prepared him well.

This paper will demonstrate the priceless value Merton placed on the inner self, its importance with regard to the recovery and reconstruction of community, and, being a Christian monk, the ever-increasing faith he had in identifying this inner self with Christ, especially the *suffering, paschal* Christ.

To Merton, the North American capitalist agenda, by freely and indiscriminately enlisting and manipulating human knowledge, research, and technology, rather than furthering the cause of humanity—its overt intention—had the reversed effect of keeping the giant unthinking machine well-oiled and self-perpetuating, albeit misdirected. To the monk, Americans of his time lived by the unquestioned assumption that their lives were inextricably linked with that self-propelling machine, and anyone disconnected from the speed, efficiency, and progress that drove the entire enterprise was somehow not fully sane and rational and outside the American dream. It distressed him how a nation which prided itself on personal liberty could so easily miss the obvious bridge between this *diminished* self and the continuous usurpation of and the facile inroads made against freedom by a sophisticated technology that seemed to have taken on a life of its own. This technology was most profoundly embodied in the military-industrial complex and an ever more powerful and self-serving mass media.

Merton harshly criticized the USA because he believed as leader of the free world his adopted country fell far short of the goods she purported to be delivering, particularly when it came to preachments regarding peace, race relations, humanity and fair play, and, above all, nuclear responsibility. He called her bluff on these and many more issues. Going beyond the more conventional social and cultural critics, the monk, seldom wasting ink on patchwork reform, insisted in *radical* social and political change related to inner transformation and the reinvention and reassessment of true brotherhood, an issue to which he was increasingly responsive as his personal correspondence extended globally and his writings diversified to cover an ever-broadening range of concerns.

One sees this urgency particularly in his letters of the 1960s to fellow writers with whom he had a special affinity beyond the commonality of generation, race and religion. Such relationships through correspondence deepened his understanding of the world. It would be well to remember that this keeping of the channels of communication open among his circle of like-minded friends was, for Merton, a matter of *personal* survival. As a monk, Merton found himself increasingly questioning the viability of his own religious community as a social unit. He vacillated over its communal authenticity, at times perceiving it as an unedifying institution that mirrored all too clearly some of the more unpromising pragmatic and utilitarian elements of the larger world beyond. Rightly or wrongly, he did not see a future in it *as it stood*, being convinced that Gethsemani with all its continuous input of middle class values did not pose as a radically different alternative to the styles of living enjoyed outside its walls. It would seem that a proper understanding of Merton's anxieties over, and protests against, his life as a cloistered monk should be seen within the framework of a search for a condition that would ground him more firmly in the poverty of Christ which, to him, held the answer to the restoration of monastic community (or, by extension, *any* community, both religious and secular). He sought a return to some semblance of sanity and authenticity in which the ideals of monasticism could once again become living tissues in the lives of its monks. Typically, for Merton, it meant a setup allowing both a deeper solitude as well as a greater embracing of universal human concerns.

Nothing meant more to Merton than living the authentic life; moreover, true vocation in which one is free to make use of one's natural gifts and a living community kept together by genuinely caring hearts in support of one's brothers (and sisters) held the key to human survival and genuine reformation of social and political life. It was both his weakness and his strength that he considered the monastic experience a basically *human* experience, not unlike any other institution engineered and maintained by human beings. In other words, Gethsemani was neither better nor worse for its being an overtly religious institution. Yet, this did not prevent him from being dismayed that even at his beloved monastery, life, by the late fifties, had become a too-real reflection of society in general.[2] The novice master often

2. In a *GEO Magazine* interview, "Father Ernesto Cardenal" (exact date uncertain, though it is most likely in 1984–85), conducted by Kenneth L. Woodward,

complained of the barren, if not total absence, of conventional cultural life and the distressingly mediocre level of consciousness among his young students, which he felt were obstacles to genuine spiritual progress. Merton's own greatness seemed to lie in his ability to nurture the subtle and creative dialectics and constant interplay he allowed himself—and, we might add, encouraged among his student novices—between a broad secular or worldly culture and the spiritual life. Being himself a poet, he never closed his heart to other artists, and he knew his friends, though they were not necessarily Christians or even theists but humanists in the broad sense, were indispensable in bringing him closer to or at least keeping him intimate with the heart of Christ.

Merton's correspondence, particularly with writers, was a conscious attempt to connect with those whose lives bore the noble burden of preserving glimmers of authentic life burning within whatever tradition they were working and living. Today, few would deny that by having kept his own end of the contemplative world open to the influences of both secular and sacred traditions, Christian monastic life now reflects a broader, deeper and more catholic spirituality. In the tradition of all genuine reformers, Merton seemed to have gone forward by having trekked backwards, certainly to the spiritually sumptuous and "open cellars" of his own rich traditions; equally important, he courageously willed to explore the multi-tiered mansion of the cosmic heart and, by an unfailing instinct, he knew his very salvation was tied with that search and unfolding. He made the task all the more difficult for himself because he never doubted that life at its core was one and paradisiacal.

Cardenal, the then Minister of Culture in the Nicaraguan Sandinista government, says the following:

> Merton said the Trappists were a very antiquated order, though he recognized that it could be very good for some people. He said the monks were much too influenced by the American way of life, and that within the monastery, which was to be a place of contemplation, they ran around like it was rush hour on the New York subway. He said the Trappists had the political mentality of middle-class North Americans and that he himself was very anti-North American. He felt Latin. He was born in France, and French was his native language. He told me he loved the poetry of Latin America and was very anti-Yankee, very much in favor of Latin America (20).

2. "Lotus-Eaters" of the North

Living in an America of unprecedented social change, Merton aimed his criticisms at his fellow citizens and religious for what he called their "intransigence" and "complacency." To Ernesto Cardenal, on the American indifference over the nuclear buildup, he wrote in harsh, angry tones:

> It is as if (North Americans) have become lotus-eaters. As if they were under a spell. As if with charmed eyes and ears they saw vaguely, through a comatose fog, the oncoming destruction . . . I resist this bad dream with all my force . . . .[3]

Then, in the same letter, he blasts the American Catholic Church, particularly its hierarchy, in having accepted

> the most secular, the most debased, the most empty of world standards. In this case, the acceptance of nuclear war. Not only that, it is glorified as Christian sacrifice, as a crusade, as the way of obedience . . . This is to me a complete nightmare (*CT*, 130).[4]

But over and above such criticisms of his own Church, Merton severely berated the more pervasive "lotus-eaters," his fellow Americans:

> (North Americans) are prisoners of a completely quantitative view of life and consequently, having no sense either of essence or existence, are out of touch with reality. It is a culture of well-fed zombies (*CT*, 133, 5/22/62, to Cardenal).

---

3. Thomas Merton, *The Courage for Truth: Letters to Writers;* selected and edited by Christine M. Bochen (New York: Farrar Straus Giroux, 1993) 129–30. Hereafter referred to in the text as *CT*.

4. See letter to James Forrest (11/7/62) which points out both the confusion and the casuistic tendencies of Catholics: " . . . the ambiguity of so many Catholics on the war question . . . is a very serious symptom of spiritual sickness in our society. It is a mark of the failure of Catholics to meet the spiritual challenge of the times. They have failed to meet it not because the Church as such has failed, because the clear statements of the Popes are there. But these statements have not been effectively interpreted or put into practice. On the contrary they have been left as pure dead letter except for clauses that give a loophole for militarists." (*The Hidden Ground of Love,* selected and edited by William H. Shannon [New York: Farrar Straus Giroux, 1985] 271. Hereafter referred to in the text as *HGL*).

In a later letter to Cardenal, he asks distressingly, "Do we have to be in a concentration camp before the truth comes home to us?" (*CT*, 137, 11/17/62).

Besides calling Americans "mealy-mouthed patriots" and "lotus-eaters" living in a "comatose fog," Merton literally bristles in a letter to Miguel Grinberg as the US had become ever more entrenched in the quagmire of Vietnam four years later:

> What is this country? If you want to know, look at Vietnam because that is where it all comes out into the open. A big bucket of sickness. But everything here (in the US) goes on in dazed tranquillity. The patient is etherized upon the table . . . The beasts chew on his flesh but he observes nothing (*CT*, 203–4, 10/8/66).

As early as the late 1950s and 1960, when he was seriously considering a move to Mexico and other points south until his hopes were dashed by authorities in his own Cistercian Order, he wrote to Paris to the exiled Polish poet, Czeslaw Milosz, who was contemplating living and teaching in the US. In strong, unguarded language one often finds in letters to fellow writers, Merton, perhaps blind to life in Eastern Europe and unable fully to assess Milosz' own heart, discouraged his coming. Yet, his words remain more prophetic than ever:

> Why live among lotus-eaters and conformists. Never was there a place where freedom was so much an illusion . . . you will find here no imagination; nothing but people counting, counting and counting, whether with great machines, or on their stupid fingers. All they know how to do is count (*CT*, 68, 5/6/60).

The sea of fire was not merely Vietnam but the various materialisms offered by the major political powers. Merton, who saw no fundamental choice between the US and the Soviet Union offered the following to Pablo Antonio Cuadra for whom he had written the splendid, "A Letter . . . Concerning Giants":

> The tyrannies and compulsions under which we live . . . are a moral affront to man, the image of God. And it is becoming more and more clear that our fundamental moral obligation is to resist complicity and submission to every form of abusive power, whether physical or moral or spiritual. And this is both complicated and perilous (*CT*, 184, 6/13/59).

And, as we know today, "complicated and perilous" applied ever more to Merton himself. He keenly anticipated such future personal difficulties when he said to Cardenal, his former novice student, on Christmas Eve, 1961: "I realize I have to be very careful how I protest because otherwise I will be silenced. And no doubt sooner or later I will be."

In hindsight, the important letters to Cardenal served to bolster the latter's courage; more significantly, they set on solid ground Cardenal's own social and political commitment to his native Nicaragua in whose cabinet he would serve two decades later as Minister of Culture. Given the nature of the Trappist vocation, its conventional expectations and the unorthodox manner in which Merton proceeded to fulfill that vocation, the monk was perceived by many as "a square peg in a round hole," the way he half-humorously described himself once in a letter to his abbot, James Fox.[5]

3. Moral and Spiritual Brutalization

Merton's writings often drive home the point that human brutalization in the twentieth century has not been restricted to war and politics. They are filled with indictments aimed at capitalist societies that he felt consciously conspired to imprison and glut our minds with their unending barrage of invented pleasures. Even in Asia, the human problem is greatly intensified by the fact that, in order to survive economically, her societies have ever more been forced to accept the global modernist package whole. The ever-present hustle, the promise of "big bucks," even the antagonisms one finds in academic circles resulting from competition for research grants and other unpleasantries that have little to do with true learning and education now add up to a generally non-conducive atmosphere for healthy personal and communal development.

As early as the mid-fifties, in the essays of *No Man Is an Island,* Merton already assumes a frame of mind so characteristic of his later writings when he writes:

> Half the civilized world makes a living by telling lies. Advertising, propaganda, and all the other forms of publicity that have taken the place of truth have taught man to take for granted that they can tell other people whatever they like provided that it

5. Thomas Merton, *The School of Charity: Letters;* selected and edited by Br. Patrick Hart (New York: Farrar Straus Giroux, 1990) 80. Hereafter referred to in the text as *SC.*

sounds plausible and evokes some kind of shallow emotional response.[6]

In the wake of cultural grotesqueries such as morally-neutralizing and language-dulling talk shows, the continuing mindless onslaught of the mass media, and the indiscriminate use of hi-tech and bogus statistics in pressing forward self- or party-serving political programs, all of which can, indeed, sound plausible and enticing and "evoke shallow emotional responses," authentic communication has become ever more difficult and improbable. One wonders, then, how Merton would have negotiated the often hazardous waters of the present, including the phenomenon of political correctness? Yet, we can perhaps answer such a query by showing in the concrete the nearly always uncompromising manner in which the monk dealt with such problems. Merton rarely opted for the useful, the cheaply gotten or the expedient.[7]

We can clearly see this in the monk's letters to Evora Arca de Sardinia who with her husband were Cuban exiles in Miami. The letters are richly textured and bring into sharp relief the difficult position he had to assume as shepherd and priest to suffering men and women seeking moral and spiritual support. In his missives to Arca de Sardinia, what he wrote was all the more delicate and poignant given the nearly impossible political circumstances in which she found herself. We can also see in them Merton's thinly-disguised aversion for the old Batista gang that the Cuban revolution had driven from the country.

6. Thomas Merton, *No Man Is an Island* (New York: Harcourt, Brace and Company, 1955), 193.

7. Merton's ventures into Asian thought can be said to be a reconfirming of his strong dislike for the "useful", the "expedient," and the merely practical and pragmatic. To James Forrest, he writes: "It is clear that everywhere we are up against a brass wall of organized stupidity and prejudice, the monumental institutionalism that says no to all truth that is inexpedient. To be without God is to be condemned to a cult of expediency" (*HGL*, letter of 11/29/61, 259).

Again, to Forrest who had been arrested during an anti-war demonstration and sentenced to a short prison term on Hart's Island in the East River, Merton seemed to have been suggesting a higher form of efficacy or was even being *Taoistic* when giving counsel on the tactic of non-violent protest: "One has to learn to see the significance of one's apparent *uselessness* and not be driven to frustration by it. The uselessness, the inactivity, the frustration are deliberately assumed as an important part of non-violent resistance" (*HGL*, letter of 3/21/62, 264, Emphasis added).

When he wrote, "How tragic it is that everywhere men (sic) fall victims to the tyranny of absurd ideologies and empty slogans, which have such far-reaching consequences,"[8] the monk was pointing to a good deal more than the political propaganda on *both* the Communist and the side of the refugees and, of course, by implication, the U.S. government. Merton, true to form, was forthright and risked both hurting and being misunderstood by this woman of simple faith. In the following, he is bold yet sensitive to the nearly impossible position she was in, her husband, after all, being a freedom fighter committed to the overthrow of Castro:

> Frankly, I think most of your troubles come from the con-
> flict of grace within your own nature and with the obscure aware-
> ness you have that all is not well with the political cause you have
> embraced, or with Christianity as a whole, as it is manifested in
> the comfortable and wealthy Catholicism of the US. The situation
> is full of ambiguities and contradictions, and *right and wrong is in-*
> *extricably mixed up on both sides.* The evil of Communism grows in
> Cuba, but *the evil of moral injustice is not absent on the American side.*
> There is no question that there *is* some truth in the accusation of
> American imperialism: in the same sense that the big money is
> what determines all the decisions . . . This is a bitter injustice, and
> you obscurely realize this: You cannot help doing so (*WT*, 82,
> 9/19/62, Emphasis added).

The voice is clearly that of a compassionate friend saying—no matter how difficult the task—what needed to be said and reading quite ac-curately the furtive hieroglyphs on the conscience of another whom one supposes only Merton the confiding monk was privy.[9] The words,

---

8. Thomas Merton, *Witness to Freedom: Letters in Times of Crisis;* selected and edited by William H. Shannon (New York: Farrar Straus Giroux, 1994), 83. Hereafter referred to in the text as *WF*.

9. A fitting tribute to Merton are the following words of Robert Coles ("Thomas Merton the Healer") in his interview of Dorothy Day: "I especially re-member Dorothy Day's remarks about him: 'He had known much pain, and he knew how to lift pain from others.' . . . (Day) knew that an essential and impor-tant part of Merton's life was his passionate desire to minister unto others, to hear from them, learn of their tensions and turmoils, and tell them of his, too. Once Dorothy Day said this about Merton . . . 'He cured with words—all the time he did! I know! I can remember those letters, the good medicine that they were to me. And I always knew that with Merton it was the doctor healing himself as well as the rest of us who were his patients.'" From *A Robert Coles Omnibus* (Iowa City: University of Iowa Press, 1993) 33–4.

simple yet neither simplistic nor patronizing, are remarkable for the way they make sense of the diverse and seemingly intractable and diffused elements of the ethical, the spiritual and the political. They are subtly and artlessly interwoven into a living and rationally integrated whole so characteristic of Merton. Empathy was closer than arm's length because the monk himself was then living out of the "ambiguities and contradictions" he speaks of above.

In later letters to the Cuban exile, he writes with a good deal of political savvy and realism. He is sensitive yet unafraid of risking possible misunderstanding:

> The ones to blame are not Castro and Khrushchev . . . We must take a far wider view: this is just one part of a huge historical and social cataclysm and the root of it all is the technological revolution with its myriad consequences (*WT*, 83, 1/1/63).

> I assure you that if the exiles take over Cuba, then the whole thing would start all over again, there would be other exiles planning bloody revenge, and the new ones in power would savagely execute their former persecutors . . . You simply cannot put your trust in American arms, but *you cannot trust in any arms* (*WT*, 84, 7/25/63 Emphasis added).

Merton was able to voice in naked form such seemingly despairing sentiments because, knowing he was addressing a person steeped in religious faith, he saw in it an opportunity to strengthen that faith and to conspire in the possible inner transformation of another person. Some of the most affecting words to her can be found in his letter of 10/29/62 (*Cold War Letter* #109, *WT*, 82): "Certainly it is hard to see your world broken up around you. No man (sic) can take that without suffering and self-questioning." Then, as if addressing and nurturing his own hurt and pain at a time of deep personal crisis when he himself often felt standing alone, he turns spiritual director *par excellence* as he consoles and encourages. Note, too, how he suggests the ever possible danger of faith degenerating into superstition and the necessity of accepting maturity *on God's terms* rather than on human terms:

> God has sent these trials to deepen your faith, not to destroy it. If you feel that it is hard to believe, this is because God is no longer presenting to you the image and idea of Him you once had. He is different from what you think He is and what you want Him to be. If He does not do things the way we want Him to, and we cease to believe in Him, then that means we only want to believe

in a God made in our own image. That is why we have to have our
faith purified and conform to His inscrutable will (*WT*, 82).

Still later, he adds, "Be detached and go forward in faith, and use
prayer as the great weapon for the liberation of your country" (*WT*, 83,
2/22/63).[10]

Such letters from the heart seem to serve the dual purpose of reminding both the recipient and the sender the impossible and futile
task of living out the Christian commitment through mere human effort; they also remind us of the extent of the spirit of poverty and surrender necessary as a prelude to the suffusion of grace in our lives.
Finally, they drive home to us the futility of holding on to some stulti-
fying and usually uninformed or trivialized notions we have regarding the Ground of Being.

Merton seems to be insisting that whatever role we may play in
our own inner transformation, as long as we are not yet resigned to the
inherent limitations of such efforts and its ultimate bankruptcy when
pushed beyond its limits, we have not yet understood the role Wisdom
plays in helping truth to emerge in us. In short, the monk rarely fails
to caution his readers that God seldom makes His appearance at our
beck and call, and that Wisdom never favors one ideology or social
program over another, or, surely in any movements that inevitably divide people into two distinct and faceless camps. Wisdom, in other
words, is likely to be present in the most unsuspecting of circumstances, when we least expect it.

Like Job, Merton the monk increasingly began to understand
through his own lived life that the only answer to any human problem

---

10. On prayer and inner transformation as the basis of social and political
change and action, writing to Forrest who was involved in a General Strike for
Peace, Merton says: "Really we have to pray for a total and profound change in the
mentality of the whole world. What we have known in the past as Christian
penance is not a deep enough concept if it does not comprehend the special problems and dangers of the present age . . . (What is) important is the complete
change of heart and the totally new outlook on the world of man. We have to see
our duty to mankind as a whole . . . / The great problem is this inner change, and
we must not be so obsessed with details that we block the deeper development in
other people and in ourselves. The strike is to be regarded . . . as an application of
spiritual force and not the use of merely political pressure. We all have the great
duty to realize the deep need for purity of soul, . . . the deep need to possess in us
the Holy Spirit . . . This takes precedence over everything else" (*HGL, Cold War
Letter 25*, 1/29/62, 262).

lay not in any facile knee-jerks nor dogmatic schemes but *in God Himself.* Or, like Christ, one becomes a "scandal," not only to one's community and the world at large but *to oneself* as well, for part of this scandal and, indeed, destitution of soul lies in the rejection of all things that were once held to be precious and sacred. Instead, being stripped of all crutches and abandoned, one finds oneself "answer-less." Even God may refuse to be the answer, for this experience is not inconsistent with Christ's own agony and suffering. Perhaps not fully realizing its full implications, the monk had been granted the greatest of Christian gifts: he was, with the help of imperceptible grace, beginning to free himself of all illusions. And his letters to friends could not help but reflect the contradictions that came with this freedom of self-surrender.

4. "The Trouble with Squares . . . "

To Czeslaw Milosz, Merton writes with great passion and a resignation reminiscent of the beleaguered Job. The following are sentiments—with large dosages of gall and sarcasm—precipitated by the visit, as he says, of "a very good and learned" European monk whose answers were "all better down the line." Yet, though intellectually he accepts them, Merton retorts almost obstinately, "something in me says 'No' to them." This letter reveals a personal defiance rarely found in his more formal writings, or even in the journals:

> I have given the impression I had answers. / . . . / . . . One is left without answers, without comfort, without companionship, without a community. That is the thing that has finally hit me. My darkness was tolerable when it was only dark night, something spiritually approved. But it is rapidly becoming "exterior" darkness. A nothingness in oneself into which one is pressed down further and further, until one is inferior to the human race and hates the inferiority. Yet clings to it as the only thing one has. Then the problem is that perhaps here in this nothingness is infinite preciousness, the presence of the God Who is not an answer, the God of Job, to whom we must be faithful above all, beyond all. But the terrible thing is that He is *not known to others,* is incommunicable. One has no sense whatever that He is mentioned or referred to ever by anyone else; hence there is great danger that it may be the devil, for God, they say, is not at all private (*CT,* 75, 6/5/61).[11]

11. Merton was perfectly aware of his walking on a theological tightrope, and he was to spell this out rather clearly, among other places, in the essay, "A Christian

Merton speaks from out of a broken heart, or a broken cistern, if you will, yet, one suspects it is in and through this desperation and sense of *angst* that Merton's own ultimate liberation and inner transformation are rooted for, in their painful existential depth, we sense (and, no doubt, he senses) an identity with humanity hitherto merely verbal and abstract, which, in a sense, was still a luxury and a cushion distancing him from his fellow men and women. They also foreshadow his later ideas of the monk *in diaspora*, of the necessity of having to stand alone in post-Christian times.

Nearly two years before, in a letter to the poet, Herbert Mason, Merton had sung a quite different, surely more optimistic and conventional tune regarding "darkness." It is classic John of the Cross, wonderfully rhapsodic yet, upon some reflection, in comparison to the Milosz letter, there are still traces of the glibly-confident Merton:

> Look, if you think about darkness you will naturally get a tired mind. And when you think about it you put a kind of light in its place, that is what makes you tired. When it is dark, it is dark, and you go in the dark as if it were light. *Nox illuminatio mea.* The darkness is our light, and that is all. The light remains, simply, our everyday mind, such as it is, floating on the sea of darkness which we do not have to observe. But it carries us with great power. It is the being carried that is, actually, its light. Float, then. And trust the words of God, which you do not see either, but they are cool (*WF*, 263, 8/24/59).

Articulate and reassuring, and even euphoric. But in the later letter to Milosz, a less-assured and bruised Merton rejects now the "sanity" of easy rejoiners, of facile affirmations not grounded strictly in experience, especially in human suffering and alienation from one-

---

Looks at Zen" (*Zen and the Birds of Appetite* [New York: New Directions 1968] 33–58. Hereafter referred to in the text as *ZBA*):

> (W)e must not neglect the great importance of experience in Christianity. But Christian experience always has a special modality, due to the fact that it is inseparable from the mystery of Christ and the *collective life of the Church*, the Body of Christ. To experience the mystery of Christ mystically or otherwise is always to transcend the merely individual psychological level and to "experience theologically with the Church" . . . . In other words, this experience must always be in some way reducible to a theological form that *can be shared by the rest of the Church* . . . (46. Emphasis added).

self and the world. In the beginning of that profound missive to the future Polish Nobel laureate, the monk admits to his failure in coping with the "basic theological questions." "There is," he says, "something wrong with the questions that are supposed to be dispensed of by answers. That is the trouble with squares. They think that when you have answers you no longer have questions." But, on the contrary, he continues,

> The more you simply stand with the questions all sticking in your throat at once, the more you unsettle the 'peace' of those who think they have swallowed all the answers. The questions cause one to be nauseated by answers. This is a healthy stance, but it is not accepted. Hence *I am nauseated by answers and nauseated by optimism*. There is an optimism which cheapens Christianity and makes it absurd, empties it. It is a silly, petty optimism which consists in being secure because one knows the right answers (*CT*, 75, 6/5/61. Emphasis added).

Merton had finally come to terms with the fact that in this "worst of all centuries" (*CT*, 77, 9/16/61) identity with mankind meant, among other things, being "spiritually excommunicated," of suffering the sort of "metaphysical torment" that marked the lives and writings of Simone Weil, of Charles Peguy, of Albert Camus, and of Milosz himself, and that such lives, though perhaps unofficially non-Christian and even atheistic were, he now perceived, *more Christian* than his own. He seemed to have found himself "on the outside" as far back as the early 1950s.[12] But his later readings, contacts and struggles over his vocation and with authorities over censorship with regard to his writings and his wish to leave Gethsemani strongly persuaded him that true sanity and humanity lay in the midst of the bleak human desert and especially among wrecked lives that indeed did not have the comfort and luxury of ready-made answers.

The Pauline "putting on Christ" began to manifest an unthought of starkness and a radical and existential encounter not with Merton's own nor with any humanly-conceived spirit of poverty but with the very "*perfect* poverty" of Christ who seemed to want to live

12. See letter to Naomi Burton Stone, Merton's agent, *WT*, 130–1, 10/10/52. Writing to his "sensible sister," the monk perhaps half-laments yet convincingly says, "I am now used to the fact that what seems to me to be prayer seems to many holy men (sic) to be folly." My own assessment is that the censorship battle over *The Sign of Jonas* radicalized Merton once and for all and convinced him that his true vocation was not to walk the well-worn monastic path of past centuries.

now in the monk and some chosen others *by being absent*. In such a modality, one is neither comforted by the presence of the self nor the presence of divinity, and grace is so stark and poor that "all is done in us but without us—*in nobis et sine nobis*" (*ZBA*, 121).

5. Conclusion: God Heals by Wrecking

In some sense, what Merton experienced in those years was even beyond Zen, for Zen can take us to purity of heart but not to the Kingdom of God which demands a greater personal price and resignation of self and sense of emptiness and destitution whereby, as Merton says, "the real work of God begins."[13] Life takes on the mode of "a dynamic gift, a fullness of love" (*ZBA*, 138) experienced at every moment in the *here and now* and yet, whose manifestations are fully undeterminable, unmediated and unconditioned by anything either exterior to or interior in us, and surely beyond anything we may wish for or expect.

This is the only *milieu* in which divine freedom can breathe, and its pulses are wholly inconsistent with the rhythms and beats of human constructs and intrusive "answers" which purport to catch anything. It is the *milieu* in which God wrecks havoc on all human plans and schemes and takes away all hopes that might obscure *His* loving and merciful Intrusion. His mercy is so great that He insists on crowning His saints with His own nobility rather than allowing His creatures to wallow in their own falsified and alloyed elements. But existentially—in his own abject poverty—man cannot face this loss of self and utter bankruptcy of reality alone and unaided.

In an inspired essay in *Zen and the Birds of Appetite*, Merton writes:

13. Merton writes in *ZBA*, echoing among others, Cassian, Evagrius Ponticus, Sts. Maximus and Gregory of Nyssa,

> Purity of heart . . . is the intermediate end of the spiritual life. But the ultimate end is the Kingdom of God. This is a dimension which does not enter into the realm of Zen.
>
> . . . Purity of heart . . . is the necessary preparation not for further struggle between good and evil, but for the real work of God . . . , the work of the *new creation*, the resurrection from the dead, the restoration of all things in Christ. This is the real dimension of Christianity, the eschatological dimension which is peculiar to it, and which has no parallel in Buddhism (132).

> (A)ll transcendent experience is for the Christian a partici-
> pation in 'the mind of Christ' . . . *who emptied himself* . . . obedient
> unto death . . . This dynamic of emptying and of transcendence
> accurately defines the transformation of the Christian conscious-
> ness in Christ. It is a kenotic transformation, an emptying of all the
> contents of the ego-consciousness to become a void in which the
> light of God or the glory of God, the full radiation of the infinite re-
> ality of His Being and Love are manifested (75).

Merton continues by quoting Meister Eckhart whose following words
D. T. Suzuki himself had once likened to the experience of *prajna*
(Buddhist wisdom): "In giving us His love God has given us His Holy
Ghost so that we can love Him with the love wherewith He loves
Himself. We love God with His own love; awareness of it deifies us"
(*ZBA,* 75). Perhaps, rather than regarding the experience as an "emptying," it may be more appropriate to take Merton's lead and see it as
a divine *crowning,* a *lifting* or *restoring* of the ego to the mind of God
whence it originates and has never really left. While the ego, or what
we may call, "limited selfhood," "simply vanish(es) out of the picture
altogether" (76), the pain of this "self-naughting," the letting go of
both attachments *and* detachments that nurture and inflate the ego and
serve as its scaffolding, nonetheless, remains intensely real because the
old Adamic pull continues to have its sway, remaining, as long as there
is human life, forever an emblem of man's willfulness. Apropos of the
monk's sense of ambiguity was the ever-hovering and humbling
awareness that he was a sinner.

Despite his strong conviction that we, without being conscious
of this great boon, are always living in the presence of this Oneness,
Merton never allowed himself to live under the delusive luxury that he
or anyone else had conquered sin and alienation once and for all.
Consequently, while he never regarded the world with all its perplex-
ities as an illusion, he nonetheless stubbornly refused to acknowledge
that the sea of fire to which we had all somehow contributed to its
making, succumbed to its seductions and which now engulfs us all
constitutes a viable and sane way of life. Its roots, in other words, lay
in duplicity and sin, the result of the Fall. And we may guess that perhaps it was this overriding awareness of seeing himself personally as
a sinner with a *similarly* duplicitous nature that finally gave him the
balance, humility and wisdom to seek ever more broadly and deeply
for further manifestations of the true brotherhood and sisterhood of
the human community in both the present and the past, and in all
races and religions of humanity.

He saw as well the need for dialogue and for connectedness with all those who similarly seek salvation—though, perhaps, *gropingly* and through a glass darkly—by contact with a cosmic heart and with people who understand instinctively the utter need for continual inner transformation and whose joys and sorrows and fecundity are as great as Christ would allow them to savor in His inner sanctum. In fact, Thomas Merton had been there all along without fully realizing where he was; paradoxically, the initial impulse of that awareness that God truly loved him was most surely felt when he first *reckoned himself out,* and he became gratefully and willingly and, we might add, *joyously,* God's or Brahma's solitary and compassionate eternal hymn to the world.

Spirituality, Scholarship and Biography: An Interview with Anthony T. Padovano

Introduced, Conducted, and Edited by Jonathan Montaldo

$\mathbf{D}$r. Anthony T. Padovano is professor of American literature and religious studies at Ramapo College in New Jersey and is adjunct professor of theology at Fordham University in New York City. He holds a doctoral degree in theology from the Pontifical Gregorian University in Rome and a Ph.D. in English language and literature from Fordham University. Since 1988 he has been the president of COR-PUS, a national organization of four thousand members working for ministerial reform in the Catholic Church. An author of twenty-five books (June 1996), Anthony Padovano has devoted critical research to the thought of Thomas Merton. In addition to *The Human Journey: Thomas Merton, Symbol of a Century* (1982), and an audiotape of twenty-four lectures on Merton entitled *Thomas Merton: A Life for Our Times* (1988), he has also authored a one-actor play, available on videotape, *Winter Rain* (1985), in which Michael Moriarity portrays Thomas Merton.

This interview of June 14, 1996, records a scholar/theologian/dramatist's reflections on one subject of his dedicated study: the life and work of Thomas Merton and Merton's influence on contemporary culture and the spiritual life. Since Thomas Merton's death in 1968, a diversity of professionals has produced a significant body of scholarship on Merton. While dedicated scholars are aware of the secondary literature directed toward Thomas Merton's legacy, the general Merton reader is understandably unaware that a wealth of reflection exists which helpfully deciphers Merton's message and its meaning. This interview with Anthony T. Padovano inaugurates plans for a series of interviews with scholars whose research about Merton holds continuing significance as Thomas Merton's appeal to both scholarship and general readership shifts toward the twenty-first century.

***

Montaldo: When did you first read Thomas Merton?

Padovano: The Seven Storey Mountain came out in 1948. I was a sophomore in high school in 1949 when I read it, and the book made a profound impression on me. So profound an impression, in fact, that the next year I took a bus trip to Gethsemani. It was an enormously moving experience. It turned out to be archetypical for a lot of what would later follow in my life and studies.

Montaldo: Did you realize that at fifteen years of age in 1950 you could have entered Gethsemani? There were actually Trappists postulants that young in those days!

Padovano: I was not aware of that, but I was thinking seriously of becoming a Trappist. I was inspired by Merton's autobiography, by the Gethsemani community and what it stood for, and by the contemplative way of life. Looking back on it now, I'm not quite sure that was the right place for me. I think the arrangement we had for seminary in the Archdiocese of Newark was effective. We were not taken out of the normal events of growing. I was able to start preparing for seminary studies as a high school freshman at a regular, private prep school, Seton Hall, in Northern New Jersey. The only difference between my course of studies and that of the regular students was that I took more Latin and Greek and I was formally registered as a divinity student. But other than that, from athletic teams to dances to the yearbook to the school paper and clubs, as a theological student you were not treated exceptionally. I think that was a good system.

Montaldo: Give me an overview of your seminary studies.

Padovano: I started seminary in 1948, when I entered high school, but for those four years, and for the first two years of college the system I have already described prevailed. In my first two years of college at Seton Hall University, I was formally registered as a seminary student but existentially I was in a position not much different from that of any other college student. In 1954, as a college junior, I formally entered Darlington Seminary for the Archdiocese of Newark. Darlington was academically affiliated with Seton Hall University from which I received my B.A. in 1956. I actually had three majors: classical languages, philosophy, and literature. In the normal course of events, I would have remained at Darlington for four more years to do theology, but I received an assignment to the North American College in Rome to study at the Gregorian University from which in 1960 I received a Licentiate in Sacred Theology (STL), which is equivalent to a master's degree. My archbishop then requested I stay another two years to finish a doctorate in theology and appointed me to the seminary faculty at Darlington. In 1962 I came back to New Jersey and started teaching at Darlington as a professor of systematic theology. I stayed with that until 1974 when I resigned and married.

Montaldo: Your wife Theresa and you have raised a family?

Padovano: We have four children. Our eldest, Mark, is twenty-one. He's in aeronautical school. Andrew is twenty and studies in the School of Foreign Service at Georgetown University. Paul is sixteen and Rosemarie is fifteen, both in high school.

Montaldo: There is a gap in your life between your personal interest in Thomas Merton, which you date from 1949, when you were fifteen years old, and the beginning of your scholarly interest in Merton. When and how did you turn your critical attention to Thomas Merton's life and work?

Padovano: My scholarly interest in Merton, as I recall, began with an essay I wrote at the request of Canadian theologian Gregory Baum for a book he was editing entitled *Journeys.* Baum had asked a dozen Canadian and American theologians to write about people who had most shaped their theological thinking and to reflect on the ways these personalities had influenced their own theological system. I chose John Henry Newman, who had been the topic of my doctoral dissertation in theology at the Gregorian, John XXIII and Merton. I knew a great deal about Newman and John XXIII, but I realized then how relatively little I knew about Merton in terms of cognitive and scholarly content. So that essay for *Journeys* led to more systematic studies of Thomas Merton.

Montaldo: Newman, John XXIII and Merton. Why these three?

Padovano: I believe strongly, and this may be a Merton influence on me from the beginning, in the fusion of biography and scholarship. I have always been less moved by Thomas Aquinas, for example, whose work is fully accessible without any reference to his biography. I am more moved by Augustine, although I disagree with him on many things. It's hard to read Augustine without knowing the life. So this reflection on how trying to figure out how your life impacts your theology, I think, was a creative idea on Baum's part. Newman, John XXIII, and Merton, I concluded, were major influences on my own theological thinking and personal-spiritual development.

Montaldo: Why Cardinal Newman?

Padovano: John Henry Newman had a great influence on me for many reasons: the drama in his own life, the eloquence with which he writes—he's a marvelous stylist—the soaring creativity of his thought. Newman was a considerable influence on Vatican II. He reached out from one century to another to shape it. Newman's themes in *The Grammar of Assent*, for example, the idea that we reach certitude by a convergence of probabilities rather than by moving from certitude to certitude, is an impressive insight. His whole idea that a thousand difficulties do not make a doubt, that to be perfect is to change often.

Montaldo: "To be perfect is to change often." That's an important insight with references to both your own life and to Thomas Merton's, isn't it?

Padovano: Ralph Waldo Emerson thought consistency the hobgobblin of little minds. This penchant that we have to be absolutely consistent all the time is a terrible problem for our lives and in our thinking, this assumption that consistency is somehow or other a mark of intellectual maturity. Obviously people can't be so capricious, so random, so idiosyncratic that one hardly knows where one is going to be from one moment to the next. But one would think that if one's mind is creative, one does move in different directions and one has to recast one's thought.

Montaldo: Returning to Newman's influence, in your series of taped lectures, *Thomas Merton: A Life for Our Times,* you speak approvingly of Newman's proposing a toast, after the ending of the First Vatican Council, in which he first lifted his glass to "Conscience" and then offered a second toast to the Pope. I imagine Newman's toast still resonates with your approval?

Padovano: Very much so. The deepest levels of Catholic theology always say that you are obliged to follow your conscience, even if your conscience is wrong. This is the supreme norm by which our integrity and authenticity is judged. By conscience—Newman himself was clear on this—I don't mean whatever we self-indulgently choose to call conscience and I certainly do not mean by conscience that you are not subjecting your conscience to the possibility of growing, of being enriched, of being enlightened and of being in dialogue with alternative viewpoints. But as one goes through the process of forming one's conscience, one has to do, after all, what one thinks is right.

If you do what is objectively the right thing—Thomas Aquinas was clear on this—but your conscience informs you it's the wrong thing, that is a sinful act in Aquinas' system. Protestantism has a tendency toward anarchy while Catholicism tends toward fascism and tyranny. If we push the Catholic principle too hard in an extreme direction, then you have no conscience: you have tyrannical control. On the other hand, if you push the Protestant principle of conscience too far, without a counterbalancing and countervailing influence of institution and community, then you have anarchy. But, in any case, I think the papacy and the Church have always to be second to the conscience of the individual. If one, after all, left the Church in good conscience, one is saved. If one stays in the Church with a bad conscience, one is lost. So I think Newman was quite correct. The problem is, as I said, that at times the category of conscience can in our own day be trivialized and identified with whatever happens to be convenient. Conscience is something far more profound than that.

Montaldo: John XXIII was a second influence.

Padovano: Emotionally I felt very connected to John XXIII because I was in the square of St. Peter's on the night he was elected to the papacy and I remember receiving word, within ninety days of his election, of his call for the Second Vatican Council which has been a major shaping influence not only on my life but on an entire era of Catholic thinkers. John XXIII represented for me, as did Newman and Merton, a movement to reach out and bring into the Church the entire world, this desire to exclude no one, yet not being, in the process of inclusion, merely arbitrary. One knew exactly where those three leaders stood even though one felt included in their life and thought. I was in Rome for all the preparations for the Council but I was due back to begin teaching at Darlington in September. The Second Vatican Council opened on October 11, 1962. I unfortunately experienced it only from a distance.

Montaldo: You were teaching systematic theology at Darlington Seminary from 1962, but your scholarly interest in Thomas Merton only began in earnest in 1974.

Padovano: Yes, it began at New York University after I had completed a master's in American literature and had started a doctoral program. I had made up my mind that I wanted to do a dissertation on Merton in both literature and theology, but I could not find any professor at NYU, this was in 1973, who was willing to direct an interdisciplinary dissertation in the fields of literature and theology especially focused on Thomas Merton. I decided I did not want to spend a few years of my life researching a dissertation in something that did not have great meaning for me, so I moved to Fordham in 1974. It happened that I also resigned from the Archdiocese of Newark in 1974 and married, but, as I recall, there was no causal connection between that decision and the decision to go in the direction of Merton.

Montaldo: You first visited Gethsemani in 1949. You revisited the abbey in 1975. Did you return to research your dissertation on Merton?

Padovano: My visit to Gethsemani in 1975 was both a scholarly and personal pilgrimage. Certainly the idea of returning to Merton and Gethsemani was spiritually and emotionally rewarding. And, of course, there was no way I could do a doctoral dissertation without first reading absolutely everything Merton had published. Secondly, I was trying to read all the available unpublished material at the Thomas Merton Center at Bellarmine College. The access to unpublished material was more limited in 1975 than it is now. Thirdly, it was important to visit the monastery, the hermitage, Louisville itself. I had the opportunity to interview the people who were key to Merton's life both at Gethsemani and in the Louisville area. I can't quite recall whether I made two or three trips while I was working on *The Human Journey,* which was the title of my published dissertation at Fordham.

Montaldo: Was your interview with Dom James Fox, Merton's abbot at Gethsemani, extensive? Did you audiotape the interview? Did you save your notes?

Padovano: Yes, I have my notes. I saved the notes on every interview. But I did not audiotape. It could have been interesting, but it might have inhibited some people. But no, I have my personal notes on all those interviews [archived in The Padovano Collection at the University of Notre Dame].

Montaldo: I want to preface my questions on *The Human Journey* by remarking that, as time passes and when all of Thomas Merton's primary material is published or accessible, it's my assessment that *The Human Journey* will remain an important and decisively perceptive study on Merton's life and influence. Your prose and your analysis resonate deeply with symbols and metaphors embedded in Merton's writing. Were Merton alive to read the secondary literature published since his death, I think he would without doubt enjoy and learn from *The Human Journey.* Rehearse for me—it has to be understandably brief—the reasons for your calling Thomas Merton "symbol for a century."

Padovano: My concern was to figure out why this man has the appeal that he does. What is there in this man that is so attractive?

Merton's appeal did not originate with any one element in his writing that in itself was so extraordinary that it merited world-class attention. For example, I did not find that his theology was first-rate or that his spiritual writing was anything like Teresa of Avila's or John of the Cross'. He was not a major poet. So as I went through the elements I kept saying "well, where's the appeal?" And the appeal seemed to be in two things: first, in the fusion of biography and theology. Secondly, and perhaps more important, Merton resonates in a subliminal way for people when they read him; he captures the dynamics of the age in which they are living. He is dealing with the same tensions, the same problems, the same prospects that his readers are, but he is solving his difficulties by holding in tension what seem to be polarities. He deals with polarities such as the sacred and the secular, east and west, male and female, conscience and authority, polarities that fuse brilliantly in his writing. And then I began to think that the tensions in these particular polarities were the issues that the twentieth century was and is dealing with more energetically and creatively than any previous century did.

In the nineteenth century, for example, the either/or mentality prevailed. One was either this or that. In the twentieth century we are trying to say that, "No, maybe we are both/and. We are both Catholic and Protestant, both male and female, both east and west." In the twentieth century the preference is toward balance. What would have been seen in the nineteenth century as a betrayal of principle—one had to be totally one thing to the exclusion of anything else—one true Church and all the others were false—in the twentieth century is seen as intellectually myopic and emotionally arrogant.

Montaldo: You said that Merton seemed to solve the problem of "dialectics," which is your own technical word for the tensions inherent between two apparently irreconcilable experiences or ideas in *The Human Journey.*

[*Padovano:* Yes.] But I would not say Merton "solved" because, to my reading, Merton's biographical tensions were solutionless. You yourself have said elsewhere that tensions exist in every aspect of our lives and that we not only cannot escape these tensions but we do not even have a right to escape them. Does Merton's writing really represent a solution to the "dialectics" of the twentieth century?

Padovano: In Merton there is what I might call an existential solution: his willingness to live with the tensions and to realize they can never be solved. What attracted Merton to Buddhism was his reaction to his and our western tendency to think we can resolve problems once and for all and get on to something else, our western penchant for problem-solving. Buddhism says that you live with the insoluble problem and that this is the solution. Merton lived fully with the tensions inherent in ideas like conscience and authority, being unable and unwilling, I think, on the deepest levels, to compromise an understanding of either conscience or authority in ways which would remove the inherent tension between them. The non-resolution—if this is not playing with words too much—the non-resolution *is* a resolution in the sense that you realize this is the creative, healthy tension that you must live with for your whole life. So, I would say that Merton "solved" the tension by saying that the ambiguity is inescapable.

Montaldo: You are a theologian by extensive training and profession. You have written that Thomas Merton is much more profound in living his theology than he is in articulating his theology.

Padovano: Karl Rahner once said that all good theology is a step or two after life, that the life happens first and then the theology later codifies it. Theology doesn't create the life, but follows the life. I think that Merton intuitively knew where to go even before he had theologically worked it out. And where he was going, I think, was theologically coherent even if he was not able to explain where he was moving with theological coherence. For example, something in Merton made him know that the secular world was good even though at times he wrote about it savagely. But he couldn't let the secular world go; he could not cut ties to the world at large. All the letters, all the articles, all the correspondence he received, had a lot to do with the need to stay in contact with the world. Merton could not let the monastery become the world or the world become a monastery, even though at times, in his autobiography at least, he wrote as if he wanted the world to be a monastery and every Catholic a monk. In his early writing he gave the impression he hated the world, but he intuitively understood that the secular world was terribly important for his own calling and his own religious life.

I think the same thing happened with his problems with conscience and authority. He wanted to be an obedient monk. He also wanted to be—and was right from the beginning, I think—a monk aware of having to follow his own path. Later, when he entered and thought through the tensions between Eastern and Western spirituality, he didn't first work everything out before he moved into experiencing and studying these tensions. He moved into the tension and then later realized how it was proper he should have explored this direction in his experience. So for these reasons, I think Merton's life was ahead of his theological synthesis. Only decades after Merton experienced these things can we begin to give them the kind of formal theological explanation for which he appears to have been either unwilling or incapable.

Montaldo: Could you share any critical reaction from your colleagues, professional theologians, to your research interests in Thomas Merton?

Padovano: I cannot recall any direct criticism. A great deal depends on how one views theology. If one is a theologian who deals with major theological thinkers only, like Edward Schillebeeckx or Karl Rahner, then you would not be impressed by Merton. I do think the more creative theologians see Merton's value. Theology, as it has been formulated for most of this century, has put theology and spirituality in different camps but I believe they are fused. Good theology is always spiritual. I can be a good literature professor or a good philosopher without necessarily moving toward spiritual dimensions in my field of study, dimensions that might change my life. But theology is a different discipline: good theology passes over into life and prayer. Good theology is profoundly meditative. A profound Christian theology should lead you to a spiritual encounter with Christ.

Montaldo: A distinctive mark of your Merton scholarship, although you are not alone, is your having taken Merton's poetry seriously. You have had an especially analytical interest in the later poetry, in *Cables to the Ace* and in Merton's "epic," *The Geography of Lograire.* Yet Merton's poetics is another element which does not, in your opinion, account for his first-class cultural influence.

Padovano: Some have described Merton's poetry as being first-rate minor poetry. I think in his own mind he wanted to be a greater poet than I, at least, see him as having been. But the deepest cast of Merton's mind is poetic. Merton is like the writer Albert Camus in this way. Camus doesn't write any poetry to speak of but the whole tone of his prose is poetic. Strange to say, Merton's poetry shows itself best in his prose. And yet, paradoxically, I believe what was most true about Merton's soul, if we want to talk this way for a moment, got through more easily in the poetry. Merton is a poetically powerful writer. When you consider solely the form of his prose, the poetry helped the prose a great deal. But in terms of Merton's actual revelation of himself, I think the poetry allows things to get through that are more guarded in the prose. Let me be concrete: in the scene in *The Seven Storey Mountain* when the young Merton in Rome has a mystical experience of his dead father's presence in his bedroom, an experience which significantly turns his life around, had Merton cast the experience into a poem there would have been little hesitation about the rightness of everything that he was experiencing. In the prose he was more conditional, not quite willing to claim that the experience in Rome was essentially mystical.

In *The Geography of Lograire*, for example, Merton makes references to his love for a "vanished nurse," to early loves and to his "wailing for a mate." He tries to reach his lost mother, now suffused into Church imagery, with his "Sing A Song to Mama."

In an earlier and more simple poem, "Grace's House," Merton encounters the charm of children in a way not revealed in his prose. And in *Cables to the Ace* Merton does not hesitate to identify the world's need for God as Father with his personal need for an abiding father figure he cannot find.

Montaldo: You raise the question of mysticism. In your analysis Merton's prose describes and reveals four significant experiences which you have characterized both as mystical and as marking turning points in Merton's life. Merton describes two of these in his autobiography: his sensing the strong presence of his father, Owen, in Rome and then the powerful experience ignited when he hears children crying *"Creo en Diós"* as he attends Mass in Cuba. The third experience, described in *Conjectures of a Guilty Bystander,* is at Fourth and Walnut Streets in Louisville. He describes the final experience in *The Asian Journal:* "Merton approaches the Buddhist monuments at Polonnaruwa in Ceylon and feels he has finally gone "beyond the shadow and the disguise." I am frankly skeptical about claims that Merton was a mystic and that these experiences are important, life turning points. These four experiences are narrated, remembered events. Perhaps "moments of clarity" for Merton, none of these recounted experiences definitively alleviates the abiding insecurities and uncertainties of his being a human being and alive. I think commentators, and we readers following their lead, have exaggerated these events as both "mystical" and "definitive turning points" in Merton's biography.

Padovano: I guess I define mystical by saying that it is that which helps us see everything as harmonious. I think the mystical experience is one in which all the contradictions and the negativities, the liabilities and the assets, fuse together: in some way one sees continuities where before there were only interruptions. So the mystical experience is holistic with a wholeness that is absolutely riveting because it is a wholeness that incorporates elements that one would have thought were excluded. The second element of mysticism, which is really a sub-set of wholeness, is the idea that one becomes aware of the deepest depths of one's own authenticity, one's own calling, one's own identity. These two things go together. Now to address what you have said was what we now call a mystical experience little other than Merton's having worked out very painfully a conclusion which could have been worked out on the level of the cognitive, of the logical, without introducing this other element of the mystical?

First of all I guess I'm willing to take the testimony the way the author presents it. I think Merton, as few people, tried to be scrupulously honest with his own life and I do think that the mystical in his life was something that embarrassed him. I mean he did not readily admit any of his experience was mystical. You get his guardedness certainly with his description of his father appearing to him in Rome. There's a tension in the way Merton describes it. The prose clearly carries Merton's emotional realization that something terribly important happened. His writing is vivid and electric in the narrating. But then he imposes a cognitive overlay, in which he questions if he's being foolish, that it really wasn't a mystical experience and maybe it was indigestion and maybe it was only a psychologically distraught situation. I believe he inserts this cognitive overlay either because the Trappist censors wanted it or he thought they might have wanted it. His own superego as a Trappist might have imposed on that experience the need to dismiss it as mystical. A reader can usually sense where a writer is emotionally very much involved. I think the appearance of his father in Rome was a deeply mysterious experience and it shattered his previous categories. It introduced him to levels of authenticity with himself that he had never before experienced. It came in a flash, a *eureka* moment. And it gave him a sense of wholeness. I think I can replicate that through the other three experiences as well. However, your point is well taken: the fact that these narrated events are put to paper at the same time that he is trying to make a painful decision about his own life probably means that the narrated event was preceded by a lot of agitated thinking. My guess, however, is that, without that kind of transcendent experience, the agitated thinking would not have led him forward. The transcendent experience convinces him of the rightness of what he is to do although the certification and validation of that rightness is coming from outside all the resources that he is able to attract to himself.

Montaldo: I sense a current exploding of texts focused on the private spiritual journey, especially among women writers. Annie Dillard was seminal in *A Pilgrim at Tinker Creek* (1974). Patricia Hampl's *Virgin Time* (1992) is another important example. Kathleen Norris' second effort in this genre, *Cloister Walk,* has just hit bookstores (1996). To what do you attribute this popular emergence of spiritual writers as journalists of their own souls?

Padovano: Some of it is deeply ingrained in the American psyche. America, although a more superficial reading would think otherwise, is not an essentially materialistic country. America from the beginning has been on a spiritual journey. That's certainly how the Puritans got here. That is even to a large extent, although we do not have time to explore all of this, how the Revolutionary War was fought, with a Declaration of Independence, a Constitution and a Bill of Rights: there was something profoundly spiritual in those documents. They were not just political documents; they were documents searching for something perfect, a utopian place for power, authority and a government to be. If one traces American literature through the nineteenth and twentieth centuries, if one really reads Hemingway, Fitzgerald, and Faulkner, and certainly if one reads Emerson, Thoreau, Hawthorne, and Melville, there is a profound spiritual yearning and hunger that has never been absent from the American soul. Alexis de Tocqueville, the French visitor to our country in the 1830s, said in his classic work *Democracy in America,* that if there is a materialism that will come about in the new country, it will be something the world has never seen before: it will be a "virtuous materialism." Nonetheless, I don't want to go too far down that road at the moment, but merely point out that Dillard, Hempl, and Norris are probably being more quintessentially American than would appear at first sight. I also think that the idea of the explicitly spiritual journey, certainly with people like Emerson and Thoreau, and even to some extent with people like Martin Luther King and Dorothy Day, and clearly with Thomas Merton, you get people very much interested in cataloging the explicit spiritual journey itself. So those two things are more traditional than one might expect. I think the third element that explains it is more contemporary and the reading on it is less benign, that is, the failure of the institutional churches to address the spiritual hungers of the age has led people to catalog and to retreat into their own spiritual journeys.

People are tending to examine their private experiences as a way of addressing their spiritual needs in ways more adequate than are being offered in traditional church structures. This is true for both Protestant and Catholic church structures although my interest is more in the Catholic, of course. I think Merton experienced the inadequacies of the religious institution.

Now, Merton's commitment to Catholicism, even on its institutional levels, was whole-hearted. But nonetheless, when one reads *The Seven Storey Mountain,* one is already beyond the boundaries a monk, and a Trappist monk especially, should have observed. In some ways I think Merton subconsciously understood that the institution would never be able to give him all the spiritual nourishment that he needed. So the journals and his own experience became a terribly important way of dealing with that. And later the inadequacy of the institution becomes more explicit as he takes stands against the institutional structures and as he moves toward the East and so on, never losing his Catholicism. Now this is always the tricky thing: people think Merton's move to the East was somehow or other a diminution of his Catholicism. I find him more Catholic at the end than he was in the beginning because he's gotten to the core of Catholicism. Paradoxically he becomes more committed now that he sees viable alternatives to Catholicism. He wants to be Catholic, but not in ways the institutional Church can easily accept.

Montaldo: One of the features which I find ties Merton to writers like Dillard, Hampl, and Norris is the turn toward nature. I don't know whether to capitalize Nature or not. Merton and these writers seem to find reflected in the rhythms and patterns of nature the rhythms of an earlier pattern for interior life which they sense as more congenial to their spiritual development than the more artificial patterns experienced in contemporary society. This turn toward nature is typically American.

Padovano: Yes, I think it's more traditional than we realize. The American Puritans were convinced that God revealed who God was both in scripture and in nature. Emerson puts the whole of his spiritual journey into nature. Certainly Thoreau does that on the shores of Walden Pond. Huckleberry Finn does that. It's out on the Mississippi River that Finn really finds God, not on the shore, not in civilization nor in institutional structures, but actually in some kind of flight from them. I think it is also quintessentially Merton who is very much attuned to nature and the soil and the natural. Merton's father, Owen, was influential here. Merton's experience of the spiritual in the patterns of nature connects him with eastern spirituality and native American spirituality as well.

Montaldo: The profusion of spiritualities and the literature expressing them disorients: Jewish spirituality, Buddhist spirituality, Womanist spirituality, St. Bernard's spirituality, Annie Dillard's and Merton's! What is spirituality and what do we mean when we attach a qualifier, like "lay" or "clerical," to spirituality?

Padovano: I think there is only one spirituality and I think both clerical spirituality and lay spirituality are misnomers. The essence of the spiritual is to encounter God on whatever transcendent reality one is seeking. Certainly if one stays within the intellectually defined resources of the human, one is not spiritual. The spiritual always transcends what seems to be only human and encounters a cosmic presence or God, as we would say. The transcendence of the familiar human categories as a definition of spirituality makes the essence of the spiritual true for both a Buddhist and a Christian. Merton's distinction between the empirical self and the real self can help us understand that. When you reach the real, you are always connected to everyone else. The empirical is divisive: it's the surface of reality. So one might say there is a clerical and a lay spirituality as long as one stays on this empirical level. But when one journeys to the inner heart of things, it doesn't matter whether John of the Cross was a priest or Teresa of Avila was a woman religious or Dorothy Day was a lay woman or John XXIII was a pope. These things which connote difference and distinction fade into insignificance in terms of their ability to witness for others what it means to move in a spiritual direction. Jesus, after all, is technically a lay person. He is not a Jewish priest. The spirituality represented by Jesus has nothing to do with whether he is lay, priest, Jewish or even first-century. There's something timeless and boundaryless when you encounter that level of spirituality. So I don't think there is a lay spirituality as such.

Montaldo: Does a person need a spiritual guide? Where can you find a spiritual guide today?

Padovano: I have ambivalent feelings about spiritual guides. One of the great problems with spiritual directors—Merton notes this himself in his book on spiritual direction—is that they can lead you to become something other than you are. What is it that Chinese Taoism says so incisively: "The leader, when he has done his job well, leads those he has led to feel that they never needed him." The best spiritual guide is the one who sets you free and doesn't try to keep you in bondage. Parents and professors, for example, may do the same thing, i.e., keep people from being free. That's the great danger, so I'm very wary of spiritual directors on that level. On the other hand, the spiritual guide who is a partner with us in dialogue and allows us to be different, but at the same time acts as a catalyst for our growth, is the healthiest guide of all. Those kinds of guides we always need, whether they are the contemporary spiritual writers you were citing before or the more traditional ones. Certainly reading the *Confessions* of Augustine or the autobiography of Newman or of Gandhi can be a tremendous help to us.

Montaldo: You have written that "spirituality is autobiography." Unpack that.

Padovano: Spirituality is autobiographical in the sense that spirituality only makes sense to us within the context of our own lives. You can't approach the spiritual without taking into account all the conditions of your own life. The spiritual journey must first be a personal journey. A spiritual guide should not impose on another a Benedictine, Franciscan, Ignatian, or Salesian kind of spirituality unless the person's own journey calls for that. Our spiritual journey is tied up with the sacred moments in our own lives. Each of us lives a sacred history. God is constantly revealing us to ourselves through the events and experiences of our own lives. Merton found God by reflecting on the sacred moments in his own life. If, on the other hand, we try to use Francis of Assisi or Teresa of Avila or Thomas Merton as concrete models, then we do not become who we have to be.

Allow me to reflect on the three people who influenced me. No one can doubt that Newman was a very unique individual. John XXIII was not trying to be Pius XII, his brilliant predecessor, next to whom he may have felt insignificant in some ways. But John XXIII was enough in touch with himself to say "This is who I am and I will follow this path." Newman did that. Newman doesn't come across as a Franciscan or a Benedictine but as Newman. In some ways Merton doesn't come across as a Trappist, although that obviously was what he was and it influenced what he became.

I get very concerned when spiritual writers, and sometimes even the institutional Church, give the impression that your personal experience must not be validated, that it is better to follow someone else's path. Merton once warned us to be wary of people who know what is best for us.

Montaldo: But is spirituality possible without its being grounded in a disciplined practice?

Padovano: Life itself has to be disciplined. Life can't work, much less be spiritual, without discipline. Love needs discipline: you can't be undisciplined and be in love. Without a structure, life, spirituality and love become random and spontaneous without any sense of substance and continuity. In the spiritual life, yes, there has to be the discipline of prayer and the discipline of *accepting the consequences* that results from one's praying. Approaching life by making definite choices from one's prayer is part of spiritual discipline. But if the structure gets too rigid you have got a problem. In *The Way of Chuang Tzu* Merton quoted with approbation Chuang Tzu's statement that "when the shoe fits, the foot is forgotten." Merton talks explicitly about the danger of over-organizing your life, of crushing your spirit. The ambiguities we were talking about earlier, Jonathan, are very much in play here. One has to have a discipline, but it must be a discipline that allows a fair amount of spontaneity and freedom. Even when Kathleen Norris goes to that Benedictine monastery in Dakota she doesn't pretend she is a Catholic and she certainly doesn't want to join the monastery, but yet she is able to gain from that exposure to Benedictine discipline enormous amounts of potentiality for development, but without losing her self. This is the great fear I have: if the self is lost, one has lost everything.

Everything we do can be done better by someone else *except* to be the person we are. That is the only thing we do better than everyone else. Someone else can be a better father, a better professor, a better physician, a better writer, a better poet, there is not a talent that you or I have that cannot be exceeded by someone else's talent. But to be Anthony and Jonathan, only we can do that. The self is terribly important for the spiritual life.

Montaldo: Merton, like Paul of Tarsus, hoped he could be "all things to all people." Especially in the last decade of his life Merton spoke of seeking to bridge gaps between the west and the east, between the latin and orthodox churches, between north and south American cultures. But can any of us really become "transcultural persons"? Doesn't an attempt to transcend cultures belie the principle of the Incarnation? How does one act transculturally?

Padovano: It depends on how one defines transcultural. I agree that one has to be who one is. The irony of it is you can't become universal without being particular. Dostoevsky used to say a lot of people love humankind but hate their neighbors. Thus on one level transculturalism can be evasive because one may say "I don't have to be anything, I can be everything," which is a way of being nothing. If I can be a Buddhist this year and a Muslim the next and a Catholic the next and Jewish the next, I am committed to nothing at all. So I think that we become universal by becoming emphatically particular. Jesus is clearly a first-century Jew. He is not a Samaritan; he is a first-century Jew limited to Israel. He doesn't go outside of Israel. He doesn't visit any other place, yet all of his universality comes from taking that particularity to its depth, by finding all the possibilities of freedom and love in his incarnation.

James Joyce does that in *Ulysses*. Leopold Bloom has one day. *Ulysses* takes place in twenty-four hours. If you have just one day in your own life you have everything. All you need is a day. We used to have a beautiful insight in pre-Vatican II spirituality, and I believe it is reappearing: the sacrament of the present moment. If I can take the present moment to its sacramental depths of mystery and infinity, then I reach everything, but I have to stay with the present moment to do that. So, I would agree with you on that level. You can't be transcultural by denying you are a male, white, American, of the twentieth century, a Catholic. At some level all of that must be affirmed without hesitation or embarrassment. But if that is taken superficially, then it is not transportable beyond one's own culture. If that is taken in depth, then one does become transcultural. What does it matter to us that Gandhi was a Hindu? It was terribly important for him, but Gandhi to me is as Catholic and American as I am in the sense that I can connect with him fully in his Hinduism. Gandhi transcends his Hinduism by the fact that he not only did not forsake his Hinduism but affirmed it in its core. So, I think transculturalism's deepest meaning comes from the affirmation of one's own biography and geography.

In its shallow meaning, transculturalism means that you can be absolutely everything to everyone. I don't think that is how Paul meant it. Let me put it another way very simply: a lover reaches everyone. John XXIII was a lover. Does anyone really care he was Italian? Or about his age? Or the fact that he was the patriarch of Venice before he was elected? It doesn't even register on the radar screen. Who cares about that? All of his particularities, of course terribly important to him, get transcended precisely because he embraced who he was. John XXIII was unmistakably Catholic, there was no doubt about that at all, and yet Protestants and Jews felt that he was their ally and their brother. At that moment, when the particular is taken to its depths, the universal is communicated for all to see.

Montaldo: You have written, "I believe non-violence is the hallmark of spirituality, [*Padovano:* (passionately) Yes.] the touchstone and measure of its authenticity and depth." [*Padovano:* Indeed!] Can you elaborate on your judgment?

Padovano: I don't think anything is more distinctive of Jesus than non-violence. Certainly that is the most concrete expression that his love takes. If Jesus indeed, as later Catholic theology affirms, is the Son of God, if that be true, the fact that Jesus is so non-violent in going to his death is enormously illustrative of what we are supposed to be as Christians. The early Christians understood that, which is why they would not bear arms for centuries and would not fight. They went to their deaths meekly at times, as Jesus did, rather than die in anger and protest. I do not think there is anything that is more corrosive to the human spirit than violence or power, not genuine authority, but oppressive power. If a church or a community or person can witness to the ability to lead life non-oppressively, that one can go through life and not take hostages and make victims of others, I think to the extent that we can demonstrate that, we can make Christianity and Christ more credible to others than in any other way. Non-violence basically means that you always see the other, not just the self but also the other, and that you find a way to reach the other. Violence says, "I want to eliminate the other." Non-violence says, "I want to include the other." This does not mean everything is permissible or that all behaviors go unprotested. Gandhi said it so well, "If you must choose between violence and cowardice, do violence." Gandhi could not think of anything worse than to use non-violence as a mask for cowardice or as a mask for not taking a position or not standing for something. It was clear what Gandhi stood for.

It was clear what Jesus stood for. It was clear what Merton stood for. But they believed that they could go about their tasks unoppressively. If we can do that, we unleash enormous creative possibilities in ourselves and in the human family, and we ignite incandescently a kind of spirituality that can enlighten and save and heal the whole world. I can't think of anything more important than non-violence as a hallmark of spirituality.

Montaldo: May your words be of benefit, Dr. Padovano. Thank you very much.

A Haven for 'Homeless Religious Minds': 1996 Bibliographic Review

George Kilcourse

In the wake of the sensationalism created by the publication of the first of seven volumes of Thomas Merton's journals last year, readers have set about the task of digesting four volumes of Merton material which arrived during 1996. While three of them are the journals (covering 1941–1952; 1952–1960; and 1960–1963), the gem among these publications as the year 1996 met 1997 is the modest but sterling collection of letters exchanged by Czeslaw Milosz and Merton between 1958 and 1968.

After assessing the merits of all this new primary material, our attention will shift to one new book about Merton, the sole contribution of this caliber during the past year. But a wide spectrum of critical essays from various journals and periodicals rounds out this year's bibliographic survey, ranging from an interest in Art and Spirituality to Merton's "Christ-Consciousness." A new bibliographic tool for reading Merton's five volumes of published letters is also noted.

I

It is disarming to recognize that Michael Mott's biography of Thomas Merton will soon be fifteen years old. Yet, as time passes, Mott's painstaking labor of love proves itself still without peer in Merton studies. It was in the pages of *The Seven Mountains of Thomas Merton* that we first appreciated the nature of the monk's correspondence with the Polish linguist and literary critic Czeslaw Milosz. Midway in Mott's biography he described their letters as "[t]he most vital exchange" for Merton in the early 1960s. Only now, with the early release of *Striving Towards Being* in late 1996 (although the book bears the 1997 date) and publication of *both* sides of this correspondence, can we begin to fathom the deep impression—perhaps the singularly transforming impact—which Milosz made on Merton and his vocation as a monk-literary figure. Readers of *The Merton Annual* deserve an immediate alert to this volume and its import for understanding the twentieth century's most celebrated monk.

A large selection of Merton's letters to Milosz were included in the fourth volume of selections from Merton's letters, *The Courage for Truth*. However, the other side of the correspondence from the recipient of the 1980 Nobel Prize in Literature has, until now, remained unpublished. Robert Faggen, professor of English literature at Claremont McKenna College in California, has edited a handsome volume to remedy that missing dimension. In the process, he has also given us a new perspective and context in which to appreciate Merton's mind and heart as the monk submitted to Milosz's challenge, his scrutiny, and his encouragement. I do not know of a more important exchange of correspondence in Merton's life.

The final line from Milosz's last letter (January 15, 1968) measures well the circumference of the two writers' exchange: "My prediction—and I wish I were wrong—is that the number of homeless religious minds will be rapidly increasing." The Polish literateur wrote before both the momentous demise of the Communist empire and the election of a Polish pope in 1979. Nevertheless, he proves prescient as he continues: "I advised Turowicz [a friend] to start a new heresy in Poland, consisting in an exact reversal of the existing trends, namely, to cling to Latin and to the traditional liturgy and to drop any concerns with sex, the pill, etc. But no heresy will come from Poland" (173). It is this sense of spiritual inertia and a lament over the alienation of religious minds that forges the strong kinship between Milosz and Merton throughout the decade of letter writing.

Merton initiated this correspondence by an enthusiastic letter brimming with questions about his Polish friend's "remarkable book" *The Captive Mind* and its analysis of the Marxist totalitarian siege in Eastern Europe. Merton is quick to point out "[t]he lamentable, pitiable emptiness of so much Catholic writing, including much of my own" in his second paragraph, and anticipates some "third position" which would refuse to be subject "to the pressures of the two massive groups ranged against each other in the world. There is wonderful self-deprecation as Merton admits the need to break out of "my own particular kind of shell." A vintage Merton sentence, replete with his own "hidden wholeness" is voiced in this initial letter: "One thing I do know," writes Merton, "is that anyone who is interested in God Who is Truth, has to break out of the ready-made shells of the 'captive' positions that offer their convenient escapes from freedom—one who loves freedom must go through the painful experience of seeking it, perhaps without success" (4).

Milosz eventually ventured to criticize Merton's romanticism in a February 1960 letter: "Every time you speak of Nature [in *The Sign of Jonas*], it appears as soothing, rich in symbols, as a veil or a curtain. You do not pay much attention to torture and suffering in Nature" (64). (Mott observes that in Merton, nature is never "red in tooth and claw" [357].) This led Milosz to suggest that Merton might write sequels to *Thoughts in Solitude* which would explore "the terrible questions"— making him something of a contemporary Paschal, a voice his Polish correspondent suggests is desperately needed. Milosz proved to be the catalyst when he challenged Merton:

> Now, when there is such chaos in the world of arts and letters, the most sane, intelligent (and of best literary style) are works of French theologians. They perform an important and lasting task. We are groping—and I say it basing upon what young Catholics in Poland write—towards completely new images permitting perhaps to grasp religion again as a personal vision. I do not invite you to write theological treatises but much can be accomplished, it seems to me, through literary criticism for instance (142).

As early as his second letter to Milosz, dated February 28, 1959, Merton had raised the issue of redefining spirituality after mentioning a copy of his "Letter to an Innocent Bystander" enclosed for his new Polish acquaintance:

> [I]t is unbearable for me to feel that I may have let myself get too far away from the actual problems of my time in a kind of pious detachment that is an indefensible luxury. There are all sorts of complicated angles to this, though. There is something much too mental and abstract, something too parochial about a great deal of Catholic thought and Catholic spirituality today. . . . So much of it all in the head. And in politics it is even worse: all the formulas, the gestures, the animosities, and the narrowness (16–17).

Merton also speaks candidly about his own misgivings over *Thoughts in Solitude*, remarking, "these notes were revised and dressed up by me and became what I take to be a little commercial and hence false." With an uncommon vulnerability, Merton asks Milosz for his appraisal, even inquiring whether *Thoughts* "bores you completely" and seems "completely alien, bourgeois etc." (19). In the same vein, he seeks perspective on his writing by asking Milosz about his "Letter to an Innocent Bystander"—"tell me if it is really a piece of presumptuous complacency" (21).

This same early letter ends with Merton voicing an animated faith in the paschal mystery:

> Milosz—life is on our side. The silence and the Cross which we know are forces that cannot be defeated. In silence and suffering, in the heartbreaking effort to be honest in the midst of dishonesty (most of all our *own* dishonesty), in all these is victory. It is Christ who drives us through a darkness to a light of which we have no conception and which can only be found by passing through apparent despair. Everything has to be tested. . . . Much has to be lost. Much in us has to be killed, even much that is best in us. But Victory is certain (19–20).

Milosz's reply, three months later on Easter Saturday, gravitates to the spiritual struggle of the writer: "Writing is suspect since love of truth can go together with an urge to oppose our 'I' to the world." He warns of the constant "danger of self-delusion as to our importance" and defers to Merton-the-monk having "to resolve [what I am saying] in the first years of your monastic life" (24–5). He ends this lengthy letter alluding to a friend's reproach "that I never write what I really think, that I am a dialectician, always speaking through the hat, perhaps a coward" (30).

Six months later Merton speaks again, referring to our "apparent despair." His reflections follow remarks about a Polish novelist whose work Milosz had sent him. Merton responds:

> If [the novelist] were not nearly in despair there would be something the matter with him: his plight is a sign that he is at least healthy enough to react. . . . We should all feel near to despair in some sense because this semi-despair is the normal form taken by hope in a time like ours. Hope without any sensible or tangible evidence on which to rest. Hope in spite of the sickness that fills us. Hope married to a firm refusal to accept any palliatives or any-

thing that cheats hope by pretending to relieve apparent despair. . . . In the end it comes to the old story that we are sinners, but that is our hope because sinners are the ones who attract to themselves the infinite compassion of God (52).

Mott nonetheless has faulted Merton for having missed Milosz's point. But he has also alerted us to the heart of the exchange summarized in the two excerpts just read. Milosz had written in the second year of their exchange that the usefulness of a book like *The Sign of Jonas* was "limited for somebody who is seriously interested in 'anatomy of faith'. . . ." But he suggests a different dilemma: "What are the contents of faith, in any case those translatable into notions and images[?]" He appreciates how Merton's diary describes "your internal country in its results" but faults it for lapsing into the "mysterious." There is, Milosz reminds, a world of difference between the diary's "noting" and the process of "distilling" (60).

A new question comes from Milosz: "[A] reader . . . is eager to learn (gradually) what is the *image* of the world in Thomas Merton[?]" He nudges Merton further, describing his journals as narrative "sequences"; but Milosz speaks for readers ready to follow Merton "in five volumes through a very vision of the world redeemed by Christ." He then gently scolds the monk: "In how many [of your] books [can we] find it if we exclude books of devotion?" Milosz quickly begs Merton not to interpret this "as an attempt to convince you to become a theologian in the Dominican tradition. . . ."

> You created a new dimension thanks to images, you change a monastery into something else than it was in the literature up to the [current] times. How to combine two contradictory exigencies I do not know (62).

The context of this challenge for Merton is Milosz's remark that the novels of Graham Greene and François Mauriac "belong to the past" because "in them religion is added, as *a Deus ex machina.*" Milosz wanted of Merton a way to engage the ultimate questions of theology: the Problem of Evil and Suffering; the Question of Guilt; the Question of Institutionalized Christianity. But he awaits answers not in the abstract but "on the border between intellect and imagination, a border," he admits, "so rarely explored today in religious thinking: we lack an image of the world. . . " (61). So, Czeslaw Milosz had reciprocated the sudden intimacy of a kindred spirit by pointing out the limitations of Merton's writing style and its devotional narrowness. More importantly, he had now summoned Merton to find a new means for groping towards new images of the world, "to grasp religion again as a personal vision."

There is much more to be mined from the rich veins of *Striving Towards Being*. Both writers share an enthusiasm for Simone Weil's life and literary works; they exchange reflections on Pasternak, with Milosz offering a Polish perspective on Merton's unbridled enthusiasm for the Russian; the Pole wants to convince the American to comment on Camus' *The Fall*, describing it as "a very ambiguous book, . . . a cry of despair and a treatise on Grace (absent)" (65). Added to this literary potpourri is an undertow of political conversation to explore how protest and witness are to be engaged with integrity by the spiritually awakened writer.

In some way these letters anticipate the openness and mutual spiritual direction which are evident in the Merton-Rosemary Ruether correspondence, although she never ventures to be as forthcoming and vulnerable as Milosz in his letters. No one who makes an effort to understand the complexity of Thomas Merton can neglect to pore over, savor, and return again and again to *Striving Towards Being*. One of Merton's last letters to Milosz admits that "my 'happiness' does not depend on any institution or establishment" and that friends like his Polish counterpart comprise his "'Church' of friends" who are far more important than any institution" (175). This volume presents a unique segment of his correspondence wherein Merton himself chronicles the development of his own "homeless religious mind." It is a conversation exchanged by intimates without peers.

We are blessed with a bounty in the more than twelve hundred pages of three new Merton journals—the second, third, and fourth in the projected seven-volume series from HarperCollins, San Francisco. Editors Jonathan Montaldo, Lawrence Cunningham, and Victor A. Kramer have untangled Merton's dense script onto the screens of their pc's and delivered texts delicately edited with only a trace of their own annotations (although readers would undoubtedly have benefited from more signs and interpretive keys on their part). I found myself reading first the indexes for each volume, gaining a quick preview of the names, titles, places, and even some themes that preoccupy Merton in these journals that span 1941–1952 (vol. II, *Entering the Silence*); 1952–1960 (volume III, *A Search for Solitude*); and 1960–1963 (vol. IV, *Turning Toward the World*).

How to attempt a "review" of the Merton journals? What impresses me most about these unalloyed pages is how, over time, they record and leave footprints of the various changes in his spirit and psyche. All these journals serve as the unfailing barometer of Thomas Merton's soul. At times they ramble, are tedious, or they volley ideas and impressions so quickly that their pages leave the reader either dizzy or disoriented. For all the piecemeal nature of the genre, they bear a remarkable fluidity. I convince myself that any writer's journal resists the reviewer's reductionism and flair for geiger countering the unsuspected factoid or the heretofore concealed peccadillo. My task, therefore, is more to identify succinctly the tenor and bent of each of the volumes in the hope of encouraging readers to immerse themselves in these pages.

Having read *The Sign of Jonas,* one cannot but begin *Entering the Silence* without some preconception of what lies ahead here. All the enthusiasm of a romance with the newly professed monk spills from these pages. But somehow Merton avoids (in the main) the saccharine that might make his zeal off-putting. I admit that I found Jonathan Montaldo's introduction distasteful for two reasons. First, while he rightly points to Merton's cultivating the spiritual discipline of writing, he unfelicitously chooses his words when he claims that Thomas Merton therefore "made himself God's bait." I cannot think of a description less compatible with the spirituality of Thomas Merton. But I found it even more condescending to be advised: "As you can, Reader, doubt everything you believe you already know about Thomas Merton and entrust yourself to his journals with an open heart." Such a willing suspension of disbelief might be a fine rhetorical flourish in Coleridge, but here it serves to render the reader less intelligent. The great value of these journals will be for the *connections* readers (and scholars) make to themes, developments, and revisions in Merton's story.

The argument with himself which Merton publicly revealed in *The Sign of Jonas* is lengthened in these ample pages. While the first volume of the journals, *Run to the Mountain,* may have left the impression of Merton constantly whining, this second volume shows how tedious he becomes over the complaints of insomnia, his identity as a contemplative, and the flirtation with leaving Gethsemani for the Carthusians or some other new monastic venture, and the lure of solitude and a hermit's hut. I found Merton claustrophobic in this journal because he is so preoccupied with the piety surrounding his passage through the orders of subdeacon, deacon, and then priestly ordination. There are devout meditations on eucharistic spirituality to give all this some ballast, of course. And I found the mention on December 8, 1948, about the noise of the guns at Fort Knox a premonition of the later Merton's writings about peacemaking and his "Rain and the Rhinoceros" essay, one of his most mature and lyric prose-poems. The election of Dom James Fox as abbot in the same year gives us a glance at first impressions (as well as some later potent and outspoken ones!) that will be confirmed throughout their relationship.

The effect of *Entering the Silence* is Merton's immersion in the ethos of the monastery, reading the Fathers and scripture, concerned with the domestic tasks of the monastery (such as arranging a "mosaic" of flowers for the altar), and trying to discover his own poverty and humility in a cenobitic community. The poet's eye always finds expression to relieve these pages' heaviness. Merton passes the bier for the monks' funerals and remarks about anticipation of its use, reveling in the fact that shirts stand on its gunwales and handkerchiefs are drying on it. Robert Speaight's visit to read from T. S. Eliot's *Murder in the Cathedral* is described with typical Merton superlatives: "a landmark in the history of Gethsemani." Knowing the later effect of Rilke upon Merton's own writing and poetry, it is fascinating to follow his initial enthusiasm for the German poet in *Entering the Silence*. Through 1952 Merton matures in his fervor as a monk. But the transition is already evident when he alludes to the monastery's growth, numbering 185 members of the community in July 1949.

Lawrence Cunningham's introduction to *A Search for Solitude* again affords us the clear, insightful sensitivity to Thomas Merton's vocation that we have come to expect from his own spiritual resources. There is a unique rapport with Merton in everything that Cunningham writes about him, and this important transitional journal is well suited to this editor's gifts as theologian and literateur. The fact that Merton writes ten books during the course of this journal makes it an especially rich resource, capturing the diverse interests as well as the frustrations for a monk whose life is growing ever more complex. Merton's role as master of scholastics and then master of novices crowds the entries of *A Search for Solitude*. In fact, the title itself aptly names his dilemma. These entries register the change with more notes recorded of his readings, more ideas and reflection upon them and less of the unrelieved introversion of the earlier journals.

So it was that Merton took his scholastics off to the woods. He also wedged his way into the confines of the tiny woodshed that he named St. Anne's hermitage, describing it as "a rampart between two existences." The happiness of this solitude mingles with his reading in 1953 of Max Picard's *The World of Silence*. His poet's eye parenthetically (and ironically) juxtaposes the subtle detail: "A train of the old time sings in my present silence, at St. Anne's, where the watch without a crystal ticks on the little desk." I am distracted by Merton's whimsy and humor. At one point he records the "news" of malt carried by the south wind from a nearby Bardstown distillery. Another distraction comes for this reviewer with Merton's journal entry following a stop at Louisville's St. Martin's Church, a critique of liturgical space rendered with an artist-priest's eye. His first errand to Louisville's "gargantuan" GE plant leaves Merton meditating on the lifelessness of industry's modernity.

It is refreshing to find Merton's enthusiasm for Stephen Spender's poetry, his inquisitiveness over Dostoevsky as a religious novelist, his meeting with J. F. Powers in Minnesota. Merton unburdens himself of reflections on that trip to St. John's in Collegeville after his devastation by the encounter with psychiatrist Gregory Zilboorg who questioned his integrity and intentions as a monk. The last half of this journal seems dominated by Merton's dreams to bolt from Gethsemani and perhaps escape to Cuernevaca, Mexico. It makes for dramatic reading, with Jean Danielou as Merton's Dutch uncle. My surprise was in watching him take to his nurturing role as master of scholastics and novices. He has a tender but self-conscious sense of his serving as midwife to a generation of monks. It engulfs him at times. But now his prayers in the journals address his evolving sense of the deeper contemplative and solitary vocation vis-à-vis both a monastic commitment and his awakening social responsibility in the world. Some of this awakening we have already seen in the pages of *Conjectures of a Guilty Bystander*—an edited version of this journal and its sequel, the fourth volume. It is helpful to see both the Zilboorg episode and the Fourth and Walnut and Proverb visions in their original context. However, I suspect some readers will be deflated when they realize that Merton edited well his own work to deliver the polished relics we revere in the familiarly quoted later versions.

The potpourri of Heschl, Suzuki, Pasternak, Marcel, Ezra Pound, and Pablo Antonio Cuadra mingle with Marx, Gandhi, and Russia's Sputniks in these pages. Merton's horizons are shifting toward the southern hemisphere. Amid it all, Merton-the-poet punctuates the entries with sublime lines that dangle with a contemplative's allure: "A red-shouldered hawk screams insistently in a very blue sky."

Victor A. Kramer is especially well-equipped to edit this fourth and pivotal volume of Merton's journals, *Turning Toward the World*. The matrix of these three years and two months proves to be the monk's struggle about whether to cut back on his writing. Kramer's *Thomas Merton: Monk and Artist* (Kalamazoo: Cistercian Publications, 1984) remains a valuable interpretation of the public data; Kramer's essays there and in other presentations alertly have analyzed *The Sign of Jonas* and *Conjectures of a Guilty Bystander* for this very dynamic. What *Turning Toward the World* presents is Merton's hammering out his mature monastic identity on the anvil of social issues like war, civil rights, nonviolence, and the political impasse of a Cold War era.

This is the era in which Merton is censured and silenced by Cistercian authorities. Yet simultaneously the Church is launching the Second Vatican Council under the leadership of Pope John XXIII, a visionary who coaxes Catholics to unimagined social responsibility. Now, "the guns of Fort Knox pound incessantly" as Merton awakens to the U.S. government's use of U2 spy planes in Russia. Meanwhile, the hermitage had appeared in the guise of a meeting place for small ecumenical conferences—but it served more and more during these years as his solitary refuge. The questions for the mid-life monk were more complex and his answers were both more measured but nonetheless forthright—I like the way Kramer describes him as "much more willing to accept mystery on many levels." His introduction points out that the journals now more frequently record reflections about items he was reading. So the stimuli add momentum to the changes evidenced in Merton.

Whether it is reading Reinhold Neibuhr to deliver Merton from "my stupor" about politics, or just accepting the complexity of the world outside the monastery, Thomas Merton in the early 1960s was engaged in a new project. The Mount Olivet "hermitage" symbolized it. Nonetheless, Merton can still wrestle with the false self in passages like the entry of April 29, 1961: "My basic trouble: it is a strictly unchristian refusal . . . *The refusal to love those I do not consider worthy of love*." For all the reading notes, the journals maintain their spiritual transparency. It is no wonder that Merton has written his Auschwitz poem and records the Mennonites in Kansas' request to publish it.

The Catholic Worker figures more prominently in Merton's life in these years of unrest. But the Milosz letters continue and offer him both challenge and solace. Perhaps most of all it is the interludes at the hermitage, in silence and immersed in nature's rhythms, that capture the maturity and prayerful search of Merton in these years of *Turning Toward the World*. If you want some of this flavor then read the entry for Holy Saturday, 1963—it is vintage Merton. Part of that day is at the hermitage, watching sunrise and "the ceremony of the birds feeding in the dewy grass"; he laments "post-Cartesian technologism . . . separates man from the world and makes him a kind of little god in his own right"; and then he shifts to a visit from two Spanish families, especially admiring the fourteen or fifteen year old "overgrown" but "charming" daughter of one family. All this, and Merton's familiarity with medieval monastic sources, French scholarly studies, contemporary poets, and the fevers of the early 1960s political arena.

My only really disconcerting experience in reading these three new volumes came with the discovery that there are indeed gaps in Merton's journals, especially in volume II when he destroyed part of one of his early journals. Nonetheless, what these 1200+ pages afford will take us decades to absorb, appreciate, and fathom fully.

II

During 1996 readers were virtually starving for book-length critical studies of Merton. Suzanne Zuercher, O.S.B., has therefore attracted considerable attention with *Merton: An Enneagram Profile* (Notre Dame, Ind.: Ave Maria Press, 1996). Her theme is "the spiritual path of Thomas Merton, a path he saw and walked from the standpoint of one of [the enneagram's] nine incarnations of human experience" (6). This is a well written, engaging volume. The text is salted with carefully selected Merton quotations and significant, if limited, excerpts from those who knew Merton-the-contemplative. Zuercher has authored two previous studies on the enneagram and brings to her interpretation of Merton a recognition that much criticism of it is "not lacking in foundation" because of "much of the superficiality of so-called enneagram study" and the trivialization of the enneagram. She offers the enneagram "as a genuine help to contemplation and not merely as a means to label people" (9).

Zuercher encourages readers unfamiliar with the enneagram not to turn away from the book, but to consider how our instinctive survival skills develop into ego-building compulsions. Then by admitting and acknowledging how these grow into exaggerated compulsions, Zuercher invites us to grow in contemplation, according to the enneagram's processes, and let go of the illusions or distortions and reclaim for our lives our innate enneagram stance in proper proportion. The application of the "4" on the enneagram scale to the images, vocabulary and emphases of "his particular kind of personality," says Zuercher, "lets us into Merton's world with a nuance not found elsewhere" (7). That 4 profile includes characteristics such as the ego-romantic, the ego-melancholic, and the over-dramatizer. In turn, the 4 exhibits tendencies to exaggeration, whining, aloofness, and doubting the goodness of one's intrinsic being; this combines with restlessness, a sense of one's "special" status, discontented envy, self-criticism and self-accusation, manipulation, and manic-depression as the erratic range of his hope and despair. *Merton: An Enneagram Profile* unfolds how his life journey reconciled him with his limitations, not eliminating them but liberating his instincts from exaggeration and distortion.

In chapter two, "The Fundamental Sin: A Figure on His Own," Zuercher fixes upon a photograph of the young Merton. She is prompted by Michael Mott's attention to this photograph and his description of some of these very traits of the 4 profile which he described in his magisterial biography, *The Seven Mountains of Thomas Merton*. Rejection, privacy, and melancholy figure prominently in Zuercher's interpretation of this instant, capturing the three generations in an impromptu portrait. She concludes that Merton "became his own god, further alienating himself from himself and others" (36), thus the original reference in the title of this chapter and its etiology of his compulsions.

A methodological issue keeps surfacing for serious readers of *Merton: An Enneagram Profile*. Put bluntly: Does not the enneagram approach risk an exaggerated categorizing or stereotyping? There is no doubt that a judicious application of the insights from this field can further enlighten us about Merton's psyche and spirituality. But at what point does this schema contradict essential Merton principles such as human freedom and the *uniqueness* of the human person? Are there other more satisfactory ways of interpreting the contradictions one finds in Merton? At what point does exegesis give way to eisegesis? (On this score, Zuercher's fine excerpts from Merton could benefit from critical attention to the context of his writings; does a 1950s text like *The Sign of Jonas* need to be measured analytically against later, more mature works such as *Zen and the Birds of Appetite*, to say nothing of his late poetry?)

Could a momentary distraction or other factor explain the young Merton's posture and facial expression in the photograph on which Zuercher (and Mott) places so much emphasis? Why is this photograph *the* definitive point of reference instead of the smiling, almost peek-a-boo glee of the young boy Thomas Merton standing at the door, a photograph featured in James Forest's *Living With Wisdom* (11)? Or the photograph (two pages later in Forest's book) of the two young brothers, Tom and John Paul, appearing quite happy and healthy? How do we interpret other, later Merton photographs, such as the serene Merton (with bottle in hand—is it a beer?) in the group photograph with psychiatrist Gregory Zilboorg when the two met at Collegeville in 1956—a devastating encounter as Merton himself recorded, but belied by the jovial camaraderie evidenced in this photograph? (Or, was this photograph antecedent to the private exchange with Zilboorg?) John Howard Griffin mused about his own experience of photographing Merton:

> Merton showed no stiffening. I wondered if he would have masks, as nearly everyone does. How many films would I have to waste before I penetrated his masks and got to the man?

> In some instances you would find it difficult to tell that [Ed Rice's and Eugene Meatyard's photographs] were photographs of the same man . . . they were so different. I have replied that all of them looked like him, or like aspects of him. Everything showed in his face. I tended to catch his face in repose, others often snapped their cameras in moments when his face was more animated. All of these views are perhaps necessary for a composite portrait of such a multifaceted man" [*A Hidden Wholeness: The Visual World of Thomas Merton* (Boston: Houghton Mifflin, 1970) 38–9].

No wonder that the most famous photograph of Thomas Merton, Griffin's Mona Lisa-like portrait of the monk, captured the complex of moods and characteristics that defy a univocal interpretation. The same range of affect is captured in the striking photographs by Sibylle Akers which have appeared in more recent publications.

The virtue of Zuercher's book is the careful and compelling case she builds in chapters 3–9 (Part Two), her enneagram's "4" profile of Merton: fearing conflict; the compulsive doer; a feeling of "specialness" and intensity; art as the life-search for meaning; dramatic intensity; the social without conflict or disapproval; despair and the awakening of feelings. Part Three ambitiously attempts to name the "Spiritual Geography" of Merton. Although its various chapters prove uneven, Zuercher explores important themes such as "homecoming" death and rebirth, and Merton's quest for wholeness and unity. Part IV investigates Merton's relationships including the monastic community, friends and colleagues, and women friends. It is refreshing to see Merton emerge as human and yet loved in the context of both his brother monks' reminiscences and Zuercher's enneagram interpretation of his mid-life crisis affair with Margie, the young nurse. Part V is especially valuable for the chapter on "The True Self," the theme that is the fulcrum of Merton's spirituality and which Zuercher weaves throughout her book.

Among the reels of taped Merton conferences with the novices, I recall one particular session when the master was discouraging his charges from psychologically analyzing one another. "Don't try to figure out what makes *that* guy tick," Merton scolded. He recommended rather that a monastic community survives by seeing the glory of God shine through one other. In effect, Merton was skeptical about "systems" such as the enneagram. No doubt someday someone will discover that somewhere else in his canon Merton uttered a word of openness to the enneagram. Perhaps it will be in the context of his study of Sufi mysticism (although Zuercher herself discredits claims that the enneagram originated among the Sufis). No matter. He resisted the univocal. And Merton readers will do well to resist any temptation to reduce him to the 4 profile as a definitive and final interpretation. Suzanne Zuercher's study is more subtle than such a simplistic verdict. However, too many will no doubt utilize this book in such a manner and thus misrepresent her work.

Zuercher's book begs for an index and one hopes that future editions will provide this necessary tool. In addition to my questions raised about her use of primary sources, Zuercher's neglect of David Cooper's provocative interpretation of Merton's childhood and later development in *Thomas Merton's Art of Denial* is a serious flaw in her work. While she acknowledges a debt to Erik Erikson's approach in her interpretation of Merton's life (8), she nowhere appraises or critiques Cooper's insightful application of Erikson in interpreting him. On the contrary, her uncritical acceptance of Robert G. Waldron's *Thomas Merton in Search of His Soul: A Jungian Perspective* needs to be balanced by the insights and caveats of Joann Wolski Conn [*The Merton Annual* 8 (1995) 258–62.] It would also be helpful for her to attend to Robert Daggy's pair of essays interpreting the young Merton and his turbulent relationship with his father in the years following his mother's death. The editorial decision to publish this enneagram interpretation *before* and without reference to the publication of the seven volumes of Merton's journals leaves readers and scholars with a new challenge. It makes it all the more incumbent upon both popular and serious readers to appreciate Suzanne Zuercher's provocative contribution which will undoubtedly be a new benchmark in Merton studies.

A final critique: notwithstanding the strengths of Zuercher's book, there is an alarming absence of any specific attention to concerns that became synonymous with Thomas Merton, e.g., peacemaking, social justice, and racial equality. While she does acknowledge the "social" side of Merton's personality, it is the lack of concrete connection between the enneagram profile and this integral Merton outreach that exposes a serious weakness in the enneagram approach. It is not enough to make a passing comment that Merton knew Daniel Berrigan and complimented him by imitating his manner of dress—in enneagram fashion. Or that the Dalai Lama remarked on Merton's honest face. Far more substantive aspects of Merton remain unexplored and unacknowledged by the enneagram profile.

III

Erlinda Paguio's "Thomas Merton and the Saints of Carmel"[1] is a carefully researched examination of how his acquaintance with the Carmelite saints is directly related to his search for God. She examines, in particular, the influence of John of the Cross, Therese of Lisieux, and Theresa of Avila on his early work. This essay is especially valuable for delineating the "first period" of his writings on the Carmelite saints (1938 to his ordination, 1949), and the "second period" beginning in the 1950s until the early sixties. Paguio builds this study into a compelling case for Merton's evolution as both a writer and devotee of the Carmelite spirituality. A case in point is the "Little Way" of St. Therese, whose absolute "trust and surrender" finds an imprint on the Trappistine, Mother Berchmans, whom Merton celebrated by writing her biography, *Exile Ends in Glory.*

Paguio's most important contribution comes by way of her interpretations of Merton's poetry vis-à-vis the Carmelite saints. She offers a poignant reading of "Elias-Variations on a Theme" with its celebration of the contemplative's "listening" emblematic of a deep

1. *Spiritual Life* 42 (Summer 1996) 74–86.

relationship with God. This poem comes from the collection *The Strange Islands*, a poorly received volume that is redeemed, in part, by her exegesis *of The Spiritual Canticle* of St. John of the Cross, the source of Merton's title. In conjunction with this contextual appreciation of St. John of the Cross, this essay includes the author's response to a meditative study on the thirty-five drawings of the Carmelite saint which Merton completed between 1946–1953. Here is a genuinely creative turn in Merton scholarship, employing non-verbal elements of the Merton archives.

Cistercian Studies Quarterly regularly includes essays about Thomas Merton. This year three authors addressed very different topics. Paul Ruttle, CP contributed "Voice of the Stranger: Merton's Penetration of the Mystery of the Maya."[2] This essay examines various texts in which Merton considered the pre-Columbian, Conquest, and modern Maya; Ruttle goes on to report upon the remarkable progress made in the study of the Maya civilization during the past five years (notably the studies of Linda Schele and David Stuart). While Merton may have worked with inaccurate data or may not have had access to the translations of eighty percent of the writings now available through the work of cultural anthropologists, Ruttle credits Merton with a greater achievement: "[He] was somehow able to grasp intuitively the vitality of the art and spirituality of this ancient people" (206). This study identifies how Merton's contemplative identity gravitated to the reality of faith of the Maya. A careful analysis of his essay from *Ishi Means Man*, "The Cross Fighters: Notes on a Race War," interprets the deep religious currents in this culture as it struggled with interracial warfare and the persecution of the Maya by Ladinos. Ruttle alertly relates this analysis to the three versions of Merton's autobiographical essay, *Day of A Stranger*. A comparison of the texts is remarkable because, as Ruttle notes, Merton removed the earlier direct references to the Maya in the third and published version of the notes, "but [he] has included them spiritually and symbolically in his mention of the *axis mundi*." When coupled with Merton's attention to the Maya in *The Geography of Lograire*'s sections IX, X, and XI where Merton again addresses the Maya culture with allusions to the metaphor of "the center" and the phenomenon of the "Miraculous Talking Cross," the mature hermit's creative reworking of the global reality of violence brims with reclaimed meaning for readers. Ruttle rounds out

2. *Cistercian Studies Quarterly* 31:2 (1996).

this excellent piece of scholarship with a chronicle of more recent political events in the jungles around Chiapas, Mexico. The effects of the North American Free Trade Act (NAFTA) and the influx of eighty thousand Maya immigrants from Guatemala have only borne out Merton's passion for peace in this sacred land.

"The Paschal Heart of Merton's Spirituality"[3] by Patrick F. O'Connell originates in response to the *Horizons* journal's 1994 review symposium on *Ace of Freedoms: Thomas Merton's Christ*. He asks whether it is possible to "move the debate" beyond the terms raised in the symposium. In that context, Christine Bochen argued that Merton is better described as "theocentric" rather than "Christocentric." As the author of *Ace of Freedoms*, I had responded in the *Horizons* forum to the way in which I see a theocentric lens distorts Merton's contribution. I do find it disingenuous for O'Connell to quote from his own essay in *The Merton Annual* 7 (1994) studying Merton's eight freedom songs, but to disregard the other review symposium on *Ace of Freedoms* in that very volume—a twenty-nine page discussion by Patrick Eastman, Diana Culbertson, O.P. and two distinguished christologians, Donald J. Goergen, O.P., and Jean-Marc Laporte, S.J.

Suffice it for me to offer two observations about O'Connell's feeble effort which never really arrives at a conclusion and certainly contributes nothing by way of a resolution to the "debate." First, readers ought to be suspicious that the overwhelming majority of Merton texts he quotes are early writings; there is a wealth of Merton material (as I demonstrate in *Ace of Freedoms*) in the last five to eight years of his life which reflects an extraordinary development of his kenotic christology, especially in his Camus and Faulkner essays as well as in his social criticism. Second, O'Connell's theological categories are not carefully delineated. To speak of the paschal mystery in Christian theology is to speak of the death and resurrection of *Jesus Christ*, and therefore it must be seen within the broader context of christology. The work of contemporary christologians has sought to reintegrate soteriology with christology. O'Connell apparently is unfamiliar with the groundbreaking research of christologian William M. Thompson, "Exploring the Christ-Experience IV: Thomas Merton's Transcultural Christ," *Jesus, Lord and Savior: A Therapeutic Christology and Soteriology* (Paulist, 1980). Since the genius of Christian theology is the mystery of the Trinity, I would suggest that O'Connell also examine the work of

3. *Cistercian Studies Quarterly* 31:3 (1996).

Catherine LaCugna and scholars who are building on her revisionist study, *God For Us: The Trinity and Christian Life* (HarperSanFrancisco, 1991). A purely theocentric approach cannot do justice to Thomas Merton's spirituality, or to *any* "Christian" spirituality. While O'Connell makes passing reference to the Trinity at a few junctures of his essay, he fails to grasp fully the methodological principle upon which LaCugna (and, I think, Merton) builds: "Christian theology must always speak about God on the basis of God's self-communication in Christ and in the Spirit." This effort is not one of his more careful or constructive contributions.

The third and final *Cistercian Studies Quarterly* essay for 1996 is Craig Helms' "Mary as the New Eve in Thomas Merton's Poetry."[4] It is encouraging to see more attention paid to Merton's religious poetry. Helms exegetes a broad collection of poems (dating from the early 1940s to the early 1960s) in terms of Merton's bringing "fresh, passionate, vibrant images and language" to both patristic and biblical Mariology. Helms thematically structures the analysis of poems around Mary's "humility, obedience, co-redemptive atonement, queenship, and role in humanization, as she reverses Eve's fault." This essay demonstrates fine historical research in patristic sources. The influences of Bernard of Clairvaux and other Cistercian spirituality combine with the gospels and psalms to create the ethos from which Merton wrote these poems. Helms examines each of the themes he has identified by interpreting particular poems: "The Evening of the Visitation," "Advent," "The Blessed Virgin Mary Compared to a Window," "The Annunciation," "Aubade—The Annunciation," "The Quickening of St. John the Baptist," "Hagia Sophia," "Canticle for the Blessed Virgin," "An Argument: On the Passion of Christ," "La Salette," "The Trappist Cemetery—Gethsemani," and "The Fall of Night." The essay is not only a valuable tool for readers unfamiliar with the Catholic traditions of Mariology and contemplation, but it also raises the issue of art's relationship to spirituality. If there is one issue in this tradition that deserves to be critiqued, however, it would be the references to Mary's role as "co-redemptrix." The Second Vatican Council carefully clarified some lingering distortions about this issue, distortions which even creep into Merton's early poems. Helms provides a valuable, insightful analysis. While it is alert to both the metaphors and imagery which Merton's imagination renders, one

4. *Cistercian Studies Quarterly* 31:4 (1996).

leaves this essay with a sense that Helms might have ventured more by way of an appraisal of the poetry *qua* poetry and not only as artifact touched by doctrine.

Annice Callahan, R.S.C.J., makes a genuine contribution to Merton scholarship with her nuanced and carefully researched essay, "The Development of Thomas Merton's Christ-Consciousness."[5] It adds to her earlier work, *Spiritual Guides for Today* (Crossroad, 1992), which included Merton as one of six contemporaries who have lived what she there calls "certain attitudes of heart with which we can identify."

Callahan traces the dramatic shift in Merton's spirituality: from the personalistic and individualized eucharistic spirituality of early works like *The Sign of Jonas* and *The Living Bread;* to the final decade of his life when "he let go of an exclusive mystical body language and branched out to dialogue with unbelievers, calling himself 'a diaspora Christian'. . . ." Her essay offers a reflective synthesis of the currents in Merton's "Christ-consciousness" ranging from his early years through his more mature openness to compassionate solidarity. She alertly insists that Merton's solitude and identity as a solitary is not to be mistaken for the stance of an individualist, but that "he was keenly aware that solitude opens us to the world's needs."

By calling attention to *New Seeds of Contemplation* and describing its newly revised chapter, "A Body of Broken Bones," "his most original chapter," Callahan carefully traces the mystery of Christ's redemptive love in our suffering solidarity. In this regard, her analysis of Merton's expansive political horizon in *Seeds of Destruction* combines with her interpretation of his changed sense of "spiritual freedom" in *Conjectures of a Guilty Bystander*. Finally, Callahan addresses Merton's growing awareness of the "transcultural" Christ without muting "Christ as the uncompromising truth of who God is, of who each person really is, and of what the world is meant to be." This is an essay worthy of any reader who is serious about understanding Thomas Merton. In Callahan's words, "By the end of his life, Merton developed not only a consciousness of Christ's presence in the world but also a consciousness of Christ's concerns and compassion for the world."

In May 1996 The Thomas Merton Society of Great Britain and Ireland convened a conference at La Sainte Union College, Southampton, England. Papers from that conference have now been

---

5. *The American Benedictine Review* 47:1 (March 1996) 99–113.

collected in *Your Heart Is My Hermitage*,[6] edited by Danny Sullivan and Ian Thomson. In addition to the three main conference addresses and a roundtable by Merton's friends, the volume collects papers presented at topics sessions devoted to "Thomas Merton and Other Traditions," "Thomas Merton on Solitude and Community," "Thomas Merton—The Early Years," and "Thomas Merton and the Human Community." While readers can profit from many of the dozen special interests reflected in those papers, as well as from the homily offered by Jim Forest at the Sunday Eucharist to conclude the conference, I call readers' attention to two particular presentations.

Canon A. M. [Donald] Allchin, President of the Society and a friend of Merton's, presented "Celebrating Thomas Merton" at the conference banquet. In his inimitable, sprightly manner, Allchin enthusiastically engaged the question of celebrating Merton as one of the "saints." He brought to this task his own knowledge of the Eastern Orthodox Church's distinct effort to "recognize" saints under the direction of the Holy Spirit: "It is through the spontaneous action of the people of God, recognizing and celebrating God's gift to his world, in and through this particular person, that the public, official recognition of the saint, can in time take place." He contrasts this with the Western (Roman) Church's more juridical and canonical procedures for "making saints." Allchin then addresses Merton's role in seeing God's presence in all the religious traditions of humanity, what Merton identified as his exploratory task. It is telling that Allchin concludes his paean to Merton's Christian faith with a quotation from the Czeslaw Milosz correspondence (he calls it "one of the most challenging but I believe one of the most important of all Merton's correspondences") that celebrates invincible "silence and the cross of which we know" and the victory of Christ's resurrection.

Robert E. Daggy has added to his special interest in Merton's childhood and his relationship with his father, Owen Merton. Although illness prevented Daggy from traveling to England for the Southampton conference, his paper "Question and Revelation: Thomas Merton's Recovery of the Ground of Birth," which I had the privilege of reading for him, his presence and the impact of this paper were inestimable there. In some ways this essay overlaps with Daggy's earlier

---

6. *Your Heart Is My Hermitage: Thomas Merton's Vision of Solitude and Community*, ed. Danny Sullivan and Ian Thomson (London: The Thomas Merton Society of Great Britain and Ireland, 1966).

essay, "Birthday Theology: A Reflection on Thomas Merton and the Bermuda Menage" which appeared in *The Kentucky Review* VII (1987). However, Daggy is developing further what he describes as Merton's interest in his own "unfinished childhood business." The legacy of Owen-the-artist, Owen-the-religious seer, and the sense of a "vocation" figured prominently in his son's search for identity.

What is most intriguing in this essay is the careful manner in which Daggy analyzes Merton's suffering in terms of a longing for his lost father (Owen died of a brain tumor just before his son's sixteenth birthday). The complex of questions posed about the unfinished "pain" vis-à-vis Thomas Merton's father revolves around the question, "Was the overblown view of Owen in his public pronouncements at variance with what he felt within himself?" Daggy presents a textured, multi-layered account which is well anticipated in his own introductory response: "The answer would seem to be both 'yes' and 'no.'" Daggy's essay will familiarize many readers with new biographical details. For one, Thomas Merton was indeed in rebellion against the idea of his recently widowed father's affair and prospects of marriage with novelist Evelyn Scott during 1922–1923 in Bermuda. This essay ends on a lyric note as it interprets Merton's August 1967 "A Letter on the Contemplative Life" in light of the monk's ongoing search for his father. All Merton readers will benefit immensely from this poignant, meticulously researched contribution.

The year does not pass without at least one significant essay on Merton and interreligious dialogue. Terry Graham's "Sufism: The Strange Subject; Thomas Merton's Views on Sufism"[7] offers a semi-popular article on the monk's interest in Islam and this mystical tradition. Triggered by correspondence with Islamic scholar, the Frenchman Louis Massignon, and Boston University's Herbert Mason, Merton's interest in Sufism grew in the final decade of his life. Correspondence with Iranian psychologist Reza Arasteh bridged Merton's interest through Arasteh's exploration of the relationship between Islam's mystics and the psychological work of both Jung and Fromm. Graham, however, points to the exchange of letters between Merton and the Pakistani scholar, Abdul Aziz as the "fertile source" for Merton's 1967–1968 series of Sunday lectures to novices at the Abbey of Gethsemani.

---

7. *Sufi* 30 (Summer 1996) 31–40.

What proves most valuable in Graham's article is his attention to two encounters "which fired what one might call the 'Sufi nature' of Thomas Merton, one on the classically spiritual plane, the other on the *eros* plane. The first was the visit of the Algerian Sufi shaikh, Sidi Abdesalam; the second, the passionate love affair with the student nurse, Margie Smith" (36). The interpretation of these events lends insight into Merton's eventual travel to Asia and his "heart-opening necessary to receive Divine or True Love" (37). Graham includes a brief synopsis and excerpts from the series of six talks which Merton gave in 1967–1968. The article is highly recommended for readers either unfamiliar with Sufism and Merton's interest, or those who heretofore have been perplexed when tackling more technical explanations.

The Elizabeth F. Cheney Foundation sponsored a loan exhibition, "Negotiating Rapture: The Power of Art to Transform Lives,"[8] at the new Museum of Contemporary Art in Chicago from June 21–October 20, 1996. Merton's Columbia University classmate, the abstract painter Ad Reinhardt was featured in the exhibition, which includes a copy of the "Small Painting for T.M." which he gave the monk in 1957; the painting hung in Merton's cell and then in the hermitage. Five of Merton's photographs were included in "Negotiating the Rapture" and reproduced (along with Reinhardt's paintings) in the exhibit's catalogue (88–91) by the same title. Martin E. Marty of the University of Chicago has written the accompanying text (78–79, 88–89, 91) for both artists' works, describing the monk's photographs as having "something of the aesthetic of Abstract Expressionism" and echoes of Samuel Palmer and William Blake. Marty addresses cogently Merton's interest in the mysticism of the West and of the East. Perhaps one of the most revealing phrases he quotes from Merton is his search for "undiluted reality" in his art. Readers who have access to this handsome volume can savor this brief but refined focus on Merton the artist.

Finally, a new research tool appeared in 1996 which should make future reading and research with Thomas Merton's correspondence an easier task and a more integral experience. *Index to the Published Letters of Thomas Merton* compiled by Patricia A. Burton is available from The Thomas Merton Society of Rochester (4095 East Avenue, Rochester, N.Y. 14618-3798). The five volumes of selected let-

---

8. *Negotiating the Rapture: The Power of Art to Transform Lives* (Chicago: Museum of Contemporary Art, 1996).

ters which have been published by Farrar Straus Giroux are: *The Hidden Ground of Love* (1985); *The Road to Joy* (1989); *The School of Charity* (1990); *The Courage for Truth* (1993); and *Witness to Freedom* (1994). They address, respectively: religious experience and social concerns; new and old friends; religious renewal and spiritual direction; writers; and times of crisis.

William H. Shannon, the general editor of the project, writes a Preface and quotes John Henry Newman's maxim that "The true life of a person is in his [her] letters" and insists "that one of the ways we will come to know this unusual monk, who keeps eluding our grasp, is a careful study of his letters." For this very reason, Burton's index is valuable because it makes possible a chronological reading of Merton's letters rather than accessing letters according to the content and various arrangements of the different volumes. Moreover, she has arranged the index by both alphabetical listing of individuals who received letters (noting the date of the first letter and the total number of letters) and by volume-by-volume detailed list by name; and also with a lengthy listing of letters sorted by date. Parallel columns provide the requisite information to locate the letters.

From these 2,227 letters and from this carefully constructed index compiled by Patricia Burton we can expect much important critical analysis of the life and thought of Thomas Merton to be written. We can also hope that a trade edition of this unique tool will follow the 8 1/2 by 11 inch offprint version in which it has made its debut. It is certainly a worthy and welcome—indeed a necessary—addition to the shelf of any serious Merton scholar.

Reviews

Thomas Merton. *Entering the Silence: Becoming a Monk and Writer / The Journals of Thomas Merton, Volume Two 1941–1952*. Edited by Jonathan Montaldo. New York: HarperCollins, 1996. 501 pages. $27.50 hardcover.

Reviewed by Jim Grote

One has either got to be a Jew or stop reading the Bible. For the Bible really cannot make sense to anyone who is not spiritually a "Semite." *Salus ex Judaeis.*

Thomas Merton

Jonathan Montaldo's editing of volume two of Merton's journals reflects the monastic virtue of simplicity. His guiding principle of "minimalism" presents Merton to the reader, unencumbered by the distractions of scholarship and footnotes about secondary sources. Montaldo allows Merton to speak directly to the reader.

Volume two of Merton's journals actually includes three separate journals. One, the brief "Novitiate Journal" (only six entries) covers the time from his formal acceptance as a postulant on December 13, 1941 through April 1942 and contains more poetry than prose. Two, "A Journal-Memoir: Dom Frederic Dunne," includes random notes about Merton's first abbot at Gethsemani (with the implication that these notes might be of use someday to a future biographer of Dom Frederic). Three, "The Whale and the Ivy," comprises the vast majority of this volume. Written between December 1946 and July 1952, this journal takes the reader from Merton's fifth anniversary at Gethsemani through his ordination as a priest and his appointment as Master of Scholastics.

Less than half of "The Whale and the Ivy" was originally published in 1953 as *The Sign of Jonas*. It is intriguing to compare *Entering the Silence* to *The Sign of Jonas* and observe Merton's editorial process at work. As Montaldo mentions in his introduction, "The Whale and the Ivy" provides us with "intimate archaeological digs" (xvi) into Merton's personality. The most prominent theme in this volume that Merton excluded from *The Sign of Jonas* is the material on his temptation to leave Gethsemani for the Carthusians.

Many of Merton's entries reflect his three crosses at Gethsemani: "writing, singing, and contemplation" (254). If conflict is the soul of plot, then these conflicts form the soul of this journal. Merton's obedience to his vocation as a writer (which his superiors encouraged [55, 128, 228, 331]) complicated his vocation as a monk. His complaints about the poor singing in choir fill many entries. But his "lamentations about not being a contemplative" (124) are at the core of his conflicts. After reading half of the text, I remarked to my wife: "Merton sure did complain a lot." To which she responded: "I could easily fill seven volumes with your complaints!" Following a brief chapter of faults, I took a vow of silence and resumed reading. While Merton's debates about becoming a hermit eventually subside (cf. 262, 415), they return in later journals.

The intensity of this conflict can be seen in a sample entry: "I am to throw myself away for Gethsemani. I am to face the danger of losing everything that I hold most high, renouncing my ideals of solitude and contemplation to work in distracting tasks that I shall hate in order that others may become in some measure contemplatives, in order that they may have what I so much desire" (88–9). While such a passage might serve as another point of entry into the endless "archaeological digs" into Merton's personality, I think the excavation of his personality was exhausted a long time ago. As Michael Downey argues, Merton studies are in dire need of an *"aggiornamento"* and a "critical turn" (*The Merton Annual,* Vol. 6, 200).

Merton's conflict between the active and contemplative life possesses a broader significance than the hackneyed psychological speculation in which some of his biographers and critics delight. These conflicts reflect the more profound question that Tertullian and the early Fathers grappled with and, as Merton's life shows, is not resolved to this day. "What, indeed, has Athens to do with Jerusalem? What concord is there between the Academy and the Church?" (*On the Prescription Against Heretics,* VII). Merton not only reflected on this question, he lived it.

In one journal entry, Merton mentions "a disturbing thesis which . . . says that there is nothing in the Gospel about the contemplative life and that the whole theory of the contemplative and of contemplation vs. action was developed by the Greek Fathers (e.g., Origen, the first to interpret Martha and Mary in this light)" (347). In another entry he exchanges barbs with a scholar in the *Thomist* who takes him to task for muddling Aquinas's distinctions between the active, contemplative, and mixed vocations (266–71). Neither entry adequately tackles the question of Athens and Jerusalem, of contemplation and charity. A challenge for future Merton studies would be to reexamine this question at length in his writings. I offer the following reflections as an impetus to such a study.

After two millennia of Western monastic tradition, it is natural to forget that contemplation was originally a pagan activity borrowed from the Greeks and justified by less that overwhelming Scriptural evidence. The Scriptures are full of patriarchs, prophets, priests, warriors, lawgivers, kings, apostles, missionaries, etc. But monks? St. John the Baptist is probably the closest thing to a monk that the Scriptures have to offer, but his primary mission was that of a prophet. St. Paul had mystical experiences, but he was a missionary. Christ may have often retreated to a lonely place to pray (e.g., Mark 6:31; Luke 5:15; John 6:15), but he always returned to active ministry.

Scriptural justifications for the contemplative life depend on allegorical interpretation. For example, St. Augustine refers to the use of Greek philosophy as "a spoiling of the Egyptians" (*On Christian Doctrine*, II, 40). The Israelites rejected the idols of the Egyptians, but secretly took with them vases of gold and silver when they fled Egypt (Exod 3:22; 11:2; 12:35). Or, St. Thomas, in his defense of the superiority of the contemplative over the active life, lists eight different arguments from Aristotle, but relies heavily on one passage from Scripture where Mary "figures" the contemplative life (cf. Luke 10:38-42 and *Summa Theologica* II-II, Q. 182, a. 1). Merton came to question such a traditional interpretation of the Martha and Mary story. By 1959 he would write: "The Gospel of Martha and Mary shows that the one thing necessary is love—not, as usually interpreted, 'The Contemplative Life.' Love whether in contemplation, or in action: love of Christ in Himself and in our brother, that and that alone is the one thing necessary" (Merton, *A Search for Solitude/The Journals of Thomas Merton, Volume Three 1952–1960*, 262). Merton's questioning of the traditional interpretation leads us to question the medieval synthesis of Athens and Jerusalem.

Contemplation (*theoria*) originates in Athens, not Jerusalem. It is a Greek discovery that corresponds to the Greek discovery of nature *(physis)*. Socrates, the archetypal contemplative in the West, was famous for his fits of abstraction. Socrates showed up late for the most famous drinking party in history because he became lost in contemplation while walking down the street on the way to the party (Plato, *Symposium* 174d). On a military expedition, he entered into a state of contemplation at dawn and remained standing for 24 hours, while the other soldiers stared with amazement (Plato, *Symposium* 220c). Yet Socrates never lived in a monastery. He not only spent his entire life in the city of Athens, but spent his days in its busiest section, the *agora* or marketplace.

Aristotle inherited this tradition of contemplation through Socrates' student, Plato. Aristotle's eight arguments for the superiority of the contemplative life (*Ethics* X, vii–viii) presuppose a pre-Socratic tradition, Pythagoras' doctrine of the Three Lives. Pythagoras compared the three different "types" of men to the kinds of people who attended the Greek festivals: the vendors, the competitors, and the spectators (see Diogenes Laertius VIII, 8). Greek thought translated these three types into the life of Enjoyment, the life of Politics *(bios politikos)*, and the life of Contemplation *(bios theoretikos)* *(Ethics* I, v). *Theoria* is a "looking at, viewing, beholding, observing, especially being a spectator at the public games" (Liddel and Scott, *Greek-English Lexicon)*. The Greek word for contemplation *(theoria)* comes from the Greek word for spectators, *theatai.*

Philosophic contemplation (which the monastic tradition later termed natural contemplation *[theoria physike])* entailed beholding the spectacle of the cosmos itself and its first principles. The Greeks assumed a split between doing and understanding. "As a spectator you may understand the truth of what the spectacle is about; but the price you have to pay is withdrawal from it" (Hannah Arendt, *Thinking*, chapter 11). Through contemplation the philosopher literally enters into the life of the divinity, which Aristotle defines as "thought thinking itself" *(Metaphysics* XII, 9). The sole activity of Aristotle's god is contemplation *(Ethics* X, 8). Aristotle's god is the contemplative, *par excellence.*

In his early years as a monk, Merton strove to attain the summit of contemplation. He saw many of his duties at Gethsemani as a distraction from pure contemplation. Later in life, this tension between action and contemplation expressed itself in a completely different way in his life. By 1957 he is making snide comments in his journal about the god of Aristotle (Merton, Vol. 3, 148) and investigating the prophetic side of his monastic vocation (Merton, Vol. 3, 150). "It is absolutely true that here in this monastery we are enabled to systematically evade our real and ultimate social responsibilities. In any time, social responsibility is the keystone of the Christian life" (Merton, Vol. 3, 151).

What does the contemplative god of Aristotle have to do with the active God of the Bible? The god of Aristotle meditates on itself and is unconcerned with the changing affairs of humans. The god of Aristotle does not suffer, but is "impassable." The God of Abraham, Isaac, and Jacob, however, shows intense concern for humankind (compassion, anger, etc.). God suffers with humanity. The God of the Bible does not attract philosophic contemplation, but commands obedient love. "He has shown you, O man, what is good; and what does the Lord require of you but to do justice, and to love kindness, and to walk humbly with your God?" (Mic 6:8). All the Hebrew prophets call Israel to repent and return to a life of obedient love. But the life of a Hebrew prophet is a far cry from the spectator sport of the Greek philosopher. The Hebrew prophets may have retired to the desert from time to time, but they remained avid participants in the divine drama of the salvation of Israel.

Merton's interest in economics, race relations, and non-violence indicates his growing participation in the affairs of humans. His vocation is gradually transformed from cloistered mystic to social prophet. The transformation reflects the tension built into the vocation of the monk. The monk is a hybrid of the Greek spectator and the Hebrew prophet. The conflict of Athens and Jerusalem is inherent to the monastic vocation.

In order to take Merton seriously, it is necessary to situate his personal "conflicts" within the greater horizon of this complex tradition he inherited, rather that the limited horizon of his biography. The tradition of Christian monasticism requires that each generation examine the foundations of that tradition. The greatest tribute to Thomas Merton is to reflect critically on this tradition. His journals are an invaluable resource for such reflection.

Thomas Merton. *A Search for Solitude: Pursuing the Monk's True Life.* The Journals of Thomas Merton, Vol. 3: 1952–1960. Edited with introduction by Lawrence S. Cunningham. Patrick Hart, O.C.S.O., General Editor. San Francisco: HarperCollins, 1996, xviii + 406 pages. $30.00 hardcover.

Reviewed by Robert Ellsberg

A Search for Solitude, the third volume of Merton's published journals, covers the years 1952 to 1960. Like all Merton's private writings, these journals reflect the paradoxical tension between an outward life of apparent calm and stability and an inner life of intense drama. For a good part of this period Merton served as master of novices. Apart from his monastic duties he carried on a vast array of writing projects (ten books were published in this period). But all the while his interior ruminations reflect an intensive debate about the meaning of his vocation and the question of remaining at Gethsemani. In previous years he had explored the possibility of joining a different monastic community—the Carthusians or Camoldolese, perhaps— which he imagined would afford an opportunity for greater solitude. But now his questions roamed in a different direction, increasingly concerned with the relation of the contemplative vocation to the wider world.

The journals of this period reflect Merton's voracious reading. To his study of the Church Fathers he added Russian spirituality, Berdyaev, Marx, Zen, the novels of Boris Pasternak (with whom, during this period, he established a warm personal relationship), and scores of books on Latin American history and culture. To the suggestion that such topics were not traditional Trappist fare, Merton insisted that "the pleasure of reading and writing poetry within certain limits 'helps me Godward.'" But the struggle to justify his questing and questioning temperament came into increasing tension with the prevailing spirit of the monastery, with its emphasis on rules and submission to the will of God (as defined by the abbot). "My interior life has become a passion, perhaps a guilty passion, for fresh air," he writes.

Upon his first visit to Gethsemani, recorded in *The Seven Storey Mountain,* Merton had looked admiringly on the monastic choir as a great dynamo of prayer. But now the monastery seemed like a different kind of machine, geared to efficiency and profit, epitomized by the thriving business in cheese. Increasingly he felt oppressed by the lack of spontaneity and freshness. "I think the monastic life as we live it here warps people. Kills their spirit, reduces them to something less than human." He found it intolerable and degrading "to have to spend my life contributing to the maintenance of this illusion. The illusion of the great, gay, joyous, peppy, optimistic, Jesus-loving, one hundred percent American Trappist monastery." Did his superiors fully appreciate the depth of his feelings? If so, it is a wonder that they continued to entrust him with the formation of novices.

In fact, a good deal of this volume is taken up with Merton's desperate fantasies about leaving Gethsemani altogether—to light out for the territories, literally, in some hermitage in Mexico, or Ecuador, or Nicaragua, or even Nevada. While writing letters to bishops around the world and spiritual advisors like Jean Danielou, studying maps, and even checking on airline routes, he explores the possibility of receiving official permission to leave the monastery to pursue the call to greater solitude and authenticity. These efforts are countered by the abbot, the formidable Dom James Fox, who is determined that Merton's true place remains at Gethsemani. Toward the end of this volume Merton's desperation for some resolution to this crisis—any resolution, it seems—has become overwhelming. In this context the arrival of a definitive answer from Rome—no to all thoughts of leaving Gethsemani—leaves Merton strangely calm. "A kind of anesthesia. . . . The letter is obviously an indication of God's Will and I accept it fully. So then what? Nothing. Trees, hills, rain. And prayer much lighter, much freer, more unconcerned, a mountain lifted off my shoulders—a Mexican mountain I myself had chosen."

Actually, Merton himself had entertained the thought that it was perhaps not necessary to leave Gethsemani to find what he wanted. What did he want? Essentially, a greater interior space to define for himself the meaning of his contemplative vocation. This was not a call to leave the monastery but to rediscover its inner meaning—rejecting the "worship of monastic concepts," the mentality of the ghetto, "closed in on itself, interpreting interpretation of interpretations."

In this volume one encounters Merton's original account of his famous experience on the corner of Fourth and Walnut in downtown Louisville, when he "suddenly realized that I love all the people and that none of them were, or could be totally alien to me. As if waking from a dream—the dream of my separateness, of the 'special' vocation to be different. My vocation does not really make me different from the rest of men or put me in a special category except artificially, juridically. I am still a member of the human race—and what more glorious destiny is there for man, since the Word was made flesh and became, too, a member of the Human Race."

Even if this is not as polished as the later version in *Conjectures of a Guilty Bystander*, it does characterize the shift in Merton's spiritual outlook that underlay the vocational crisis of these years. His earlier sense of the monastic life did certainly stress the "specialness" of this vocation. The challenge now was to find a style of contemplative life that did not rely on the "dream of separateness." Reading his old writing he observes, "I cannot go back to the earlier fervor or the asceticism that accompanied it. The new fervor will be rooted not in asceticism but in humanism." The tension he experiences is the pain of death and rebirth. "I am finally coming out of the chrysalis. . . . Now the pain and struggle of fighting my way out into something new and much bigger. I must see and embrace God in the whole world."

By the end of this period Merton has achieved a degree of peace with his circumstances. By 1960 he is exploring the foundation of the retreat house that will eventually become his hermitage on the monastery grounds. He has observed that "it does not much matter where you are, as long as you can be at peace about it and live your life. The place certainly will not live my life for me, I have found that out. I have to live it for myself." Where will he find the solitude he seeks? "Here or there makes no difference. Somewhere, nowhere, beyond all 'where.' Solitude outside geography or in it. No matter."

And so, after a fairly frantic crescendo, *The Search for Solitude* ends on a remarkably quiet note. If Merton had had his way it would have ended quite differently—in Puerto Rico or some remote island off the coast of Nicaragua. But then perhaps he would not have faced so directly the challenge to find the "solitude outside geography or in it."

Thomas Merton. *Turning Toward the World: The Pivotal Years. The Journals of Thomas Merton, Volume 4: 1960–1963.* Edited with introduction by Victor A. Kramer. Patrick Hart, O.C.S.O., General Editor. San Francisco: HarperCollins, 1996. xix + 360 pages. $30.00

Reviewed by Daniel Carrere, O.C.S.O.

In this fourth tome of Merton's seven volume saga, we observe a gifted but sometimes adolescent and archetypal monk maturing into a kenoticly real human being. In a comprehensive embrace, the transformation unifies the dichotomy of divine and secular, paradoxically, through Merton's increasingly eremitical praxis. Long seeking a monastic discipline "capable of understanding the mystery of the contemporary world" (330), Merton reflects (under the journal's concluding date) that the hermit "returns" concretely to history as an agent of divine love, dwelling "fully in a world which is for him no longer bewitched" (349).

Be that as it may, much if not most of the journal's political comment is simplistic and without nuance. If there was ever a concern that Merton's peace writings represented one who was ambivalent about Communism, this volume makes it clear that he was a partisan anti-Communist. Thus, and in part due to his romantic and emotional links with pre-Castro Cuba, Merton fails to register any awareness of the horror that life under Batista was often a cruel and unusual punishment and that the calamity of the revolution was that its promise of liberation short-circuited with the vicious substitution of one oppression for another.

At other moments Merton is impossibly abrupt and vague; one is unable to discern whether he is superficial anew or privy to genuine understanding. Lamenting our government's failure to be "a real leader in democracy for both Americas," he observes from the cloister that "Castro gave the U.S. first chance to assume this role, and the U.S. did not respond" (13). Might this be a hint of awareness about the greatest tragedy of the Cuban fiasco? Truman (in Merle Miller's *Plain Speaking* [New York: Berkley, 1974]) insisted that the Soviet usurpation of Cuba need not have occurred and that what became the threatening malignancy at the heart of Latin America and the costly distraction on our Caribbean flank was the result of Eisenhower's failure to act presidentially. Instead of immediately intervening with direct, personal diplomacy upon Castro's success, inviting the victor to Washington and offering whatever assistance the beleaguered island desired, the general sat at his desk awaiting staff reports to direct his thinking. The history of the hemisphere could have been altered profoundly, but Merton's entry is too cryptic to ascertain the depth of his comprehension.

At odd moments, Merton places his finger on the eternal dilemma of the U.S. psyche and of our international motivations. Proclaiming democracy, we are nevertheless content to export only capitalism: "We have political *ideals* that are more and more removed from and in contradiction with what we intend to do, what we 'must do,' because we are bound above all and before all else to 'make money' and to safeguard our profits" (20, Merton's emphasis). Thus, in the arena of foreign affairs—he seems to assert—capitalist pragmatics are confused with and supplant democratic ideals, all redounding to our advantage as the market economies of other peoples fortify our own coffers and standard of living.

Elsewhere, Merton naively adopts the propaganda of cold war paranoia, excoriating the "optimism of F.D.R., who was fooled by Stalin" (103). Presumably, he alludes to the partition of Easter Europe into the Soviet camp at Yalta. With the collapse of the Communist empire, this complaint may be set aside if not recognized for its opacity: Discounting the fact that Russia had suffered the greatest traumas in subduing the Nazis and that only ignobility could have ignored its demands for a European buffer, Merton's position fails to perceive that Winston Churchill, shrewd student of global politics and of the turbulent Balkans and Eastern Europe in particular, sat indomitably at Roosevelt's side. It is more than likely these two strategists knew exactly what they were doing. What appeared to Merton and to many as a sad gratuity proved to be a Trojan horse. *Inter alia*, it was the centrifugal forces of its captive provinces that agitated the U.S.S.R. incessantly and ultimately forced Gorbachev to dismantle the cumbersome empire. Without the cacophony of its satellites, Communist Russia might have entrenched itself indefinitely.

Finally, the reader is aghast at Merton's shockingly cruel assessment of the Red Chinese multitudes (for whom he professes "great love and compassion") in "their fabulous sacrifices and suffering" to industrialize the feudal country. "The system is terrible," Merton summarily dismisses its tyranny, "but the work has to be done, and there is no doubt that capitalism was helpless to do it" (146). In other words, in this instance, means are permitted to justify ends. The curious irony, as Merton devotees will immediately recognize, is that Merton vigorously protested the advance of industrialization and technology in the ambiance of his own existence.

The predominant focus of Merton's "turn to the world" targets his concern for peace amid the escalating tension of superpower hostility. An unexpected but important clarification arises in the discovery that Merton is no monolithic or doctrinaire pacifist. Reading of the Battle of Britain as prelude to German invasion of England, Merton is compelled to reflect that "[t]here is no question possible of absolute, unqualified pacifism in the light of this. The Nazis had to be fought and were fought bravely by my people. . . . There is no question *Dictatorship must be fought,* if possible non-violently. But if that is not possible, then violently" (114–5, Merton's emphasis and majuscule).

For Merton, peace is not capitulation. While there is no doubt in his mind that "for all our faults, we represent a better and more decent life than Russia or China ever could" (116), the contemporary situation appeared overwhelmingly apocalyptic; only madness could entertain a nuclear arms race, atmospheric testing, or flirt with the specter of annihilation.

Merton's anti-war essays were spurred, in large measure, by the scandalous ecclesial and ethical environment: the aggressive predilections of bishops, "prejudices of fat men with vested interests" (178, most notably New York's Cardinal Spellman), the paleolithic obtuseness of theologians, and the peculiar proclivity of Jesuits to champion, in the early 1960's the machine-gunning defense of one's personal fallout shelter against encroaching neighbors. There can be no doubt, however, that an equally significant stimulant was Merton's ongoing conflict with Abbot James Fox. The peace enterprise sublimated Merton's own hostile energies. In fact, one interpretation of the journal's data indicates that Gandhi's non-violence was first embraced as a resolution to Merton's personal war; once this transformative praxis quieted his own bellicose environment, he was free to contemplate broader horizons and spontaneously applied Gandhi's philosophy to the cold war crisis. When the head of the Order blocked publication of his "peace book" because, Merton conjectured, the French cleric was adamant that his own government should secure the bomb, Merton turned his energies to the problems of racial equality then cauterizing the nation.

In spite of the title, the book's principal value concerns Merton's personal odyssey and transformation. Just as a reader, familiar with volume three, approaches the midpoint verging on despair that this tome is simply more of the same carping, ad nauseam, one senses a reorientation of Merton's psychic and spiritual climate—not unlike that which transpires in Hammarskjöld's *Markings*. Before this perception can be questioned, Merton registers his own awareness, noting the possibility of "a new turning, a new attitude, an inner change" (167). Within the month he senses anew the emergence of "a turning point in my spiritual life," and this consciousness burgeons into a celebration: "I am happy that I have turned a corner, perhaps the last corner in my life . . . homegoing joy" (172, 173).

It is almost scandalous that an adult of forty-six years was such a problem to himself, but this is to neglect the foundational hermeneutic of kenosis. The very contortions of Merton's drama indicate a healthy spirit robustly facing the challenges of incarnation; its testimony offers an encouragement that if he can remain faithful to his deepest, most authentic aspirations, so can we.

It is here that we begin to comprehend the graced but monumental achievement of Thomas Merton. Rather than being overcome by, or simply surviving, a vapid, bankrupt spirituality and institutional pathology, Merton creatively and sapientially embraced—relying utterly upon a faithful God—an exodus beyond the mindless but structured evasions of what Kierkegaard has called "Christendom." Merton is an exemplar of the pathos that Kierkegaard has underscored is the only task worthy of a lifetime: becoming a Christian in Christendom. Challenged by his monastic precincts to a deeper life (and although he is too facilely called a mystic by some), the solution toward which Merton is working—not systematically but experientially—might be called incarnational mysticism or, better and only apparently redundant, incarnational humanism.

What these journals are bearing witness to is a process of dissolution and rebirth. Plagued by a romantic disposition that Kierkegaard called the "aesthetic," Merton spent his early monastic years absorbed narcissisticly in the immediacy of religious symbolism. The symbols had not yet given rise to thought. Only when his milieu betrayed those romantic symbols could Merton experience the questions asked of him by Life; yet he remained trapped—as the journal so frequently attests—within the dead artifacts of tribal worship and cultural religion, the futile hegemony of aesthetic symbolism.

In something of an epiphany that corroborated his inclination to solitude, Merton gleaned from his reading that the true function of a symbol is to "serve as an agent of release—into *nada*"—so that one is disengaged from the symbol's protection "to meet directly the *mysterium tremendum* of the unknown" (241).

In the kenotic space of a hermitage, Merton could meditatively face the absolute mystery, discovering and learning to embody, through the kenotic and life-giving Spirit, the simple but graced humanity of the incarnating Word. Through these pivotal years, it was the solitary praxis of this all-embracing Word that led Merton to affirm that the "great question today is really the question of Christian humanism" (143).

It is most interesting that Merton moved gradually into solitude through ecumenical dialogue. What eventually proved to be a hermitage was initially constructed to house occasional but ongoing discussion with visiting Methodists, Baptist, Episcopalians, and Presbyterians who came to Gethsemani in the atmosphere of Vatican II. Significantly, Pope John XXIII remained an avid, if distant, witness to these collegial gatherings.

Readers will find it rewarding to compare, as the editor suggests, select entries with their edited and annotated appearances in *Conjectures of a Guilty Bystander.* While a comparison with the original holograph would result in a number of corrections, anyone who has seen Merton's handwriting recognizes the extraordinary task Victor A. Kramer and his fellow editors have performed.

One editorial policy must be protested. Merton was in the habit of identifying, often parenthetically, those of whom he wrote. With regard to private persons, these identifications are irrelevant in all instances of negative or critical comment. The editors have egregiously compounded the infraction by identifying some individuals through the bracketed insertion of full names or surnames. It is unconscionable to lionize Merton at the expense of others.

Suzanne Zuercher. *Merton: An Enneagram Profile*. Notre Dame, Ind.: Ave Maria Press, 1996. 215 pages. $9.95.

Review by John P. Mossi, S.J.

Merton: An Enneagram Profile examines the family structure, complex personality, and diverse writings of Thomas Merton from the perspective of the enneagram. In essence, the book presents the author's interpretation of Merton's primary motivations which led him to embrace monastic life and which remained as the developing force in his personality.

Suzanne Zuercher, O.S.B., President of Saint Scholastica Academy in Chicago, has previously authored two books: *Enneagram Spirituality* and *Enneagram Companions*. Zuercher's interest in the enneagram serves as the dominate framework for her analysis of Merton. This book is divided into five major sections: "The Enneagram, the Spiritual Journey, and Thomas Merton," "Instinct, Compulsion, and Gift: Vice and Virtue in the Life of Thomas Merton," "The Spiritual Geography of Thomas Merton," "Relationship Brings Meaning: The People in Merton's Life," and "Merton's Spiritual Message." These classifications provide the rationale for predicating of Merton one of the nine enneagram personalities.

In fairness to the reader, who will invest time and money in this book, a few assumptions need to be clarified. First, while the enneagram is a popular topic for workshops and self-help manuals, its typology, which is attributed to the Islamic mystical sect of the Sufis, is not recognized by professional psychology associations nor can its theories be propounded with certainty by any measurable criteria, be they cognitive or behavioral. At best, the enneagram is a parapsychological tool whose value is under scrutiny by the academy. Second, in order to engage this book in a critical fashion, the reader will have to be well versed in the enneagram framework, since Zuercher's text presumes familiarity with it. If the reader does not possess such understanding, the blueprint of Zuercher's book will not be helpful in assisting a reader in arriving at the author's conclusions. Lastly, since the book's principal focus is to provide an enneagram profile for Merton's personality, it would seem to me that the dedicated reader would need to possess a lively curiosity to explore this rather arcane topic.

As a reviewer, I harbor serious reservations concerning the research method and conclusions of *Merton: an Enneagram Profile*. My major objection is that the methodology provides an interpretation of Merton's life and writings rather than a disciplined inquiry. The chapters begin with gratuitous descriptions of characteristics or traits attributed to the *artistic* type, which according to the enneagram's numerical structure is referred to as a *Number Four*. In essence, the *Four* is postulated of the creative artist, who as inspired, highly intuitive and poetic, manifests depressive tendencies and feels exempt from living as others do. From inchoate samples of Merton's writings, which are often uncontextualized and inadequately analyzed, the author "discerns" that Merton most likely was a *Four*. Throughout this text, it seems that the author's enthusiasm for the enneagram overrides an intelligent dialogue with Merton's writings.

Chapter Seven, entitled "Life as Drama," which features excerpts from *Conjectures of a Guilty Bystander*, serves as one of many examples of personality theory which is invoked to serve as a justification for the interpretation of Merton's thought. Zuercher sees Merton as a "character who is on stage in this scene [as] the suffering, misunderstood martyr." An examination of the quote from *Conjectures* yields that it has nothing to do with drama, theater, suffering or martyrdom. Instead it clearly addresses the topic of rigorous, truthful self-examination (74). Assertions, in this chapter and elsewhere, are freely made and inadequately analyzed. Throughout, it is assumed that the validity of the author's assumptions are to be uncritically accepted by the reader.

In Chapter Two, entitled "The Fundamental Sin: A Figure on His Own," Zuercher attempts to diagnose a family portrait which features Merton as a little boy. The author writes:

> Children not only make choices about how they will live their lives, they do so from their characteristic instinct or gesture or stance. Were Tom Merton not a 4, he would have judged reality and behaved other than he did.

> In the photo of the four-year old Tom we see captured on camera one moment when he learned about living. This and similar learnings shaped his articulation of issues in the spiritual journey. The picture itself may have been a significant moment in his memory. Surely, at least it made concrete the gesture that characterized Merton's future living and writing.

From the interpretation of this one photograph, the reader is asked to accept the conclusion that the *Four* personality type was already ineluctably established in Merton as a youngster.

In a word, I found *Merton, An Enneagram Profile* to be a tedious and confusing work. It is freighted with assumptions and implausible interpretations. The writing is repetitious, lacks critical development, and so, provides a simplistic and dubious portrait of Thomas Merton.

Michael Casey. *Toward God: The Ancient Wisdom of Western Prayer.* Ligouri, Mo.: Triumph Books, 1996. 180 pages. $12.95 paper; Michael Casey. *Sacred Reading: The Ancient Art of Lectio Divina.* Ligouri, Mo.: Triumph Books, 1996. 151 pages. $12.95 paper.

Reviewed by Mary Margaret Funk, O.S.B.

Michael Casey, a Trappist monk of Tarrawarra Abbey in Victoria, Australia, could be a reincarnation of Jean Leclercq, O.S.B., according to Patrick Hart, O.C.S.O. My generation (fifty something) is fortunate to have him at the time when many of us have awakened to the splendors of *lectio divina* and contemplation.

Toward God is Caseys' personal statement about prayer: "How I feel about prayer at this stage of my life." (vii). He positions prayer as a journey toward God and away from self: "To turn towards God means, first, turning away from whatever is untrue or delusory . . . no matter how much comfort it brings" (5). Casey's monastic life experience shows through these pages. He speaks from experience. His style is candid, straight, and quite readable. He writes, for example:

> Suffering does not always produce prayer. . . . Suffering can narrow our horizons, making us concentrate on our selves and our misery, rather than transcending self and becoming detached from the limited satisfactions human life offers. With grace . . . what began as a function of pain is transformed into an element of faith (1).

This book is for the practitioner who wants help in praying. Casey's advice: On God's part, prayer is total gift. On our part, prayer is total receptivity (171). "What we can do is to create an empty space in our consciousness and put other considerations aside for the time being so that we can be shaped by whatever comes from the heart." (38)

Especially noteworthy is the author's sharp *catechesis* or, rather, *mystogogia* on spiritual delight, compunction, and the gift of tears. Also noteworthy is the attention given to the dark side of prayer. His treatment of spiritual direction is also quite good. He does not treat direction as a way through hard times, as much as a way to tell one's story to another soul friend. The strongest part of *Toward God*, however, is the chapter entitled "The Gift of Time." Often those of us who try to teach prayer are soft about prayer's burden on our time. But Casey reminds us:

> Time given to God is time withdrawn from other activities. This means that if I am an achiever, I will achieve less. If I am self-indulgent, I will be less gratified. If I thrive on human contact, I will have to learn a measure of solitude. Time given to God is time not available for self. . . . Time spent in prayer is time lost to temporal gain. It is bread cast onto the waters of eternity (48).

The treatment of *lectio divina* in *Toward God*, brief yet profound, is developed more fully in *Sacred Reading*. Casey draws from Scripture and the Fathers of the Church. Since Casey's aim is practical, he provides insight regarding eight factors in the life of prayer: regular time; place; posture; attention to breathing; physical health; emotional equilibrium; social harmony; "winding down" time.

The author provides a script for a meditation period (115). His suggested practice leaves room for intuition and receptivity. Compared to a strict practice of "centering prayer" that relies on a more prescriptive method, Casey's approach is somewhat more flexible. For example, he writes: "I allow the prayer to act as my guide" (116). The author is to be admired for speaking of his own prayer practice for the purpose of giving others a gauge by which to evaluate their own.

Casey presents mystery as constitutive to union with God. Before union with God there is a need for radical purgation. Everything in us that is hostile to God must be uncovered and its bitterness tasted, before we can eliminate it (158). He attends to the place of the cross of Jesus Christ, central to the Christian understanding of union. He describes the Christian's union with God in terms of both the experience of sin and separation and the immersion with Christ into resurrection and glory. Casey's insights will be a welcome addition to the ongoing monastic interreligious dialogue, since the cross and death of Jesus remain a point of bewilderment to the monks of the religions of the far east.

Sacred Reading fills a gap. To date there is no book-length "postgraduate treatment of the art of *lectio divina* from within the monastic tradition" (vii). Casey speaks of *lectio* as preparation for contemplation. The Bible, the focus of the art of sacred reading, is not an easy book to read, and so Casey provides some advice as to what to look for and how to read it. He speaks of his own difficulty with inattention, hardheartedness, blindness, and forgetfulness. Other obstacles to fruitful *lectio* are identified: "inner noise" that speaks of residual echoes of the past, *acedia*, overconcern with external projects, divided heart or double soul, alienation from the church or other unconscious factors.

Casey discusses the importance of honoring the integrity of the text, with attention to its internal dynamic of context and content. Those serious about the practice of *lectio* will avoid using the Bible as a medicine chest, or cutting the Bible like a deck of cards in search of just the right message. Similarly, he urges against grazing the Scriptures to suit one's tastes, or flipping through the Bible's pages for inspiration in the way that folks today surf hundreds of TV channels for just the right kind of entertainment. He suggests that random selection of a passage for *lectio* rarely captures the text's profundity as does *lectio continua*. It usually takes months and even years to engage in dynamic of *lectio divina* with a single book of Scripture. Casey writes:

> If we are going to follow St. Benedict's recommendation and read biblical books in their entirety we will need to be prepared for a prolonged exposure to a particular book. If we choose to read the prophet Jeremiah or the Gospel of John, for instance, we can expect that either of these will fill the time available for lectio for three to six months" (14).

What is required is fidelity, regularity, repetition, and perseverance to allow the layers and layers of meaning to unfold. An attitude of reverence is required. Obedience and listening anoint the mind with subtleness for spiritual realities. Lack of reverence is an indication of deficient understanding and points to a certain grossness of mind that is unable to perceive the true nature of spiritual reality.

Particularly noteworthy is Casey's notion that compunction is the world of sensibility to God. He recommends: "allow God to act upon us not only by the medium of ideas but also through our feelings . . . we cannot relate to God feeling nothing" (32). The chapter on a theology of *lectio* is a bit lean. But it still offers many helpful insights.

The levels of meaning of Scripture are covered in an expose of the "four senses" of Scripture: literal, christological, behavioral and mystical. Casey relates these to the faculties of intellect, memory, conscience, and spirit, and to the four moments of prayer: *lectio, meditatio, oratio, and contemplatio.* This is then related to an understanding of prayer involving four interrelated functions: understanding the text, contextualizing the meaning, living the meaning, and meeting God in the text (56).

Casey makes the important point that we are to move from reading to prayer through the discipline of *lectio,* but this takes time. It is important to note that *lectio divina* is not a method for one session. The process of *lectio* requires that one start with the literal sense, then live what has been read, and then gradually grasp what God has revealed. The process involves discipline and effort. There is no room for pious laziness.

Beyond the Scriptures, Casey suggests reading the Church Fathers for *lectio divina.* He provides a brief introduction to reading the Fathers, drawing from his own experience: "Being lucky enough to have acquired a facility of some of the relevant languages, I try to read these texts in the original. I feel this also brings me closer to the author and to the experience that is the source of the text"(108). Casey does not underestimate the difficulties in understanding the Fathers' culture and spirituality, and has a wonderful way of sharing the Fathers' experience of the Christ event.

In conclusion, *Toward God* and *Sacred Reading* each provides helpful quotes from the best of Christian literature. Readers will appreciate the notes for further reading. These books are recommended for monastics and laypersons alike. Casey's survey of patristic literature will be helpful to librarians in monastery, college, and university. Though the books are presented as companions, each is a free standing work on a topic related to the other. Each offers both invitation and challenge to grow in the practice of *lectio divina* that draws us toward God.

Kathleen Norris. *The Cloister Walk.* New York: Riverhead
Books, 1996. 384 pages. $23.95.

Reviewed by David Bock, O.C.S.O.

Kathleen Norris presents the reader of *Cloister Walk* with a series of reflections and autobiographical sketches, many of which show
the influence of her encounter with American monasticism. The book
is presented as an "immersion into a liturgical world" and is loosely
structured in following a sanctoral and seasonal calendar. The chapters
sometimes take the form of entries in a journal, sometimes of autobiographical reminiscences, and sometimes of minor essays or editorials.
A glance at the titles of the seventy-five chapters (from one to twenty
pages in length) should warn the reader that this is a highly personal
exposition and selection of topics.

The book is carried by the author's capacity to write extremely
well. Her prose is vivid, immediate, and confronting. She is hard to ignore. There is something worthwhile in reading her descriptions and
explanations of commonplace activities. In the title chapter "Cloister
Walk," she describes experiencing the transformation of the familiar
space of St. John's Abbey Church into a wild place that "could roar like
the sea" (265). The landscape of open country, the persistence and
"brooding, comforting presence" of trees, the sunrises and sunsets
"that ground me in the present" are hallowed by attentive descriptions. "I often think I live here because I'm a frustrated painter, drawn
to painting this landscape with words" (351). As in her previous book
Dakota: A Spiritual Geography, Norris continues to find in nature a
source of spiritual insight and understanding.

The author does seem to be working in the *genre* of what is
called the "literature of nature." Douglas Burton-Christie describes
this as literature which "is characterized by an acute attention to the
particular, by its local character, by focus on experience, by its valua-
tion of imagination, by an implicit, oblique evocation of the transcendent, and by an enduring ethical impulse" ("The Literature of
Nature and the Quest of the Sacred," *The Way Supplement* 1994/81, 5).
In the Preface, Norris acknowledges that her apprenticeship as a writer
"was in essence a religious quest" (xi). She has discovered in the

monastic world an experience and tradition which illumines, informs, and supports her own vocation as a poet.

One of the valuable gifts of this volume is the description from within that Norris gives of the poet's vocation. The task of the poet is "not to convince but to suggest, evoke, explore" ". . . speaking without reference to authority but simply because the words are given you. . . ." (37). The poet, the prophet, and the monk are called to "see things as they are" even though this is at the price of putting themselves at a distance from conventional culture. As Norris puts it, "monks and poets are the best degenerates in America" (146). Both share a developed sense of the sacred potential in all things; live from symbol, image and metaphor; eschew the utilitarian; develop attitudes of attentive waiting; attempt to pay close attention to objects, events, and natural phenomena "that otherwise would get chewed up in the daily grind" (266). The author finds possible antidotes for some cultural ailments in monastic tradition, in its cultivation of simplicity, in its oral environment of liturgy, *lectio*, and ritual. However, she seems a bit too ready at times to slip into an editorializing mode, trying to persuade her readers of a wider human value of some monastic practices.

Two concerns which receive repeated attention in several chapters of the book are metaphor and celibacy. Interestingly, both have to do with the negotiating of boundaries, literal and bodily. "It is fear of metaphor that in some ways defines American culture" she somewhat surprisingly declares (211). Metaphor has to do with "fuzzy boundaries" where definitions give way (58). It is metaphor which has the capacity to yoke together sacred and secular, the natural, psychological, and spiritual worlds. It is obviously at the heart of her own creative expression. And she explores celibacy and virginity at some length. Her method in discussing celibacy is largely to collate the conversations and experiences of several Benedictines—mostly women. It is presented as a path of potential freedom in relationships, of availability, non-possessiveness and hospitality to the other. Her discussion of virginity seems to make it solely a feminine capacity and one which today would allow a woman to redefine her identity apart from social and sexual roles imposed by a male-dominated culture. Her treatment of Maria Goretti seems to be influenced by the same politicizing she finds objectionable when used by "nineteenth century hagiographers."

There is an unmistakable feminist agenda working its way through the book. This is particularly true in her treatment of virginity and her treatment of the relationships of women with men and the institutional church. The saints and poets she chooses to discuss are predominantly women. She stays close to topics of clothing, the body, sexuality, the earth, geography, and her family. She is concerned with relationships and the sense of exclusion and displacement that comes from vocational and personal differences. Hospitality is a key notion for Norris, and it captures the sense of passage, of boundaries, of receiving and letting go that she struggles with in this work.

Norris has found that her experience of monastic life and tradition has given her new perspectives to incorporate in her own life and she suggests that this may be valuable for others. She is hardly complete in her portrayal of monastic living. She does not discuss the corporate nature of Catholic liturgy and ritual, nor how the traditional sense of Scripture might be at work in *lectio*. Surprisingly, she does not mention the work of Merton which deals with the experience of someone who was a monk and poet. The value of the work lies in the perceptions and insights that Norris makes as an outsider, from the margins. As a poet, she feels part of the contemporary world and culture and able to mediate the experience of a monastic world and culture. She invites the reader to look with fresh and new eyes at familiar experiences. She does not explore new territory, but works the soil of human experience to uncover a renewed appreciation of its depth.

Contributors

Alan Altany teaches in the Department of Religious Studies at Marshall University, Huntington, West Virginia.

Emily Archer wrote her dissertation on Denise Levertov and has published articles in several scholarly journals as well as reviews of Levertovs' work (including a review in *The Merton Annual*, Vol. 7).

Claire Hoertz Badaracco is Director of Graduate Studies in Communications at Marquette University. She published an earlier study about Merton and contemporary women writers in *Merton Annual*, Vol. 8, and her book *Trading Words* (John Hopkins) appeared in 1995.

Beatrice Bruteau has a background in science and a Ph.D. in philosophy from Fordham. She is author/editor of seven books and over a hundred articles in philosophy and religion. Founder of the Schola Contemplationis (a correspondence network), she offers retreats and workshops.

David Joseph Belcastro teaches at Capitol University in Columbus, Ohio and is a contibutor to *The Merton Annual*, Vol. 7.

David Bock, O.C.S.O., is a monk of New Melleray Abbey near Dubuque, Iowa.

Daniel Carrere, O.C.S.O., is a monk of Gethsemani and is editor of the series *Gethsemani Studies in Psychological and Religious Anthropology* to be published by The University of Notre Dame Press.

David D. Cooper, Acting Director of American Studies at Michigan State University, is author of *Thomas Merton's Art of Denial: The Evolution of a Radical Humanist* (University of Georgia Press, 1989) and editor of *Thomas Merton and James Laughlin: Selected Letters* (W. W. Norton, 1997).

Robert Ellsberg is editor-in-chief of Orbis Books and the author of *All Saints: Daily Reflections on Saints, Prophets, and Witnesses for Our Time.*

Margaret Funk, O.S.B., is a Benedictine of Our Lady of Grace Monastery in Beech Grove, Indiana. She is executive director of the Monastic Interreligious Dialogue.

Jim Grote is associate director of stewardship for the Archdiocese of Louisville. With John McGeeney he is the author of *Clever as Serpents: Business Ethics and Office Politics* (The Liturgical Press, 1997).

Patrick Hart, O.C.S.O., former editor of *The Merton Annual,* and long-time editor of Merton, serves as the general editor of the *Complete Journals of Thomas Merton.*

George Kilcourse, Professor of Theology at Bellarmine College, is an editor of *The Merton Annual* and is the author of *Ace of Freedoms: Thomas Merton's Christ.* He has published widely on Merton and as well on aspects of ecumenism.

Victor A. Kramer is a founding editor of *The Merton Annual* (Vols. 1–5, A.M.S. Press) and continuing editor (Vols. 6–10). He is editor of the fourth volume of Mertons' complete journals, *Turning Toward the World: The Pivotal Years (1960–1963).*

Jonathan Montaldo is an independent scholar and lecturer. He has done extensive Merton work, and is the editor of volume two of the complete journals, *Entering the Silence: Becoming a Monk and Writer (1941–1952).*

John P. Mossi, S.J., author of *Prayers from the Cross: Solace for all Seasons,* teaches in the Religious Studies department at Gonzaga University in Spokane.

Patrick O'Connell is associate professor in the Departments of English and Theology at Gannon University, Erie, Pennsylvania. He served as president of The International Thomas Merton Society (1995–1997).

Mark O'Keefe, O.S.B., is president-rector and associate professor of moral theology at St. Meinrad School of Theology. He is the author of *Becoming Good, Becoming Holy: On the Relationship of Christian Ethics and Spirituality* (Paulist, 1995).

Anthony Padavano has written many books about theology and literature, as well as a play about Thomas Merton.

Johan Seynnaeve teaches in the Department of Foreign Languages, West Virginia University, Morgantown.

Bradford T. Stull teaches in the English Department at Rivier College in Nashua, New Hampshire. He is the author of *Religious Dialectics* and *Pain and Imagination*.

Wendy M. Wright is professor in the Department of Religion at Creighton University, Omaha, Nebraska, and has published widely.

John Wu, Jr. has taught in the Departments of English, Philosophy, and now Religion at universities in Taiwan for over two decades. His presentation, "The Zen in Thomas Merton," was recently included in *Your Heart is My Heritage* (papers at the Southampton Conference of the Thomas Merton Society of Great Britain and Ireland, May 1996).

Index